Beyond Self-Interest

Beyond Self-Interest

Edited by Jane J. Mansbridge

The University of Chicago Press / Chicago and London

The University of Chicago Press, Chicago 60637
The University of Chicago Press, Ltd., London
© 1990 by the University of Chicago
All rights reserved. Published 1990
Printed in the United States of America

99 98 97 96 95 94 93 92 91   5 4 3 2

Library of Congress Cataloging-in-Publication Data

Beyond self-interest / edited by Jane J. Mansbridge.
    p.   cm.
Includes bibliographical references.
    ISBN 0-226-50359-3 (alk. paper).—ISBN 0-226-50360-7 (pbk. : alk. paper)
    1. Consensus (Social sciences)   2. Common good.   3. Self-interest—Moral
and ethical aspects.   4. Altruism.   5. Cooperation.
I. Mansbridge, Jane J.
JC328.2.B47   1990
320′.01′1—dc20   89-38629
                                                                         CIP

Contents

Preface

The essays in this book constitute a manifesto. They reject the increasingly prevalent notion that human behavior is based on self-interest, narrowly conceived. They argue for a more complex view of both individual behavior and social organization—a view that takes into account duty, love, and malevolence. Focusing on the "pro-social" motivations, the essays acknowledge individuals' commitment to moral principles, concern for others, "we-feeling," and readiness to cooperate when cooperation does not serve self-interest narrowly conceived. They recognize the extent to which existing institutions depend on public standards and a public spirit.

Because research on motivation that goes beyond self-interest has evolved simultaneously in several different academic disciplines, and because even within their home disciplines several of the authors are "mavericks" working outside the dominant self-interest model, the cumulative potential of these ideas has not been widely recognized. This volume introduces, sometimes to one another, leading practitioners in different fields in the social sciences, summarizing a key book, article, or life's work. Together their impact ought to modify almost every discipline in the social sciences.

None of these authors claims that self-interest is unimportant, or that everyone is concerned with the welfare of others. Self-interest explains most of human interaction in some contexts, and it plays some role in almost every context. Institutions that allow self-interest as a primary motive, like the market and majority rule, are indispensable when vast groups of people who have no other contact with one another need to coordinate their activities or make collective decisions.

This book, however, aims to make thinking about self-interest more subtle, showing that when people think about what they want, they think about more than just their narrow self-interest. When they define their own interests and when they act to pursue those interests, they often give great weight both to their moral principles and to the interests of others.

The essays examine most closely the political realm, where democratic institutions have a complicated dual task. In moments of irresolvable conflict, these institutions must find a way to aggregate individuals' selfish interests and to harness for the public good some of the direction and energy that derive from the pursuit of self-interest. At the same time, these institutions must encourage citizens and legislators to put the public interest above their own self-interest. As many observers have pointed out, institutions that do the first often undo the second. It is hard for a polity simultaneously to legitimate self-interest and to persuade its citizens to make the common good their own. The task becomes harder when political scientists, economists, and psychologists insist that common interests are a myth and that appeals to such interests are either mystification or a waste of effort.

While a few passages in these essays may suggest that social scientists cannot or should not try to calculate the costs and benefits for the individual of individual actions, that is not the argument of the collection as a whole. Most of the writers in this volume are comfortable both with taking the individual as the unit of analysis for many calculations and with making cost-benefit comparisons. This is not, therefore, a manifesto against "rational choice" modeling, at least if the aim of such models is simply to work out, with or without the aid of numbers and Greek letters, how individuals would act if they were trying to maximize benefits while minimizing costs. Rather, it is a sustained argument in favor of the idea that people often take account of both other individuals' interests and the common good when they decide what constitutes a "benefit" that they want to maximize.

The notion of maximizing can itself distort reality. It does not capture the subjective experience of most individuals as they act, fail to act, choose, or fail to choose. Jeremy Bentham had to invent the word "maximize" to encompass meanings that had not earlier crystallized into a single word, and that word, still carrying with it some of the connotations of conscious calculation that Bentham's system gave it, does not describe well the experience of a devout believer, an alcoholic on a binge, or even the full experience of a comparison shopper. Nor can a moral account framed in maximizing language capture the meaning of certain goods and virtues. Even if viewed from the outside, as describing only behavior rather than subjective experience, "maximizing" describes many actions less accurately than "satisficing," which takes account of information and decision costs, or "quasi-rational behavior," which takes account of cognitive biases and the emotions. While several authors in this book will take note of such problems in the maximization assumption, the essays will focus on the assumption of self-interest.

The essays in this volume represent new thinking. Before modern social science began to rely so exclusively on self-interest to explain human action, most major thinkers realized that human beings had benevolent and malevolent as well as self-interested motives. Returning to this earlier understanding of motivation does not mean dropping the advances in analysis that have occurred in the last fifty years. Eighteenth- and nineteenth-century writers like Hume or de Tocqueville, for example, argued, in terms that today seem somewhat vague, that individuals' "remote" self-interest, or "self-interest rightly understood," was congruent with the common good. In the second half of the twentieth century, game theorists, economists, and others began to parse out a more precise logic of collective action, demonstrating how each individual's narrow self-interest will in some circumstances undermine the collective good. In the last ten years, as the essays in this volume suggest, scholars in each of the social sciences have added to this new logic the recovered recognition that love and duty, hatred and factional feeling, animate much of human action, and must be integrated with any emerging understanding of collective behavior.

These essays spell out some of the varieties of altruism and how these differ from narrow self-interest. They rethink "prisoners' dilemma" interactions from the viewpoint of long-run self-interest, commitment to principle, and genuine we-feeling. They integrate our growing understanding of altruistic motivation with evolutionary models that explain how such behavior can reproduce itself. They investigate the role of altruism in citizen and legislative behavior. They demonstrate that the view of democracy inherent in existing interpretations of the United States Constitution is not based on self-interest. They conclude that a prudent reliance on empathy and principle may enhance, rather than undermine, international interdependence and stability. They suggest how one can model the motivations of public spirit and self-interest in a single individual. They sketch some alternatives to self-interest in human evil, orneriness, and mothering. They end with a penetrating feminist critique of the "contract" model of human interaction based on self-interest. All the essays either take for granted or aim to demonstrate the critical importance of motivations that go beyond self-interest.

With the exception of the last two philosophical essays in the volume, these essays derive from thinkers trained in an empirical tradition. Indeed, the primary aim of the volume is empirical—to make our understanding of human behavior more accurate. My aim has been to bring together important empirical work that philosophers should know and important philosophical work that empirical researchers should know, even when the language of each raises problems for the other. Both the philosophical and the empirical essays address the question of accurate description.

Yet the essays all have normative implications. The empirical description is often underlaid with implicit, and sometimes explicit, prescriptive claims. Assuming that the description of human motivation is correct, what are the implications for prescription?

It does not follow from a description of human nature as motivated by benevolence (and malevolence) as well as self-interest that we should promote love and duty indiscriminately in place of self-interest. Although most moral systems praise acts done for the good of others, acting from self-interest does not automatically generate either bad consequences or bad character. Nor do duty and love, which can produce tyrannical consequences and personalities, deserve only praise.

In the women's liberation movement of the late 1960s and early 1970s, consciousness-raising groups helped women realize that actions they had implicitly justified as helping a larger collective, like their family or the enterprise in which they worked, were sometimes not good for them as individuals. That realization did not turn social beings into selfish ones, but helped women renegotiate the terms of their sociality. In some cases, justice required a renegotiation that left one party, the woman, better off in narrowly self-interested terms and another party, the husband or employer, worse off. But in some cases, both parties are better off when each openly espouses and negotiates for his or her self-interest under fair procedural rules than when both try to subordinate all self-interest to a higher good. Normative systems that make self-interest morally unacceptable also make it hard, if not impossible, to recognize and handle those self-interested impulses that continue to exist.

Larger democratic polities must also balance techniques and institutions that assume self-interest and those that assume public spirit. At the moment, techniques and institutions geared to self-interest probably have far more weight in liberal democracies, and especially in the United States, than is compatible with the long-run public good. Prescriptively, therefore, it makes sense to try to redress this imbalance by revitalizing or creating institutions that foster a commitment to the common good.

Yet efforts at revitalization will not be undertaken if policymakers have concluded in advance that such efforts will not work. This fact gives purely empirical points about human behavior an underlying prescriptive thrust.

Designing institutions when participants have both selfish and unselfish motives requires attention to variation in contexts, individuals, and the way individuals learn from institutions. The seemingly cautious strategy of designing institutions to work only on self-interest, so that if there is little or no public spirit the institutions will work anyway, will in some conditions erode whatever public spirit might otherwise exist. But the alternative strategy of assuming a high level of public spirit also entails serious risks, since public spirit may not survive when it is too strongly at odds with self-interest. Observation and experimentation should make it clearer which conditions are likely to generate each of these patterns, when changing an institution actually affects motivation, and when making motivation more public-spirited produces good rather than harmful results.

Robyn Dawes and Richard Thaler conclude a recent article on cooperation with the following observation:

> In the rural areas around Ithaca it is common for farmers to put some fresh produce on a table by the road. There is a cash box on the table, and customers are expected to put money in the box in return for the vegetables they take. The box has just a small slit, so money can only be put in, not taken out. Also, the box is attached to the table, so no one can (easily) make off with the money. We think that the farmers who use this system have just about the right model of human nature. They feel that enough people will volunteer to pay for the fresh corn to make it worthwhile to put it out there. The farmers also know that if it were easy enough to take the money, someone would do so. (1988:145)

The farmer's produce stand demonstrates that human institutions *can* be predicated on mixed motives. I would argue that most human institutions, including the family, elections, tax collection, and war, to name some obvious examples, are predicated on equally mixed motives. As empirical social science stops ignoring this reality and starts exploring duty and love with the same intensity it has recently given self-interest, the resulting analyses are likely to become more useful to those engaged in collective action.

JANE J. MANSBRIDGE

I Introduction

1   The Rise and Fall of Self-Interest in the Explanation of Political Life

Jane J. Mansbridge

In political science, a theory of "adversary" democracy, founded on both conflict and self-interest, has been evolving from the seventeenth century. When the "rational choice" school in the second half of the twentieth century made explicit the underlying assumptions of adversary democracy, the ensuing clarity had a dual effect. It inspired some to work out, in provocative detail, the implications for actual politics of the logic of self-interested action. It provoked others to challenge the factual accuracy of the theory.

Empirical research in political science today thus has some earmarks of a crisis in the natural sciences. The anomalies the reigning adversary theory cannot explain have, under challenge, become worrying enough to demand a new explanatory model.

Preparing the Normative Ground

The idea that politics can legitimately be based on self-interest did not begin with Hobbes or with capitalist economic relations. In the fourth and fifth centuries B.C. in Athens, several thinkers—loosely those whom Plato labeled Sophists—argued that human beings came together in political association for the self-interested reason of mutual defense; that the laws of any polity, including Athens, were ultimately reducible to self-interest; and that human nature was self-interested: by nature human beings simply desired the maximum power to hurt others with the minimum risk to them-

For comments on this and other essays of mine in this book, I thank David Beam, Joseph Cropsey, Steven Elkin, Richard Fenno, Bernie Grofman, Russell Hardin, Carol Heimer, Don Herzog, Alfie Kohn, Eric Kramer, Michael Loriaux, Ronald Mansbridge, Kristin Monroe, Benjamin Page, Arthur Stinchcombe, and Sidney Verba, as well as the contributors to this volume. I particularly thank Christopher Jencks for his critical advice and support. On the logistical front, I am gratefully indebted to Jennifer Dreyfus, Christine Kidd, and Laura Leavitt for research assistance, to the federal work-study program that paid a good portion of their salaries, to Northwestern University's Dispute Resolution Research Center, and to Northwestern University and the Center for Urban Affairs and Policy Research at Northwestern for the released time that made possible this volume and my chapters within it. An abridged version of this chapter appeared as "Self-Interest in Political Life," *Political Theory* vol. 18, no. 1, © 1990 by Sage Publications. Used by permission of Sage Publications, Inc.

selves. It is hard to know how current these ideas were in their day, or even to explore their implications, for they have been preserved primarily in fragments or in the writings of Plato and Aristotle, who opposed them. Yet they provide the first extant attempts—attempts probably made by democratic philosophers—to ground political life in self-interest.[1]

During the fifteen hundred-odd years that Christianity dominated Western thought, the notion that self-interest could serve as a legitimate foundation for political order found little support. When it survived, it was in the undeveloped contract theories of the eleventh through the six-teenth centuries. The eleventh-century prior, Manegold of Lautenbach, for example, advanced against Emperor Henry IV a revealing and mixed analogy: if a man discovered his hired swineherd stealing, slaughtering, and losing his pigs, he would fire the swineherd; so if a people discovered that the king they had chosen to coerce the wicked and defend the good was in fact a tyrant and had thus been the first to break the compact for whose sake he had been appointed, that king should deservedly fall from the dignity entrusted to him.[2] While the swineherd analogy suggests a polity established to promote individual self-interest, the specific duties of the king—to coerce the wicked and defend the good—suggest a polity established to promote a common good.

By the mid-seventeenth century in England, the widely understood goal of the founding contract (whether between people and sovereign, or people and people) had become the preservation of property—a comparatively self-interested individual good—as much as the enforcement of justice. At the same time, the aftermath of religious and factional war had left disbanded armies and landless peasants roaming the highways, with thousands drifting to the cities to settle outside their walls and laws. Religious authority faltered under the impact of factional and dynastic disputes. In this world of "masterless men,"[3] self-interest seemed to thinkers like Thomas Hobbes the only predictable base on which to build a polity.

Social contract theorists before Hobbes had conceived of conflict in the state of nature as involving the crimes of some against others, not as a "war of all against all."[4] Thomas Hobbes, following the advanced scientific method of his day, reduced the world to its analytic components of individual self-interest and built it up again from this single base. In this manner, he derived from self-interest a state of universal, irreconcilable conflict. Although some individuals might be content with sufficiency, he reasoned, self-preservation required that even these seek infinitely more power in order to protect themselves against the predations of the insatiable.[5] The universal structural position of vulnerability combined with self-interest to produce the war of all against all, which Hobbes proposed could end only with the decision to submit to a superordinate authority, the sovereign.

Today's rational choice theorists[6] have pointed out that Hobbes's theory of third-party control is a crude but effective solution to the prisoners' dilemma in which a strategy that is self-interestedly rational for each individual ("collect as much power as possible for yourself") produces collective outcomes that are not in any individual's interest. Self-interest by itself can lead one voluntarily to submit to a sovereign, authorizing the sovereign's actions as if they were one's own; self-interest can thus provide the basis for political legitimacy.

Hobbes's legitimation of self-interest, and the atheism this often was held to imply, so appalled many of his contemporaries that they made "Hobbism" grounds for expulsion from political or religious service. As one of them put it, "where [Hobbesian] principles prevail, adieu honour and honesty and fidelity and loyalty; all must give place to self-interest."[7] On the Continent, however, and even in England, the idea of grounding political legitimacy in self-interest found its adherents.[8]

In England, expanding markets and incipient capitalism had produced an upheaval in economic thought. In the second half of the seventeenth century, pamphlets on economic issues, often written by churchmen, argued against the traditional notions of just price, fair wages and controlled interest, and defended the "undeniable maxime, That every one by the light of nature and reason will do that which makes for his greatest advantage."[9] Interest, they implied, was predictable, and therefore a firm basis on which to build.[10] These pamphlets argued not only the necessity of self-interest, but also its ultimate good for the larger polity: "The advancement of private persons will be the advantage of the publick."[11] A key element in this reasoning was that the pursuit of self-interest was "natural," and trying to regulate it by, say, imposing fixed interest rates was unnatural and doomed to failure. "The supream power," wrote one pamphleteer, "can do many things, but it cannot alter the Laws of Nature, of which the most original is, That every man should preserve himself."[12]

The Dawn of Adversary Democracy

The mid-seventeenth century saw self-interest advanced as a weapon against a monarch who used the language of public interest to promote foreign adventure.[13]

It also saw the beginning of a democratic theory that incorporated a legitimate role for self-interest. Colonel Rainborough argued in 1647 that if the poor did not have the vote, the rich would "crush" them.[14] This was a new argument, justifying the vote as a means of protecting one's interests. Departing from the medieval understanding of majority vote as the best way, without endless discussion, to ascertain the good of the whole,[15] it was the first step toward the claim in full-fledged adversary theory of moral neutrality between one set of interests and another.

Hobbes' model of individuals pursuing power after power without end, like Galileo's stones never stopping once set in motion, suggests that, if the individuals or stones come in contact, they will clash. The ideas of self-interest and conflicting interest, while analytically distinct, thus have a logical connection once one posits an asocial self. Historically, the first steps toward legitimating self-interest came at the same time as the first steps toward legitimating conflict. In the mid-seventeenth century, Parliament, which had made almost all its decisions by consensus, began making most decisions by majority vote.[16] Representatives to Parliament, who had usually been selected in various ways without contest, began to compete for office through elections. Counties began to produce divided votes, and the outcome began to be decided by polling individuals rather than by "acclamation" (shouts) or "view" (standing together). Political parties began to develop into ongoing organizations that remained in conflict from one election to another, and the word *party* began to lose its unsavory connotation of a faction opposed to the common good.[17] Theorists like John Locke began to stress the necessity of accepting conflict. Religious toleration was required, Locke wrote, because "diversity of opinions . . . cannot be avoided." Majority rule was required, he wrote, by the "contriety of interests, which unavoidably happen in all collections of men."[18]

In short, several currents in the seventeenth century led writers to recommend recognizing and adapting to, rather than trying to fight, the unshakable facts of self-interest and opposing interests in the polity. As Albert Hirschman has shown, one important strand of thought in this century and the next praised self-interest as less damaging to the public good than the passions, particularly the passion for glory and honor, upon which people acted without thought to their future.[19] Self-interest, or "rational self-love," could calm the passions of caprice, zeal, faction, even undue curiosity, shame, love of imitation, humor, and indolence.[20] Indeed, by the eighteenth century, Helvetius was claiming self-interest as the basis for the scientific study of politics: "As the physical world is ruled by the laws of movement so is the moral universe ruled by laws of interest."[21] Moralists, he wrote, "might succeed in having their maxims observed if they substituted . . . the language of interest for that of injury."[22] Even if most people acted from public spirit, it might be argued, nations should design their institutions to work as if everyone acted from self-interest. Public spirit would be reinforced by sanction, and the public good would be preserved against the narrowly self-interested.[23]

The framers of the United States Constitution mixed the growing reliance on self-interest that had developed in both England and the Continent with other strands from Scotland and the Continent that stressed virtue among citizens and representatives, and the constant danger of corruption.[24] During the revolutionary war, when citizens were being asked for a short time to give voluntarily both their money and their lives to the cause, the language of many American thinkers stressed commitment to the public good. Twelve years later, designing a constitution to work in ordinary times, their language stressed an accommodation to self-interest. Gordon Wood argues, on the basis of this change in rhetoric, that in these few years American thinkers experienced the "beginnings of a fundamental shift of thought," which would replace "individual self-sacrifice for the good of the state" with "a total grounding of government in self-interest."[25]

Wood's claim must be tempered by recognizing the role of self-interest in proto-constitutional thinking since the mid-seventeenth century. Even during the revolutionary war General Washington had urged:

> I do not mean to exclude altogether the Idea of Patriotism. I know it exists, and I know it has done much in the present Contest. But I will venture to asert, that a great and lasting War can never be supported on this principle alone. It must be aided by a prospect of Interest or some reward. For a time, it may, of itself push Men to Action; to bear much, to encounter difficulties; but it will not endure unassisted by Interest.[26]

Nor did attention to the public good die out in 1787. In 1788, James Madison argued not only that no government could eliminate the "causes of faction"—self-love and self-interest combined with differing economic circumstances—but also that representatives selected for wisdom could discern and pursue the "true interest of their country." Madison's constitutional proposals always had two prongs: one based on using self-interest, and one on repressing it. To bend self-interested impulses to the good of the whole, he proposed that the nation's institutions be designed to regulate the "various and interfering interests" in a way that actually "involves the spirit of party and faction in the necessary and ordinary operations of the government." To control the ineradicable impulses of self-interest, he proposed that the nation's selection processes be designed to generate representatives "fit to comprehend and pursue great and national objects," with the capacity to "refine and enlarge the public views."[27]

Madison was not a scientist like Hobbes, nor was he writing in a disintegrating world in which one could trust only the motive of self-interest. But he and his contemporaries understood that the constitution they were creating would have large and terrible consequences if it embodied inadequate assumptions regarding human motivation. Like their contemporary Adam Smith, they thus recognized and tried to set to work the power of both self-interested and non-self-interested motivation.[28]

The constitutional tension they created set the framework for an Anglo-American political theory that continued to advocate tapping for public purposes the dual motivations of self-interest and public spirit, though the emphasis on public spirit became at times extremely weak. In the nineteenth century, Jeremy Bentham put his version of the balance nicely when he wrote of designing governmental institutions: "For diet, nothing but self-regarding affection will serve: but for a *dessert*, benevolence . . . is a very valuable addition" (1818–19/1843:511).

Establishing the Descriptive Paradigm

While the first half of the twentieth century saw various attempts to build a descriptive political science on the basis of self-interest,[29] it was not until after World War II that a theory developed grounding government totally in self-interest. Joseph Schumpeter's ground-breaking work in 1942 laid the intellectual foundations for scrapping entirely the prevailing theory of dual motivation and constructing a democratic theory, both descriptive and normative, on the foundations of self-interest alone.

In Schumpeter's descriptive theory of "adversary democracy," there is no common good or public interest.[30] Voters pursue their individual interests by making demands on the political system in proportion to the intensity of their feelings. Politicians, also pursuing their own interests, adopt policies that buy them votes, thus ensuring accountability. In order to stay in office, politicians act like entrepreneurs and brokers, looking for formulas that satisfy as many and alienate as few interests as possible. From the interchange between self-interested voters and self-interested brokers decisions emerge that come as close as possible to a balanced aggregation of individual interests.

The theory also had a normative side, which Schumpeter did not explore. Normatively, the aggregation of interests is legitimated when each individual's interests are weighted equally. That equal weighting is in turn legitimated both by the equal moral worth of each individual's interests and by the absence of accepted standards for arguing that some interests deserve greater weight than others.[31]

The gradual evolution of the theory and practice of adversary democracy from the seventeenth century to the present had made possible democracy on the level of the nation-state. Transforming the conception of majority rule from a substantive measure of the good of the whole to a procedure that only summed competing individual preferences had made it possible to generate democratically, rather than through monarchy or elite consensus, a single will that could speak for the nation as a whole. Previous understandings of democracy had assumed a single substantive common good, applicable to the whole nation. As nations increased in size, as the interests of their citizens diverged, and as the goal of a unanimous citizenry in either fact or fiction became untenable, unity may have seemed to require investing the common good in a single person, the monarch, rather than in the citizenry. The new conception of majority rule, which did not require the majority to be right but only to understand and promote its own interests, made it possible to produce on the scale of a modern nation-state democratic, unified, and legitimate political decisions without substantively resolving underlying conflicts. It is true that when decisions derive their legitimacy from a procedure that in principle gives each individual's interests equal weight, few decisions in any polity can be fully legitimate. But the theory evolved slowly, and its strong egalitarian implications did not have a major impact on democratic thought until the second half of the twentieth century.[32]

The procedures of adversary democracy have the great advantage of making decisions possible under conflict. But the theory has both prescriptive and descriptive weaknesses. Because adversary democracy takes preferences as given, and because it assumes both self-interest and irreconcilable conflict, it does not meet the deliberative, integrative, and transformative needs of citizens who must not only aggregate self-interests but choose among policies in the name of a common good. Framers of actual democratic institutions have, accordingly, always built in arenas for deliberation and for the discovery and creation of a public good—at least among the representatives and occasionally even among the citizens themselves. Indeed, as Cass Sunstein argues in this volume, adversary democracy by itself—the battle of interest against interest decided by, say, the procedure of majority rule—may fail to meet the criteria for democracy implicit in the decisions of the United States Supreme Court.

Yet despite the descriptive weaknesses of the theory, which derive from ignoring or misunderstanding institutions designed to discover or create a common good, after World War II the profession of political science began to describe the democratic process primarily in adversary terms. The political scientists who studied pluralism and interest groups—who gets what, where, when, and how—typically both assumed a dominant role for self-interest and expected interests to conflict. Even critics of democracy in the United States stressed the inequalities of power that allowed the interests of corporations and the wealthier classes to prevail over those of the working and lower classes. While Marxist critics pointed to structural imbalances involving massive inequalities of political power, mainstream critics of existing institutions found that "those who may need governmental assistance the least participate the most" (Verba and Nie 1972:12). Without making the self-protective basis of the vote explicit, the United States Supreme Court began to evolve a doctrine entitling all citizens to equal votes.[33]

Both mainstream political science and the Left critique had normative reasons for stressing self-interest. For mainstream political scientists, pluralism, ethical relativism, trade-offs, and adjustments among competing selfish desires posed an ethically attractive, egalitarian alternative to a potentially totalitarian single view of the public interest.[34] Disillusion with the Progressives' goal of entrusting public policy to experts, the rediscovery of human evil in Hitler's Germany, and the cold-war concern for avoiding nuclear destruction helped make the rationality of self-interest seem the soundest base on which to build an edifice of both fairness and self-preservation. For Marxists and others on the Left, talk of a public interest obscured underlying class, race, or gender conflict in a way that kept the less powerful from understanding or acting on their interests.[35] The conviction of the Left that dominant ideas are usually the self-serving ideas of the ruling class[36] and the conviction of the Right that big government had the same motives as big business helped reduce putatively public-spirited ideas to rationalizations of self-interest.

The postwar determination to make political science a genuine science contributed to the "hard-nosed" approach of a politics based on self-interest. But as important as the attraction of science was the attraction of scientific elegance. Beginning in 1957 with Anthony Down's *Economic Theory of Democracy,* "rational choice" or "public choice" modeling—which, like economic modeling, assumed self-interest as the sole human motivation—became in the 1970s the most elegant strand of thought in the adversary paradigm. Political scientists with a flair for mathematics began to explore the ways a few key simplifications and a formal model could extend the power of the human brain. The discovery of regularities that explain a wide range of relationships elegantly and parsimoniously has its own motivation and its own reward. Looking at the territory economists had covered in their field, political scientists were drawn to similar methods. Looking at the uncharted waters of political life, economists were drawn to this ocean of new material.

The intellectual insights of rational choice require modeling, and modeling requires simplification. The earliest entrepreneurs in this field, being economists, adopted the central economic simplification, namely, the notion that human beings have the single motive of self-interest. As Anthony Downs postulated in his classic early work, "We assume that every individual, though rational, is also selfish."[37]

Like other good thinkers in this field, Downs did not assert that the assumption of self-interest accurately described reality. Rather, he wrote,

> In reality, men are not always selfish, even in politics. They frequently do what appears to be individually irrational because they believe it is socially rational—i.e., it benefits others even though it harms them

personally. For example, politicians in the real world sometimes act as they think best for society as a whole even when they know their actions will lose votes. In every field, no account of human behavior is complete without mention of such altruism; its possessors are among the heroes men rightly admire. (1957:29)

"Nevertheless," he continued in the next sentence, "general theories of social action always rely heavily on the self-interest axiom."

Downs was wrong. Talcott Parsons's *The Structure of Social Action*, written in 1937 and perhaps the most important general theory of social action at the time Downs was writing, argues that social stability is grounded in cooperation and consensus, not merely in exchange or conflict. Anthropology has long been dominated by Lévi-Strauss and others who find symbolic, consensual bases for social order. But Downs was an economist and perhaps acquainted primarily with economic theories of social action. He thus concluded, with no further attempt at generating evidence, that Adam Smith's reasoning that we get our dinner from the butcher, brewer, and baker's "regard to their own self-interest" and not "from their benevolence only," applies "equally well to politics. Therefore we accept the self-interest axiom as a cornerstone of our analysis." [38]

Downs was elaborating a formal model, in which simplification to a single motive allows the modeler to work out, in some detail, a set of intellectually provocative consequences. But while he tried to keep the boundary between model and real world clear, it fuzzed beneath his pen. Because of the stature of this early work, it is worth looking closely at the following paragraph, in which Downs tries to distinguish between modeling and reality. Here the words "almost," "purely," "every," and "usually" war against one another (and against Downs's earlier statement that people "frequently" act to benefit others even though it harms them personally), failing in the end to compose a coherent picture of the "real world":

> Even in the real world, almost nobody carries out his function in the division of labor purely for its own sake. Rather every such function is discharged by someone who is spurred to act by private motives logically irrelevant to his function. Thus social functions are usually the by-products, and private ambitions the ends, of human action. (1957:29)

Almost everyone would agree with the first sentence's claim that motives are usually mixed. Therefore almost everyone should disagree with the implication of the second sentence that motives are in every function self-interested. What we need to study is when we can expect self-interested motivation, what forms self-interest will take, when we can expect non-self-interested motivation, what forms (both good and bad) it will take, and, crucially, which contexts promote which kinds of motives. Downs resolves these critical questions in the third sentence with his simple assertion that social behavior is "usually" self-interested.

Shortly after its inception the rational choice school evolved a set of practitioners who did not require the self-interest assumption but only the assumption that rational actors would act consistently and maximize whatever ends they preferred. Yet the version of rational choice that restricted its modeling to self-interest predominated at the start. Extremists in the self-interest school concluded "as a result of empirical research . . . the average human being is about 95 percent selfish in the narrow sense of the term."[39] Others, like Downs, slid from modeling the world according to self-interest into assuming that self-interest, often in its narrowest form, is "usually" the end toward which political actors strive.

In the heyday of this restricted version of rational choice, from 1960 to 1980, two books on the United States Congress seemed to argue that members of Congress were solely interested in reelection.[40] Because the United States Congress is the most studied democratic assembly on the planet, their claims had important consequences for understanding democracy more generally. While neither researcher in fact actually claimed that representatives cared only about reelection, they argued either that one could reinterpret all professed concern with public policy as in some way self-interested or, more narrowly, that because of the great uncertainty surrounding the circumstances of reelection, including the possibility that a challenger might raise even the most obscure vote into issue, enough representatives acted as if they were primarily concerned with reelection enough of the time to make predictions on that basis valuable.[41]

For the profession, the main impact of these books was to take the self-interest assumptions of rational choice modeling into the real world as a description of the stable motivations of members of Congress. Indeed, some of the entrepreneurs in the field began proselytizing actively for descriptions of politics based solely on self-interest. As Gordon Tullock put it, triumphantly, in 1979, "the traditional view of government has always been that it sought something called 'the public interest,'" but "with public choice, all of this has changed." In the profession of political science, "the public interest point of view" is now obsolete, although it "still informs many statements by public figures and the more old-fashioned students of politics."[42]

As Thomas Kuhn points out, however, the social sciences differ from the natural sciences in the degree to which models that describe the way the world works are both disputed and allowed to coexist with others that challenge their most fundamental premises. So it was with rational choice. As rational choice modelers made clearer the self-interested premises and implications of the larger theory of adversary democracy, that larger theory itself came under attack.

Partial Anticipations

Along with the development of adversary theory through rational choice, empirical political science after World War II had also seen both partial anticipations of the coming crisis and holdovers from an earlier tradition. In a 1961 article, James Q. Wilson and Peter Clark distinguished among what they called "material," "solidary," and "purposive" incentives. In several empirical studies over the next ten years, Wilson continued to make the point that the second two motives, of wanting solidarity with a group and wanting to promote a cause, account in some contexts for a large fraction of political motivation.[43] In 1964, Wilson and Edward Banfield used patterns of citizen voting for expenditures to suggest that some cultural groups in the United States tended to vote for "public-regarding" reasons, others more according to self-interest.[44] While the "public-regarding" studies provoked a decade or so of research in political science and then faded, Wilson's three categories of motivation became quasi-canonical, co-existing uneasily with the increasing emphasis in the profession on self-interest.

Wilson and Banfield may have been mavericks,[45] but another figure whose work did not fit the paradigm fell directly within the mainstream. Richard Fenno's classic 1973 congressional study, *Congressmen in Committees,* pointed out that members of certain congressional committees tried to get on those committees because they wanted to help make good public policy. This insight, like Wilson's emphasis on purposive and solidary motivation, found no opposition in the profession. Subsequent researchers confirmed the existence of a "policy orientation" among members of Congress, although younger scholars might have made their reputations by showing such an orientation had declined or had never existed.[46]

In a pattern more like the one Kuhn would predict, two journalists outside the academy also discovered and tried to publicize the commitments of certain legislators to the public good. Elizabeth Drew quoted an important lobbyist as saying, "You got to understand what motivates the politician. Dummies, even in this town, think that politicians just want to be reelected. Well [when I talk about public policy with these legislators], I'm talking merits with most of them." In response to the by now almost hegemonic assumption that legislators acted only on self-interest, Bernard Asbell entitled his book *The Senate Nobody Knows.*[47]

The Awareness of Anomaly

Some political scientists stumbled on anomalies in adversary theory in the course of field research. To take a personal example, in the research for *Beyond Adversary Democracy* I had particularly selected for study a town in which conflicts of material interest dramatically split the populace. In interviewing, I had probed for conflict. Only in the next case study, a collective like one in which my own membership had given me the eye of an insider, did I recognize extensive identification with the common interest. Rereading my earlier notes, I now noticed the citizens who told me how they made the good of "the town" their own. Each polity had within it, and I concluded needed within it, both adversary and deliberative procedures. As the adversary procedures helped manage irreconcilable and often self-regarding interests, the deliberative arenas helped citizens discover and create their common interest, often by transforming self-interested preferences.

After 1980, other researchers studying legislatures also attacked the adversary paradigm. In 1982, William Muir's *Legislature: California's School for Politics* argued that legislators can learn, want to learn, and often act upon what they have learned. They want to not look stupid, to matter, and to make good public policy. Specific governmental institutions, like those in the California legislature, encourage these nonelectoral motivations. In 1983, Arthur Maass's *Congress and the Common Good* argued that members of the United States Congress deliberate to reach agreement on the standards of the common life at least as much as they aggregate particular self-interests. In 1985, David Vogler and Sidney Waldman's *Congress and Democracy* applied to Congress the distinction between adversary and unitary democracy, specifying individuals and instances in which members of Congress appeared genuinely concerned with what they called in private a "bad bill," or in public "legislation detrimental to the long-term well-being of the American people" (1985:11). In the same year, Martha Derthick and Paul Quirk's *The Politics of Deregulation* (see Quirk, chap. 11, this vol.) reported hundreds of legislators and other political actors acting orthogonally to or against their own self-interest because they had been convinced by the idea that deregulation was in the public interest.

Meanwhile, in the study of social movements the evidence for the importance of non-self-interested motivation had become incontrovertible. One could not understand the decisions proponents and opponents made in the political struggle for the Equal Rights Amendment, for example, without plumbing motivations only remotely related to self-interest.[48]

But of all the anomalies that perplexed researchers, "the paradox of the rational voter" had the most classic Kuhnian form. As Morris Fiorina succinctly put it, this was "the paradox that ate rational choice theory"

(1986:10). In Downs's original formulation, the value of a single citizen's vote (its likelihood of having a decisive impact) is "tiny; hence it is outweighed by a very small cost of voting," for example, the time it takes to vote. Looking only at returns to self-interest, then, it is not rational to vote (Downs 1957:267). Yet many people do vote. The obvious conclusion is that voters are acting for "irrational," that is, non-self-interested, reasons. They may vote because they are calculating incorrectly. But they also may vote because they feel solidarity with a group, because they have never thought of voting in cost-benefit terms, or because they believe in a principle that prompts their actions.

If intellectual stimulation is the goal of modeling, as I believe it ought to be, failing to predict voting behavior would not destroy the usefulness of a model based on self-interest. The model would still function effectively to explain the consequences of self-interest, even in contexts where self-interest predicted very little. But as Downs's uncertainty about the relation of the rational choice model to the real world suggests, many modelers want more than this. "Theoretical models," Downs states, "should be tested primarily by the accuracy of their predictions rather than by the reality of their assumptions."[49] If accurate prediction is the goal, a model based on self-interest does not do well. When voter turnout rises to 60 percent, the model does not predict accurately 60 percent of the time—even presuming that the 40 percent who do not vote abstain for the reasons that model assumes.

Kuhn describes a crisis in the natural sciences as beginning with "a pronounced failure in the normal problem solving activity" (1970:74–75). Confronted with this failure, the defenders of the paradigm "will devise numerous articulations and *ad hoc* modifications of their theory in order to eliminate any apparent conflict" (p. 78). When an anomaly calls "into question explicit and fundamental generalizations of the paradigm, . . . the transition to crisis and to extraordinary science has begun. The anomaly now comes to be more generally recognized as such by the profession. More and more attention is devoted to it by more and more of the field's most eminent men" (p. 83).

By the late 1970s, the paradox of the rational voter had taken on this cast. In 1974 and 1975, for example, the *American Political Science Review* devoted eight articles to Morris Fiorina and John Ferejohn's thesis that it was rational to vote if, in the extremely improbable case that your favored candidate lost the election by one vote, you would feel a regret so extreme as to make the small cost of voting a reasonable price to pay for not taking that gamble. This explanation met with immediate opposition and did not win many converts.[50] Other possible explanations, none commanding general assent, appeared in the pages of *Public Choice*.[51] By 1984, a distinguished economist had produced an analysis of a two-candidate election proving that in equilibrium no one at all would vote.[52] As Kuhn (1970:91) puts it, "the proliferation of competing articulations, the willingness to try anything, the expression of explicit discontent, the recourse to philosophy and to debate over fundamentals, all these are symptoms" of oncoming scientific crisis. By 1980 political scientists were paying attention to Brian Barry's earlier conclusions from Riker and Ordeshook's data, which showed that believing in the importance of voting (sometimes called "citizen duty") has a greater effect on whether one votes than does thinking an election will be close or caring who wins. Since believing in the importance of voting is the strongest determinant of voting using these measures, and since, in Barry's words, voting is not therefore "undertaken with any expectation of changing the state of the world, it fails to fit the minimum requirements of the means-end model of rational behavior."[53] Nor does it fit the requirements of a model based on self-interest.

Crisis

In the last ten years, at the same time that economists were advancing rational choice models based on self-interest to explain phenomena as varied as industry regulation, marital stability, and suicide,[54] social science disciplines other than political science were preparing the theoretical and empirical ground for a massive revision both of the larger adversary paradigm and of the rational choice strands within it.

In economics, Amartya Sen fired the first major theoretical salvo at the self-interest assumptions of economists and rational choice theorists with his classic 1977 paper, "Rational Fools" (reprinted here as chap. 2). Sen argued that sympathy for other people and commitment to a principle produce two key departures from self-interest, and that commitment, which involves counterpreferential choice, "drives a wedge between personal choice and personal welfare" while "much of traditional economic theory relies on the identity of the two."[55] He suggested the now highly influential concept of a "meta-ranking" of preferences to explain how one might place commitment above a subjective preference.[56] In 1978, David Collard's *Altruism and Economy* supported the thesis that "human beings are not entirely selfish, even in their economic dealings" (1978:3), with copious illustrations from empirical work on games, wages, communes, charity, and disasters. Albert Hirschman's "Against Parsimony" in 1985 criticized the parsimonious postulate of a "self-interested, isolated individual" and argued for a new focus on changes in values (rather than "wanton" tastes), on noninstrumental action, and on the practice of an ability (where use augments supply rather than depleting it). Thomas Schelling, followed by Jon Elster, argued for models of a "divided self," in which one self uses on another the strategies of constraint or persuasion. Michael McPherson and Robert Frank added theoretical and empirical arguments against the dominance of self-interest, while Lester Thurow criticized the entire theory of equilibrium supply and demand. In empirical studies James Kau and Paul Rubin argued that beliefs about the structure of the world and ways of improving it explain congressional votes on regulatory legislation better than do the economic interests of constituents or campaign contributors, and Joseph Kalt and Mark Zupan argued that "ideological shirking" (ignoring reelection concerns for the sake of "individuals' altruistic, publicly interested goals") is an important political phenomenon in certain congressional contexts.[57]

Cognitive psychologists joined these renegade economists. Daniel Kahneman, a psychologist, teamed up with economists Jack Knetch and Richard Thaler to investigate, with phone and classroom surveys, the kinds of economic behavior people think is fair,[58] teasing out of their results principles that were not always intuitively obvious and making on this basis testable predictions about consumer and labor markets. They found that the public usually considers unfair behavior that violates the implicit commitments of an ongoing relationship or "deliberately exploits the special dependence of a particular individual."[59] These determinants of fairness have economic effects, because consumers will try to find ways to reward and punish firms they see as behaving fairly and unfairly.[60]

In departments of psychology, management, and economics, hundreds of recent experiments with prisoners' dilemma and other games that reward self-interested behavior at the expense of the group indicate a stubborn refusal on the part of a significant fraction (usually 25 percent to 35 percent) to take rational self-interested action, even under conditions of complete anonymity with no possibility of group punishment. Those who insistently take the cooperative stance usually say that their motive was to "do the right thing" (Dawes and Thaler 1988: 194). Experimenters can raise the level of cooperative behavior to 85 percent by allowing discussion and other procedures that increase feelings of group identity (see Dawes, van de Kragt, and Orbell, chap. 6 this vol.). On the other hand, they can raise the level of self-interested behavior by raising the payoff (indicating that morality can have a price), having the cooperators lose over and over (indicating that morality can be extinguished), or by using economics students (indicating that self-interested people choose to study economics, or that socialization into the profession generates a self-interested outlook, or both).[61]

In political psychology, survey research by David Sears (Sears and Funk, chap. 9, this vol.) and others shows that on several issues self-interest has less effect than political principles on political attitudes. Thinking of oneself as a liberal or conservative, for example, explains one's opposition to busing more than having a child in a school liable to be integrated through busing. It explains one's views on Vietnam more than having a relative or friend fighting there, one's views on national health insurance more than being privately insured or not, and, among corporate executives, one's views on foreign policy more than whether one's company has defense contracts or investments overseas.[62] Tom Tyler's work (chap. 10, this vol.) shows that citizens evaluate courts, police, and political figures more positively if they conclude that these institutions and individuals acted fairly than if they benefit personally from the decisions. Even convicted criminals think more highly of legal authorities, law, and government when they believe the procedures in their case were fair than when they get a low sentence (Tyler, Casper, and Fisher, in press).

Other psychologists have been studying the roots of "prosocial behavior" in innate responses, personality, early childhood training, group norms, and immediate context. They find, for example, that even newborns experience "primitive" empathy, crying more when they hear another infant's crying than when they hear other equally loud and aversive sounds. Two-year-olds spontaneously proffer help to others they see in distress; older children add cognitive filters, helping those they believe to be deserving.[63] While researchers had earlier found it difficult to get a hearing for anything other than a self-interested model of human behavior, by 1980 "prosocial behavior had moved from a marginal, hardly permissible topic of research to one that was vigorously investigated."[64]

The sociological profession, traditionally the stronghold of academic concern for non-self-interested motivation, has produced the strongest statement against the self-interested model of motivation. Pulling together evidence from a wide variety of disciplines, Amitai Etzioni contends that the "most important bases of choice," the "majority of choices," and the "natural" forms of choice both as to means and ends are "affective and normative" rather than rational and self-interested (1988:4, 90, 93, 151).

In the last ten years, biologists have shown that social contexts affect human and animal biology. Menstruation in one woman causes menstruation in another. Eliminating a higher-ranking vervet monkey in a dominance hierarchy causes a rise in serotonin in the second ranked.[65] As evidence mounts that even the biological self is socially constituted, the very concept of self-interest becomes more complex.

Within sociobiology, theorists have been trying to explain how groups can select for altruism and cooperation if individual human beings select for self-interest. The question is why the genes of the self-interested do not perpetuate themselves and the genes of those who sacrifice themselves for anyone but their close genetic kin do not die out. Donald Campbell has argued for more than a decade that cultural evolution must explain the persistence of cooperative norms (1975, 1982, 1983, 1986). Christopher

Jencks (chap. 4, this vol.) and others have also pursued this argument. Boyd and Richerson (chap. 7, this vol.) now suggest at least one mechanism—"conformist transmission" or "frequency dependent bias"—by which group selection outcomes might survive in the face of individual selection processes. They argue that if information costs lead most individuals to copy the behavior they find most frequent among them, populations with a majority of cooperators can sustain themselves against individuals learning to defect, and can multiply through their advantages in the struggle for group survival.

In the more restricted domain of small groups that expect repeated interaction, Axelrod and others have demonstrated the evolutionary feasibility of reciprocal altruism (e.g., "Tit for Tat").[66]

Finally, in political science, the years 1987 and 1988 alone have seen a small surge of books and articles aimed at undermining the adversary paradigm.[67] Steven Kelman's 1987 *Making Public Policy* documented the motivation for making good public policy in Congress, and Robert B. Reich's 1988 edited volume, *The Power of Public Ideas,* brought together likeminded colleagues at the Kennedy School, including Kelman, Gary Orren, Mark Moore, and Philip Heymann, with further evidence on the importance of public spirit among both citizens and policymakers. Kristen Monroe has suggested incorporating within rational actor theory the human needs for sociability and group identity, and Carol Uhlaner has produced a rational choice model explaining political participation through citizens wanting to belong to a group and electorally relevant leaders wanting to strengthen their partisans' group-oriented motives.[68] Roger Friedland and Alexander Robertson's *Beyond the Marketplace* (1989) challenges the primacy of individual material self-interest in economic action, and new work by Anthony Downs (1989) softens the stress on self-interest that characterized his earlier book.

The Near Irrelevance of Philosophy

In 1990 we see a minirevolt, in almost all empirical branches of the profession of political science, against the self-interested model of the way a democratic polity actually works. The surprise is how tangentially this revolt is related to the strands in normative democratic theory that since World War II have come to focus on this issue.

Deliberation was the essence of democracy in the empirical description as well as the normative prescriptions of major nineteenth- and early twentieth-century writers such as Bagehot and Barker. After World War II, as empirical description focused more and more on self-interest, the normative concern for a politics that transcended self-interest was preserved in several almost independent philosophical traditions—the antimodernist tradition associated with Leo Strauss, the Republican virtue tradition associated with the historical work of J. G. A. Pocock, the communal tradition associated with Sheldon Wolin, and the Frankfurt tradition associated with Jurgen Habermas. Many contemporary democratic theorists, most notably Benjamin Barber in *Strong Democracy*, but also Hannah Pitkin and others, stressed transformation of self and polity through communal deliberation.[69] Recent influential "communitarian" theorists such as Michael Sandel (1982) and Charles Taylor (1989) put collective attributes at the core of individual identity, pointing out that the self must always be "situated" and "encumbered," and that many goods, like language, are "irreducibly social." Feminist theorists in particular have turned political thinking toward relationships and mutuality from rights and individuality,[70] suggesting, for example, that mothering is a model of human behavior as applicable as contract to political life (Held, chap. 17, this vol.). Yet while the insights of rational choice have informed political philosophy,[71] the concerns of philosophers for deliberation and the transformation of interests through political discourse have had relatively little effect on either rational choice or empirical political science.

What Now?

On the narrow question of "rational choice," it would be absurd to give up the extraordinarily useful insights into political behavior that rational choice as an enterprise has given us, or to give up the intellectual power that modeling with reduction to a single motive can provide. To rational choice we owe ideas such as central clustering in a two-party system, models of retrospective voting, income redistribution from the tails to the center, unanimity through side payments, political rent-seeking, and free riding in the provision of collective goods. These ideas have invigorated theory and stimulated revealing empirical investigations. Rational choice theories provoke thought. By pointing out that certain outcomes flow logically in certain circumstances from self-interest, they challenge the researcher to explain deviations from those outcomes.

But the claim that self-interest alone motivates political behavior must be either vacuous, if self-interest can encompass any motive, or false, if self-interest means behavior that consciously intends only self as the beneficiary. Some rational choice theorists equivocate on this point, most of the time making the false claim, and backing off to the vacuous claim under critical fire.[72] Others, "inclusive" modelers, are in principle happy to abandon the claim that self-interest is the sole operative motive and willing to work with any motive, provided only that the decision maker maximize and be consistent.[73] Inclusive modelers can now expand the range of motives beyond self-interest, experiment with new forms of modeling, and, most importantly, begin to specify the contexts in which narrowly self-interested behavior is most and least likely to appear (Mansbridge, chap. 15, this vol.).

Specifying context allows us to move easily between the descriptive arena and the normative. Normatively, if we conclude that some outcomes are good, or find the outcomes acceptable and want to promote the motive as good in itself, we can use the degree to which models accurately predict behavior and outcomes in different contexts as guides to designing contexts, or institutions, that are likely to encourage certain motives and discourage others.

In 1986 James Buchanan won the Nobel Prize in economics for applying to politics a "rational choice" model based on self-interest. In the same year, however, he repudiated the single motive of self-interest in favor of looking at context. "There has not been enough attention paid," he concluded then, "to the interdependence between the predicted patterns of political outcomes and the rules or institutions that constrain the political actors." Both those who imagine a world of benevolent public servants following only the public interest and those who "have modelled politicians and bureaucrats as self-interested maximizers" share "a fatal flaw."

> Both images are widely interpreted, by their own proponents, to be descriptions of a total reality of politics, when, in fact, both images are partial. Each image pulls out, isolates, and accentuates a highly particularized element that is universal in all human behavior. To an extent, political agents, elected politicians and bureaucrats, as well as voters, act in pursuit of what they genuinely consider to be the "general interest." But also, to an extent, these political participants act in pursuit of what they estimate to be their own pecuniary interest. Each political actor, regardless of his role, combines both of these elements in his behavior pattern, along with many other elements not noted here.
>
> The whole point of constitutional inquiry is the proposition that the constraints, rules, and institutions within which persons make choices politically can and do influence the relative importance of the separate motivational elements.[74]

Buchanan's argument suggests that, like Madison and Hamilton before us, we should try to design institutions to encourage motivations that we believe on normative grounds are either good in themselves or will lead to good and just outcomes. We need institutions based primarily on self-interest as well as those based primarily on altruism, recognizing that each may well require some admixture of the other set of motives. We need particularly to understand better the internal dynamics of various mixtures of motives in specific institutions, investigating the contexts in which different forms of self-interest either undermine or sustain specific forms of concern with others. We need to accommodate issues on which citizens have, or can come to have, a common interest, as well as issues on which citizens' interests conflict. On most issues, which mix common and conflicting interests, we need deliberative processes as well as adversary ones.

Buchanan's recognition that institutions influence motivation, and that motivation can be at least public- and self-interested, invites empirical political scientists to engage with those contemporary political philosophers who analyze the political transformation of preferences. Here we need to understand, among many other things, what political forms encourage individuals to replace self-interest with a concern for the collective good; to what extent elections in a representative system can transform the electorate's preferences (Schwartz 1988); the potential for good and ill in such transformations; how ritual, symbols, schema, and scripts work in the transformative process (Johnson, 1988); how people take on political identity; how the different arenas for deliberation—courts, legislatures (staff members as well as legislators), the executive branch and its agencies, interest groups, universities, grant-making foundations, the media, the citizenry, and the interaction among these—contribute to and detract from political life (Mansbridge 1988); and how we can distinguish usefully among the components of deliberation—bargaining according to self-interest under different constraints on power, negotiation that appeals both to principled standards and to what the other parties actually want, and arguments, with evidence, on questions of the common good.[75]

It is critical, in these investigations, to recognize the transformative power of self-interest as well as altruism. If a central goal of participation in politics is to come to understand one's interests better, self-interest must have a legitimate role in the body politic. Consciousness-raising groups cannot have altruism as their only mandate. Leaving aside the philosophical problem of whose interests a society of people who cared only for others would promote, self-awareness requires the legitimation of self-interest. Awakened, conscious adults must be able to understand their own interests and negotiate for them in moments of conflict in ways that would not be possible in a culture that prescribed only "a disinterested attachment to the public good, exclusive and independent of all private and selfish interest."[76]

Just as, after three centuries of evolution, normative democratic theory and the empirical study of democratic practice are now at a point where each can accommodate both conflict and common interest, so too both these enterprises should have approached the point where they can begin to give both self-interest and concern for the common good a significant role in political action.

II   Dimensions of the Problem

2   Rational Fools: A Critique of the Behavioral Foundations of Economic Theory

Amartya K. Sen

I

In his *Mathematical Psychics,* published in 1881, Edgeworth asserted that "the first principle of Economics is that every agent is actuated only by self-interest."[1] This view of man has been a persistent one in economic models, and the nature of economic theory seems to have been much influenced by this basic premise. In this essay I would like to examine some of the problems that have arisen from this conception of human beings.

I should mention that Edgeworth himself was quite aware that this so-called first principle of Economics was not a particularly realistic one. Indeed, he felt that "the concrete nineteenth century man is for the most part an impure egoist, a mixed utilitarian."[2] This raises the interesting question as to why Edgeworth spent so much of his time and talent in developing a line of inquiry the first principle of which he believed to be false. The issue is not why abstractions should be employed in pursuing general economic questions—the nature of the inquiry makes this inevitable—but why would one choose an assumption which one believed to be not merely inaccurate in detail but fundamentally mistaken? As we shall see, this question is of continuing interest to modern economics as well.

Part of the answer, as far as Edgeworth was concerned, undoubtedly lay in the fact that he did not think the assumption to be fundamentally mistaken in the *particular* types of activities to which he applied what he called "economical calculus": (i) war and (ii) contract. "Admitting that there exists in the higher parts of human nature a tendency towards and feeling after utilitarian institutions," he asked the rhetorical question: "could we seriously suppose that these moral considerations were relevant to war and trade; could eradicate the 'controlless core' of human selfishness, or exercise an appreciable force in comparison with the impulse of self-interest."[3] He interpreted Sidgwick to have dispelled the "illusion" that "the interest of all is the interest of each," noting that Sidgwick found the "two supreme

This chapter was first published in H. Harris, ed., *Scientific Models and Men* (London: Oxford University Press, 1978), 317–44.

principles—Egoism and Utilitarianism" to be "irreconcilable, unless indeed by religion." "It is far from the spirit of the philosophy of pleasure to deprecate the importance of religion," wrote Edgeworth, "but in the present inquiry, and dealing with the lower elements of human nature, we should have to seek a more obvious transition, a more earthy passage, from the principle of self-interest to the principle, or at least the practice, of utilitarianism."[4]

Notice that the context of the debate is important to this argument. Edgeworth felt that he had established the acceptability of "egoism" as the fundamental behavioral assumption for his particular inquiry by demolishing the acceptability of "utilitarianism" as a description of actual behavior. Utilitarianism is, of course, far from being the only non-egoistic approach. Furthermore, between the claims of oneself and the claims of all lie the claims of a variety of groups—for example, families, friends, local communities, peer groups, and economic and social classes. The concepts of family responsibility, business ethics, class consciousness, and so on, relate to these intermediate areas of concern, and the dismissal of utilitarianism as a descriptive theory of behavior does not leave us with egoism as the only alternative. The relevance of some of these considerations to the economics of negotiations and contracts would be difficult to deny.

It must be noted that Edgeworth's query about the outcome of economic contact between purely self-seeking individuals had the merit of being immediately relevant to an abstract enquiry that had gone on for more than a hundred years already, and which was much discussed in debates involving Herbert Spencer, Henry Sidgwick, and other leading thinkers of the period. Two years before Edgeworth's *Mathematical Psychics* appeared, Herbert Spencer had published his elaborate analysis of the relation between egoism and altruism in *The Data of Ethics*. He had arrived at the comforting—if somewhat unclear—conclusion that "general happiness is to be achieved mainly through the adequate pursuit of their own happinesses by individuals; while, reciprocally, the happiness of individuals are to be achieved in part by their pursuit of the general happiness."[5] In the context of this relatively abstract enquiry, Edgeworth's tight economic analysis, based on a well-defined model of contracts between two self-seeking individuals, or between two types of (identical) self-seeking individuals, gave a clear answer to an old hypothetical question.

It appeared that in Edgeworth's model, based on egoistic behavior, there was a remarkable correspondence between exchange equilibria in competitive markets and what in modern economic terms is called "the core" of the economy. An outcome is said to be in "the core" of the economy if and only if it fulfills a set of conditions of unimprovability. These conditions, roughly speaking, are that not only is it the case that no one could be made better off without making somebody else worse off (the situation is what is called a "Pareto optimum"), but also that no one is worse off than he would be without trade, and that no coalition of individuals, by altering the trade among themselves, could on their own improve their own lot. Edgeworth showed that given certain general assumptions, any equilibrium that can emerge in a competitive market must satisfy these conditions and be in "the core." Thus, in Edgeworth's model the competitive market equilibria are, in this sense, undominated by any feasible alternative arrangement, given the initial distribution of endowments. More surprising in some ways was the converse result that if the number of individuals of each type were increased without limit, the core (representing such undominated outcomes) would shrink towards the set of competitive equilibria; that is, the core would not be much more extensive than the set of competitive equilibria. This pair of results has been much elaborated and extended in the recent literature on general equilibrium with similar models and with essentially the same behavioral assumptions.[6]

Being in the core, however, is not as such a momentous achievement from the point of view of social welfare. A person who starts off ill-endowed may stay poor and deprived even after the transactions, and if being in the core is all that competition offers, the propertyless person may be forgiven for not regarding this achievement as a "big deal." Edgeworth took some note of this by considering the problem of choice between different competitive equilibria. He observed that for the utilitarian good society, "competition requires to be supplemented by arbitration, and the basis of arbitration between self-interested contractors is the greatest possible sum-total utility."[7] Into the institutional aspects of such arbitration and the far-reaching implications of it for the distribution of property ownership, Edgeworth did not really enter, despite superficial appearance to the contrary. On the basis of the achievement of competition, however limited, Edgeworth felt entitled to be "biased to a more conservative caution in reform." In calculating "the utility of pre-utilitarian institutions," Edgeworth felt impressed "with a view of Nature, not, as in the picture left by Mill, all bad, but a first approximation to the best."[8]

I am not concerned in this essay with examining whether the approximation is a rather remote one. (This I do believe to be the case even within the structure of assumptions used by Edgeworth, but it is not central to the subject of this paper.) I am concerned here with the view of man which forms part of Edgeworth's analysis and survives more or less intact in much of modern economic theory. The view is, of course, a stylized one and geared specifically to tackling a relatively abstract dispute with which Spencer, Sidgwick, and several other leading contemporary thinkers were much concerned—namely, in what sense and to what extent would egoistic behavior achieve general good? Whether or not egoistic behavior is an accurate assumption in reality does not, of course, have any bearing on the accuracy of Edgeworth's answer to the question posed. Within the structure of a limited economic model it provided a clear-cut response to the abstract query about egoism and general good.

This particular debate has gone on for a long time and continues to provide motivation for many recent exercises in economic theory today. The limited nature of the query has had a decisive influence on the choice of economic models and the conception of human beings in them. In their distinguished text on general equilibrium theory, Kenneth Arrow and Frank Hahn state (*General Competitive Analysis,* pp. vi–vii):

> There is by now a long and fairly imposing line of economists from Adam Smith to the present who have sought to show that a decentralized economy motivated by self-interest and guided by price signals would be compatible with a coherent disposition of economic resources that could be regarded, in a well-defined sense, as superior to a large class of possible alternative dispositions. Moreover, the price signals would operate in a way to establish this degree of coherence. It is important to understand how surprising this claim must be to anyone not exposed to the tradition. The immediate "common sense" answer to the question "What will an economy motivated by individual greed and controlled by a very large number of different agents look like?" is probably: There will be chaos. That quite a different answer has long been claimed true and has indeed permeated the economic thinking of a large number of people who are in no way economists is itself sufficient ground for investigating it seriously. The proposition having been put forward and very seriously entertained, it is important to know not only whether it *is* true, but whether it *could* be true. A good deal of what follows is concerned with this last question, which seems to us to have considerable claims on the attention of economists.

The primary concern here is not with the relation of postulated models to the real economic world, but with the accuracy of answers to well-defined questions posed with preselected assumptions which severely constrain the nature of the models that can be admitted into the analysis. A specific concept of man is ingrained in the question itself, and there is no freedom to depart from this conception so long as one is engaged in answering this question. The nature of man in these current economic models continues, then, to reflect the particular formulation of certain general philosophical questions posed in the past. The realism of the chosen conception of man is simply not a part of this inquiry.

II

There is another nonempirical—and possibly simpler—reason why the conception of man in economic models tends to be that of a self-seeking egoist. It is possible to define a person's interests in such a way that no matter what he does he can be seen to be furthering his own interests in every isolated act of choice.[9] While formalized relatively recently in the context of the theory of revealed preference, this approach is of respectable antiquity, and Joseph Butler was already arguing against it in the Rolls Chapel two and a half centuries ago.[10] The reduction of man to a self-seeking animal depends in this approach on careful definition. If you are observed to choose *x* rejecting *y,* you are declared to have "revealed" a preference for *x* over *y.* Your personal utility is then defined as simply a numerical representation of this "preference," assigning a higher utility to a "preferred" alternative. With this set of definitions you can hardly escape maximizing your own utility, except through inconsistency. Of course, if you choose *x* and reject *y* on one occasion and then promptly proceed to do the exact opposite, you can prevent the revealed-preference theorist from assigning a preference ordering to you, thereby restraining him from stamping a utility function on you which you must be seen to be maximizing. He will then have to conclude that either you are inconsistent or your preferences are changing. You can frustrate the revealed-preference theorists through more sophisticated inconsistencies as well.[11] But if you are consistent, then no matter whether you are a single-minded egoist or a raving altruist or a class-conscious militant, you will appear to be maximizing your own utility in this enchanted world of definitions. Borrowing from the terminology used in connection with taxation, if the Arrow-Hahn justification of the assumption of egoism amounts to an *avoidance* of the issue, the revealed-preference approach looks more like a robust piece of *evasion*.

This approach of definitional egoism sometimes goes under the name of rational choice, and it involves nothing other than internal consistency. A person's choices are considered "rational" in this approach if and only if these choices can *all* be explained in terms of some preference relation consistent with the revealed-preference definition, that is, if all his choices can be explained as the choosing of "most preferred" alternatives with respect to a postulated preference relation.[12] The rationale of this approach seems to be based on the idea that the only way of understanding a person's real preference is to examine his actual choices, and there is no choice-independent way of understanding someone's attitude towards alternatives. (This view, by the way, is not confined to economists only. When, many years ago, I had to take my qualifying examination in English Literature at Calcutta University, one of the questions we had to answer concerning *A Midsummer Night's Dream* was: Compare the characters of Hermia and Helena. Whom would you choose?)

I have tried to demonstrate elsewhere that once we eschew the curious definitions of preference and welfare, this approach presumes both too little and too much: *too little* because there are non-choice sources of information on preference and welfare as these terms are usually understood, and *too much* because choice may reflect a compromise among a variety of considerations of which personal welfare may be just one.[13]

The complex psychological issues underlying choice have recently been forcefully brought out by a number of penetrating studies dealing with consumer decisions[14] and production activities.[15] It is very much an open question as to whether these behavioral characteristics can be at all captured within the formal limits of consistent choice on which the welfare-maximization approach depends.[16]

III

Paul Samuelson has noted that many economists would "separate economics from sociology upon the basis of rational or irrational behavior, where these terms are defined in the penumbra of utility theory."[17] This view might well be resented, for good reasons, by sociologists, but the cross that economists have to bear in this view of the dichotomy can be seen if we note that the approach of "rational behavior," as it is typically interpreted, leads to a remarkably mute theory. Behavior, it appears, is to be "explained in terms of preferences, which are in turn defined only by behavior." Not surprisingly, excursions into circularities have been frequent. Nevertheless, Samuelson is undoubtedly right in asserting that the theory "is not in a technical sense *meaningless*."[18] The reason is quite simple. As we have already discussed, the approach does impose the requirement of internal consistency of observed choice, and this might well be refuted by actual observations, making the theory "meaningful" in the sense in which Samuelson's statement is intended.

The requirement of consistency does have surprising cutting power. Various general characteristics of demand relations can be derived from it. But in the present context, the main issue is the possibility of using the consistency requirement for actual *testing*. Samuelson specifies the need for "ideal observational conditions" for the implications of the approach to be "refuted or verified." This is not, however, easy to satisfy since, on the one hand, our love of variety makes it illegitimate to consider individual acts of choice as the proper units (rather than *sequences* of choices) while, on the other hand, lapse of time makes it difficult to distinguish between inconsistencies and changing tastes. There have, in fact, been very few systematic attempts at testing the consistency of people's day-to-day behavior, even though there have been interesting and useful contrived experiments on people's reactions to uncertainty under laboratory conditions. What counts as admissible evidence remains unsettled. If today you were to poll economists of different schools, you would almost certainly find the coexistence of beliefs (i) that the rational behavior theory is unfalsifiable, (ii) that it is falsifiable and so far unfalsified, and (iii) that it is falsifiable and indeed patently false.[19]

However, for my purposes here this is not the central issue. Even if the required consistency were seen to obtain, it would still leave the question of egoism unresolved except in the purely definitional sense, as I have already noted. A consistent chooser can have any degree of egoism that we care to specify. It is, of course, true that in the special case of pure consumer choice over private goods, the revealed preference theorist tries to relate the person's "preference" or "utility" to his *own* bundle of commodities. This restriction arises, however, not from any guarantee that he is concerned only with his own interests, but from the fact that his own consumption bundle—or that of his family—is the only bundle over which he has direct *control* in his acts of choice. The question of egoism remains completely open.

I believe the question also requires a clearer formulation than it tends to receive, and to this question I shall now turn.

IV

As we consider departures from "unsympathetic isolation abstractly assumed in Economics," to use Edgeworth's words, we must distinguish between two separate concepts: (i) sympathy and (ii) commitment. The former corresponds to the case in which the concern for others directly affects one's own welfare. If the knowledge of torture of others makes you sick, it is a case of sympathy; if it does not make you feel personally worse off, but you think it is wrong and you are ready to do something to stop it, it is a case of commitment. I do not wish to claim that the words chosen have any very great merit, but the distinction is, I think, important. It can be argued that behavior based on sympathy is in an important sense egoistic, for one is oneself pleased at others' pleasure and pained at others' pain, and the pursuit of one's own utility may thus be helped by sympathetic action. It is action based on commitment rather than sympathy which would be non-egoistic in this sense. (Note, however, that the *existence* of sympathy does not imply that the action helpful to others must be *based on* sympathy in the sense that the action would not take place had one got less or no comfort from others' welfare. This question of *causation* is to be taken up presently.)

Sympathy is, in some ways, an easier concept to analyze than commitment. When a person's sense of well-being is psychologically dependent on someone else's welfare, it is a case of sympathy; other things given, the awareness of the increase in the welfare of the other person then makes this person directly better off. (Of course, when the influence is negative, the relation is better named "antipathy," but we can economize on terminology and stick to the term "sympathy," just noting that the relation can be positive or negative.) While sympathy relates similar things to each other—namely, welfares of different persons—commitment relates choice to anticipated levels of welfare. One way of defining commitment is in terms of a person choosing an act that he believes will yield a lower level of personal welfare to him than an alternative that is also available to him. Notice that the comparison is between *anticipated* welfare levels, and therefore this definition of commitment excludes acts that go against self-interest resulting purely from a failure to foresee consequences.

A more difficult question arises when a person's choice happens to coincide with the maximization of his anticipated personal welfare, but that is not the *reason* for his choice. If we wish to make room for this, we can expand the definition of commitment to include cases in which the person's choice, while maximizing anticipated personal welfare, would be unaffected under at least one counterfactual condition in which the act chosen would cease to maximize personal welfare. Commitment in this more inclusive sense may be difficult to ascertain not only in the context of others' choices but also in that of one's own, since it is not always clear what one would have done had the circumstances been different. This broader sense may have particular relevance when one acts on the basis of a concern for duty which, if violated, could cause remorse, but the action is really chosen out of the sense of duty rather than just to avoid the illfare resulting from the remorse that would occur if one were to act otherwise. (Of course, even the narrower sense of commitment will cover the case in which the illfare resulting from the remorse, if any, is *outweighed* by the gain in welfare.)

I have not yet referred to uncertainty concerning anticipated welfare. When this is introduced, the concept of sympathy is unaffected, but commitment will require reformulation. The necessary modifications will depend on the person's reaction to uncertainty. The simplest case is probably the one in which the person's idea of what a "lottery" offers to him in terms of personal gain is captured by the "expected utility" of personal welfare (that is, adding personal welfares from different outcomes weighted by the probability of occurrence of each outcome). In this case, the entire discussion is reformulated simply replacing personal welfare by *expected* personal welfare; commitment then involves choosing an action that yields a lower expected welfare than an alternative available action. (The broader sense can also be correspondingly modified.)

In the terminology of modern economic theory, sympathy is a case of "externality." Many models rule out externalities, for example, the standard model to establish that each competitive equilibrium is a Pareto optimum and belongs to the core of the economy. If the existence of sympathy were to be permitted in these models, some of these standard results would be upset, though by no means all of them.[20] But this would not require a serious revision of the basic structure of these models. On the other hand, commitment does involve, in a very real sense, counterpreferential choice, destroying the crucial assumption that a chosen alternative must be better than (or at least as good as) the others for the person choosing it, and this would certainly require that models be formulated in an essentially different way.

The contrast between sympathy and commitment may be illustrated with the story of two boys who find two apples, one large, one small. Boy *A* tells boy *B*, "You choose." *B* immediately picks the larger apple. *A* is upset and permits himself the remark that this was grossly unfair. "Why?" asks *B*. "Which one would *you* have chosen, if you were to choose rather than me?" "The smaller one, of course," *A* replies. *B* is now triumphant: "Then what are you complaining about? That's the one you've got!" *B* certainly wins this round of the argument, but in fact *A* would have lost nothing from *B*'s choice had his own hypothetical choice of the smaller apple been based on sympathy as opposed to commitment. *A*'s anger indicates that this was probably not the case.

Commitment is, of course, closely connected with one's morals. But moral this question is in a very broad sense, covering a variety of influences from religious to political, from the ill-understood to the well-argued. When, in Bernard Shaw's *The Devil's Disciple,* Judith Anderson interprets Richard Dudgeon's willingness to be hanged in place of her husband as arising from sympathy for him or love for her, Richard is adamant in his denial: "What I did last night, I did in cold blood, caring not half so much for your husband, or for you as I do for myself. I had no motive and no interest: all I can tell you is that when it came to the point whether I would take my neck out of the noose and put another man's into it, I could not do it."[21]

The characteristic of commitment with which I am most concerned here is the fact that it drives a wedge between personal choice and personal welfare, and much of traditional economic theory relies on the identity of the two. This identity is sometimes obscured by the ambiguity of the term "preference," since the normal use of the word permits the identification of preference with the concept of being better off, and at the same time it is not quite unnatural to define "preferred" as "chosen." I have no strong views on the "correct" use of the word "preference," and I would be satisfied as long as both uses are not *simultaneously* made, attempting an empirical assertion by virtue of two definitions.[22] The basic link between choice behavior and welfare achievements in the traditional models is severed as soon as commitment is admitted as an ingredient of choice.

V

"Fine," you might say, "but how relevant is all this to the kind of choices with which economists are concerned? Economics does not have much to do with Richard Dudgeon's march to the gallows." I think one should immediately agree that for many types of behavior, commitment is unlikely to be an important ingredient. In the private purchase of many consumer goods, the scope for the exercise of commitment may indeed be limited and may show up rather rarely in such exotic acts as the boycotting of South African avocados or the eschewing of Spanish holidays. Therefore, for many studies of consumer behavior and interpretations thereof, commitment may pose no great problem. Even sympathy may not be extremely important, the sources of interpersonal interdependence lying elsewhere, for example, in the desire to keep up with the Joneses or in being influenced by other people's habits.[23]

But economics is not concerned only with consumer behavior; nor is consumption confined to "private goods." One area in which the question of commitment is most important is that of the so-called public goods. These have to be contrasted with "private goods" which have the characteristic that they cannot be used by more than one person: if you ate a piece of apple pie, I wouldn't consider devouring it too. Not so with "public goods," for example, a road or a public park, which you and I may both be able to use. In many economic models private goods are the only ones around, and this is typically the case when the "invisible hand" is given the task of doing visible good. But, in fact, public goods are important in most economies and cover a wide range of services from roads and street lighting to defense. There is much evidence that the share of public goods in national consumption has grown rather dramatically in most countries in the world.

The problem of optimal allocation of public goods has also been much discussed, especially in the recent economic literature.[24] A lot of attention, in particular, has been devoted to the problem of correct revelation of preferences. This arises most obviously in the case of subscription schemes where a person is charged according to benefits received. The main problem centers on the fact that it is in everybody's interest to understate the benefit he expects, but this understatement may lead to the rejection of a public project which would have been justified if true benefits were known. Analysis of this difficulty, sometimes referred to as the "free rider" problem, has recently led to some extremely ingenious proposals for circumventing this inefficiency within the framework of egoistic action.[25] The reward mechanism is set up with such ungodly cunning that people have an incentive to reveal exactly their true willingness to pay for the public good in question. One difficulty in this solution arises from an assumed limitation of strategic possibilities open to the individual, the removal of which leads to an impossibility result.[26] Another difficulty concerns the fact that in giving people the incentive to reveal the truth, money is handed out and the income distribution shifts in a way unguided by distributional considerations. This effect can, of course, be undone by a redistribution of initial endowments and profit shares,[27] but that action obviously raises difficulties of its own.

Central to this problem is the assumption that when asked a question, the individual gives that answer which will maximize his personal gain. How good is this assumption? I doubt that in general it is very good. ("Where is the railway station?" he asks me. "There," I say, pointing at the post office, "and would you please post this letter for me on the way?" "Yes," he says, determined to open the envelope and check whether it contains something valuable.) Even in the particular context of revelation of preferences for public goods the gains-maximizing behavior may not be the best assumption. Leif Johansen, one of the major contributors to public economics, is, I think, right to question the assumption in this context:

> Economic theory in this, as well as in some other fields, tends to suggest that people are honest only to the extent that they have economic incentives for being so. This is a homo oeconomicus assumption which is far from being obviously true, and which needs confrontation with observed realities. In fact, a simple line of thought suggests that the assumption can hardly be true in its most extreme form. No society would be viable without some norms and rules of conduct. Such norms and rules are necessary for viability exactly in fields where strictly economic incentives are absent and cannot be created.[28]

What is at issue is not whether people invariably give an honest answer to every question, but whether they always give a gains-maximizing answer, or at any rate, whether they give gains-maximizing answers often enough to make that the appropriate general assumption for economic theory. The presence of non-gains-maximizing answers, including truthful ones, immediately brings in commitment as a part of behavior.

The question is relevant also to the recent literature on strategic voting. A number of beautiful analytical results have recently been established showing the impossibility of any voting procedure satisfying certain elementary requirements and making honest voting the gains-maximizing strategy for everyone.[29] The correctness of these results is not in dispute, but is it appropriate to assume that people always do try to maximize personal gains in their voting behavior? Indeed, in large elections, it is difficult to show that any voter has any real prospect of affecting the outcome by his vote, and if voting involves some cost, the expected net gain from voting may typically be negative. Nevertheless, the proportion of turnout in large elections may still be quite high, and I have tried to argue elsewhere that in such elections people may often be "guided not so much by maximization of expected utility, but something much simpler, viz, just a desire to record one's true preference."[30] If this desire reflects a sense of commitment, then the behavior in question would be at variance with the view of man in traditional economic theory.

VI

The question of commitment is important in a number of other economic contexts.[31] It is central to the problem of work motivation, the importance of which for production performance can hardly be ignored.

It is certainly costly and may be impossible to devise a system of supervision with rewards and punishment such that everyone has the incentive to exert himself. Every economic system has, therefore, tended to rely on the existence of attitudes toward work which supersedes the calculation of net gain from each unit of exertion. Social conditioning plays an extremely important part here.[32] I am persuaded that Britain's present economic difficulties have a great deal to do with work-motivation problems that lie outside the economics of rewards and punishments, and one reason why economists seem to have so little to contribute in this area is the neglect in traditional economic theory of this whole issue of commitment and the social relations surrounding it.[33]

These questions are connected, of course, with ethics, since moral reasoning influences one's actions, but in a broader sense these are matters of culture, of which morality is one part. Indeed, to take an extreme case, in the Chinese "cultural revolution" one of the primary aims was the increase of the sense of commitment with an eye on economic results: "the aim of the Great Proletarian Cultural Revolution is to revolutionize people's ideology and as a consequence to achieve greater, faster, better and more economical results in all fields of work."[34] Of course, China was experimenting with reducing dramatically the role of material incentives in production, which would certainly have increased the part that commitment was meant to play, but even within the traditional systems of payments, much reliance is usually placed on rules of conduct and modes of behavior that go beyond strictly economic incentives.[35] To run an organization *entirely* on incentives to personal gain is pretty much a hopeless task.

I will have a bit more to say presently on what might lie behind the sense of commitment, but I would like to emphasize at this stage that the morality or culture underlying it may well be of a limited kind—far removed from the grandeur of approaches such as utilitarianism. The "implicit collusions" that have been observed in business behavior in oligopolies seem to work on the basis of a system of mutual trust and sense of responsibility which has well-defined limits, and attempts at "universalization" of the same kind of behavior in other spheres of action may not go with it at all. There it is strictly a question of business ethics which is taken to apply within a fairly limited domain.

Similarly, in wage negotiations and in collective bargaining the sense of solidarity on either side may have well-defined limits, and may not fit in at all with an approach such as that of general utilitarianism. Edgeworth's implicit assumption, on which I commented earlier, that egoism and utilitarianism exhaust the possible alternative motivations, will be especially unhelpful in this context. While the field of commitment may be large, that of commitment based on utilitarianism and other universalized moral systems may well form a relatively small part of it.

VII

The economic theory of utility, which relates to the theory of rational behavior, is sometimes criticized for having too much structure; human beings are alleged to be "simpler" in reality. If our argument so far has been correct, precisely the opposite seems to be the case: traditional theory has *too little* structure. A person is given *one* preference ordering, and as and when the need arises this is supposed to reflect his interests, represent his welfare, summarize his idea of what should be done, and describe his actual choices and behavior. Can one preference ordering do all these things? A person thus described may be "rational" in the limited sense of revealing no inconsistencies in his choice behavior, but if he has no use for these distinctions between quite different concepts, he must be a bit of a fool. The *purely* economic man is indeed close to being a social moron. Economic theory has been much preoccupied with this rational fool decked in the glory of his *one* all-purpose preference ordering. To make room for the different concepts related to his behavior we need a more elaborate structure.

What kind of a structure do we need? A bit more room up top is provided by John Harsanyi's important distinction between a person's "ethical" preferences and his "subjective" preferences: "the former must express what this individual prefers (or, rather would prefer), on the basis of impersonal social considerations alone, and the latter must express what he actually prefers, whether on the basis of his personal interests or on any other basis."[36] This dual structure permits us to distinguish between what a person thinks is good from the social point of view and what he regards as good from his own personal point of view. Presumably sympathy enters directly into the so-called subjective preference, but the role of commitment is left somewhat unclear. Insofar as a person's "subjective" preferences are taken to "define his utility function," the intention seems to be to exclude commitment from it, but an ambiguity arises from the fact that these are defined to "express his preferences in the full sense of the word as they actually are." Is this in the sense of choice, or in the sense of his conception of his own welfare? Perhaps Harsanyi intended the latter, since "ethical" preferences are by contrast given the role of expressing "what he prefers only in those possibly rare moments when he forces a special impartial and impersonal attitude on himself."[37] But what if he departs from his personal welfare maximization (including any sympathy), not through an impartial concern for all,[38] but through a sense of commitment to some particular group, say to the neighborhood or to the social class to which he belongs? The fact is we are still short of structure.

Even in expressing moral judgments from an impersonal point of view, a *dual* structure is deficient. Surely a preference ordering can be *more* ethical than another but *less* so than a third. We need more structure in this respect also. I have proposed elsewhere—at the 1972 Bristol conference on "practical reason"—that we need to consider *rankings of preference rankings* to express our moral judgments.[39] I would like to discuss this structure a bit more. A particular morality can be viewed, not just in terms of the "most moral" ranking of the set of alternative actions, but as a moral ranking of the rankings of actions (going well beyond the identification merely of the "most moral" ranking of actions). Let X be the set of alternative and mutually exclusive combinations of actions under consideration, and let Y be the set of rankings of the elements of X. A ranking of the set Y (consisting of action-rankings) will be called a meta-ranking of action-set X. It is my claim that a particular ranking of the action-set X is not articulate enough to express much about a given morality, and a more robust format is provided by choosing a meta-ranking of actions (that is, a ranking of Y rather than of X). Of course, such a meta-ranking may include *inter alia* the specification of a particular action-ranking as the "most moral," but insofar as actual behavior may be based on a compromise between claims of morality and the pursuit of various other objectives (including self-interest), one has to look also at the relative moral standings of those action-rankings that are *not* "most moral."

To illustrate, consider a set X of alternative action combinations and the following three rankings of this action-set X: ranking A representing my personal welfare ordering (thus, in some sense, representing my personal interests), ranking B reflecting my "isolated" personal interests ignoring sympathy (when such a separation is possible, which is not always so),[40] and ranking C in terms of which actual choices are made by me (when such choices are representable by a ranking, which again is not always so).[41] The "most moral" ranking M can, conceivably, be any of these rankings A, B, or C. Or else it can be some other ranking quite distinct from all three. (This will be the case if the actual choices of actions are not the "most moral" in terms of the moral system in question, and if, furthermore, the moral system requires sacrifice of some self-interest and also of "isolated" self-interest.) But even when some ranking M distinct from A, B, and C is identified as being at the top of the moral table, that still leaves open the question as to how A, B, and C may be ordered vis-à-vis each other. If, to take a particular example, it so happens that the pursuit of self-interest, including pleasure and pain from sympathy, is put morally above the pursuit of "isolated" self-interest (thereby leading to a partial coincidence of self-interest with morality), and the actual choices reflect a morally superior position to the pursuit of self-interest (perhaps due to a compromise in the moral direction), then the morality in question precipitates the meta-ranking M, C, A, B, in descending order. This, of course, goes well beyond specifying that M is "morally best."

The technique of meta-ranking permits a varying extent of moral articulation. It is not being claimed that a moral meta-ranking must be a *complete* ordering of the set Y, that is, must completely order all rankings of X. It can be a *partial* ordering, and I expect it often will be incomplete, but I should think that in most cases there will be no problem in going well beyond the limited expression permitted by the twofold specification of "ethical" and "subjective" preferences.

The rankings of action can, of course, be ordered also on grounds other than a particular system of morality: meta-ranking is a general technique usable under alternative interpretations of the meta-ranking relation. It can be used to describe a particular ideology or a set of political priorities or a system of class interests. In quite a different context, it can provide the format for expressing what preferences one would have preferred to have ("I wish I liked vegetarian foods more," or "I wish I didn't enjoy smoking so much"). Or it can be used to analyze the conflicts involved in addiction ("Given my current tastes, I am better off with heroin, but having heroin leads me to addiction, and I would have preferred not to have these tastes"). The tool of meta-rankings can be used in many different ways in distinct contexts.

This is clearly not the occasion to go into a detailed analysis of how this broader structure permits a better understanding of preference and behavior. A structure is not, of course, a theory, and alternative theories can be formulated using this structure. I should mention, however, that the structure demands much more information than is yielded by the observation of people's actual choices, which would at most reveal only the ranking *C*. It gives a role to introspection and to communication. To illustrate one use of the apparatus, I may refer to some technical results. Suppose I am trying to investigate your conception of your own welfare. You first specify the ranking *A* which represents your welfare ordering. But I want to go further and get an idea of your *cardinal* utility function, that is, roughly speaking, not only which ranking gives you more welfare but also by how much. I now ask you to order the different rankings in terms of their "closeness" to your actual welfare ranking *A,* much as a policeman uses the technique of photofit: is this more like him, or is that? If your answers reflect the fact that reversing a stronger preference makes the result more distant than reversing a weaker intensity of preference, your replies will satisfy certain consistency properties, and the order of rankings will permit us to compare your welfare *differences* between pairs. In fact, by considering higher and higher order rankings, we can determine your cardinal welfare function as closely as you care to specify.[42] I am not saying that this type of dialogue is the best way of discovering your welfare function, but it does illustrate that once we give up the assumption that observing choices is the only source of data on welfare, a whole new world opens up, liberating us from the informational shackles of the traditional approach.

This broader structure has many other uses, for example, permitting a clearer analysis of *akrasia*—the weakness of will—and clarifying some conflicting considerations in the theory of liberty, which I have tried to discuss elsewhere.[43] It also helps in analyzing the development of behavior involving commitment in situations characterized by games such as the Prisoners' Dilemma.[44] This game is often treated, with some justice, as the classic case of failure of individualistic rationality. There are two players and each has two strategies, which we may call selfish and unselfish to make it easy to remember without my having to go into too much detail. Each player is better off personally by playing the selfish strategy *no* matter what the other does, but both are better off if both choose the unselfish rather than the selfish strategy. It is individually optimal to do the selfish thing: one can only affect one's own action and not that of the other, and given the other's strategy—no matter what—each player is better off being selfish. But this combination of selfish strategies, which results from self-seeking by both, produces an outcome that is worse for both than the result of both choosing the unselfish strategy. It can be shown that this conflict can exist even if the game is repeated many times.

Some people find it puzzling that individual self-seeking by each should produce an inferior outcome for all, but this, of course, is a well-known conflict, and has been discussed in general terms for a very long time. Indeed, it was the basis of Rousseau's famous distinction between the "general will" and the "will of all."[45] But the puzzle from the point of view of rational behavior lies in the fact that in actual situations people often do not follow the selfish strategy. Real life examples of this type of behavior in complex circumstances are well known, but even in controlled experiments in laboratory conditions people playing the Prisoners' Dilemma frequently do the unselfish thing.[46]

In interpreting these experimental results, the game theorist is tempted to put it down to the lack of intelligence of the players: "Evidently the run-of-the-mill players are not strategically sophisticated enough to have figured out that strategy DD [the selfish strategy] is the only rationally defensible strategy, and this intellectual short-coming saves them from losing."[47] A more fruitful approach may lie in permitting the possibility that the person is *more* sophisticated than the theory allows and that he has asked himself what type of preference he would like the other player to have, and on somewhat Kantian grounds has considered the case for himself having those preferences, or behaving *as if* he had them. This line of reasoning requires him to consider the modifications of the game that would be brought about by acting through commitment (in terms of "revealed preferences," this would look *as if* he had different preferences from the ones he actually had), and he has to assess alternative behavior norms in that light. I have discussed these issues elsewhere;[48] thus I shall simply note here that the apparatus of *ranking of rankings* assists the reasoning which involves considering the merits of having different types of preferences (or of acting as if one had them).

VIII

Admitting behavior based on commitment would, of course have far-reaching consequences on the nature of many economic models. I have tried to show why this change is necessary and why the consequences may well be serious. Many issues remain unresolved, including the empirical importance of commitment as a part of behavior, which would vary, as I have argued, from field to field. I have also indicated why the empirical evidence for this cannot be sought in the mere observation of actual choices, and must involve other sources of information, including introspection and discussion.

There remains, however, the issue as to whether this view of man amounts to seeing him as an irrational creature. Much depends on the concept of rationality used, and many alternative characterizations exist. In the sense of *consistency* of choice, there is no reason to think that admitting commitment must imply any departure from rationality. This is, however, a weak sense of rationality.

The other concept of rationality prevalent in economics identifies it with the possibility of justifying each act in terms of self-interest: when act x is chosen by person i and act y rejected, this implies that i's personal interests are expected by i to be better served by x than by y. There are, it seems to me, three distinct elements in this approach. First, it is a consequentialist view: judging acts by consequences only.[49] Second, it is an approach of *act* evaluation rather than *rule* evaluation. And third, the only consequences considered in evaluating acts are those on one's own interests, everything else being at best an intermediate product. It is clearly possible to dispute the claims of each of these elements to being a necessary part of the conception of rationality in the dictionary sense of "the power of being able to exercise one's reason." Moreover, arguments for rejecting the straightjacket of each of these three principles are not hard to find. The case for actions based on commitment can arise from the violation of any of these three principles. Commitment sometimes relates to a sense of obligation going beyond the consequences. Sometimes the lack of personal gain in particular *acts* is accepted by considering the value of *rules* of behavior. But even within a consequentialist act-evaluation framework, the exclusion of any consideration other than self-interest seems to impose a wholly arbitrary limitation on the notion of rationality.

Henry Sidgwick noted the arbitrary nature of the assumption of egoism:

> If the Utilitarian has to answer the question, "Why should I sacrifice my own happiness for the greater happiness of another?" it must surely be admissible to ask the Egoist, "Why should I sacrifice a present pleasure for one in the future? Why should I concern myself about my own future feelings any more than about the feelings of other persons?" It undoubtedly seems to Common Sense paradoxical to ask for a reason why one should seek one's own happiness on the whole; but I do not see how the demand can be repudiated as absurd by those who adopt views of the extreme empirical school of psychologists, although those views are commonly supposed to have a close affinity with Egoistic Hedonism. Grant that the Ego is merely a system of coherent phenomena, that the permanent identical "I" is not a fact but a fiction, as Hume and his followers maintain; why, then, should one part of the series of feelings into which the Ego is resolved be concerned with another part of the same series, any more than with any other series?[50]

The view of rationality that identifies it with consequentialist act-evaluation using self-interest can be questioned from any of these three angles. Admitting commitment as a part of behavior implies no denial of reasoned assessment as a basis for action.

There is not much merit in spending a lot of effort in debating the "proper" definition of rationality. The term is used in many different senses, and none of the criticisms of the behavioral foundations of economic theory presented here stands or falls on the definition chosen. The main issue is the acceptability of the assumption of the invariable pursuit of self-interest in each act. Calling that type of behavior rational, or departures from it irrational, does not change the relevance of these criticisms, though it does produce an arbitrarily narrow definition of rationality. This paper has not been concerned with the question as to whether human behavior is better described as rational or irrational. The main thesis has been the need to accommodate commitment as a part of behavior. Commitment does not presuppose reasoning, but it does not exclude it; in fact, insofar as consequences on others have to be more clearly understood and assessed in terms of one's values and instincts, the scope for reasoning may well expand. I have tried to analyze the structural extensions in the conception of preference made necessary by behavior based on reasoned assessment of commitment. Preferences as rankings have to be replaced by a richer structure involving meta-rankings and related concepts.

I have also argued against viewing behavior in terms of the traditional dichotomy between egoism and universalized moral systems (such as utilitarianism). Groups intermediate between oneself and all, such as class and community, provide the focus of many actions involving commitment. The rejection of egoism as description of motivation does not, therefore, imply the acceptance of some universalized morality as the basis of actual behavior. Nor does it make human beings excessively noble.

Nor, of course, does the use of reasoning imply remarkable wisdom.

It is as true as Caesar's name was Kaiser,
That no economist was ever wiser,

said Robert Frost in playful praise of the contemporary economist. Perhaps a similarly dubious tribute can be paid to the economic man in our modified conception. If he shines at all, he shines in comparison—in contrast—with the dominant image of the rational fool.

3   Selfishness and Altruism

Jon Elster

In the state of nature, nobody cares about other people. Fortunately, we do not live in this dismal state. Sometimes we take account of other people's success and well-being, and are willing to sacrifice some of our own for their sake.[1] Or so it appears. But perhaps altruistic behavior really springs from self-interest? For instance, isn't it in my long-term self-interest to help others, so that I can receive help in return when I need it? Isn't the patron of a charity motivated by his own prestige rather than by the needs of the beneficiaries? What matters to him is that his donations be visible and publicized, not who benefits from them.[2] Some argue that people are always and everywhere motivated by self-interest, and that differences in behavior are due only to differences in their opportunities.[3] Civilized society, on this view, depends on having institutions that make it in people's rational self-interest to speak the truth, keep their promises, and help others—not on people having good motivations.

I believe this argument is plain wrong, and I'll explain why in a moment. Let us first, however, get a few things out of the way. The proposition that self-interest is fundamental could be understood in two other ways besides that just set out.[4] It could mean that all action is ultimately performed for the sake of the agent's pleasure or that self-interest has a certain methodological priority. The first view, again, is plain wrong. The second is true, but unhelpful as a guide to understanding behavior.

Consider first the view that all rational action must be self-interested because it is ultimately motivated by the pleasure it brings to the agent. An illustration could be love, often defined as taking pleasure in another person's pleasure. If I give a present to someone I love, am I not simply using that person as a means to my own satisfaction? Against this view, it is sufficient to point out that not all altruistic actions are done out of love.

This chapter was adapted from Jon Elster, *Nuts and Bolts for the Social Sciences* (Cambridge: Cambridge University Press, 1989), and Jon Elster, *The Cement of Society* (Cambridge: Cambridge University Press, 1989).

Some are done out of a sense of duty and need not provide any kind of pleasure. A person who is motivated solely by the warm glow that comes from having done one's duty is not acting out of duty, but engaging in narcissistic role-playing. And in any case, the means-end theory of love is inadequate. I choose the gift to satisfy the other person's desire, and my own satisfaction is simply a by-product.[5]

There is a sense, though, in which self-interest is more fundamental than altruism. The state of nature, although a thought experiment, is a logically coherent situation. But we cannot coherently imagine a world in which everyone had exclusively altruistic motivations. The goal of the altruist is to provide others with an occasion for selfish pleasures[6]—the pleasure of reading a book or drinking a bottle of wine one has received as a gift.[7] If nobody had first-order, selfish pleasures, nobody could have higher-order, altruistic motives either. Some of the excesses of the Chinese cultural revolution illustrate the absurdity of universal altruism. All Chinese citizens were told to sacrifice their selfish interests for the interests of the people—as if the people were something over and above the totality of Chinese citizens. The point is just a logical one. If some are to be altruistic, others must be selfish, at least some of the time, but everybody *could* be selfish all the time. The assumption that all behavior is selfish is the most parsimonious we can make, and scientists always like to explain much with little. But we cannot conclude, neither in general nor on any given occasion, that selfishness is the more widespread motivation.[8] Sometimes the world is messy, and the most parsimonious explanation is wrong.

The idea that self-interest makes the world go round is refuted by a few familiar facts. Some forms of helping behavior are not reciprocated and so cannot be explained by long-term self-interest. Parents have a selfish interest in helping their children, assuming that children will care for parents in their old age—but it is not in the selfish interest of children to provide such care.[9] And still many do. Some contributors to charities give anonymously and hence cannot be motivated by prestige.[10] Some forms of income redistribution are perhaps in the interest of the rich. If they don't give to the poor, the poor might kill them. But nobody was ever killed by a quadriplegic.[11] From a self-interested point of view, the cost of voting in a national election is much larger than the expected benefit. I might get a tax break of a few hundred dollars if my candidate wins, but that gain has to be multiplied by the very small probability that my vote will be decisive—much smaller than the chance that I'll be killed in a car accident on my way to voting. And still large numbers of people vote. Many people report their taxable income and tax-free deductions correctly, even when tax evasion would be almost riskless.

Some of these examples invite a counterargument. It *is* in children's rational self-interest to help their parents, because if they don't their friends would criticize and perhaps desert them. It *is* selfishly rational to vote, because if one doesn't one will be the target of informal social sanctions, ranging from raised eyebrows to social ostracism. Against this, I would simply like to make two points. It is not clear that it is in the rational self-interest of other people to impose these sanctions. And in any case the argument does not apply to behavior that cannot be observed by others. Anonymous contributions fall in this category, as does voting in many electoral systems.

Pure nonselfish behavior is represented by anonymous contributions to impersonal charities. Gifts to specific persons could be explained (although I don't really think so) by the donor's pleasure in giving pleasure. Publicly visible gifts could be explained by the prestige of donating or by the social sanctions imposed on nondonors. Only gifts from unknown to unknown—voluntary donation of blood is perhaps the purest example—are unambiguously nonselfish. On average, such transfers amount to about one percent of people's income—not quite enough to make the world go around, but not negligible either if there are few recipients. When we add abstention from riskless tax evasion the amount increases. Ambiguously nonselfish transfers are quite large. Since, in my opinion, the ambiguity can often be resolved in favor of the nonselfish interpretation, this makes the amount even bigger.

Let us look at the fine grain of altruistic motivation. Helping or giving out of love is instrumental behavior, that is, concerned with outcomes. If I help my child, I seek the best means to make that child happy. (Behavior can be rational and instrumental and not yet be selfish, contrary to a widespread but vulgar view that equates rationality with selfishness.) The concept of duty is more ambiguous: it can be instrumental or squarely noninstrumental. To begin with the latter, consider Kant's "categorical imperative" which, roughly speaking, corresponds to the question, But what if everyone did that? What if everyone cheated on their taxes? What if everyone stayed home on voting day or refused to help the poor? This powerful appeal is not concerned with actual outcomes, with what would happen if *I* took a certain course of action. It is concerned with what would happen, hypothetically, if everyone took it. Suppose I am moved by the categorical imperative and try to decide how much I should contribute to charity. I decide on the total amount of charitable contributions that is needed, divide by the number of potential donors, and donate the sum that comes out. If everyone did that, things would be just fine.

In the real world, however, not everyone is going to do that. Many people give nothing. Knowing that, some would argue that it is their duty to give more than what would be needed if everyone did the same. They are motivated by actual outcomes of action under actual circumstances, not by outcomes under hypothetical circumstances. Because they are sensitive to outcomes and to circumstances, they give more the less others give. Conversely, if others give much, they reduce their contribution. To see why, it is sufficient to invoke the decreasing marginal utility of money. If many have already given much, the recipients have a relatively high income, at which a further dollar adds less to their welfare than it does at lower levels. If one is concerned with the instrumental efficacy of giving, the motivation to give is reduced.

Kantians are concerned neither with outcomes nor with circumstances. The people discussed in the last paragraph—they are often called utilitarians—are concerned with both. A third category of people is concerned with circumstances, but not with outcomes. They look at what others are doing and follow the majority. If others give little, they follow suit, and similarly if others give much. The underlying motivation is a norm of *fairness*. One should do one's share, but only if others are doing theirs. This motivation is insensitive to outcomes, as shown by the fact that it leads to exactly the opposite pattern of outcome-oriented utilitarianism. Suppose that we have had a big party and that next morning there is a lot of cleaning up to be done. Everyone joins in, although the kitchen is small and we are tripping over each other's feet, so that the work is actually done less efficiently than it would be if some of us went instead to sit on the back porch. But the norm of fairness forbids free riding, even when everyone would benefit from it.[12]

Giving and helping are supposed to be in the interest of the recipients or beneficiaries. But how do we tell what is in their interest? The answer seems obvious: we find out by asking them. Sometimes, however, they cannot answer. Small children and mentally incompetent persons cannot tell us whether they want our help. We have to rely on some notion of objective interest, and usually that is not too difficult. Hard cases arise when people's expressed interest differs from what we, the donors, believe to be their real interest. The expressed interest might reflect an excessive preoccupation with the present, whereas we, the donors, want to improve their life as a whole. Such *paternalism* is relatively easy to justify when the relation is literally that of parent to child, but harder when the recipients are adults with full civic rights, including the right to vote. Giving food stamps instead of money is an example. If the recipients had voted for this mode of transfer, it would be an unobjectionable form of self-paternalism, but that is not how these decisions are made. They are taken by the welfare bureaucracy.

Paternalistic decisions should not be taken lightly. For one thing, the opportunity to choose—including the right to make the wrong choices—is a valuable, in fact, indispensable, means to self-improvement. For another, there is a presumption that people are the best judges of their own interest. From the point of view of a middle-class welfare official the values and priorities of the poor may look crazy, but that is not really any of his business. His life-style probably appears the same way to them. Paternalism is appropriate only when freedom to choose is likely to be severely self-destructive, especially when it will also harm other people.

Paternalism, even when misguided, is concerned with the well-being of the recipient. Gift giving can also, however, be a technique of domination and manipulation. It can serve the interests of the donor, against—and not through—the interests of the recipients. I can do no better here than to quote at some length from Colin Turnbull's account of gifts and sacrifices among the Ik:

> These are not expressions of the foolish belief that altruism is both possible and desirable: they are weapons, sharp and aggressive, which can be put to divers uses. But the purpose for which the gift is designed can be thwarted by the non-acceptance of it, and much Icien ingenuity goes into thwarting the would-be thwarter. The object, of course, is to build up a whole series of obligations so that in times of crisis you have a number of debts you can recall, and with luck one of them may be repaid. To this end, in the circumstances of Ik life, considerable sacrifice would be justified, to the very limits of the minimal survival level. But a sacrifice that can be rejected is useless, and so you have the odd phenomenon of these otherwise singularly self-interested people going out of their way to "help" each other. In point of fact they are helping themselves and their help may very well be resented in the extreme, but it is done in such a way that it cannot be refused, for it has already been given. Someone, quite unasked, may hoe another's field in his absence, or rebuild his stockade, or join in the building of a house that could easily be done by the man and his wife alone. At one time I have seen so many men thatching a roof that the whole roof was in serious danger of collapsing, and the protests of the owner were of no avail. The work done was a debt incurred. It was another good reason for being wary of one's neighbors. [One particular individual] always made himself unpopular by accepting such help and by paying for it on the spot with food (which the cunning old fox knew they could not resist), which immediately negated the debt. (1972:146)

Now, it would not be possible to manipulate the norm of reciprocity unless it had a grip on people, since otherwise there would be nothing to manipulate. Turnbull's account demonstrates both the fragility of altruism and its robustness.

Selfishness has a bad name, but compared to some other motivations it can look positively altruistic. When people are motivated by envy, spite, and jealousy, they have an incentive to reduce other people's welfare. The hard way to doing better than others is to improve one's own performance. The easy way is to trip up the competition. Taking pleasure in other people's misfortune is probably more frequent than actively promoting it, but sometimes people do go out of their way to harm others at no direct gain to themselves. When a good—such as custody of a child—cannot be divided between the claimants, one response is, "If I can't have it, nobody shall." A depressing fact about many peasant societies is that people who do better than others are often accused of witchcraft and thus pulled down to, or indeed below, the level of others. Against this background, ruthless selfishness can have a liberating effect.

To have this effect, however, selfishness must be restrained. Traditional societies governed by envy and the principle of not sticking one's neck out can be suffocating, but the state of nature in which short-term self-interest dictates every decision is just as bad. Consider a firm that has reached a wage agreement with its workers. If wages are paid at the end of the production period, the following game arises. At the beginning of the period, workers have the choice between working and not working. If they decide to work, the firm has the choice, at the end of the period, between paying them the agreed-upon wage and not paying them. If this were all there was to the story, it is clear that a rational, selfish management would decide not to pay them and that rational workers, anticipating nonpayment, would decide not to work. Any promise of payment that the firm might make would lack credibility. As a consequence, both the firm and the workers would end up worse off than if the promise of payment had been credible.

One restraining principle could be codes of honor. If people pursue their selfish ends subject to the constraint of not telling lies or breaking promises, more cooperation can be achieved than if lies are made and promises broken whenever it seems expedient. This is not altruism, although it may have similar effects. Rather, being honest when it does not pay to do so is a form of irrationality. This characterization may seem to offend common sense. The same argument can, however, be made with respect to threats (see Frank, chap. 5, this vol.). When a person vows to exact revenge if others act against his interest, the question arises whether the threat is credible. Avenging oneself when it does not pay to do so is a form of irrationality. Rational persons let bygones be bygones. But if the person is irrational, his threats command greater respect. If this conclusion is accepted, the parallel argument with respect to honesty may seem more acceptable. (A fuller discussion of similarities and differences between threats and promises is found in the appendix.)

In some cases, unilateral honesty ensures gains for both parties. The example of wage payment illustrates this case: if the management is known to be honest, it is in the self-interest of the workers to come to work. In other cases, both parties have to be honest. Figure 3.1 illustrates this case.

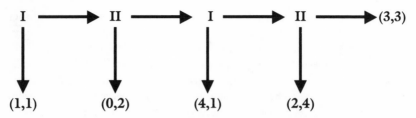

Fig. 3.1. The wage-payment game.

In this game, the parties take turns moving. If they choose to move "down," the game ends. If they move "across," the game continues up to the last node, at which player II has a choice between terminating the game by either moving down or across. When the game is terminated, the players receive payoffs as indicated, the first number being the payoff accruing to I and the second that of II. In this game, both parties must believe each other to be honest for a cooperative outcome to be realized. (At least, I shall tell a story in which this is a plausible conclusion.) Suppose first that I is honest but that II is rational rather than a man of honor. In that case I could move across at the first node and promise to move across at the third node, knowing that II will then move down at the last node. But if I is a man of honor, he may resist being taken advantage of in this way. Rather than accept the unequal outcome (2,4) he moves down at the first node. Suppose next that II is honest but believes I to be rational. II will then anticipate that at the penultimate node I will play down rather than across, even if II has made a credible promise to play across at the last node. Knowing this, II will play down at the second node. Knowing this, I will play down at the first node.

Note that honesty is not the same as altruism. In the game of figure 3.1, assume that I is an altruist in the sense of always maximizing the sum of the two rewards but that II is purely selfish. Neither is honest, that is, neither can be counted on to keep a promise unless it is in his (altruistic or selfish) interest to do so. This will ensure the outcome (2,4). II will know that at the penultimate mode, I will play across to ensure a joint gain of six rather than five. Knowing this, II will play across at the second node. Knowing this, I will play across at the first node. Altruism may yield socially desirable outcomes even in the absence of honesty.

Conversely, cut-throat competitiveness in the market may coexist with stable norms of honesty, if the agents are motivated by self-interest without guile. For instance, this has always been considered the ideal form of capitalism. Cut-throat competitiveness without honesty, that is, self-interest with guile or opportunism, is a much uglier creature. Superficially, most societies would seem to exhibit more honest behavior than what the opportunistic model would predict. Yet we must be wary in inferring from the fact that observed behavior is consistent with norms of honesty that it is actually *sustained* by these norms. It could also be sustained by a motivation neglected up to this point in the argument, namely, long-term self-interest.

Consider again the wage payment problem. If there is a single period of production and wages are paid at the end of that period, the promise to pay will not be credible. If, however, there are many periods and wages are paid at the end of each of them, the promise can be sustained even if managers are known to be dishonest. They will know, namely, that if they don't pay the workers, the latter will not come to work in the next week. More precisely, workers can follow the rule "Always work in the first week. In later weeks, work if and only if wages were paid at the end of the preceding week." Against this "Tit-for-Tat" strategy the rational response of management usually is to pay wages.[13] Long-term self-interest can mimic the norm of honesty.

Why, then, are we not in the state of nature? There is no general answer to this question. Altruism, codes of honor, and long-term self-interest all enter into the explanation. What seems clear is that self-interest cannot be the whole story.

Appendix

To bring out the formal similarity between threats and promises, consider the decision tree in figure 3.2. In threats as well as promises, the payoffs to Eve are constrained by $a > c$ and $a > d$. The threat or promise is in-

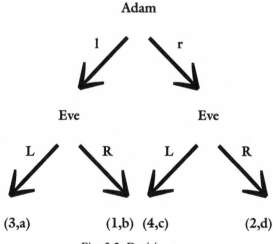

Fig. 3.2. Decision tree.

tended to induce Adam to move left so that she can ensure for herself a gain that is greater than what she would get if he moved right. Suppose first that $a > b > c > d$. Then Eve can threaten to move right if Adam moves left. But this threat is not credible. He knows she will not cut off her nose to spite her face by moving right; hence he moves right, knowing she will move left. The outcome will be worse for Eve and better for Adam than it would have been if the threat had been credible. Suppose next that $b > a > d > c$. Then Eve can promise to move left if Adam moves left. Once again, however, this promise is not credible. Adam knows that once he has moved left it will be in her self-interest to move right. As a result he will move left and Eve will move right, leaving them both worse off than if her promise had been credible. Suppose finally that $b > a > c > d$. Here Eve can brandish both the carrot and the stick, promising to move left if he moves left and threatening to move right if he moves right. Neither communication is credible; Adam moves right, Eve moves left; he is better off and she is worse off than if the promise/threat had been credible.

4   Varieties of Altruism

Christopher Jencks

One of the classic puzzles—perhaps *the* classic puzzle—of social theory is how society induces us to behave in ways that serve not our own private interest, but the common interest of society as a whole. Social scientists have developed a bewildering variety of vocabularies for analyzing this question, invoking concepts like "socialization," "operant conditioning," and "deterrence." In this essay I explore the advantages of reverting to a more primitive vocabulary. I think we can learn something by formulating the tension between public and private interests in traditional moral terms, that is, as a problem of selfishness versus unselfishness.

For these terms to be useful, however, they must be fairly precisely defined. I describe individuals as "selfish" (or "egoistic") if (1) their subjective definition of their welfare does not include the welfare of others; or (2) their actual behavior indicates that they are not concerned with the welfare of others; or (3) their concern with the welfare of others is merely an instrumental means for promoting their own longer-term selfish ends, and ceases once these selfish ends can be more easily realized in some other way. A man with a sick business partner is thus "selfish" if (1) he does not care whether his partner recovers; or (2) he does not take obvious steps that would help his partner to recover; or (3) he only takes those steps if he believes that his partner's recovery will increase his own income. I describe individuals as "unselfish" (or "altruistic") when they feel and act as if the long-term welfare of others is important *independent* of its effects on their own welfare.

Every motive or act falls somewhere on a spectrum between extreme selfishness and extreme unselfishness, depending on the relative weight we give our own interests and the interests of others. Most ethical theories

This chapter was adapted from Christopher Jencks, "The Social Basis of Unselfishness," in Herbert J. Gans, Nathan Glazer, Joseph Gusfield, and Christopher Jencks, eds., *On the Making of Americans: Essays in Honor of David Riesman* (Philadelphia: University of Pennsylvania Press, 1979), 63–86.

imply that we should place the same weight on other people's interests as on our own when choosing a course of action. We should, in other words, pursue the greatest good of the greatest number, counting our own good as neither more nor less important than anyone else's. I call this ideal "complete" unselfishness. In practice, few people live up to this "disinterested" ideal. Most of us do, however, take *some* account of the interests of the individuals affected by our behavior. I call this "partial" unselfishness. In a few cases we may go to the opposite extreme, weighing other people's individual interests *more* heavily than our own. I call this "extreme" unselfishness.

I also distinguish three sources of unselfishness: empathy, community, and morality. What I call "empathic unselfishness" derives from the fact that we "identify" with people outside ourselves. We incorporate their interests into our subjective welfare function, so that their interests become our own. As a result, our "selfish" interests are no longer synonymous with the interests of the biological organism in which our consciousness resides. When this process goes far enough, we say that we "love" the other individuals whose welfare concerns us.

What I call "communitarian unselfishness" involves identification with a collectivity rather than with specific individuals. This collectivity can take virtually any form, but the most common examples in modern societies are probably the family, the work group, the nation-state, and the species. In each case we redefine our "selfish" interest so that it includes our subjective understanding of the interests of a larger collectivity of which we are a part. In large complex societies we usually identify at least partially with more than one such collectivity. This means that we can easily find ourselves in situations where the claims of different collectivities (for example, family and nation) conflict with one another as well as with our narrow self-interest.

Communitarian unselfishness can also take a more extreme form, at least in small homogeneous groups. In what Redfield called a "folk society," individuals identify so completely with the group to which they belong that they do not even imagine the possibility that their private interests could diverge from those of the group. By limiting imagination in this way, a society can, at least in theory, prevent individuals from even developing a sense of "self," and hence from conceiving courses of action that are "selfish" in the modern sense. While I find it hard to believe that any society is completely successful in doing this, what Tönnies characterized as "Gemeinschaft" and what Durkheim called "mechanical solidarity" both seem to assume something close to this result.

Moralistic unselfishness involves the incorporation of external moral ideals into our sense of "self." These moral ideals are usually derived from the collective culture of a larger group. For reasons I discuss later, they usually imply that we should behave in ways that take account of other people's interests as well as our own. Once we have internalized such ideals, failure to follow them produces some sort of inner conflict (for example, between "superego" and "id"). Since such conflict is painful, we are often willing to sacrifice the interests of the id in order to quiet the superego.

These three varieties of unselfishness can lead to quite different forms of behavior. Empathy, for example, usually induces us to promote the interests of some specific individual, whereas communitarian unselfishness encourages us to promote the interests of a larger group. The two can therefore conflict. Likewise, moralistic unselfishness involves the subordination of self to some principle, the application of which may well conflict with the interests of other individuals with whom we empathize, as well as with our own selfish interests. Many of the moral dilemmas that fascinate philosophers and novelists involve precisely such conflicts between varieties of unselfishness, rather than just conflicts between selfishness and unselfishness.

All three varieties of unselfishness involve a redefinition or transformation of the self so as to incorporate "outside" elements. Once the self is transformed in this way, there is a sense in which all acts are selfish. Because of this, some cynics like to argue that unselfishness is impossible. Every voluntary act, even if it leads to death, must serve some "selfish" end, since otherwise we would not have chosen it. But such reasoning still leaves us with the problem of distinguishing behavior that takes no account of the ultimate welfare of others from behavior that is at least partially concerned with the welfare of others. Labels like "selfish" and "unselfish" allow us to make this useful distinction, which is why they persist despite efforts to get by without them.

The psychological mechanisms that lead to unselfishness also play a major role in selfish behavior. At least as ordinarily conceived, selfishness involves concern with one's own welfare *over time*. To be selfish is to be concerned not just with the welfare of the person I now am, but with the welfare of the person I will become in a day, a year, or even fifty years. Those who are indifferent to the welfare of these future selves are usually described as "irrational." The mechanisms that make us take account of the welfare of our future selves are, I think, much the same as the mechanisms that make us take account of others. One reason for altruism vis-à-vis our future selves is that we empathize with the person we will later become and anticipate how he or she will feel if we choose a given course of action. We save for our old age, for example, because we imagine what it would be like to be old and poor. If we cannot imagine this, we may not save. A second reason for altruistic acts vis-à-vis our future selves is that we have internalized the general principle that we ought to be "prudent." Not saving for our old age, for example, makes some of us feel guilty. A third, less common, reason for altruism vis-à-vis our future selves is that we identify with a larger group. ("If I get drunk tonight, I will not play well tomorrow, and that would be letting down the team.") Individuals who cannot empathize with the person they will eventually become (for example, adolescents), and who do not feel guilty when they act imprudently, are likely to act selfishly vis-à-vis their future selves.

The remainder of the essay has three parts. In the first I argue that, contrary to the claims of many influential social theorists since Hobbes, a complex society cannot survive if all its members are governed by exclusively selfish motives. In the second I explore the effects of genetic selection on the evolution of unselfish behavior. In the third I discuss the implications of cultural selection, which are quite different from those of genetic selection.

Hobbes and Beyond

Virtually all of us assume that when interests conflict, most of our neighbors will habitually place their own interest ahead of other people's. When this does not happen, we are pleasantly surprised. Most people also see this tendency toward selfishness as one of the prime sources of human misery. There are two distinct responses to this situation, one of which I label "idealistic," the other "cynical."

Idealists respond to human selfishness by trying to reduce its prevalence. Christianity, for example, exhorts the faithful to do unto others as they would have others do unto them. Maoism urges its adherents to "serve the people" selflessly. Indeed, virtually every movement for radical social change seeks to transform not only social institutions but also individual consciousness in such a way as to make people less selfish.

Cynics dismiss all attempts to reduce the prevalence of selfishness as "utopian." Instead, they concentrate on trying to limit the damaging consequences of pervasive selfishness. This means arranging social institutions so that the private pursuit of selfish advantage also promotes the common good. This ideal has dominated Anglo-American economic thought for the past three hundred years. Its most elegant and influential expression is probably *The Wealth of Nations,* where Adam Smith shows that under certain conditions, competitive markets ensure that the pursuit of private advantage will maximize economic output. The same general approach has also pervaded Anglo-American political theory. Classical liberal theorists argued that the purpose of the state was to maximize citizens' freedom to pursue their selfish ends. More recently, many democratic theorists have argued that if politicians compete for votes in the same way that merchants compete for customers, these politicians will tend to adopt policies that promote the greatest good of the greatest number. In all these visions, society is simply a machine for resolving conflicts among selfish individuals and perhaps helping them to pursue shared objectives more effectively. It is not a system for making people less selfish or even reshaping their selfish impulses.

Thomas Hobbes was the first English theorist to argue that society could be organized around selfish motives. Since his *Leviathan* (1651) presages most of what has come since, it provides a convenient illustration of the problems posed by this view. *Leviathan* argues that men are driven by "a perpetual and restless desire of Power after power, that ceaseth only in Death." In the absence of some collective restraint on this natural impulse, such a populace would engage in a permanent "war of all against all." The result would be anarchy, in which life was, in Hobbes's most famous phrase, "solitary, poore, nasty, brutish, and short." The only way to end this war is through a contract. Whatever its form, the aim of the contract is to bring "peace." Its substance is that each citizen should forswear violence and "be contented with so much liberty against other men, as he would allow other men against himselfe."

It is clear why people agree to such a contract. Given the dangers of the war of all against all, we want to restrain others' depradations against ourselves. But having agreed to such a contract, why abide by it? From a strictly selfish viewpoint, our interest is merely to persuade *others* to abide by the contract. We have no reason for sticking to the contract ourselves unless violating it would encourage others to do the same at our expense. If we can violate the contract without detection, why not do so?

Hobbes saw only two possible reasons why men might abide by the social contract: "either a Feare of the consequence of breaking their word; or a Glory or Pride in not appearing to breake it." Pride, he argued, was seldom sufficient to ensure that individuals kept to the contract, so fear had to be the dominant motive. Fear could come in either of two varieties: fear of the "Power of Spirits Invisible" or fear of "the Power of those men they shall therein Offend." Of these two, Hobbes wrote, "though the former be the greatest Power, yet the feare of the latter is commonly the greater Feare."[1]

Fear of detection and punishment may well suffice to enforce the social contract in small communities where nobody has much privacy and few people have dealings with strangers. Those who violate rules against prohibited forms of selfishness are likely to be detected, and once detected they can easily be punished, either formally or informally. But in a large society, where one is often dealing with strangers and where one also has a certain amount of privacy even vis-à-vis others whom one knows, we can no longer be certain that prohibited forms of selfishness will be detected. We do not usually know, for example, when someone fails to report a fire.

We simply assume that the fire was unnoticed. Even when we know that *someone* has violated a rule, the culprit may be impossible to identify or punish. Large complex societies develop formal policing systems to deal with this problem, but this is not in itself sufficient. If *everyone* responds to privacy and anonymity by pursuing his or her selfish interests, the number of individuals who violate established norms will soon be very large. This will lower the odds that any individual cheater will be caught and punished, leading to a further increase in cheating. Eventually this vicious circle will lead to a collapse of the established social order and a return to the war of all against all. Policing is only feasible when violations are relatively infrequent and when the police themselves are relatively committed to the norms they enforce.

Some argue, of course, that even if only a small proportion of cheaters are caught, society can deter violations by making the penalties for cheating much larger than the potential benefits. If there is "too much" cheating, according to this view, society can always increase the severity of the penalties against those whom it catches. This changes the expected cost of a violation, at least in a mathematical sense. Experience suggests, however, that neither the probability nor the severity of punishment explains most of the variance in crime rates. The cleanliness of public parks does not, for example, bear much relationship to the number of police patrolling the park or the size of the fine for littering. This does not mean that deterrence is completely ineffective, but it does suggest that Hobbes's analysis of our reasons for conforming to the social contract is incomplete.

The missing element is not far to seek. We abide by the social contract partly because we have moral ideas. We ask not only whether acts are prudent or imprudent, but whether they are right or wrong. For Hobbes, moral ideas seem to reflect our anticipation of divine retribution. But if that were their main source, they should have disappeared with the rise of religious skepticism in the eighteenth century. Since this did not happen, an alternative explanation is needed. Perhaps the best is Adam Smith's *Theory of Moral Sentiments* (1759).

Smith argues that moral ideas derive from our capacity for what he calls "sympathy," or what we would now call "empathy." Because we are capable of experiencing the pleasure and pain of others, we *cannot* be completely selfish. Furthermore—and this is vitally important—Smith asserts that we *value* sympathy with others as an end in itself. We want to experience the pleasure and pain of others and to have them experience ours. (Even for Hobbes, one of the drawbacks of the state of nature was its being "solitary.") But to maintain this kind of emotional interchange with others, Smith argues, we must protect ourselves against one of its most common consequences: casual or unjust judgments of our behavior by others. We therefore develop standards of what others "ought" to think about our conduct. To do this, we try to see our behavior objectively, that is, as others would see it. This means trying to evaluate our behavior from a perspective in which our selfish interests count no more than the interests of others. These moral standards are, in principle, independent of any particular individual's judgment.

The linkage between moral ideas and selflessness recurs over and over in subsequent theories. Rawls, for example, argues that we carry out the social contract not merely because we are afraid to break it, but because we are positively attracted to a "just" society, and because we feel rules are "just" if they are the rules we would agree to if we did not know our selfish interests. Our capacity to imagine such rules is, I think, inextricably tied to our ability to experience the disapproval others would express if they knew we had broken such rules. We know what others would say or feel, and we know how we would respond. Such vicarious feelings are not likely to be as strong as feelings about real events, but for most people this is a difference of degree, not of kind.

If this argument is correct, the viability of the social contract depends not just on society's capacity to inspire fear in the hearts of potential violators, but on its capacity to develop the empathic tendencies from which moral sentiments derive. If a society can do this, it can expect its members to act unselfishly at least some of the time. When we calculate the costs and benefits of a particular action, we will include not only its costs and benefits to ourselves, but also its costs and benefits to the others who populate our imagination. The weight we attach to the presumed judgments of these "significant others" may be less than the weight we attach to our own selfish judgment, but it will seldom be zero. (When it is, we judge an individual "morally deficient" or "psychopathic.") The views we impute to those imaginary others may not be altogether accurate, but they are seldom completely fanciful. (When they are, we judge an individual psychotic.)

Empathy is not, of course, the primary mechanism for enforcing the social contract on a day-to-day basis. Rather, enforcement depends on the fact that people have moral ideas. These ideas have a life of their own. They can, indeed, prevent us from acting unselfishly vis-à-vis those with whom we empathize when such actions would, at least in theory, have negative consequences for others with whom we do not empathize. When Lawrence Kohlberg asked respondents whether a man should steal a drug to save his wife's life, for example, respondents often thought they were being asked whether they endorsed a universalistic morality based on concern for anonymous others or a particularistic morality based on empathy.

Furthermore, while the existence of moral ideas probably depends on our collective capacity for empathy, the force of these ideas in the lives of particular individuals seems to depend on many factors besides the intensity with which they empathize with others. In the caricature version of psychoanalytic theory, for example, the development of empathy depends on a warm, loving mother, while the development of moral standards depends on a powerful, punitive father. Whether for this reason or others, there are plenty of people whose behavior seems to be deeply influenced by moral ideals that demand a high level of unselfishness, but who nonetheless show little sign of participating vicariously in the pleasure or suffering of those whom their unselfishness benefits. This suggests that we should not equate cultural dynamics with psychodynamics, or assume that the logic of cultural evolution is the same as the logic of individual development.

One reason cultural dynamics differ from psychodynamics is that patterns of behavior that are desirable from a cultural viewpoint are often undesirable from an individual perspective. It seems clear, for example, that society as a whole would be better off if the combined effect of empathy, community, and morality were to ensure that everyone always abided by the social contract. Yet we know that no society has ever come close to achieving this goal. In order to understand why this has never happened, it is helpful to look more closely at the mechanisms by which natural selection operates.

The Genetic Trap

Our genetic heritage limits the likely range of human behavior in innumerable ways. Genes, for example, provide the physiological basis for being able to imagine the feelings of others, a capacity that appears to be limited to a few species—though it is, of course, hard to be sure of this. Physiology also ensures that we will almost always experience our own pleasure or pain more vividly than we experience the pleasure or pain of others. Humans are thus "partial empathizers." This is a quite predictable by-product of spontaneous variation and natural selection over many generations.

Consider the likely fate of a "complete empathizer." Suppose that genetic mutations occasionally produced individuals who empathized completely with the pleasures and pains of those around them. These mutants would presumably act completely unselfishly vis-à-vis everyone they encountered. If they saw a fellow human attacked by a predator, for example, they would come to the victim's aid whenever the likely benefit to the victim exceeded the likely risk to themselves. This would be a very satisfactory state of affairs if the victims were also complete empathizers, and therefore reciprocated whenever the tables were turned. But if the victims were only partial empathizers, they would often fail to reciprocate. A complete empathizer's chances of surviving and leaving altruistic progeny would therefore be less than a partial empathizer's chances of doing so. The genes that led to total empathy would therefore be subject to negative selection and would eventually be eliminated from the population.

Next consider the fate of a "nonempathizer." At first glance it might seem that natural selection would favor nonempathizers over partial empathizers, since a nonempathizer would not be likely to take *any* risks on behalf of others, and would therefore have a greater chance of leaving surviving offspring. There are, however, three common circumstances in which failure to take risks for others will reduce the odds that our genes will be represented in later generations. The most obvious circumstance is where the risks are taken on behalf of our own offspring. I know of no hard evidence that empathy is essential for effective parenting, but the assumption is widely shared by parents, social workers, pediatricians, and psychiatrists. If partial empathizers took better care of their offspring than nonempathizers, the genes responsible for partial empathy would gradually spread through the entire population.

A second hazard of nonempathy is its likely effect on one's behavior toward other relatives. Individuals share more of their genes with their immediate relatives than with other members of their species. Siblings, for example, share about half the genes that ordinarily vary within a species. This means that if I engage in altruistic acts that increase my siblings' chances of survival, I have a 50–50 chance of facilitating the survival of my own genes, including those that make me act altruistically. This means that there will be positive selection over time for altruistic acts that increase my siblings' chances of survival by more than twice as much as they reduce my chances of survival.[2] If altruism toward relatives depends on empathy, nonempathizers' genes may be less likely to survive over time than partial empathizers' genes.

The third problem posed by the absence of empathy is its likely effect on what Robert Trivers calls "reciprocal altruism."[3] By this he means an ongoing pattern of interaction in which I help you, then you help me, and so on. If each helpful act involves some risk to the actor but a greater benefit to the recipient, such interactions will eventually benefit both parties. Genetic selection will favor such acts in relatively small closed systems, where each party can expect the other to reciprocate, though not in large open systems, where there is a low probability that those for whom I take risks will be in a position to reciprocate or can be induced to do so. Within a small closed system, genetic selection will also favor what Trivers calls "moralistic aggression," that is, punitive behavior toward those who are not sufficiently altruistic toward me. At the same time, genetic selection will favor what Trivers labels "subtle cheating," that is, behavior that *looks* altruistic (and thus forestalls moralistic aggression), but that really minimizes the risk to the actor.

What Trivers calls reciprocal altruism is not really altruistic in my sense of the term; rather, it is a matter of "enlightened self-interest." But the label is not critical in the present context. The important point is that reciprocal altruism among humans seems to depend on what we ordinarily call trust, and trust probably depends to some extent on empathy. If nonempathizers never trusted anyone, they would never engage in reciprocal altruism, and this would probably reduce their chances of leaving surviving offspring.

If the foregoing analysis is correct, we would expect genetic selection to eliminate *both* empathizers *and* nonempathizers, leaving a population composed entirely of partial empathizers. We would also expect greater empathy vis-à-vis offspring, relatives, and acquaintances with whom one has a reciprocal relationship. As a practical matter, we cannot control empathy this precisely. We do, however, seem to empathize primarily with individuals who occupy roles that are usually occupied by kin, offspring, or acquaintances, that is, those with whom we have frequent and prolonged visual contact. Rationing empathy in this way minimizes altruistic acts vis-à-vis strangers, and therefore minimizes the likelihood of unproductive risk taking.

To the extent that human behavior depends on genes, then, we expect it to be only fitfully and partially unselfish, with continuous subtle cheating by nominal adherents to the social contract and flagrant cheating by strangers, who are not part of an ongoing system that can enforce the social contract. This pattern of behavior is by no means ideal from the viewpoint of the species as a whole, since it implies that humans will often fail to help one another in circumstances where such help would increase the overall survival rate of the species.

Suppose, for example, that a committee is charged with drawing up guidelines on how we should respond when we see someone drowning, and that the committee's sole objective is to multiply the human race as fast as possible—an admittedly tawdry goal. The committee would presumably suggest that we first estimate the number of additional offspring both we and the victim could expect if we both survived. This would presumably depend on our age, marital status, physical health, and the like. Then the committee would suggest that we estimate the likelihood of saving the victim and the likelihood of drowning ourselves if we adopted various courses of action. Finally, it would tell us to choose the course of action that maximized the number of offspring both we and the victim could expect to produce in the future, paying no attention to whether these offspring were our own or the victim's. The committee would, in short, tell us to be complete altruists.

Genetic selection would almost never favor this response. If our behavior depended entirely on our genes, and if these had been selected for optimal fitness in this specific situation (an admittedly unlikely situation), we would first determine whether the victim was a relative, an acquaintance who could be expected to help us at some future date, or a stranger. If the victim were a relative, we would attempt a rescue only if this increased the probability that our genes would be represented in future generations. This would depend on the fraction of our genes we shared with the victim, our expected fertility relative to that of the victim, and the relative risk to us and the victim of various courses of action. If our expected future fertility were the same as the victim's, we would always respond in partially rather than completely altruistic ways. Much the same logic would apply to acquaintances. We would try to rescue them only if the risk to ourselves were smaller than the combined probability that by taking this risk we would *both* save the victim *and* allow the victim to save us at some future date. Since the second contingency is never absolutely certain, we would never respond as complete altruists. Finally, if the victim were a complete stranger, genetic selection would give us no reason to attempt a rescue.

The fact that genes are passed on by individuals, not groups, thus means that genetic selection favors behavior that is far from optimal for the group. To escape this genetic trap a group must devise some way of modifying the effects of genetic selection on individual behavior.

Cultural Selection

Human behavior depends not only on genes but also on past experience. This means that we can sometimes structure other people's experience so as to alter behavior that does not work to our advantage. In general, each of us has an interest in persuading others to act altruistically toward us. One possible way of doing this is to get others to empathize with us. Another possibility is to convince them that unless they are unselfish they will be severely punished (via moralistic aggression). Still another possibility is to get others to internalize altruistic norms, so that they punish themselves for violations. We all try to manipulate other people's behavior in such ways, but other people also resist our efforts. Unless we are larger or cleverer than the other person—as we are vis-à-vis our children—our individual efforts to manipulate others are seldom very successful.

But when the number of individuals attempting to manipulate a given person's behavior becomes large, resistance becomes increasingly difficult. This happens, for example, when a group collectively tries to manipulate the behavior of its individual members. If the group is united, it can sometimes drastically alter patterns of behavior favored by genetic selection. It can, for example, induce members of the group to sacrifice their lives for the group's welfare. It can also induce them to place more value on principles like "honor," "friendship," and "loyalty" than on survival.

All cultures engage in such collective efforts at manipulating individual behavior. But not all cultures promote the same kinds of behavior, and those with similar goals are not all equally successful in attaining them. While the range of cultural variation over the centuries is far from exhaustive, it is still impressive. This means that there has been considerable room for cultural as well as genetic selection.

While the principles of cultural selection are far from clear, a norm's chances of surviving are related to at least two factors. First, the norm must be compatible with the development of military organizations that can protect those who accept the norm. Second, for a norm to become widespread today, it must be compatible with reasonably efficient organization of economic production and distribution. This is partly because efficient economic organization provides a surplus to support military activities and partly because it allows population growth.

One prerequisite of both military and economic efficiency, I believe, is effective inhibition of many kinds of selfishness. Let us begin with an extreme case: military combat. Members of a combat unit must be willing to risk death. If they take this risk only when they fear a court martial, they will not make a very effective unit. First, they will avoid engaging the enemy whenever possible. Then, if engagement is unavoidable, they will minimize risks to themselves individually, even when this increases the risks to other members of the unit. Such behavior will lower the unit's overall survival rate while raising the enemy's survival rate. The more nearly altruistic the members of a unit are relative to one another, the higher their overall survival rate is likely to be, and the lower the likely survival rate of the enemy.

We can formulate this general argument somewhat differently by noting that efficient organizations usually have two distinctive features. First, they coordinate the activities of many people who are virtual strangers to one another. In order to operate efficiently, a large organization must dissuade such strangers from exploiting every available opportunity for personal advantage. In cultures where taking advantage of strangers is the norm, large organizations have great difficulty imposing sanctions that are sufficient to make the organization function smoothly. This is partly because sanctions themselves are hard to implement in an unprincipled system, since the prospective victims find it easy to buy off the enforcers.

A second distinctive feature of efficient organizations is that they provide many of their members with a significant amount of individual discretion in their behavior. This means that individuals have many opportunities for subtle cheating. If all members engage in subtle cheating, the organization must reduce the amount of discretion through more extensive policing. Yet this often lowers morale and thereby encourages even more cheating in the remaining areas of discretion. This forces still further reductions in discretion, leading to further reductions in morale. This downward spiral eventually produces the GI mentality, in which everyone is completely cynical about the organization's goals and nobody does more than absolutely necessary.

The pivotal role of unselfishness emerges in somewhat different form if we consider the social prerequisites of urbanization. Some degree of urbanization clearly enhances economic efficiency by reducing communication and transportation costs. But urbanization also increases the number of potential interactions among strangers. There is no way of policing all these potential interactions. Thus if all strangers deal completely selfishly with one another, the crime rate will be extremely high. If all opportunities for profitable crime were taken, urban life would be impossible. Society would have to revert to smaller, more physically separated communities that could police themselves internally and restrict access by strangers.

The foregoing examples suggest that cultures are likely to spread to the degree that they can inhibit individual selfishness and induce their members to abide by behavioral norms laid down by the group as a whole. But if complete subordination of individual interests to collective goals facilitates the survival and spread of cultures, why have no cultures actually achieved this end? Or to use a slightly different language, why is socialization not more effective? The answer appears to be that while cultural selection favors complete altruism, genetic selection favors limited altruism vis-à-vis kin, subtle cheating vis-à-vis acquaintances, and complete egoism vis-à-vis strangers. Powerful as culture is, it cannot fully overcome this genetic heritage.

The fact that cultural selection favors different behavior patterns from genetic selection has many complex consequences. If each selection system operated independently of the other, observed behavior would be a mixture of selfishness and unselfishness. But each selection system also tries to modify the other. Genetic selection, for example, not only encourages varieties of selfishness that are not favored by cultural selection, but encourages defensive rationalizations about the social value of such selfishness. These rationalizations then become part of the culture. Indeed, Donald Campbell interprets the bulk of twentieth-century psychotherapy in this light.[4] I would say the same about Social Darwinism and the Chicago school of economics. At the same time, however, cultural support for altruism can modify the effects of natural selection on the gene pool. In the simplest case, a culture may encourage its members to kill off individuals who are insufficiently altruistic. Genetic selection also favors this kind of moralistic aggression, but only when the benefit to specific aggressors exceeds the cost. Cultural selection may favor it even when the risks to specific aggressors are high, so long as the aggression increases the overall survival rate for the group as a whole. Cultural selection may also favor changes in breeding patterns that alter gene frequencies. If altruistic risk takers find it easier to attract or keep mates, for example, this may lead to positive rather than negative selection for altruistic risk taking.

The interpretation of genetic and cultural selection systems also allows unusually powerful individuals or groups within a society to manipulate cultural norms so as to promote their selfish ends. Their success in doing this will be directly proportional to their capacity to persuade others that the norms in question actually promote the common good rather than the good of a particular subgroup. As a result, the culture as a whole is likely to embody a complex mix of partially contradictory norms, some of which promote the common good, some of which merely appear to promote the common good while actually promoting the interests of powerful subgroups, and some of which explicitly assert the legitimacy of individual selfishness.

It is also important to emphasize that the tension between genetic and cultural selection involves only those traits that can affect either our own chances of survival or our chances of leaving surviving offspring. This is an important limitation. Most human behavior, including unselfish behavior, has no direct effect on anyone's chances of surviving. Instead, it is directed toward enhancing the subjective well-being of individuals whose survival depends on other factors. Behavior that affects only subjective well-being is subject to genetic selection only if it is caused by underlying propensities, like empathy or guilt, that also affect our chances of surviving or leaving surviving offspring. If there are forms of unselfishness that do not depend on traits that affect survival, these forms of unselfishness will not be subject to negative genetic selection.

This points to a more fundamental difficulty. While it is analytically useful to label many different forms of behavior as "selfish" or "unselfish," the use of a single label encourages the illusion that there is a single underlying trait ("unselfishness") that determines whether an individual engages in all these different forms of behavior. This seems unlikely. While I know of no systematic data on the extent to which an individual's propensity to act unselfishly in one context predicts his or her propensity to act unselfishly in other contexts, casual observation suggests that different kinds of unselfishness are only loosely related to one another. This is hardly surprising, given the multitude of motives that affect unselfish behavior. Intense empathy with another individual, strong identification with a larger group, and a strong propensity to follow universalistic rules need not arise in the same individuals. Furthermore, none of these three sources of unselfishness is itself a unitary trait. Those who empathize intensely with one person may not empathize with another, and the same holds for those who identify with one or another larger group. Even the intensity of an individual's commitment to universalistic moral rules will vary according to his or her past experience with the specific rule and the situation to which it nominally applies.

In the same way, we cannot simply assume that because a culture induces people to engage in one variety of unselfish behavior, it will be equally successful in getting them to engage in other varieties of unselfish behavior. Thus there is no guarantee that we will be able to characterize cultures as unusually successful in promoting unselfishness as a whole. Indeed, even if we could characterize cultures in this way, there is no guarantee that cultural selection will favor cultures that promote unselfishness in general. Rather, cultural selection is likely to favor those forms of unselfishness that contribute to military and economic success. It may be quite indifferent to other forms of unselfishness, even though they contribute in important ways to the subjective well-being of those who participate in the culture.

III An Ecological Niche for Altruism

5   A Theory of Moral Sentiments

Robert H. Frank

On New Year's night of 1888, the Hatfields attempted to end their feud with the McCoys once and for all. Led by James Vance, their strategy was to set fire to the McCoy farmhouse, then shoot the McCoys as they tried to escape. Young Alifair McCoy was the first cut down as she emerged from the kitchen door.

> Upon hearing that Alifair had been shot, Sarah McCoy, her mother, rushed to the back door . . . and continued toward her dying daughter. Vance bounded toward her and struck her with the butt of his rifle. For a moment she lay on the cold ground, stunned, groaning, and crying. Finally, she raised herself on her hands and knees and tried to crawl to Alifair. . . . she pleaded with the attackers, "For God's sake let me go to my girl." Then, realizing the situation, she cried, "Oh, she's dead. For the love of God, let me go to her." Sarah put out her hand until she could almost touch the feet of Alifair. Running down the doorsill, where Alifair had fallen, was blood from the girl's wounds. Johnse [Hatfield], who was standing against the outside wall of the kitchen, took his revolver and crushed Sarah's skull with it. She dropped to the ground and lay motionless. (Rice 1982: 62–63)

Although Alifair and her brother Calvin were killed, and their mother and several others in the family seriously injured, many of the McCoys escaped. The feud continued, in the end spanning more than three decades.

The costs of acting on vengeful impulses are often ruinous. It is often clear at each juncture that to retaliate will produce still another round of bloodshed. Yet families, tribes, and even nations persist.

What prompts such behavior? Surely not a clear-headed assessment of

This chapter was adapted from Robert H. Frank, *Passions within Reason: The Strategic Role of the Emotions* (New York: W. W. Norton, 1988), © copyright 1988 by Robert H. Frank, chaps. 1 and 3, research support for which was provided by NSF grant numbers SES-8707492 and SES-8605829. Used with permission.

self-interest. If a rational action is one that advances the actor's material interests,[1] it is manifestly irrational to retaliate in the face of such devastating costs.

The self-destructive pursuit of vengeance is not the only way we ignore our narrow, selfish interests. We trudge through snowstorms to cast our ballots, even when we are certain they will make no difference. We leave tips for waitresses in restaurants in distant cities we will never visit again. We make anonymous contributions to private charities. We often refrain from cheating even when we are sure we would not be caught. We sometimes walk away from profitable transactions whose terms we believe to be "unfair." We battle endless red tape merely to get a $10 refund on a defective product. And so on.

Behavior of this sort poses a fundamental challenge to those who believe that people generally pursue self-interest. Philosophers, behavioral biologists, economists, and others have invested much effort trying to account for it. Their explanations generally call attention to some ancillary gain implicit in the seemingly irrational action. Biologists, for example, tell us that someone may give up her life to save several of her immediate relatives, thereby increasing the survival rate of genes like the ones she carries. Or economists will explain that it makes sense for the Internal Revenue Service to spend $10,000 to prosecute someone who owes $100 in taxes because it thereby encourages broader compliance with the tax laws.

Much of the time, however, there appear to be no such ancillary gains. The war between the British and the Argentines over the Falklands is a clear case in point. The Argentine writer Jorge Luis Borges likened it to "two bald men fighting over a comb." Both sides knew perfectly well that the windswept, desolate islands were of virtually no economic or strategic significance. At one point in history, it might have made sense for Britain to defend them anyway, as a means of deterring aggression against other, more valuable parts of its far-flung empire. But today there is no empire left to protect. For much less than the British spent in the conflict, they could have given each Falklander a Scottish castle and a generous pension for life. And yet very few British citizens seem to regret having stood up to the Argentines.

Many actions, purposely taken with full knowledge of their consequences, *are* irrational. If people did not perform them, they would be better off and they know it. As will become clear, however, these same actions are often part of a larger pattern that is anything but irrational. The apparent contradiction arises not because of any hidden gains from the actions themselves, but because we face important problems that simply cannot be solved by rational action. The common feature of these problems is that they require us to make commitments to behave in ways that may later prove contrary to our interests.

The Commitment Problem

Thomas Schelling (1960) provides a vivid illustration of this class of problems. He describes a kidnapper who suddenly gets cold feet. He wants to set his victim free, but is afraid the victim will go to the police. In return for freedom, the victim gladly promises not to do so. The problem, however, is that both realize it will no longer be in the victim's interest to keep this promise once he is free. And so the kidnapper reluctantly concludes that he must kill him.

Schelling suggests the following way out of the dilemma: "If the victim has committed an act whose disclosure could lead to blackmail, he may confess it; if not, he might commit one in the presence of his captor, to create a bond that will ensure his silence" (1960: 43–44). The blackmailable act serves here as a *commitment device,* something that provides the victim with an incentive to keep his promise. Keeping it will still be unpleasant for him once he is freed, but clearly less so than not being able to make a credible promise in the first place.

In everyday economic and social interaction, we repeatedly encounter commitment problems like the one confronting Schelling's kidnapper and victim. My thesis is that specific emotions act as commitment devices that help resolve these dilemmas.

Consider a person who threatens to retaliate against anyone who harms him. For his threat to deter, others must believe he will carry it out. But if others know that the costs of retaliation are prohibitive, they will realize the threat is empty. Unless, of course, they believe they are dealing with someone who simply *likes* to retaliate. Such a person may strike back even when it is not in his material interests to do so. But if he is known in advance to have that preference, he is not likely to be tested by aggression in the first place.

Similarly, a person who is known to "dislike" an unfair bargain can credibly threaten to walk away from one, even when it is in her narrow interest to accept it. By virtue of being known to have this preference, she becomes a more effective negotiator.

Consider, too, the person who "feels bad" when he cheats. These feelings can accomplish for him what a rational assessment of self-interest cannot, namely, they can cause him to behave honestly even when he *knows* he could get away with cheating. And if others realize he feels this way, they will seek him as a partner in ventures that require trust.

Being known to experience certain emotions enables us to make commitments that would otherwise not be credible. The clear irony here is that this ability, which springs from a *failure* to pursue self-interest, confers genuine advantages. Granted, following through on these commitments will always involve avoidable losses—not cheating when there is a chance to, retaliating at great cost even after the damage is done, and so on. The problem, however, is that being unable to make credible commitments will often be even more costly. Confronted with the commitment problem, an opportunistic person fares poorly.

Emotions as Commitments

The irony of the commitment problem is that it arises because material incentives at a given moment prompt people to behave in ways contrary to their ultimate material interests. The conventional way to solve commitment problems is to alter the relevant material incentives. Schelling's kidnap victim, for example, resolved his dilemma by giving the kidnapper self-incriminating evidence to ensure his silence.

It will often be impractical, however, to alter material incentives in the desired ways. Fortunately, there is a potentially fruitful alternative approach. Material incentives are by no means the only force that governs behavior. Even in biological models, where these incentives are the ultimate concern, they play no *direct* role in motivation. Rather, behavior is directly guided by a complex psychological reward mechanism.

The system that governs food intake provides a clear illustration of this mechanism. Man or beast, an individual does not eat in response to a rational calculation about food intake. Instead, a complex of biological forces causes it to "feel hungry" when its stomach contents, blood sugar level, and other nutritional indexes fall below various threshold values. To feel hungry is to experience a subjective sensation of displeasure in the central nervous system. Experience, and perhaps even inborn neural circuits, tell us that food intake will relieve this sensation.

In a proximate sense, this is *why* we eat. There is a material payoff to eating, to be sure. Any organism that did not eat obviously would not be favored by natural selection. The important point is that the relevant material payoffs are more likely to be realized if eating is motivated directly through the reward mechanism. Intense feelings of hunger, apparently, are more expedient than rational reflections about caloric intake for motivating a starving individual to focus on the most important threat to its survival.

The fit between the behaviors favored by the reward mechanism and those favored by rational calculation is at best imperfect. The reward mechanism provides rules of thumb that work well much of the time, but not in all cases. Indeed, when environmental conditions differ substantially from the ones under which the reward mechanism evolved, important conflicts often arise.

The reward system governing food intake again provides a convenient illustration. It is now believed that food shortages were a common occurrence during most of evolutionary history. Under such conditions, it paid to have a reward mechanism that favored heavy food intake whenever abundant food was available. People thus motivated would be more likely to fatten up as a hedge against periods of famine. In modern industrial societies, however, people are much more likely to die of heart attacks than of starvation. A rational calculation of self-interest currently dictates that we stay slim. This calculation, needless to say, is at war, often on the losing side, with the reward mechanism.

That the reward mechanism often defeats intentions motivated by rational assessment of material payoffs is not to say that rational assessment is unimportant for survival. On the contrary, our ability to make purposeful, rational calculations has surely played a major role in our ability to persist in competition with animal species that are far stronger, faster, and more prolific than we are.

The critical point, for present purposes, is that rational calculations play only an indirect role. Suppose, for example, a hungry person calculates that being fat is not in his interests, and for this reason refrains from eating. His rational calculation has clearly played a role, but it is an indirect one. It is still the reward mechanism that directly governs his behavior. The rational calculation informs the reward mechanism that eating will have adverse consequences. This prospect then triggers unpleasant feelings. And it is these feelings that compete directly with the impulse to eat. Rational calculations, understood in this way, are an *input* into the reward mechanism.

Feelings and emotions, apparently, are the proximate causes of most behaviors. The biochemical workings of some of them—hunger, anger, fear, and mating urges, for example—are sufficiently well understood that they can be induced by electrical stimulation of specific brain sites. Others are less well mapped. Yet they are so consistently recognized across cultures that they, too, are likely to have some neuroanatomical basis.

Certain of the emotions—anger, contempt, disgust, envy, greed, shame, and guilt—were described by Adam Smith as moral sentiments. The reward theory of behavior tells us that these sentiments, like feelings of hunger, can and do compete with the feelings that spring from rational calculations about material payoffs. My thesis is that, for exactly this reason, they can help people solve the commitment problem.

It is clear, at any rate, that these sentiments can alter people's incentives in the desired ways. Consider, for example, a person capable of strong guilt feelings. This person will not cheat even when it is in her material interest to do so. The reason is not that she fears getting caught but that she simply does not *want* to cheat. Her aversion to feelings of guilt effectively alters the payoffs she faces.[2] It is not necessary to monitor such a person to prevent her from cheating, which thus avoids the problem that there is often no practical way to do so.

By the same token, someone who becomes enraged when dealt with unjustly does not need a formal contract to commit him to seek revenge. He will seek revenge because he *wants* to, even when, in purely material terms, it does not pay. His feelings of anger will offset his material incentives.

This same sense of justice can serve as the commitment device needed to solve bargaining problems. Smith may be in a weak bargaining position, for example, because he needs money more than Jones does. But if Smith is concerned not only about how much money he gets, in absolute terms, but also about how the total is divided, he will be much more inclined to reject an unfair proposal made by Jones. Being concerned about justice is like signing a contract that prevents him from accepting the short end of a one-sided transaction.

Commitment problems in close personal relationships are likewise better solved by moral sentiments than by awkward formal contracts. The best insurance against a change in future material incentives is a strong bond of love. If ten years from now one partner falls victim to a lasting illness, the other's material incentives will be to find a new partner. But a deep bond of affection will render this change in incentives irrelevant, which opens the door for current investments in the relationship that might otherwise be too risky.

By themselves, however, the described changes in incentives are not sufficient to solve the commitment problem. Granted, strong feelings of guilt *are* enough to prevent a person from cheating. And the satisfying feeling someone gets from having done the right thing is, in a very real sense, its own reward. But our task here, once again, is to explain how such sentiments might have evolved in the material world. We can't eat moral sentiments. Given that these sentiments often cause people to incur substantial avoidable costs, they must also confer some sort of compensating advantage in order to have persisted.

The potential gain from being honest, recall, is to cooperate with others who are also honest. In order for the noncheater to benefit in material terms, others must thus be able to recognize her as such, and she, in turn, must be able to recognize other noncheaters. The impulse to seek revenge is likewise counterproductive unless others have some way of anticipating that one has it. The person in whom this sentiment resides unrecognized will fail to deter potential predators. And if one is going to be victimized anyway, it is better *not* to desire revenge. For similar reasons, a sense of justice and the capacity to love will not yield material payoffs unless they can be somehow communicated clearly to others.

But how do people know that a person's feelings commit him to behave honestly in the face of a golden opportunity to cheat? Or that he will seek revenge, even when it is too late to undo the injury he has suffered? Or that he really will walk away from an unfair bargain, even when he would do better by accepting it? It is insufficient merely to *declare* one's emotional predispositions ("I am honest. Trust me."), but subtle clues of facial expression, voice, and gesture often reveal them very clearly. This fact plays a central role in the workings of the commitment model.

Clues to Behavioral Predispositions

One fall day, almost twenty years ago, black activist Ron Dellums was the speaker at a large rally on the University of California campus in Berkeley. Polls suggested he would soon become the Berkeley–North Oakland district's first radical congressman. Crowds were easily galvanized in those days, and this one was in especially high spirits. But at least one young man was not moved by Dellums's speech. He sat still as a stone on the steps of Sproul Plaza, lost to some drug, his face and eyes empty of expression.

Presently a large Irish setter appeared, sniffing his way through the crowd. He moved directly to the young man sitting on the steps and circled him once. He paused, lifted his leg, and, with no apparent malice, soaked the young man's back. He then set off again into the crowd. The boy barely stirred.

Now, the Irish setter is not a particularly intelligent breed. Yet this one had no difficulty locating the one person in that crowd who would not retaliate for being used as a fire hydrant. Facial expressions and other aspects of demeanor apparently provide clues to behavior that even dogs can interpret. And although none of us had ever witnessed such a scene before, no one was really surprised when the boy did nothing. Before anything even happened, it was somehow *obvious* that he was just going to go right on sitting there.

Without doubt, however, the boy's behavior was unusual. Most of us would have responded angrily, some even violently. Yet we already know that no real advantage inheres in this "normal" response. After all, once the boy's shirt was soaked, it was already too late to undo the damage. And since he was unlikely ever to encounter that particular dog again, there was little point in trying to teach the dog a lesson. On the contrary, any attempt to do so would have courted the risk of being bitten.

Our young man's problem was not that he failed to respond angrily, but that he failed to communicate to the dog that he was *predisposed* to do so. The vacant expression on his face was somehow all the dog needed to know he was a safe target. Merely by wearing "normal" expressions, the rest of us were spared.

A burgeoning literature describes how we draw inferences about people's feelings from subtle behavioral clues. Posture, the rate of respiration, the pitch and timber of the voice, perspiration, facial muscle tone and expression, movement of the eyes, and a host of other signals guide us in this task. We quickly surmise, for example, that someone with clenched jaws and a purple face is enraged, even when we do not know what, exactly, may have triggered his anger. And we apparently know, even if we cannot articulate, how a forced smile differs from one that is heartfelt.

At least partly on the basis of such clues, we form judgments about the emotional makeup of the people with whom we deal. Some people we feel we can trust, but of others we remain ever wary. Some we feel can be taken advantage of, others we know instinctively not to provoke.

Being able to make such judgments accurately has always been an obvious advantage. But it may be no less an advantage that others be able to make similar assessments about our own propensities. A blush may reveal a lie and cause great embarrassment at the moment, but in circumstances that require trust, there can be great advantage in being known to be a blusher.

The Problem of Mimicry

If there are genuine advantages in being vengeful or trustworthy and being perceived as such, there are even greater advantages in appearing to have, but not actually having, these qualities. A liar who appears trustworthy will have better opportunities than one who glances about furtively, sweats profusely, speaks in a quavering voice, and has difficulty making eye contact.

We know of people who can lie convincingly. In a September 1938 meeting, for example, Adolf Hitler managed to persuade British prime minister Neville Chamberlain that he would not go to war if the borders of Czechoslovakia were redrawn to meet his demands. Shortly thereafter, Chamberlain wrote in a letter to his sister: "in spite of the hardness and ruthlessness I thought I saw in his face, I got the impression that here was a man who could be relied upon when he gave his word" (Ekman 1985: 15, 16).

Clues to behavioral predispositions are obviously not perfect. Even with the aid of all their sophisticated machinery, experienced professional polygraph experts cannot be sure when someone is lying. Some emotions are more difficult to simulate than others. Someone who feigns outrage, for example, is apparently easier to catch than someone who pretends to feel joyful. But no matter what the emotion, we can almost never be certain. Indeed, the forces at work are such that it will always be possible for at least *some* people to succeed at deception. In a world in which no one cheated, no one would be on the lookout. A climate thus lacking in vigilance would create profitable opportunities for cheaters. So there will inevitably be a niche for at least some of them.

Useful lessons about this problem are contained in the similar instances of mimicry that abound in nature. Some butterflies, like the monarch, have developed a foul taste that defends them against predators. This taste would be useless unless predators had some way of telling which butterflies to avoid, so predators have learned to interpret the monarch's distinctive wing markings for this purpose. This has created a profitable opportunity for other butterflies, like the viceroy, who bear similar wing markings but lack the bad taste that normally accompanies them. Merely by looking like the unpalatable monarchs, viceroys have escaped predation without having to expend the energy needed to produce the objectionable taste itself.

In such instances, it is clear that if mimics could *perfectly* simulate the wing marking with neither cost nor delay, the entire edifice would crumble: the comparatively efficient mimics would eventually overwhelm the others, and the predators' original reason for avoiding that particular marking would thereby vanish. So in cases where mimics coexist alongside the genuine article for extended periods, we may infer that perfect mimicry either takes time or entails substantial costs. The fact that the bearer of the genuine trait has the first move in this game will often prove a decisive advantage.

Similar considerations apply in the case of those who mimic emotional traits. If the signals we use for detecting these traits have no value, we would have long since ceased to rely on them. And yet, by their very nature, they cannot be perfect. Symptoms of character, after all, cannot be scrutinized without effort. If no one ever cheated, it would never pay to expend this effort. The irony, of course, is that this would create golden opportunities to cheat.

The inevitable result is an uneasy balance between people who really possess the character traits at issue and others who merely seem to.[3] Those who are adept at reading the relevant signals will be more successful than others. There is also a payoff to those who are able to send effective signals about their own behavioral predispositions. And, sad to say, there will also be a niche for those who are skillful at pretending to have feelings they really lack.

Indeed, at first glance it might appear that the largest payoff of all goes to the shameless liar. In specific instances, this may well be true, but we must bear in mind the special contempt we reserve for such persons. Most of us will go to great trouble to inform others when we stumble upon someone who lies with apparent sincerity. Thus, even if such persons are caught only very rarely, it is far from clear that they command any special advantage.

The ecological balance between more and less opportunistic strategies is in harmony both with the view that self-interest underlies all action and with the opposing view that people often transcend their selfish tendencies. The key to resolving the tension between these views is to understand that the ruthless pursuit of self-interest is often self-defeating. As Zen masters have known intuitively for thousands of years, the best outcome is sometimes possible only when people abandon the chase. Here we see that self-interest often requires commitments to behave in ways that will, if triggered, prove deeply contrary to our interests.

Much of the time, the practical means for accomplishing these commitments are emotions that have observable symptoms. Some of these emotions, apparently, are inborn. But even if they were transmitted only by cultural indoctrination, they would serve equally well. What is necessary in either case is that people who have them be observably different, on the average, from those who do not.

For convenience, I use the term *commitment model* as shorthand for the notion that seemingly irrational behavior is sometimes explained by emotional predispositions that help solve commitment problems. The competing view that people always act efficiently in the pursuit of self-interest I call the *self-interest model*.

The commitment model's point of departure is that a person who is believed always to pursue self-interest will be excluded from many valuable opportunities. For example, no one would willingly hire such a person for a managerial position that involved failsafe opportunities to embezzle cash from the company. By contrast, a person who is believed to have a strong conscience is a much more attractive candidate for this position. The strict calculus of self-interest would still dictate that he steal the money, but a sufficiently strong emotional commitment to honesty can overcome this calculus.

On purely theoretical grounds, the commitment model thus suggests that the moving force behind moral behavior lies not in rational analysis but in the emotions. This view is consistent with an extensive body of empirical evidence reviewed by developmental psychologist Jerome Kagan. As he summarizes his interpretation of that evidence: "Construction of a persuasive rational basis for behaving morally has been the problem on which most moral philosophers have stubbed their toes. I believe they will continue to do so until they recognize what Chinese philosophers have known for a long time: namely, feeling, not logic, sustains the super-ego" (1984: xiv). The emotions may indeed sustain the superego, but the commitment model suggests that it may well be the logic of self-interest that ultimately sustains these emotions.

Illustration: The Cheating Problem

To illustrate the workings of the contest between honest and dishonest behavior, it is helpful to examine the details of a simple ecology in which the two types are pitted against one another in a struggle to survive. The commitment problem to be solved is the classic prisoner's dilemma. The specific version of it is a joint venture—the monetary payoffs given by the entries in figure 5.1. These payoffs depend on the particular combination of strategies chosen by the participants. Note that Jones gets a higher pay-off by defecting, no matter what Smith does, and the same is true for Smith. If Jones believes Smith will behave in a self-interested way, he will predict that Smith will defect. And if only to protect himself, he will likely feel compelled to defect as well. When both defect, each gets only a two-unit payoff. The frustration, as in all dilemmas of this sort, is that both could have easily done much better. Had they cooperated, each would have gotten a four-unit payoff.

Now suppose we have not just Smith and Jones but a large population. Pairs of people again form joint ventures, and the relationship between behavior and payoffs for the members of each pair is again as given in figure 5.1. Suppose further that everyone in the population is one of two types—cooperator or defector. A cooperator is someone who, possibly through intensive cultural conditioning, has developed a genetically en-dowed capacity to experience a moral sentiment that predisposes him to cooperate. A defector is someone who either lacks this capacity or has failed to develop it.

In this scheme, cooperators are hardcore altruists in the sense that they refrain from cheating even when there is no possibility of being detected. Viewed in the narrow context of the choice at hand, this behavior is clearly contrary to their material interests. Defectors, by contrast, are pure op-portunists. They always make whatever choice will maximize their per-sonal payoff. Our task, again, is to determine what will happen when people from these two groups are thrown into a survival struggle against one another. The key to the survival of cooperators, we will see, is for them to devise some means of identifying one another, thereby to interact selec-

Jones

	Cooperate	Defect
Cooperate	4 for each	0 for Y 6 for X
Defect	6 for Y 0 for X	2 for each

Smith

Fig. 5.1. Monetary payoffs in a joint venture.

tively and avoid exploitation with defectors. But the first step in the argument is to investigate what happens when voluntary, selective interaction is not possible.

Population Movements When Cooperators and Defectors Look Alike

Suppose, for argument's sake, that cooperators and defectors look exactly alike. In this hypothetical ecology, this means they will pair at random. Naturally, cooperators (and defectors, for that matter) would like nothing better than to pair with cooperators, but they have no choice in the matter. Because everyone looks the same, they must take their chances. The expected payoffs to both defectors and cooperators therefore depend on the likelihood of pairing with a cooperator, which in turn depends on the proportion of cooperators in the population.

Suppose, for example, the population consists almost entirely of cooperators. A cooperator is then virtually certain to have a cooperator for a partner, and so expects a payoff of nearly four units. The rare defector in this population is similarly almost certain to get a cooperator for a partner and can expect a payoff of nearly six units. (The defector's unlucky partner, of course, gets a payoff of zero, but his singular misfortune does not significantly affect the average payoff for cooperators as a group.)

Alternatively, suppose the population consists of half cooperators, half defectors. Each person is then just as likely to pair with a defector as with a cooperator. Cooperators thus have equal chances of receiving either zero or four units, which gives them an average payoff of two units. Defectors, in turn, have equal chances of receiving two or six units, so their average payoff will be four units. In general, the average payoffs for each group will rise with the proportion of cooperators in the population—the cooperator's because he is less likely to be exploited by a defector, the defector's because he is more likely to find a cooperator he can exploit. The exact relationships for the particular payoffs assumed in this illustration are shown in figure 5.2.

When cooperators and defectors look exactly the same, how will the population evolve over time? In evolutionary models, each individual reproduces in proportion to its average payoff: those with larger material payoffs have the resources necessary to raise larger numbers of offspring.[4] Since defectors always receive a higher average payoff here, their share of the population will grow over time. Cooperators, even if they make up almost the entire population to begin with, are thus destined for extinction. When cooperators and defectors look alike, genuine cooperation cannot emerge. In a crude way, this case epitomizes the traditional sociobiological characterization of behavior.

Population Movements When Cooperators Are Easily Identified

Now suppose everything is just as before except that cooperators and defectors are perfectly distinguishable from each other. Imagine that cooperators are born with a red *C* on their foreheads, defectors with a red *D*. Suddenly the tables are turned. Cooperators can now interact selectively with one another and be assured of a payoff of four units. No cooperator need ever interact with a defector. Defectors are left to interact with one another, for which they get a payoff of only two units.

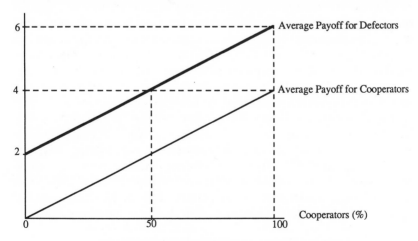

Fig. 5.2. Average payoffs when cooperators and defectors look alike.

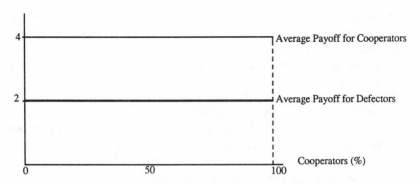

Fig. 5.3. Average payoffs when cooperators and
defectors are perfectly distinguishable.

Since all element of chance has been removed from the interaction process, payoffs no longer depend on the proportion of cooperators in the
population (see fig. 5.3). Cooperators always get four; defectors always
get two.

This time the cooperators' larger payoffs enable *them* to raise larger
families, which means they will make up an ever growing share of the population. When cooperators can be easily identified, it is the defectors who
face extinction.

Mimicry without Cost or Delay

The defectors need not go quietly into the night, however. Suppose there
arises a mutant strain of defectors, one that behaves exactly like other defectors, but in which each individual has not a red *D* on his forehead but
a red *C*. Since this particular strain of defectors looks exactly the same as
cooperators, it is impossible for cooperators to discriminate against them.
Each imposter is therefore just as likely to interact with a cooperator as a
genuine cooperator is. This, in turn, means that the mutant defectors will
have a higher expected payoff than the cooperators.

The nonmutant defectors—those who continue to bear the red *D*—
will have a lower payoff than both of these groups and, as before, are destined for extinction. But unless the cooperators adapt in some way, they
too face the same fate. When defectors can perfectly mimic the distinguishing feature of cooperators with neither cost nor delay, the feature
loses all power to distinguish. Cooperators and the surviving defectors
again look exactly alike, which again spells doom for the cooperators.

Imperfect Mimicry and the Costs of Scrutiny

Defectors, of course, have no monopoly on the power to adapt. If random
mutations alter the cooperators' distinguishing characteristic, the defec-

tors will be faced with a moving target. Imagine that the red *C* by which cooperators originally managed to distinguish themselves has evolved over time into a generally ruddy complexion—a blush of sorts—and that some defectors have a ruddy complexion as well. But because cooperators actually experience the emotions that motivate cooperation, they have a more intense blush, on the average.

In general, we might expect a continuum of intensity of blushes for both groups.[5] For the sake of simplicity, however, suppose that complexions take one of only two discrete types: (1) heavy blush and (2) light blush. Those with heavy blushes are cooperators, those with light blushes defectors. If the two types could be distinguished at a glance, defectors would again be doomed. But suppose it requires effort to inspect the intensity of a person's blush. For concreteness, suppose inspection costs one unit. For people who pay this cost, the veil is lifted: cooperators and defectors can be distinguished with 100 percent accuracy. For those who don't pay the one-unit cost of scrutiny, the two types are perfectly indistinguishable.

To see what happens this time, suppose the payoffs are again as given in figure 5.1 and consider the decision facing a cooperator who is trying to decide whether to pay the cost of scrutiny. If he pays it, he can be assured of interacting with another cooperator and will thus get a payoff of 4 − 1 = 3 units. If he does not, his payoff is uncertain. Cooperators and defectors will look exactly alike to him, and he must take his chances. If he happens to interact with another cooperator, he will get four units. But if he interacts with a defector, he will get zero. Whether it makes sense to pay the one-unit cost of scrutiny thus depends on the likelihood of these two outcomes.

Suppose the population share of cooperators is 90 percent. By not paying the cost of scrutiny, a cooperator will interact with another cooperator 90 percent of the time, and with a defector only 10 percent. His payoff will thus have an average value of $(.9 \times 4) + (.1 \times 0) = 3.6$. Since this is higher than the three-unit net payoff he would get if he paid the cost of scrutiny, it is clearly better not to pay it.

Now suppose the population share of cooperators is not 90 percent but 50 percent. If our cooperator does not pay the cost of scrutiny, he will now have only a 50–50 chance of interacting with a defector. His average payoff will thus be only two units, or one unit less than if he had paid the cost. On these odds, it would clearly be better to pay it.

The numbers in this example imply a breakeven point when the population share of cooperators is 75 percent. At that share, a cooperator who does not pay the cost has a 75 percent chance at a payoff of four units, and a 25 percent chance of getting zero. His average payoff is thus three units, the same as if he had paid the cost. When the population share of coop-

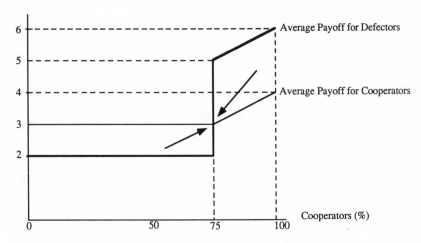

Fig. 5.4. Average payoffs with costs of scrutiny.

erators is below (above) 75 percent, it will always (never) be better for him to pay the cost of scrutiny.

With this rule in mind, we can now say something about how the population will evolve over time. When the population share of cooperators is below 75 percent, cooperators will all pay the cost of scrutiny and get a payoff of three-units by cooperating with one another. It will not be in the interests of defectors to bear this cost, because the keen-eyed cooperators would not interact with them anyway. The defectors are left to interact with one another and get a payoff of only two units. Thus, if we start with a population share of cooperators less than 75 percent, the cooperators will get a higher average payoff, which means that their share of the population will grow.

In populations that consist of more than 75 percent cooperators, the tables are turned. Now it no longer makes sense to pay the cost of scrutiny. Cooperators and defectors will thus interact at random, which means that defectors will have a higher average payoff. This difference in payoffs, in turn, will cause the population share of cooperators to shrink.

For the values assumed in this example, the average payoff schedules for the two groups are plotted in figure 5.4. As noted, the cooperators' schedule lies above the defectors' for shares smaller than 75 percent, but below it for larger shares. The sharp discontinuity in the defectors' schedule reflects the fact that, to the left of 75 percent, all cooperators pay to scrutinize while, to the right of 75 percent, none of them do. Once the population share of cooperators passes 75 percent, defectors suddenly gain access to their victims. The evolutionary rule, once again, is that higher relative payoffs result in a growing population share. This rule makes it clear that the population in this example will stabilize at 75 percent co-operators.

Now there is obviously nothing magic about this 75 percent figure. Had the cost of scrutiny been higher than one unit, for example, the population share of cooperators would have been smaller. A reduction in the payoff when cooperators pair with one another would have a similar effect on the equilibrium population shares. The point of the example is that when there are costs of scrutiny, there will be pressures that pull the population toward some stable mix of cooperators and defectors. Once the population settles at this mix, members of both groups have the same average payoff and are therefore equally likely to survive. There is an ecological niche, in other words, for both groups. This result stands in stark contrast to the traditional sociobiological result that only opportunism can survive.

A Simple Thought Experiment

The critical assumption behind the commitment model, again, is that people can make reasonable inferences about character traits in others. Because this assumption is so central, let us focus on it more closely.

First a simple point of clarification: *reasonable inference* does not mean that it is necessary to be able to predict other people's emotional predispositions with certainty. Just as a weather forecast of 20 percent chance of rain can be invaluable to someone who must plan outdoor activities, so can probabilistic assessments of character traits be of use to people who must choose someone to trust. It would obviously be nice to be accurate in every instance. But it will often suffice to be right only a fraction of the time.

Is it reasonable to assume we can infer emotional predispositions in others? Imagine you have just gotten home from a crowded concert and discover you have lost $1,000 in cash. The cash had been in your coat pocket in a plain envelope with your name written on it. Do you know anyone, not related to you by blood or marriage, who you feel certain would return it to you if he or she found it?

For the sake of discussion, I assume that you are not in the unenviable position of having to answer no. Think for a moment about the person you are sure would return your cash; call her Virtue. Try to explain why you feel so confident about her. Note that the situation was one where, if she had kept the cash, you could not have known it. On the basis of your other experiences with her, the most you could possibly know is that she did not cheat you in every such instance in the past. Even if, for example, she returned some lost money of yours in the past, that would not prove she didn't cheat you on some other occasion. (After all, if she had cheated you in a similar situation, you wouldn't know it.) In any event, you almost certainly have no logical basis in experience for inferring that Virtue would not cheat you now. If you are like most participants in this thought experiment, you simply believe you can fathom her inner motives: you are sure she would return your cash because you are sure she would feel terrible if she did not.

The thought experiment also calls attention to the fact that such emotional predispositions may depend on circumstance. Think, for example, about your relationship with Virtue. Typically, she is a close friend. This is a natural outcome for at least two reasons. First, you have had much more opportunity to observe the behavior of close friends, and if situations that shed light on a person's character occur only rarely, it is much more likely you will have witnessed one. But second, and perhaps more important, you are much more inclined to trust a friend because you believe she feels a special loyalty to you. Indeed, your belief that Virtue will return your cash does not necessarily imply a belief that she would have returned an envelope bearing the name of a perfect stranger. Her predisposition to return your money may be contingent on her relationship to you.

Your intuitions may also tell you that the amount of cash in the envelope could matter. Most people feel they know many more people who would return $100 but not $1,000. By the same token, a person who would unhesitatingly return $1,000 might instead hang onto an envelope containing $50,000.

People's feelings of right and wrong are clearly not the only forces that govern their behavior. As Walter Mischel (1968) and other social psychologists have long emphasized, behavior of almost every sort is strongly influenced by the details and nuances of context. But despite the obvious importance of situational factors, they do not tell the whole story. On the contrary, most participants in this thought experiment respond that they know someone they feel sure would return the cash of a perfect stranger, or indeed even that of someone deeply disliked, no matter how large the amount. In one sense, of course, the social psychologists are correct. It is a mistake to pretend that character traits account for all important differences in behavior. But it is perhaps a more serious error to suppose that behavior is guided only by context.

Of course, the fact that you may feel sure a particular person would return a stranger's cash does not necessarily make it so. Plenty of apparently trustworthy people have let even close friends down in situations like the one in the thought experiment. What the experiment does establish (on the assumption that you responded affirmatively) is that you accept the crucial premise of the commitment model.

Are Inherited Capacities Necessary?

According to the commitment model, the survival of trustworthiness derives in part from a tendency to be receptive to cultural training. In this respect, it is no different from the story told by critics of the biological model, who insist that culture is the sole explanation for human altruism. Yet the critics' story runs into difficulty in the case of people who are relatively unreceptive to cultural conditioning. Specifically, it does not explain why these people would not eventually dominate. And since we know there are many such people, this is a substantive difficulty.

If we are to account for altruism within a purely materialist framework, receptiveness to cultural training is not sufficient. In order for a behavioral predisposition to help solve the commitment problem, recall, it is essential that others be able to discern that we have it. It is easy to imagine that cultural training could instill a moral sentiment. But it is far from clear that it could, by itself, also account for a blush or some other observable symptom of the sentiment.

To the traditional story about the role of culture, we must thus add some mechanism whereby a person who has internalized a cultural message becomes observably different in a way that is at least partly insulated from purposeful control. In the case of physical symptoms like a blush, it is hard to see how this mechanism could be completely nonbiological. Critics of the biological approach may continue to insist that it is purely by accident that an honest person blushes when he tells a lie. Many symptoms of emotional arousal apparently did indeed originate for reasons quite independent of their role as signals of intention (see Frank 1988, chap. 6). But if altruistic behavior is to have a material payoff, at least some sort of biological symptom of emotion, accidental or not, appears necessary.

The Role of Economies of Scale

An important force behind the emergence of unopportunistic behavior in the commitment model is strength in numbers—"economies of scale" in the economist's parlance. If two could not produce more efficiently than one, there would be no reason to expose ourselves to the possibility of being cheated by interacting with another person. Nor would there be any reason to spend effort haggling over how to divide the fruits of collective efforts. It would be much easier simply to work alone.

The marriage problem is perhaps the most conspicuous example of the gains from specialization. One person acting in isolation will never get far trying to raise a family.

Of the specific commitment problems discussed, the deterrence problem depends least on the existence of scale economies. But even it is affected by them. Deterrence would never be required if it were practical to isolate ourselves completely from interaction with other persons. Economies of scale, however, are a powerful reason to avoid isolation. To take advantage of them, we must engage in social interaction. The more closely we interact, the more opportunities for predation arise and the greater need for an effective deterrence strategy.

This is not to say that vengeance seekers will always benefit in the presence of economies of scale. It would be an obvious mistake, for example, to claim that the Hatfields and the McCoys did better because of a moral sentiment that compelled them to seek revenge. But this is not my claim. Rather, it is that persons endowed with such a sentiment may do better, *on the average,* than persons who lack it. The potential usefulness of the sentiment lies in its capacity to deter aggression. When it works, they obviously do better. When it fails, as with the Hatfields and McCoys, they do worse. As things turned out, either family would have done much better to leave the area once the first shot was fired. But this does not imply that in general a person would do better to be born without the tendency to seek revenge.

Sociologist Jack Weller notes that crime rates in Appalachian communities are very low, which he attributes to the "unwillingness of mountaineers to do anything that neighbors might construe as interference with them or that otherwise might stir ill will" (1965; quoted by Banfield 1985: 278). With the vivid history of the Hatfields and McCoys in mind, it is easy to imagine the source of this unwillingness. The important point, for our purposes, is that it is advantageous not to be victimized by our neighbors. Provided the violent tempers that deter such aggression are not tested too frequently, those tempers can be very advantageous indeed.

The issues are similar in the case of perilous rescue attempts. It would be absurd to maintain that soldiers who threw their bodies atop live grenades did better because of their impulse to save the lives of their comrades. But again, that is not my claim. The payoff, if there is one, lies in such people being observably different—and more attractive—to others, which puts them in a better position to reap the material benefits of social cooperation. Thus, as in the deterrence example, it is a gamble to be a strongly empathic person. If the conditions that trigger a rescue attempt happen to arise, you probably lose. Otherwise, you win. We *like* empathic people and are more likely to favor them with out trust. If rescue attempts motivated by strong feelings of empathy are sufficiently infrequent, such feelings can obviously be useful. Moral sentiments could not emerge under the commitment model, however, if there were not substantial economies of scale in social interaction.

A Note on Rational Behavior

The notion that moral sentiments might solve the commitment problem helps clarify some of the ambiguity about what it means to behave in a rational way. The philosophical literature distinguishes at least two main accounts of rational behavior (see, e.g., Parfit 1984). In the so-called present aim theory, rationality is taken to be the efficient pursuit of whatever aims one has at the moment of deliberation and action. A person who, for example, refrains from cheating because of guilt feelings would thus be considered rational by this standard, even if there is no possibility that the cheating could have been detected.

By the same token, a person who drank cyanide because he felt a compelling desire to do so would also be considered rational under the present aim standard. The obvious difficulty of this standard is that it permits us to call virtually any behavior rational merely by asserting that a person prefers it.

The second account of rationality, the self-interest theory, tries to get around this problem. It says an act is rational if it efficiently promotes the interests of the person who performs it. A person—even one motivated by moral sentiments—who does not cheat when he could get away with cheating is thus judged, by the self-interest standard, to have acted irrationally.

Ironically, however, the self-interest version allows us to say that a self-interested person might very well *want* to be motivated by precisely such moral sentiments (provided, again, that their presence is recognizable by others). He may even take purposeful steps to enhance the likelihood that he will develop these sentiments. (He may join a church, for example, or look for opportunities to practice honesty.) Once he acquires the sentiments, of course, the behavior they provoke will still be officially categorized as irrational by the self-interest standard. But the commitment model may at least help us understand why such behavior, rational or not, might be widespread.

The commitment model is like the conventional evolutionary account in that it predicts the inevitability of opportunistic behavior. In at least one critical respect, however, it differs: opportunistic behavior here is not the *only* viable strategy. There is also room, possibly even a wide berth, for behavior that is unopportunistic in the truest sense.

I must stress again that the commitment model does not view cooperators as automatons, genetically programmed to eschew self-interest. On the contrary, it allows—indeed, in some cases almost certainly requires— a central role for cultural conditioning in the acquisition of moral sentiments. People may even make rational choices about the sorts of conditioning they expose themselves to. Thus, according to the model, a tendency to cooperate may or may not be a trait that some people inherit. The model can function even if its biological component is confined to an inherited complex of symptoms that manifests itself in people who have assimilated a cooperative predisposition. Surely not even the fiercest critic of biological theories will find this requirement unacceptable.

The honest individual in the commitment model is someone who values trustworthiness for its own sake. That he might receive a material payoff for such behavior is completely beyond his concern. And it is precisely because he has this attitude that he can be trusted in situations where his behavior cannot be monitored.

Trustworthiness, provided it is recognizable, creates valuable opportunities that would not otherwise be available.[6] The fact that trustworthy persons *do* receive a material payoff is of course what sustains the trait within the individual selectionist framework. But even if the world were to end at midnight, thus eliminating all possibility of penalty for defection, the genuinely trustworthy person would not be motivated to cheat.

Tit-for-tat (see Axelrod 1984), reciprocal altruism (see Trivers 1971), kin selection (see Hamilton 1964), and other conventional evolutionary accounts of unopportunistic behavior paint a very different picture of human nature. Indeed, for all their obvious value, these accounts do not explain genuinely unopportunistic behavior at all (see, for example, Frank 1988, chap. 2).

Of course, a brief example involving people with *C*s and *D*s on their foreheads is hardly much better. If the claim that we can benefit from a predisposition to cooperate is to be made plausible, much more must be said about how, exactly, this predisposition arises and can be identified by others. This issue is of crucial importance,[7] and I have examined it in great detail elsewhere (Frank 1988).

The Importance of Tastes

The self-interest model assumes certain tastes and constraints, and then calculates what actions will best serve those tastes. The model is widely used by economists and other social scientists, game theorists, military strategists, philosophers, and others. Its results influence decisions that affect all of us. In its standard form, the model assumes purely self-interested tastes, namely, for present and future consumption goods of various sorts, leisure, and so on. Envy, guilt, rage, honor, love, and the like typically play no role.[8]

The commitment model, by contrast, emphasizes the role of these emotions in behavior. The rationalists speak of tastes, not emotions, but for analytical purposes, the two play exactly parallel roles. Thus, for example, a person who is motivated to avoid the emotion of guilt may be equivalently described as someone with a "taste" for honest behavior.

Tastes have important consequences for action. The inclusion of tastes that help solve commitment problems substantially alters the predictions of self-interest models. We will see that it may pay people to feel envious, because feeling that way makes them better bargainers. But people who feel envious will accept different jobs, earn different salaries, spend money in different ways, save different amounts, and vote for different laws than predicted by self-interest models.[9]

Feelings of envy are also closely linked to feelings about fairness. Without taking feelings about fairness into account, we cannot hope to predict what prices stores will charge, what wages workers will demand, how long business executives will resist a strike, what taxes governments will levy, how fast military budgets will grow, or whether a union leader will be reelected.[10]

The presence of conscience also alters the predictions of self-interest models. These models predict that when interactions between people are not repeated, people will cheat if they know they can get away with it. Yet evidence consistently shows that most people do not cheat under these circumstances. Self-interest models also suggest that the owner of a small business will not contribute to the lobbying efforts of trade associations. Like one man's vote, her own contribution will seem too small a part of the total to make any difference. Yet many small businesses do pay dues to trade associations, and many people do vote. Charitable institutions also exist on a far grander scale than would ever be predicted by self-interest models.

There is nothing mystical about the emotions that drive these behaviors. On the contrary, they are an obvious part of most people's psychological makeup. My claim here is that their presence is in perfect harmony with the underlying requirements of a coherent theory of rational behavior.

The self-interest model has proven its usefulness for understanding and predicting human behavior. But it remains seriously incomplete. Most analysts regard "irrational" behavior motivated by the emotions as lying beyond the scope of the model. Yet it is neither necessary nor productive to adopt this view. With careful attention to the things people care about, and to why they care about them, we can gain a much clearer understanding of why we behave as we do.

Motives for Honesty

When an opportunistic person is exhorted to behave morally, his immediate, if unspoken, question is What's in it for me? The traditional rationale for the maxim "Honesty is the best policy" responds that penalties for cheating are often severe and you can never be sure of not getting caught. The rationale goes on to argue that living up to your promises on one occasion creates the impression you will do so in the future. This, in turn, makes people more inclined to trust you, which is often a decisive advantage.

In some cases it is easy to see why honesty might indeed be the best policy for the reasons traditionally given. Consider, for example, the practice of tipping in restaurants, which is clearly built on trust. Because, by custom, tips are left at the end of the meal, the waiter or waitress must rely on the diner's implicit promise to reward prompt and courteous service.[11] Having already received good service, the diner is in a position to stiff the waiter. But while this occasionally happens, it would not be a sensible strategy for most people, who eat repeatedly in the same restaurants. A person who leaves a generous tip each time he visits his favorite restaurant may thus be viewed as making a rational investment in obtaining good service in the future. Living up to his implicit promise is clearly consistent with—indeed, required by—the vigorous pursuit of self-interest.

The difficulty is that the tipper's behavior here does not really capture what we understand by the term *honesty.* It is perhaps more fittingly described as prudence. He has lived up to his implicit promise, to be sure; but since failure to do so would have led to bad service on future occasions, we cannot conclude that fidelity to the implicit promise was an important motivating factor.

Whether people honor their agreements when they expect to interact repeatedly with us is obviously important. But in much of life, we are concerned instead with how they behave either in fleeting encounters or in ones where their behavior simply cannot be observed. These cases, after all, are the ones that seriously test a person's character. In them, an honest action will be one that, by definition, requires personal sacrifice. The tip left in a restaurant in a distant city is a clear example. When a traveler breaks the implicit promise to tip he will save some money, and his disgruntled waiter will have no opportunity to retaliate. The difficulty with traditional self-interest appeals to morality is that they suggest no reason not to cheat in situations like these, where detection is all but impossible.

The commitment model suggests an altogether different rationale for honesty, one that is both self-interested and at the same time relevant for situations where cheating cannot be detected: If character traits such as honesty are observable in a person, an honest person will benefit by being able to solve important commitment problems. He will be trustworthy in situations where the purely self-interested person would not, and will therefore be much sought-after as a partner in situations that require trust.

The decision to tip in the distant city is in part a decision about the kinds of character traits one wishes to cultivate. For while modern biologists have established that the capacity to develop various character traits is inherited, no one has successfully challenged the nineteenth-century view that indoctrination and practice are required for them to emerge. The direction of causality between character and behavior thus runs both ways. Character influences behavior, of course. But behavior also influences character. Despite our obvious capacities for self-deception and rationalization, few people can maintain a predisposition to behave honestly while at the same time frequently engaging in transparently opportunistic behavior.

The opportunist's goal is to appear honest while availing himself of every prudent opportunity for personal gain. He wants to seem like a good guy to the people who count, but at the same time to refrain from tipping in distant cities. If character traits are observable, however, this may not be possible. In order to *appear* honest, it may be necessary, or at least very helpful, to *be* honest.

In these observations lie the seeds of a very different reason for leaving a tip in the distant restaurant. The motive is not to avoid the possibility of being caught, but to maintain and strengthen the predisposition to behave honestly. My failure to tip in the distant city will make it difficult to sustain the emotions that motivate me to behave honestly on other occasions. *It is this change in my emotional makeup, not my failure to tip itself, that other people may apprehend.*

Moral philosophers and others have long stressed the adverse social consequences of the unbridled pursuit of self-interest. Utilitarians, for example, urge us to practice restraint because the world would be a better place if everyone did so. For opportunistic persons, however, such appeals have not proved compelling. They reason, with seemingly impeccable logic, that their own behavior will not much affect what others do. Because the state of the world is largely independent of how they themselves behave, they conclude that it is best to take what they can and assume others will do likewise. As more and more people adopt this perspective, it becomes increasingly difficult for even basically honest persons not to do so.

Many of my friends, and I too in years past, have complained of feeling like chumps for paying all of our income taxes when so many people evade theirs so brazenly. More recently, however, my work on the commitment model has sharply altered my feelings on this issue. I am still annoyed if a plumber asks me to pay in cash, but now my resentment is tempered by thinking of my own tax compliance as an investment in maintaining an honest predisposition. Virtue is not only its own reward here; it may also lead to material rewards in other contexts. Whether this outside payoff is larger than what I could safely steal from the government, I cannot be sure. But there is evidence that it might be (see, for example, Frank 1988).

This possibility profoundly transforms a person's choice about whether to cultivate an honest predisposition. On traditional views of morality, opportunists have every reason to break the rules (and to teach their children to do likewise) whenever they can profitably do so. The commitment model challenges this view at its very core, which for me is by far its most exciting message. By suggesting an intelligible answer to the pressing question of What's in it for me? it encourages even the most hardened cynic to feel genuine regard for others.

6 Cooperation for the Benefit of Us— Not Me, or My Conscience

Robyn M. Dawes, Alphons J. C. van de Kragt, and John M. Orbell

Social dilemmas occur when outcomes that are good for each group member acting individually are bad for the group as a whole. In the language of game theory, they occur when payoffs to each participant yield dominating decision strategies that converge on a deficient equilibrium. Examples abound: decisions of whether to donate to public radio and television, whether to ride a bicycle rather than drive a car during a pollution alert, whether to dispose of industrial waste in the atmosphere or rivers when no laws prohibit doing so, whether to add to the earth's already strained, if not overstrained, carrying capacity by adding the most exploitive and polluting agent yet known—another human being. In all these examples, a noncooperative, or "defecting," option (e.g., not contributing, driving a car) is dominating, because no matter what others choose, the personal rewards are higher for choosing it than for making a cooperative choice. If, for example, others contribute to public broadcasting and we don't, we can use it free; if they don't and we don't, we have avoided wasting our money. If others use their bicycles and we don't, we drive our cars in comfort as the problem goes away, while if they don't and we don't, we roll up our windows to avoid their exhausts (which we can't do if we're riding a bicycle). The result of choosing these domination options, however, is that we all lose (e.g., no public broadcasts, worse pollution). Because we all prefer the result that occurs if we do not choose these dominating strategies, the result of choosing them is deficient.

Historically, theorists have concentrated on four proposals to resolve such dilemmas, that is, to encourage (gently or otherwise) people to es-

This chapter constitutes a slight revision and extension of "Not Me or Thee but We: The Importance of Group Identity in Eliciting Cooperation in Dilemma Situations: Experimental Manipulations," *Acta Psychologica* 68 (1988): 83–97. This article, in turn, was based on a paper presented at three conferences. We have thus benefited from the comments of many colleagues in those audiences, as well as the comments of Bernd Rohrmann, editor of *Acta Psychologica,* and Jane Mansbridge, editor of this volume. This work was supported by NSF grant SES-8605284.

chew choice of the dominating strategy in favor of one that avoids the outcome no one involved desires.[1]

1. *Leviathan* (Hobbes 1651/1947). Here, a central state mandates cooperation by punishing defection. People accept this state's authority because the alternative is the dilemma situation of the "warre of alle against alle." (Hobbes himself adds a second, ethical legitimating device—the "authorization" of the people.) The unpleasantness of that alternative makes accepting the state's authority worthwhile, even when the state consists of a hated minority using the cooperation of others primarily for its own benefit.

2. *Reciprocal altruism* (Axelrod 1984). Through some mechanism, perhaps biological (Trivers 1971), cooperation on the part of one individual in a dilemma situation enhances the probability that others will cooperate later in that same situation or a similar one. When such "reciprocal altruism" is likely, an individual's "enlightened self-interest" is to cooperate in hopes of eliciting reciprocity. In computer tournaments, Axelrod has studied the success of Anatol Rapoport's Tit-for-Tat strategy (Rapoport and Chammah 1965) (cooperate on trial 1 and then make the same choice that the other interacting individuals did on the previous trial) and demonstrated that it garners more profit for itself in the long run than do any competing strategies; moreover, Axelrod has demonstrated that in an evolutionary context in which strategies' probability of replication is positively related to profit, Tit-for-Tat can become predominant.[2]

3. *Mutual coercion mutually agreed upon* (Hardin 1968). Rather than being punished for defection by a (potentially arbitrary) central authority, freely choosing people agree to provide punishments to each other for choosing a dominating defecting choice. While the coercive agent itself may consist of a centralized authority, its existence is maintained through the consent of the governed, rather than their mere acquiescence.

4. *Socially instilled conscience* (Campbell 1975). While externally provided payoffs may define a social dilemma, social training can lead to such a "bad" conscience for choosing a dominating strategy which harms collective welfare—or to such heightened self-esteem for eschewing such strategies in favor of cooperation—that the individual is better off cooperating, irrespective of external consequences. While not widely publicized outside psychology, Campbell's solution was quite controversial within it, in part because it supported traditional morality and constraint in contrast to challenging these as irrational and urging people to "do their own thing." The point of socialization, according to Campbell, is to instill such internal "side-payments," in the form of good or bad feelings, that a socially harmful option that appears dominating when analyzed in terms of external payoffs is no longer so when analyzed in terms of the decision makers' utilities. According to Campbell, "social evolution"—through

moral teachings and the resulting cooperative behavior—keeps "biological evolution" from running amok only to drain into a sink of universal defection.

These four "solutions" have one characteristic in common; they turn an apparent dilemma into a nondilemma by manipulation (conscious or automatic) of the consequences *accruing to the individual* for cooperation or defection. The first three proposals concentrate on external payoffs per se, while the fourth postulates the development of an individual utility for "doing the right thing" that overwhelms the utility from the social rewards of defection. Manipulation of behavior through egoistic incentives (the payoffs resulting from such consequences) is compatible with (1) psychoanalytic beliefs in the preeminence of primitive drives; (2) behaviorist beliefs in the automatic and omnipotent effects of reward and punishment (circularly defined as "reinforcement" by all but a few theorists); (3) economic theory, assuming the optimization of utilities based on "revealed preference"; (4) social exchange theory; (5) the insistence of sociobiologists that altruism be compatible with "inclusive fitness" (characteristics positively related to the probability of reproduction);[3] and (6) the obvious success in current U.S. society of appeals to personal payoffs (e.g., "are *you* better off than you were four years ago?"—italics added).

We agree that any or all of the mechanisms postulated above encourage cooperation; certainly, for example, beliefs that one will go to jail or be tortured by guilt for defection enhance a tendency to cooperate, as do the social rewards accruing to an individual with a reputation for being cooperative and trustworthy (Taylor 1976; Axelrod 1984; Frank 1988). We have, however, conducted a series of experiments over the past ten years, the results of which have led us, somewhat reluctantly at first, to conclude that the cooperation rate can be enhanced in the absence of egoistic incentives. In particular, we conclude that we can enhance cooperation dramatically above a base rate that can be ascribed to a habit of cooperating in situations outside our experiments that are like those within them, perhaps for reasons such as expected reciprocity or internal rewards. Our experiments have led us to conclude that cooperation rates can be radically affected by one factor in particular, which is independent of the consequences for the choosing individual. That factor is group identity. Such identity—or solidarity—can be established and consequently enhance cooperative responding in the absence of any expectation of future reciprocity, current rewards or punishment, or even reputational consequences among other group members. Moreover, this identity operates independently of the dictates of conscience. In other words, our experiments indicate that group solidarity increases cooperation independently of the side payments—either external or internal—often associated with such identity.

It is, of course possible to define any incentive as an egoistic one; hence, cooperation due to group identity must serve some individual goal, by virtue of the fact of cooperation. The point here is that group identity, unlike the incentives outlined above (such as a reward from anticipated reciprocity, or a feeling of heightened self-esteem), cannot be *defined and characterized* independent of membership in the particular group with which the individual is identified.

While rewards, punishments, expectations of reciprocity, moralizing, and lack of anonymity have all been shown to "work," these variables have in general been manipulated in others' experiments without a comparison with what happens in their absence. The clearest example of this lack can be found in the experimentation on two-person dilemmas (estimated to consist of at least two thousand studies). In almost all of these prisoner's dilemma games, the subjects play has been iterated. (In fact, we have been able to find only two instances in the literature prior to our own work in which players make a single choice: Deutsch 1960 and Wrightsman 1966.) The hypothesis supposedly supported by numerous results is that cooperation is due to the successful or attempted establishment of reciprocal altruism through engaging in such strategies as Tit-for-Tat. But in the absence of any evidence that people do *not* cooperate when the games are *not* iterated, this interpretation is dubious. Moreover, claims that cooperation results from the rewards accruing to individuals qua individuals approach vacuity, given the standard instructions to subjects to "get as many points for yourself as you can." Experimental subjects who are cooperative thus face a dilemma of cooperating with other subjects by foregoing dominating strategies or cooperating with the experimenter by embracing them in order to maximize their own payoffs. When experimenters avoid substantial payments by having a prize for the subject who garners the most points, they are implicitly instructing subjects to seek not just maximal gain, but maximal *relative* gain—a strange task for studying cooperation.

Our experimental work systematically compares the presence of what we might expect to be explanatory factors with their absence. We have eliminated all side payments by simply prohibiting them. We have eliminated concern with reputation among members of the group by having all choices be anonymous. We have eliminated the possibility of reciprocal altruism by having our subjects make a choice in our dilemma situations only once. We nevertheless obtain substantial rates of cooperation. Could this cooperation be due simply to factors affecting egoistic payoffs that, because they are usually present outside our experiments, lead some subjects to cooperate out of habit? The answer is no, because we can manipulate a variable having nothing to do with any of these factors in a way that will yield cooperation rates—given the same egoistic payoffs—ranging from 25 percent to 100 percent. That variable is, as mentioned above, group identity. In this paper, we describe conditions from the three most recent series of experiments in which such identity is manipulated. Let us first mention, however, that our standard way of manipulating it is to allow subjects in groups to talk for up to ten minutes about the dilemma with which we present them. We then compare these with those who cannot communicate. We do not allow our subjects in our discussion conditions to make deals, agreements to meet later, or even agreements to tell each other what they choose; moreover, we make every effort to use groups of strangers. We are not claiming that this kind of discussion is the only way to create a group identity, but discussion works, and it does so in the absence of the other potentially explanatory factors listed at the beginning of this paper.[4]

Experimental Results: I

In the first series of studies (van de Kragt et al. 1986), using monetary incentives, we discovered that discussion between group members not only enhanced cooperation when people had at least a mild egoistic incentive to contribute, but, and most importantly, when it would have been individually rational for the members not to contribute. Specifically, we found that allowing discussion enhances cooperation in a game in which all receive $10 if most (five or more) contribute $5.

Let us explain the method used in these studies in some detail. First, subjects were recruited for a one-hour "group decision-making experiment" from advertisements in local student and town newspapers promising "from $4 to $19 depending upon what you and the other group members decide." Only those responding who were over eighteen years of age (by self-report and judgment of telephone voice) were invited to participate. Subjects who called indicating an interest for groups were scheduled for separate experimental sessions, and a list was maintained to make sure that all subjects participated in only one.

Upon arrival, subjects were run in groups of nine. All were paid $4 for "showing up," including any extra subjects we had scheduled to make sure we would have nine participants in each group. At the beginning of the experiment itself, all were given a "promissory note" for $5, which was theirs to keep if they chose. They were also told that there was the possibility of receiving a $10 bonus, depending on how many people chose to "give away" their $5 to the group. At the time of the initial instructions, subjects were told that the choice of whether to give away the $5 was anonymous; to assure anonymity, they would make their choice by placing a check mark on one of two lines in a "response form" that others couldn't see, and we would pay each subject one at a time, making certain that the previous subject had left the area before the next was paid—which we did. Subjects were individually "quizzed" about the payoff structure to make sure they understood it. The experimenters explained it again in those few instances where errors indicated lack of understanding, and the experiments did not proceed until all answers to subsequent quizzes were correct.

One factor in our design was defined by the rule according to which each subject did or did not receive the $10 bonus.

Noncontingent rule: If four or more subjects *other* than the choosing subject give away their $5, that subject receives the $10 bonus.

Contingent rule: If five or more subjects, one of whom *can be* the choosing subject, give away their $5, every person in the group receives the $10 bonus.

Under the noncontingent rule, not giving the money away is the dominating strategy. A subject can keep and thereby retains the $5 regardless of others' actions. In addition, if four or more others contribute, that subject receives a total of $15. Under the contingent rule, not giving the money away is also a possible strategy. In this case, as in the noncontingent rule, a subject who keeps, retains the $5 regardless of others' actions. In addition, however, under the contingent rule, subjects have a chance to influence through their own contribution the likelihood that a sufficient number of people will contribute to earn the $10 bonus. Thus, according to both rules, a subject who gives away the $5 loses it. Such a subject receives $10 according to both rules if four or more of the other subjects give the $5 away, otherwise the subject receives zero (except for the flat $4 for attending the experiment). A subject who keeps the $5 receives either $15 or $5, depending on whether enough of the other subjects give away their $5 (five or more in the contingent-rule games, four or more in the noncontingent ones). The $10 bonus is not strictly a "public good" in the noncontingent-rule experiments, given that subjects can receive different payoffs. Suppose, for example, that four subjects contribute their $5. They would *not* receive the $10 bonus in either condition—in the contingent one because fewer than five subjects in total gave away the $5, in the noncontingent one because for these subjects fewer than four others had contributed. The remaining five subjects would *not* receive the $10 bonus according to the contingent rule (because less than five had contributed), but *would* according to the noncontingent rule (because four others had contributed).

In half of the groups in each rule condition we let the subjects discuss the choice for up to ten minutes, and in half they had to remain silent. Previous research (van de Kragt, Orbell, and Dawes 1983) has demonstrated that subjects develop an awareness of the equilibrium in the contingent condition, and when allowed to discuss will designate—by a combination of volunteering and a lot—exactly *which* five should give away the \$5 (thereby creating an "assurance game" for these five individuals; see Sen 1967). To prevent subjects in the discussion condition from making such a designation, we told them how many giveaway choices were required for the bonus only after they had completed their discussion. Most groups hit on the idea of numbering themselves and requiring people numbered 1 through k to give away the \$5 after the experimenters announced the number k necessary to provide the bonus. The experimenters simply told subjects in such groups that "you can't do that," and being thus prohibited they were unable to implement the idea.

The effects, both of the rule and of discussion, are significant ($p < .04$ and $p < .001$ respectively; for more details, see the original paper).[5] What is striking, however, is that the effect of discussion per se is the stronger of the two. Without discussion, using the noncontingent rule, 30 percent of the subjects contributed their \$5. Also, without discussion, using the contingent rule, 45 percent of the subjects contributed. With discussion, however, 75 percent of the subjects contributed even under the noncontingent rule and 85 percent under the contingent rule. While the results show an effect of self-interest (the contingent rule elicits higher cooperation rates), such interest cannot explain either the 30 percent who gave their \$5 away without discussion, or the high 75 percent rate after discussion in the noncontingent condition—a condition, it will be remembered, in which subjects *always* receive the higher payoff for keeping the \$5. The results are graphed in figure 6.1.

Experimental Results: II

In a subsequent series of studies (Orbell, van de Kragt, and Dawes 1988), we addressed the question of whether the discussion effects we previously found to be important may have served to arouse "conscience" and its associated payoffs, or whether the results could be better accounted for by concern with others' actual outcomes—and if so, how that concern related to group identity.

To pit conscience against caring, we varied the identity of the beneficiaries of cooperation: other group members versus strangers. If discussion triggers conscience, and our contributing subjects are acting to satisfy its demands, then discussion should enhance contribution to strangers. If, however, discussion elicits caring about group members, then it should enhance contributions only to people in the groups with whom one interacts.

Our basic condition was a giveaway-dilemma game involving seven people. Subjects began with promissory notes for \$6, which they could either keep or give away (anonymously, again) for the group benefit. Each

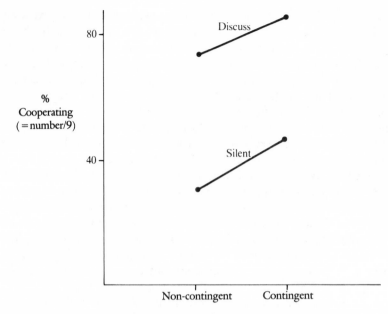

Fig. 6.1. Results: Experiment I.

$6 given away was augmented to $12 by the experimenters, and the total was divided among the six other players, with $2 going to each. Thus if a subject gave away the $6, and no one else did, he or she would get nothing back. If one of these persons gave away the $6, the subject would get $2 back and so on. The situation is a dilemma, because each subject is $6 better off keeping the money, but if all give it away all receive $12, while all receive $6 if all keep.

We recruited groups of fourteen subjects, using the same methods as in the previous experiment, who were then randomly divided into groups of seven which met in separate rooms. Again, we crossed discussion with no discussion. We varied the games, however, by telling half the groups that the augmented $12 would be divided among the other six members of their own group and half that it would be divided among six comparable members of the other group—with subjects' own potential bonuses being dependent, respectively, on what members of their own or the other group did. In all conditions, the $6 was kept by the subjects themselves if they chose not to give it away.

Finally, three minutes before the final choice, we switched the group membership of the relevant others in half the conditions. For example, in a switch condition, a subject discussed the choice believing the $12 would go to subjects in his or her own group and that he or she might receive money from them, but was subsequently told it would go to subjects in the other group—and that money would (might) come from choices in this other group. In an equal number of instances subjects believed that the relevant subjects were in the other group, and were then told that they were their own group members. Half the time we made no such switch. No further discussion in the discussion conditions was allowed after the switch.

We thus crossed three factors: the initially understood locus of relevant others (own group versus other group), interaction (discussion versus no discussion), and actual locus of relevant others (own group versus other group). We ran eight groups in each of the resulting eight conditions (number of groups = 64; number of subjects = 448). The results are presented in figure 6.2.

With group cooperation rate as the unit of analysis, all main effects are significant beyond the .001 level. That is, discussion had an effect, thinking one's group would be the recipient had an effect, and having one's

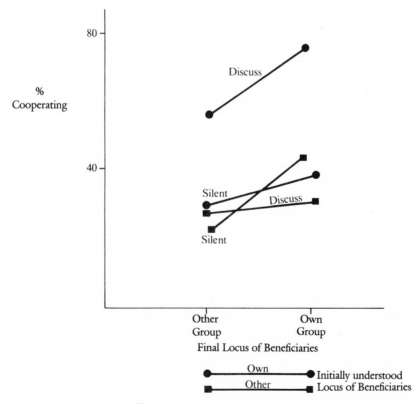

Fig. 6.2. Results: Experiment II.

group be the recipient had an effect. Of greatest importance, however, is the interaction of discussion with belief about locus of benefit. With discussion, the cooperation rate averaged 69 percent when people first believed that relevant others would be in their own group, but only 31 percent when they believed they would be in the other. The comparable figures for the no-discussion conditions were 34 percent and 33 percent. Thus, discussion does *not* enhance contribution when beneficiaries are strangers, counter to the clear-conscience hypothesis. Moreover, there is *no* ingroup-outgroup effect in the absence of discussion. Finally, the believed locus of relevant others when the subjects first considered their choices was more important than the actual (subsequent) locus (est. $\omega^2 = 30\%$ versus 10%).

Because discussion promotes cooperation vis-à-vis the parochial group but not the group with which there was no contact, we had to consider the importance of group identity as a factor. (Recall, again, that choices were single ones made in total anonymity.) Also, however, we noted a great deal of promising to give the money away in the high-cooperation condition, and it appeared to be effective. Slightly over 11 percent of coded subject-predicate utterances across all conditions were commitments to give (as opposed to 3.1 percent commitments to keep, which most often occurred when the beneficiaries of giving were believed to be in the other group), and the product moment correlation between number of commitments to give and cooperation rate in the group was .59 ($p < .01$, using groups as the unit of measurement). Thus, we were led in a subsequent experiment to investigate the importance of three other factors.

1. *Group identity.* Research in the "minimal group" paradigm (e.g., Tajfel and Turner 1979; Tajfel 1974, 1978; Turner 1975; and the papers contained in Turner and Giles 1981) has repeatedly demonstrated that allocative decisions can be sharply altered by manipulations substantially weaker than ten minutes of discussion. For example, a "common fate" group identity—amount of payoff dependent on the same coin toss—can lead subjects to attempt to "compensate" for defecting people in their own group by decreasing their withdrawals from a depleting (monetary) resource, while simultaneously increasing withdrawals when the defecting people are believed to be in the other group, even when the identities of all people are unknown (Kramer and Brewer 1986).

2. *The desirable and binding nature of promising.* Even though subjects' choices are anonymous, similar choices in the world outside our experiments typically are not. In general, it is to a promiser's long-term best interests to develop a reputation for cooperativeness and reliability (Axelrod 1984; Taylor 1976). Thus, while there are no reputational effects of not promising or reneging on promises made in our particular experimental

situation, it may be psychologically similar to situations in which there are such effects—similar enough that it does not elicit clearly distinct behavior. Alternatively, subjects may adopt cooperative promising and fulfillment of promises as a good rule of thumb ("heuristic"), given that in most situations such behavior is desirable from the perspective of future consequences. Irrationalities in a particular situation may appear less irrational when the situation is viewed as one of a class of situations that might require too much "mental accounting" to distinguish among them (Thaler 1985).

3. *Expectations derived from others' promises.* A single individual who keeps the $6 while *all* others give away their money receives $18; if that individual gives away the $6 while all others give, the payoff is $12. In contrast, an individual who keeps the $6 when no others give away their $6 receives only that $6, while the payoff for giving away the $6 when there are no other gifts is zero. Perhaps, consistent with Fechner's law, the difference between $18 and $12 is psychologically less than the difference between $6 and zero. And in general, while there is a constant $6 incentive to defect, this incentive may become less psychologically dominant as more others are expected to give away the $12. But other incentives, for example, desire to "do the right thing," may simultaneously remain constant. If the difference between cooperation and defection becomes less important the more other people cooperate, while the utility of conscience or we-feeling remains constant, perhaps (see Dawes 1980:191) we are seeing a reaction to decreasing marginal returns. The more other people expected to cooperate, according to this hypothesis, the less important the $6 incentive. Promises may, then, perform the self-exacerbating role of leading to expectations that a sufficient number of others will cooperate such that the choosers themselves are motivated to cooperate. The .59 correlation between promises made and cooperation appears to support this interpretation, but it is important to note that these promises are not equivalent to the number of people who promised, because we did not identify individuals.

Experimental Results: III

A third series of experiments (Orbell, van de Kragt, and Dawes 1988) assessed the impact of these factors. (It also concerned others not relevant here, which is why it is quite complex.) Subjects meeting in groups of fourteen were informed that they would be subsequently divided at random into two subgroups of seven and then faced with a trinary choice: (1) choose to keep $5 for themselves; (2) choose a $12 option, with $2 going to each of the other people in their seven-person subgroup; (3) choose a $21 option, with $3 going to each of the people in the other subgroup. After being told that both subgroups would either be allowed to discuss the choice or would have to remain silent, all fourteen-person groups were given up to ten minutes to discuss the problem. This fourteen-person discussion was monitored by two experimenters who coded whether or not *each subject* made at least one promise—or otherwise indicated a commitment—to give away the $21 to the members of the other subgroup once the groups were divided.

What is of importance for this paper is that in almost precisely half (13 of 24) of the fourteen-person groups, all subjects made a verbal commitment to give away the $21 to the other subgroup members. Eighty-four percent of the subjects in these *universal-promising* groups actually did so. In contrast, only 58 percent of the subjects from the other eleven groups gave away the $21. The difference (again using groups as the unit of analysis) was highly significant, $p < .01$.

That finding was not surprising, because it follows from all three factors—group identity, the desirable and binding nature of promises, and expectations that others' promises predict cooperation, which will yield reasonable payoffs for cooperating oneself. In contrast, the relationship between promising and actual choice in the eleven groups without universal promising was striking. There was none. First, the correlation across groups between the number of people who promised to give away the $21 and the number who subsequently did was only .09. Second, the correlation (phi value) at the individual level between promising to give away the $21 and actually doing so was only .03. Finally, the correlation between each individual's choice to give away the $21 or not and the number of others in the group who promised to give away the $21 was, again, .03. The hypothesis that promises are binding implies a positive correlation between commitment and choice. The hypothesis that cooperation is due to expectations of a "reasonable" payoff if others are expected to cooperate implies a positive correlation between choice and the number of commitments made by others in the group. Neither correlation occurs in the data.

Conclusions

What is left are two hypotheses: (1) group identity is indicated by universal promising, but it is the solidarity—not commitments per se—that leads to the higher level of cooperation in the universal promising groups; and (2) promises are effective, but only in a context of universal promising.

The present data do not distinguish between these interpretations. Nor do they address the question of whether solidarity elicits promising or vice versa (or—more likely—whether the relationship between the two variables is one of reciprocal augmentation). Cooperation is a function of group interactions.

Even the quickest glance at the transcripts of this and other experiments supports our group-identity hypothesis. Moreover, this hypothesis is compatible with coded "explanations for behavioral questionnaires administered after choice." In the absence of discussion, most cooperators cite "doing the right thing" as their major motive; with discussion the majority cite "group welfare." In contrast, defectors cite their personal payoffs. (See Caporael et al. 1989 for a presentation of these results.) In discussion, people immediately start discussing what "we" should do, and spend a great deal of time and effort persuading others in their own group to cooperate (or defect!), even in situations where these others' behavior is irrelevant to the speaker's own payoffs. In fact, in the first experiment reported in this paper there were frequent statements that the best results would occur if *we* all keep and *they* all give to *us*. In contrast, in all our experiments not allowing discussion, our results can be explained on the purely egoistic basis of anticipated external gain or good internal feelings. That generalization has held true over the last ten years for 27 different no-discussion conditions with 1,188 subjects in 178 groups, and for 12 different discussion conditions with 637 subjects in 95 groups. All 39 variations we have developed lead to the same conclusion: with no discussion, egoistic motives explain cooperation; with discussion, group identity—alone or in interaction with verbal promises—explains its dramatic increase.

Can that generalization fit into an evolutionary framework in which *individual* inclusive fitness must be correlated with whatever evolves? Yes, provided we postulate, as does Caporael et al. (1989), that *sociality* is primary for humans and historically precedes other changes. Then it is clear that ease in forming group identity could be of individual benefit. It is not just the successful group that prevails, but the individuals who have a propensity to form such groups. Moreover, we need not be too concerned with the problem of hypocrisy (i.e., positive selection for those only faking group identity within groups; see D. S. Wilson 1983). As the late Sen. Sam Ervin once pointed out: "The problem with lying is that you have to have a perfect memory to remember exactly what you said." None of us do. (For more on hypocrisy or mimicry, see Frank, chap. 5, this vol.)

Theorists have recently been concerned with speculating about what leads to sociality—usually in the form of some individual incentives for becoming social ("All D [defection] is the primeval state"; Axelrod 1984:99). In contrast, we don't speculate. We only point out that there have been no findings indicating that humans ever *were not* social. It is fun and somewhat romantic to speculate about how isolates developed our most cherished characteristic, our ties to other humans. But once again, such speculations must be evaluated in terms of our knowledge of how humans behaved without such ties, and there is no evidence we ever did.

Finally, we wish to point out that group identity does not equal morality. It is fragile, easily manipulated, and at times draconian—as when the good group member Rudolf Hoess, the commandant at Auschwitz, systematically murdered 2.9 million members of an outgroup—despite the claims in his autobiography (Hoess 1959) that he himself suffered great emotional pain from the suffering he inflicted on others. For the greater good of his National Socialist group, he claims, he "stifled all softer emotions." Group identity can do that, as well as lead to self-sacrificial acts that we regard as moral.

The casual observer of modern economic theory might conclude that our major motivation is supplied by a short looped tape cycling in our heads continually asking the question, Have you improved your asset position today? Modern psychological theory is worse: the tape asks, Have you raised your self-esteem today? Love, sex, friendship, beauty, art, knowledge, contentment, peak experiences, and even the joy of doing something well for its own sake are all what behaviorists used to term "secondary reinforcers"—the primary one being the ability to supply an affirmative answer to the nagging question. We interpret our experimental results as implying that there are other primary motivations—in particular the parochial one of contributing to one's group of fellow humans. We do not, for example, deny that an affirmative answer to the question "Are *you* better off than you were four years ago?" (italics added) provides a powerful incentive for such actions as voting. What we question—or rather, what our data question—is whether all, or even a majority of, group-regarding behaviors can be "ultimately" related to such egoistic concerns.

7   Culture and Cooperation

Robert Boyd and Peter J. Richerson

> I am dying not just to attempt to end the barbarity of the H-block,
> or gain the rightful recognition of a political prisoner, but primarily
> what is lost here is lost for the Republic.
> —Bobby Sands, from his strike diary

On May 5, 1981, Bobby Sands died after sixty-six days on hunger strike
in Long Kesh prison, Northern Ireland. He was the first man to die in a
strike aiming to force the British to treat IRA inmates as political prisoners
rather than common criminals, and to galvanize public opinion against
British policies in Ulster. Nine more men died before the strike ended on
August 10 without achieving its stated goal. The strikers had all volunteered, from a group of sixty IRA prisoners. All but three of the fasters
either died or were still on fast when the strike ended. Of these three, two
were fed on the instructions of relatives after they had lapsed into a coma,
and the third was removed by the strike leadership because a bleeding ul-
cer would have caused him to die too rapidly (Clarke 1987).

The hunger strikes at Long Kesh provide evidence that people sometimes make choices that are personally costly in order to benefit the group
or society to which they belong. The strikers chose to participate, while
many other IRA prisoners did not. They had to reaffirm their choice three
times a day when food was brought to their hospital rooms, and later by
resisting the pleas of relatives that they accept medical treatment. The
choice was clearly costly—it resulted in weeks of terrible suffering, followed often by death. These men were not serving life sentences. If they
had not volunteered, they would eventually have been released. It is also
clear that the strikers believed their deaths would benefit the other IRA
inmates and the Republican cause in general. Borrowing terminology
from game theory, we say that such behavior, intended to benefit a group
at a cost to the individual, represents "cooperation."

Robert Boyd's work was funded by the John Simon Guggenheim Foundation.

Chapter Seven

The hunger strikes at Long Kesh are not an isolated instance of human cooperation. Self-sacrifice in the interest of the group is a common feature of human behavior. Among hunter-gatherers, game is typically shared by all members of the group regardless of who makes the kill (e.g., Kaplan and Hill 1985; Lee 1979; Damas 1971). In stateless horticultural societies, men risk their lives in warfare with other groups (e.g., Meggit 1977; Peoples 1982). In contemporary societies, people contribute to charity, give blood, and vote, even though the effect of their own contributions on the welfare of the group is negligible. Indeed some authors (Sen, chap. 2, this vol.; Jencks, chap. 4, this vol.; Campbell 1975) argue that the existence of complex urban society is evidence for at least a degree of unselfish cooperation. (See Olson 1965/1971, 1982; and Elster, chap. 3, this vol., for further examples.) Psychologists and sociologists have also shown that people cooperate unselfishly under carefully controlled laboratory conditions, albeit for small stakes (e.g., Marwell and Ames 1979; Dawes, van de Kragt, and Orbell, chap. 6, this vol.; see Dawes 1980 for a review of such experiments).

Human cooperative behavior is unique in the organic world because it takes place in societies composed of large numbers of unrelated individuals. There are other animals that cooperate in large groups, including social insects like bees, ants, and termites (Wilson 1971), and the naked mole rat, a subterranean African rodent (Jarvis 1981). Multicellular plants and many forms of multicellular invertebrates can also be thought of as eusocial societies made up of individual cells (Buss 1987). In each of these cases, the cooperating individuals are closely related. The cells in a multicellular organism are typically members of a genetically identical clone, and the individuals in insect and naked mole rate colonies are siblings. In other animal species cooperation is either limited to very small groups or is absent altogether.

The observed pattern of cooperation among nonhumans is consistent with contemporary evolutionary theory. Evolutionary biologists reason that cooperative behavior can evolve only when cooperators are more likely than noncooperators to receive the benefits of the cooperative acts of other cooperators (Hamilton 1975; Brown, Sanderson, and Michod 1982; Nunney 1985). Suppose that this condition is not satisfied, and noncooperators receive the same benefits as cooperators from the cooperative acts of others. Then, because noncooperators receive the same benefits but do not suffer the costs of cooperative behavior, they will, on the average, leave more offspring than cooperators—over the long run cooperation will disappear.

Kinship is one important source of nonrandom social interaction. Relatives have a heritable resemblance to one another. Thus, cooperators whose behavior disproportionately benefits genetically related individuals have a greater than random chance of benefiting an individual who is similarly predisposed. (For introductory reviews see Krebs and Davies 1981, or Trivers 1985.)

Reciprocity is the other important source of nonrandom social interaction. Here cooperators discriminate based on the previous behavior of others—I will cooperate with you only as long as you cooperated in previous encounters. If individuals commonly employ some such rule, cooperative interactions among reciprocators will persist, while interactions of reciprocators and noncooperators will quickly cease. Thus reciprocators will be more likely than noncooperators to receive the benefits of the cooperative acts of others. Theoretical work (Axelrod and Hamilton 1981; Boyd and Richerson 1988b) suggests that reciprocity can readily lead to the evolution of cooperation, but only in quite small groups.

Thus the fact that humans cooperate in large groups of unrelated individuals is an evolutionary puzzle. Our Miocene primate ancestors presumably resembled nonhuman primates in cooperating only in small groups, mainly made up of relatives. Such social behavior was consistent with our understanding of how natural selection shapes behavior. Over the next five to ten million years something happened that caused humans to cooperate in large groups. The puzzle is: What caused this radical divergence from the behavior of other social mammals?

Several authors have suggested that selection among cultures is the solution to the puzzle. People's behavior is shaped by the beliefs, attitudes, and values that they acquire growing up in a particular culture. Cultures differ in the extent to which they motivate people to behave cooperatively. If cooperators discriminate in favor of group members, costly acts of cooperation are likely to be directed toward helping fellow group members who are inclined to cooperate with members of the groups. Because economic and military success requires a high degree of interdependence, cooperative cultures will tend to persist longer than less cooperative cultures. Thus, cooperative cultures will tend to replace less cooperative ones as a result of a selective process acting at the level of cultural groups (Campbell 1975; Jencks, chap. 4, this vol.). On this hypothesis, human behavior represents a compromise between genetically inherited selfish impulses and more cooperative, culturally acquired values. This cultural argument, however, lacks accounts of both the mechanisms that maintain cultural variation among groups and the ways these mechanisms may have arisen in the course of human evolution.

We need an account of the mechanisms that maintain cultural variation because group selection works only when cultural differences persist among groups. Yet many processes, such as intermarriage, cultural borrowing, and people's self-interested decisions, erode variation among groups. When noncooperative beliefs arise in largely cooperative groups, they will increase in number because they are beneficial to individuals. Intermarriage, selfish decisions, and cultural diffusion will cause selfish beliefs to spread to infect other groups of cooperators. Models of group selection in population biology suggest that the two processes of growing noncooperation and eroding variation will usually work faster than the processes promoting cooperation, which depend on group extinction. In short, selection among groups, which produces cooperation, will have little influence without social or psychological mechanisms that maintain cultural differences among groups.

We also need an account of the ways difference-maintaining mechanisms may have arisen, because cooperation is maladaptive from a genetic point of view. We need to explain how whatever social or psychological mechanisms lead to cultural group selection could have evolved in the face of countervailing evolutionary tendencies at the level of genes.

Several recent models of cultural change assume that the transmission of culture in humans constitutes a system of inheritance (Boyd and Richerson 1985; Pulliam and Dunford 1980; Cavalli-Sforza and Feldman 1981; Durham 1978, 1982; Lumsden and Wilson 1981; Rogers 1988). Humans acquire attitudes, beliefs, and other kinds of information from others by social learning, and these items of cultural information affect individual behavior. Cultural transmission leads to patterns of heritable variation within and among human societies. While individual decisions are important in determining behavior, these decisions depend on individuals' beliefs, often learned from others, about what is important and valuable, and how the world works. Human decision-makers are enmeshed in a web of tradition; individuals acquire ideas from their culture, and in turn make modifications of what they learn, which modifications become part of the cumulative change of the tradition.

To understand cultural evolution, we must account for the processes that increase the frequency of some variants and reduce that of others. Why do some individuals change traditions or invent new behaviors? Why are some variants transmitted and others not? As in the analogous case of organic evolution, individual level processes have to be scaled up to the whole population and marched forward in time to understand how a behavior such as cooperation might become part of a cultural tradition despite the costs that noncooperators can impose.

In the analysis that follows, we illustrate how this sort of model can be used to evaluate the cogency of the cultural group selection arguments like Campbell's and Jencks's. The model suggests that certain specific factors must be present in the cultural evolutionary process for group selection to be any more important than it seems to be in the genetic case.

Cultural Transmission and Group Selection

We begin by imagining that individuals live in subpopulations embedded in a larger population. The subpopulations represent the "societies" whose extinction drives cultural group selection. Suppose, for simplicity, that each individual in the population is characterized by one of two cultural variants. One variant causes individuals to place a high value on group goals compared to personal gain. Under the right circumstances, these "cooperators" will act in the group interest even if it is personally costly. The other cultural variant causes individuals to place a low value on group goals compared to personal gain. In the same circumstances, these "defectors" will not cooperate. This assumption does not entail the view that culture can be broken down into independent, atomistic traits. Each cultural variant could easily represent a large, tightly coupled complex of beliefs. Moreover, change in any one trait might easily depend on other beliefs that people hold. (It is also possible to build models with a larger number of variants, or a continuum of variants: see Cavalli-Sforza and Feldman 1981; Boyd and Richerson 1985.)

Evolutionary analysis requires constructing a framework for evaluating each process that affects whether the variants will increase or decrease relative to each other. In a "life cycle" of cultural transmission, we need to specify when and from whom an individual first acquires a belief, what later events might cause an individual to change beliefs, and finally, how holding different beliefs affects the chance that an individual will serve as a model for others. Let us assume the following life cycle:

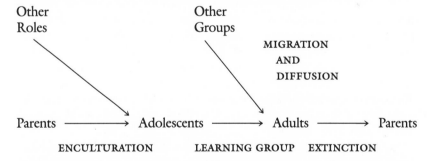

In this model, we focus on four processes: enculturation, individual learning, the flow of ideas among societies, and the extinction of societies. Real human life-cycles are much more complex than this. However, more realism would complicate matters greatly and distract from our attempt to see the essence of how the group selection process might work in human societies. The model is like a caricature, but, like a good caricature, it is in-

tended to highlight some real attributes of our subject (for a more elaborate defense of deliberately simplified models, see Richerson and Boyd
1987).

Next we describe what happens to individuals in a subpopulation during each step of the life cycle. We begin with the enculturation of children.
In this initial model, we assume that enculturation involves faithful copying. That is, children initially acquire a disposition to be either cooperators
or defectors by unbiased imitation of the adults among whom they grow
up. Many different models can have this property. For simplicity, suppose
that children imitate only one of their biological parents. Then, if both
cooperators and defectors have the same number of children, cultural
transmission will not change the proportion of cooperators in the population on the average. However, if subpopulations are small there may be
random changes due to sampling variation. (The appendix contains a brief
sketch of how the ideas in this section are formalized.)

Next, children mature to become adults. During this period, they learn
about the consequences of holding different beliefs about the importance
of group goals. Part of their information will come from their own experience. In accordance with the assumption that cooperation is costly to the
individual but beneficial to the group, we postulate that they will tend to
learn that their own cooperative acts do not yield personal benefits. Part
of their information will come from observing the consequences of the
behavior of others. They will see that defectors do not suffer as a result of
their noncooperation. As a result, some people will change their beliefs.
Some who began adolescence cooperating by copying their parents will
learn that they can get by without cooperating and will switch to defection. If learning is costly, however, most people may simply retain the beliefs acquired from parents (Boyd and Richerson 1985:116–17). If the
observations people make in the course of individual learning are prone to
error, some people may decide (incorrectly) that cooperation is individually beneficial. However, if cooperation is costly to the individual, as we
assume, cooperators will be more likely to switch to defection than vice
versa. This imbalance will usually cause the proportion of cooperators in
the population to decrease.

To say more than this one must specify the details of the individual
learning process. Let us suppose that in the course of adult individual
learning each person encounters a single other "role model," and, if the
role model's beliefs are different from the beliefs that an individual has
copied as a child, people then evaluate the costs and benefits of the alternative beliefs and adopt the one that seems better. The magnitude of the
change will depend on how easily individuals can discern the consequences of the alternatives available to them. If it is easy to see that adopting cooperative beliefs is costly, then many cooperators will switch to de-

fection and few defectors will switch to cooperation. If it is hard for individuals to discern the costs and benefits of alternative beliefs, there will be only a small increase in the fraction of defectors.

No society is completely isolated from other societies. People leave and are replaced by immigrants who bring with them different culturally acquired beliefs and values. People also borrow ideas from people in other societies. Both kinds of inputs lead to changes in the cultural composition of subpopulations. The exact nature of change depends on the details of the mixing process. For simplicity, let us assume that cooperators and defectors are equally likely to emigrate, and immigrants are drawn randomly from the population as a whole. Then if a fraction of each subpopulation emigrates or shares their beliefs, mixing will cause the proportion of cooperators in each subpopulation to approach the average proportion in the population as a whole. In other words, migration will cause subpopulations to become more alike.

The final step in the life cycle is the extinction of subpopulations. The group selection model assumes that cooperative societies are more likely to persist than noncooperative societies. Let us assume, then, that the probability that a subpopulation becomes extinct is negatively related to the proportion of cooperators—the more cooperators, the lower the probability of extinction. Empty habitats are recolonized by immigrants drawn from other subpopulations.

By combining all of these steps, we obtain a model of events during one generation that change the cultural composition of the population. This set of equations (one for each subpopulation) captures the nature of the evolutionary process on a microscopic time scale. To predict the longer-run course of evolution, the equations are iterated recursively, stepped forward from one time period to the next, to determine how the frequency of different variants changes through time, and perhaps reaches some equilibrium, a set of values at which the proportions of the two variants in each subpopulation become constant. Thus we can ask: Will the cooperators or the defectors increase and come to dominate the population? How will changing the size of subpopulations, or the ease with which individuals can discern the costs and benefits of alternative cultural variants, affect the outcome?

The model we have just sketched is closely analogous to "interdemic group selection" models studied by population geneticists, differing only in that learning rather than natural selection leads to the spread of selfish behavior within subpopulations. Extensive analysis of such models (Eshel 1972; Levin and Kilmer 1974; Wade 1978; Slatkin and Wade 1978; Boorman and Levitt 1980; Aoki 1982; Rogers, forthcoming) indicates that populations will eventually become composed almost completely of defectors unless subpopulations are extremely small, that there is little mixing among groups, and that it is very hard for individuals to discern the costs and benefits of alternative beliefs. This conclusion applies to many of the possible models of cultural transmission as well as to the genetic case; the existence of culture is, by itself, no guarantee that cooperation will evolve.

To understand this result it is useful to distinguish among processes that act within and processes that act among societies. Processes within societies, according to our assumptions, produce the result that, if there were no extinction of subpopulations, cooperation would disappear. However, the differential extinction of societies creates a process of selection among groups that increases the frequency of cooperators.

Selection among groups in this model fails to increase cooperation because in order for group selection to work, groups must differ persistently in degree of cooperation. Yet the tendency of migration to make all groups the same by mixing is powerful, while processes that generate differences among groups—random fluctuations due to small population size and small numbers of individuals colonizing empty habitats—are weak unless groups are very small. Given the cultural processes that we have assumed to operate, this logic will cause selection among culturally different groups to be ineffective at generating the scale of cooperation observed in humans.

At this point, the reader may remark that in the real world differences sufficient to provide the raw material for group selection do seem to persist. We agree, but we also believe that the preliminary model just presented is useful nevertheless. It shows that one must specifically account for the mechanisms that maintain cultural differences among groups. Our model incorporates two basic features of the enculturation process: children faithfully copy the beliefs and values of adults in their society, and people through individual learning tend to modify their beliefs in the direction of their own self-interest. Surprisingly, even with only small amounts of mixing, these processes do not maintain enough variation among groups for group selection to be important. This cultural model has the same behavior as genetic models of interdemic group selection, despite the assumed differences between cultural and genetic transmission incorporated into the model. Extensive analysis of genetic models indicates that many other elements can be added without changing the qualitative conclusion: group selection for cooperation is a weak effect (Eshel 1972; Levin and Kilmer 1974; Wade 1978; Slatkin and Wade 1978; Boorman and Levitt 1980; Aoki 1982; Rogers, forthcoming). Most evolutionary biologists, and social scientists influenced by evolutionary biologists, are properly impressed with the argument against group selection. If culture plays some role in human cooperation, it must be due to some specific attributes, not simply to the existence of a nongenetic means of acquiring behavior by tradition.

Conformist Cultural Transmission

Let us now consider an additional cultural process that could act to maintain variation among groups. In the model of group selection described above, we assumed that social learning was unbiased, meaning that it involved faithful copying plus random error. Social learning, however, could be biased in many ways, as individuals exercise conscious and unconscious choices about which variants to adopt. (For a more general discussion see Boyd and Richerson 1985, chap. 5 and references therein.) One form of biased transmission, which we call "conformist cultural transmission," is interesting and potentially important because it can maintain enough variation for group selection to be effective.

Conformist transmission occurs whenever children are *disproportionately* likely to acquire the variant that is more common among the adult role models. A naïve individual uses the frequency of a variant among his role models to evaluate the merit of the variant. For example, in the most extreme form of conformist transmission, children would always adopt the variant exhibited by a majority of their adult role models. Conformist transmission causes the frequency of the more common variant in population to increase, all other things being equal. For example, if more than half of the parents are cooperators, then there will be more cooperators among children than among their parents. If less than half of the parents are cooperators, then cooperation will decrease in frequency.

Group Selection Again

Adding conformist transmission to the model of group selection completely changes its results. When conformist transmission is strong, it can create and maintain differences among groups, and, as a result, group selection can cause cooperation to predominate even if groups are very large and extinction infrequent.

To see why, consider a subpopulation in which cooperation is common. When conformist transmission is weak compared to the effect of learning and mixing, the result is the same as in the previous model: these within-group forces act rapidly to reduce the frequency of cooperators in each subpopulation below the average frequency in the population as a whole. As in the previous model, the only stable long-run state is total defection. (Once again, see the appendix for more detail.) When the effect of conformist transmission is strong, the outcome is quite different—the effect of conformist transmission will exactly balance combined effects of learning and mixing so that subpopulations with a large fraction of cooperators persist indefinitely.

If conformist transmission is sufficiently strong, and if the mode of colonization is by single or relatively unmixed subpopulations, the process of group selection will increase the frequency of cooperators even if extinction rates are low, mixing is substantial, and subpopulations are very large (see Boyd and Richerson 1985, chap. 7, for a proof of this assertion). Once cooperation becomes sufficiently common in a subpopulation, conformist transmission acts to counter the processes of learning and mixing, leading to a stable equilibrium at which cooperation is common. The existence of such equilibria means that the long-run outcome in the population depends only on the among-group processes: extinction and colonization. Subpopulations in which cooperators are more common are less likely to go extinct than those in which cooperators are less common. Thus, differential extinction acts to increase the frequency of cooperation in the population as a whole. If the colonization of empty habitats is by a single subpopulation, then variation among groups is heritable at the group level. Groups in which cooperation is common can produce similar "offspring" groups. When these conditions hold, the results are strikingly different from those in the previous model, because conformist transmission acts to preserve variation between groups.

The Evolution of Conformist Transmission

Conformist transmission, thus, might allow the evolution of beliefs and values leading to self-sacrificial cooperation. To an evolutionist there is an obvious objection. The human cognitive capacities that allow the acquisition of culture must have been shaped by natural selection. If conformist transmission leads to excessive cooperation from the genetic point of view, it could evolve only if it has some compensating benefit. The following model of the evolution of conformist transmission suggests such a benefit.

We begin with exactly the same life cycle and model of conformist transmission used above. However, we now assume that the environment is heterogeneous, meaning that one cultural variant is better in some habitats, while the other cultural variant is better than others. To model the evolution of biased transmission we assume that individuals vary in the extent to which they are prone to adopt the more common type, and that this variation has a heritable genetic basis. We then combine the effects of biased social learning, individual learning, and natural selection to estimate the net effect of these processes on the joint distribution of cultural and genetic variants in the population. To project the long-run consequences, we repeat this process over and over. We then ask what amount of conformist transmission will be favored by natural selection.

In heterogeneous environments the answer is: always as strong a bias as possible (Boyd and Richerson 1985, chap. 7; Boyd and Richerson, in press). In the simplest model in which there are two cultural variants, the favored cultural transmission rule is: Always adopt the more common variant among your role models. Natural selection will favor such a transmission rule because in a heterogeneous environment both individual learning and selection will tend to make the most fit variant in a subpopulation the most common variant in that subpopulation. Commonness among role models provides naïve individuals with an estimate of the commonness of the variant in the local environment. The rule "imitate the common type" (or, When in Rome, do as the Romans do) provides a good way to increase the chance of acquiring the best behavior without costly individual learning.

As an example of how conformist inclinations might have evolved, consider a population of early humans in the process of expanding their range. Environments at the margin of their range differ from those at the center of their range. People at the center live in a tropical savanna, those at the margins in temperate woodland. Different habitats favor different behaviors. This is obviously true of subsistence behaviors—the foods that have the highest payoff, the habits of prey, the methods of constructing shelter, and so on. However, different habitats also favor different beliefs and values affecting social organization: What is the best group size? When is it best for a woman to be a second wife? What foods should be shared? It will be difficult and costly for individuals to learn what is best regarding many of these questions, particularly those affecting social behavior. Pioneering groups on the margin of the range will thus converge only slowly on the most adaptive behavior. Their convergence will be opposed by the flow of beliefs and values from the savanna, with the result that a minority will often hold beliefs more appropriate to life in the savanna than life in the woodland. Any system of enculturation that involves unbiased reproduction will simply reproduce these locally inappropriate beliefs and values. If individuals do not simply copy the beliefs and values of their elders faithfully, but instead adopt the most common cultural variants they see, they will adapt to the new environment more quickly. Since individual learning will eventually make the best variants the most common, those who in their social learning copy the most common variant will have no chance of acquiring beliefs that are more appropriate elsewhere. If this "conformist" tendency is genetically heritable, it will be favored by natural selection.

To sum up, group selection can lead to the evolution of cooperation if humans inherit at least some portion of the values, goals, and beliefs that determine their choices by way of conformist cultural transmission. To explain the evolution of human cooperation, we therefore need to account for the evolution of a human capacity for conformist culture transmission. We have seen that conformist transmission may be favored in heterogeneous environments because it provides a simple, general rule that increases the probability of acquiring behaviors favored in the local habitat. Averaged over many traits and many societies, this effect could plausibly compensate for what is, from the genes' "point of view," the excessive cooperation that may also result from conformist transmission. There are other peculiarities of the cultural inheritance system that may lead to a similar point (Boyd and Richerson 1985, chap. 8). We believe that such explanations of human altruism are attractive because they give us a plausible account for why we may be an exception to the powerful argument against group selection.

Cultural Endogamy

People belong to many different groups based on age, size, skin color, language, and so on. Often the interests of different groups conflict. Our model can be interpreted to yield predictions about which groups should cooperate. When (1) individuals acquire behaviors culturally from other members of the group via frequency-dependent cultural transmission and (2) the flow of cultural traits from outside the group is restricted (the group is "culturally endogamous"), group selection acting on cultural variation will favor cooperators—individuals whose behavior reduces their own welfare but increases the probability that their subpopulation will escape extinction.

Different social groupings may be culturally endogamous for some traits but not for others. For traits acquired by young children from members of their family, the culturally endogamous group might resemble the genetic deme. That is, an individual's cultural parents would be drawn from the same social grouping as its genetic parents. The culturally endogamous group for a trait acquired disproportionately from parents of one sex may differ from the culturally endogamous group for a trait acquired from parents of both sexes. For example, suppose that beliefs about what constitutes acceptable behavior during warfare are acquired exclusively from males. In patrilocal societies, where wives move to the kinship group of the males, the culturally endogamous group for these beliefs could be very small (sometimes so small as to require substantial amendments to the model). In the same societies, the culturally endogamous group for behaviors acquired from both sexes—for example, language or religious belief—could be very large. In contrast, in matrilocal societies, where husbands move to the kinship group of the wives, the culturally endogamous group might be the same for warfare, language, and religion. For traits acquired as an adult, the culturally endogamous group may be different again. For example, in modern corporations people acquire through cultural transmission from individuals who precede them many aspects of individual behavior, including professional goals, work norms, and beliefs about the nature of the product and the marketplace (Van Maanen and Schein 1979). For these behaviors, the culturally endogamous group is the firm. For other traits, the culturally endogamous group may be a fraternal organization, craft guild, or academic discipline.

Cultural Extinction Does Not Require Mortality

When conformist cultural transmission prevails, the extinction of a group need not entail the physical death of individuals; the breakup of the group as a coherent social unit and the dispersal of its members to other groups will suffice. Imagine that the members of a subpopulation are dispersed randomly to all the other subpopulations. Because the members of any subpopulation are either mostly cooperators or mostly defectors, their dispersal will change the frequency of cooperators in the other subpopulations during the generation in which the dispersal takes place. The small change will perturb each of the subpopulations from its equilibrium value, but if the number of migrants is small compared to the host population, and if they do not enter at a moment in which a crisis in individual learning is moving the host population toward a new equilibrium point, the perturbation will be overcome by the forces tending toward the original equilibrium. Each subpopulation will eventually reach the same equilibrium that it would have reached if the members of the dispersal group had never entered it. The dispersal of a group is thus equivalent to extinction because conformist transmission favors the more common variant. Cooperators persist in cooperative groups because they are most common in those groups. If they are dispersed, their numbers will usually be insufficient to cause the frequency of cooperators in defector groups to exceed the threshold necessary to cause a change to a cooperative equilibrium, and vice versa.

As we have seen, the model suggests that group selection will be more effective when vacant habitats are recolonized by individuals drawn from a single subpopulation. This model of colonization seems plausible in the human case for several reasons: First, in a social species in which division of labor and cooperative activities are important for subsistence, individuals may often immigrate as a social unit to colonize empty habitats. Second, in warfare, individuals from a single victorious group may disperse defeated groups and replace them. Finally, even if a vacant habitat is colonized by groups that originated in more than one subpopulation, behavioral isolating mechanisms may prevent them from mixing to form one larger group.

Cooperation Is Most Likely for Hard-to-Learn Traits

As we have seen, the model suggests that group selection will be important only if conformist transmission is strong compared to learning. This condition is most likely to be satisfied regarding cultural traits about which it is difficult and costly to make adaptive choices in real environments. The natural world is complex, hard to understand, and varies from place to place and time to time. People can make some intelligent guesses about complex questions like the reality of witchcraft, the causes of malaria, the effect on natural events of human pleas to their governing spirits, or the existence of an afterlife in which virtue is rewarded. But compared to the variation we observe in others' behavior, the number of alternatives we can investigate in detail is quite limited.

When determining which beliefs are best is costly or difficult, individual learning will tend to be weak, and thus group selection may be important. Consider, for example, belief in an afterlife in which virtue is rewarded. If external signals are weak and individual learning difficult, some atheists will, through individual learning, interpret some natural phenomena as confirming the existence of the afterlife and become believers. Some believers, through the same process, will despair for lack of convincing proofs and apostasize. The net effect of such decisions on the fraction of the population that believes will be relatively small, and therefore neither belief will spread rapidly at the expense of the other. If, however, such beliefs have strong effects on group persistence—if, for example, a society of believers is more able to mobilize individuals to provide education, participate in warfare, and so on—then group selection may cause believing to increase.

So far we have concentrated on behavioral differences between people who hold different culturally acquired beliefs. If the cultural environment is taken as given, however, much behavioral variation may still be explained in terms of self-interest. People who hold the same beliefs in different circumstances will make different choices. Because such choices may often be self-interested, much observed behavioral variation may conform to a selfish model of human behavior. If, for example, first sons have more to lose than second sons by joining the Crusades, then second sons will be more likely to join even if eldest sons' beliefs in Christianity are equally fervent. Given Christianity, such choices are self-interested. However, it may be very difficult to account for militant Christianity in terms of self-interest. (See Richerson and Boyd 1989 for a more extended version of this argument.)

Evolution of Ethnic Cooperation

One human grouping that seems generally to satisfy the requirements of the model is the ethnic group. The flow of cultural traits within the ethnic group is often much greater than the flow between ethnic groups. The model predicts that group selection acting on culturally transmitted traits will favor cooperative behavior within ethnic groups and noncooperative behavior toward members of other groups. Table 7.1 lists the traits of ethnocentrism that, according to LeVine and Campbell (1972), characterize human ethnic groups. These traits seem consistent with the predictions of

Table 7.1   Traits Identified with the Syndrome of Ethnocentrism

Attitudes and Behaviors toward In-group	Attitudes and Behaviors toward Out-group
See selves as virtuous and superior	See out-group as contemptible, immoral, and inferior
See own standards of value as universal, intrinsically true; see own customs as original, centrally human	
See selves as strong	See out-group as weak
	Social distance
	Out-group hate
Sanctions against in-group theft	Sanctions for out-group theft or absence of sanctions against
Sanctions against in-group murder	Sanctions for out-group murder or absence of sanctions against out-group murder
Cooperative relations with in-group members	Absence of cooperation with out-group members
Obedience to in-group authorities	Absence of obedience to out-group authorities
Willingness to remain an in-group member	Absence of conversion to out-group membership
Willingness to fight and die for in-group	Absence of willingness to fight and die for out-groups
	Virtue in killing out-group members in warfare
	Use of out-groups as bad examples in the training of children
	Blaming of out-group for in-group troubles
	Distrust and fear of the out-group

Source: LeVine and Campbell 1972.

the model. Sanctions against theft and murder within the group provide civil order—a public good that benefits group members. Few sanctions protect outgroup members. Cooperative behavior typifies interactions between group members, while lack of cooperation typifies interactions between members of different groups. Individuals are willing to fight and die for their own group in warfare against other groups. In recent times, actions on behalf of the ethnic group, like movements for ethnic autonomy, have even been taken in direct opposition to the authority and power of the modern state. These ethnic groups are often very large—too large to suggest that reciprocal arrangements are responsible for the observed behavior.

Variation in behavior among ethnic groups also provides support for the hypothesis of group selection acting on culturally transmitted behavior. LeVine and Campbell point out that in "socially divisive" ethnic groups, patrilocality or local-group endogamy helps develop a parochial loyalty structure and generates warfare among segments of the ethnic community. In "socially integrative" groups, the dispersion of males fosters loyalties to wider groupings and prevents such warfare. They go on to argue that while socially divisive societies are characterized by extensive feuding and violence, they are rarely involved in large-scale warfare, and when they are involved in warfare, alliances are formed on the basis of immediate military contingencies. In contrast, while socially integrative societies have much less violence within their own society, they readily cooperate in large-scale conflict (see also Otterbein 1968). Again, it appears that the unit upon which group selection works is the culturally endogamous group. If this unit is small, as in the case of socially divisive societies, then so is the unit within which social cooperation takes place. In socially integrated societies, the culturally endogamous unit is larger (at least with regard to traits transmitted by males) and the scale of conflict larger as well.

Conclusion

The simple model of cultural group selection outlined here is not, strictly speaking, verified by data concerning ethnic cooperation. Nor does it claim to account for all cooperative behavior in humans. The model illustrates what we believe is a crucial property of the evolution of cultural species: if the rules of cultural transmission are different from the rules of genetic transmission, similar selective regimes will result in different evolutionary behavior. The model also suggests one transmission rule, a rule of conformist transmission, that might explain human cooperative behavior. Such a rule allows group selection to be a strong force in determining human behavior in different societies. While it may still be possible to defend an egoistic theory of human society, this and similar models of cultural evolution undermine any purely deductive argument against group selection. Conformist transmission provides at least one theoretically cogent and empirically plausible explanation for why humans differ from all other animals in cooperating, against their own self-interest, with other human beings to whom they are not closely related.

Appendix

Group Selection with Unbiased Transmission

Cultural Transmission

Suppose that a subpopulation is made up of N individuals. At the end of generation $t - 1$, x_{t-1} of these individuals are cooperators, and y_{t-1} are defectors. These individuals mate and have f offspring per mating. Then the number of cooperators among offspring at the beginning of generation t, x_t, is

$$x_t = (\tfrac{1}{2}) f x_{t-1}$$

The right side of this equation is multiplied by one-half because each child has two parents, and so under our assumed rule of transmission, each parent will on average transmit the trait to half of them. The equation describing the socialization process for defectors is similar:

$$y_t = (\tfrac{1}{2}) f y_{t-1}$$

We can simplify the model considerably, without sacrificing anything for most purposes, by keeping track of frequencies or proportions of the variants instead of the numbers. Let q_t be the frequency of cooperators among offspring. Then

$$q_t = x_t/N$$

Since at this or any other state of the life cycle the proportion of defectors is just one minus the proportion of cooperators $(1 - q_t)$, we need an equation for only one of the two types to specify the model completely. We assume that cooperation is costly to the individual but beneficial to the group. Thus it is plausible that cooperators may, on the average, have fewer children than defectors. If so, the proportion of cooperators among children will be smaller than among parents, a change due to natural selection acting on cultural variation. For simplicity, however, let us suppose that both cooperators and defectors have the same number of children. A little algebra then shows that the cultural transmission does not change the proportion of cooperators in the population, or,

$$q_t = q_{t-1}$$

Thus cultural transmission does not change the frequency of cooperators in a subpopulation. This result can be obtained for a much wider range of models (see Boyd and Richerson 1985).

Learning

Assume that each individual encounters a single other role model. If the role model has the same behavior as the focal individual, the focal individual does not change his or her behavior. However, if the role model has a different behavior, the focal individual evaluates the two behaviors and adopts the one that seems best. Then the frequency of cooperation in the subpopulation after learning, q_t, is

$$q'_t = q_t - Bq_t(1 - q_t)$$

The magnitude of the parameter B depends on the accuracy of the evaluation process. If it is easy to evaluate the merit of the two variants then B will be near one, and learning will substantially reduce the frequency of cooperation within the subpopulation. If identifying the best variant is difficult, then B will be near zero, and learning will cause only small reductions of cooperation during a single generation. (See Boyd and Richerson 1985, chaps. 4, 5, and 8, 1988a, and in press; and Rogers, in press, for detailed analysis of a variety of alternative models that link learning and cultural transmission.)

Migration

If m is the fraction of each population that emigrates, then the frequency after migration, q''_t, is

$$q''_t = (1 - m)q'_t + m\bar{q}_t$$

where $\bar{q}_t$ is the average frequency of cooperators in the population as a whole.

Group Selection with Conformist Transmission

Conformist Transmission

The following model is a very simple example of conformist transmission. Assume two cultural variants, cooperate (c) and noncooperate (d), but

Table 7.2   Conformist Transmission

| Model | | | Probability of Acquiring | |
1	2	3	*c*	*d*
c	*c*	*c*	1	0
c	*c*	*d*		
c	*d*	*c*	$(2+D)/3$	$(1-D)/3$
d	*c*	*c*		
d	*d*	*c*		
d	*c*	*d*	$(1-D)/3$	$(2+D)/3$
c	*d*	*d*		
d	*d*	*d*	0	1

now suppose that children acquire their initial beliefs from three adults, say, their parents and a teacher. The probability that an individual acquires variant *c*, given that he or she is exposed to a particular set of adults, is shown in table 7.2. This model of cultural transmission is particularly simple because each of the adults is assumed to have the same role. It does not matter which adults are cooperators, only how many are cooperators. The parameter *D* measures the extent to which cultural transmission is biased. If *D* is equal to zero, the probability that a child acquires either cultural variant is proportional to the frequency of that variant among the child's adult role models. Assuming that each set of adults is a random sample of the population, then it can be shown (Boyd and Richerson 1985, chap. 7) that the frequency of *c* among naïve individuals after transmission is given by

$$q_t = q_{t-1} + Dq_{t-1}(1 - q_{t-1})(2q_{t-1} - 1)$$

When $D > 0$, cultural transmission creates a force increasing the frequency of the more common variant in the population.

Interaction of Conformist Transmission, Learning, and Migration

To see how conformist cultural transmission can preserve variation among groups, we compare the net effect of transmission, learning, and migration when transmission is conformist with the case in which transmission is unbiased.

First consider the case in which transmission is unbiased. Figure 7.1 plots the change in the frequency of a subpopulation over one generation as a function of the frequency of cooperators in the subpopulation in a subpopulation that does not suffer extinction. If the frequency of cooperators in a particular subpopulation is higher than the average frequency in the population as a whole, they will decrease in frequency—both because

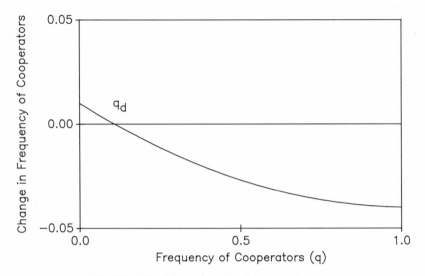

Fig. 7.1. This figure plots the change in the frequency of cooperators in a subpopulation over one generation as a function of the frequency cooperators already in the subpopulation assuming unbiased transmission. It is assumed that the subpopulation does not suffer extinction and that enculturation involves faithful copying.

of immigration and, more importantly, because people will individually learn the deleterious consequences of holding cooperative beliefs and will switch to defecting. If cooperators make up a lower than average proportion of the subpopulation, cooperators will either increase in the subpopulation due to immigration or will decrease if the consequences of individual learning are greater than those of immigration. Thus, within each subpopulation the proportion of cooperators moves toward the value labeled q_d. Notice that q_d is less than the average frequency of cooperators in the population as a whole. Within-group processes tend to lower the average frequency of cooperators in the whole population because the same processes act in every subpopulation.

Now suppose that there is strong conformist transmission. Figure 7.2 plots the change in the frequency of a subpopulation over one generation as a function of the frequency cooperators in a subpopulation that does not suffer extinction. Notice that now there are three values of q_t for which the change in the proportion of cooperators over one generation is zero. If the focal subpopulation were to reach exactly one of these values it would remain there, in equilibrium, until some external event occurred.

When cooperators are rare, conformist transmission and learning both act to reduce their numbers. As long as there are some subpopulations composed primarily of cooperators, mixing will prevent the processes from completely eliminating cooperators, and instead the subpopulation will stabilize at a low frequency of cooperators, here labeled q_d. This equilibrium is "stable," meaning that the subpopulation will return to this value after small departures from it. There are two other equilibria, labeled q_u and q_c, at which the effects of conformist transmission, learning, and migration also balance. The equilibrium labeled q_c is also stable. In contrast, the equilibrium labeled q_u is unstable: if the frequency of cooperators is increased a small amount, the subpopulation will evolve toward q_c; if the frequency of cooperators is reduced a little, eventually the subpopulation will evolve toward q_d. Thus, if for some reason the frequency of cooperators in a subpopulation increases above q_u, the subpopulation will reach a stable equilibrium at which cooperators are common. If conformist transmission is strong enough, this may occur in a subpopulation, even if every individual in the larger population is a defector.

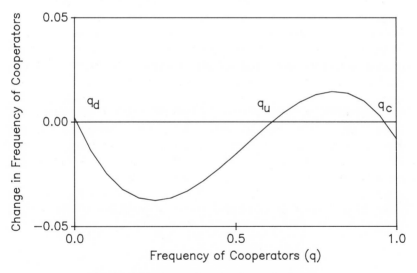

Fig. 7.2. This figure plots the change in the frequency of cooperators in a subpopulation over one generation as a function of the frequency cooperators already in the subpopulation under conformist transmission. It is assumed that the subpopulation does not suffer extinction and that enculturation involves conformist transmission that is strong compared to mixing.

The Effect of Extinction and Recolonization

Consider a population made up entirely of defectors. Even in these circumstances, if conformist transmission is strong, cooperation can increase whenever colonists of a vacant habitat are drawn from a single other population and that population has a majority of cooperators. Algebraically,

$$\begin{pmatrix} \text{probability of} \\ \text{extinction of sub-} \\ \text{populations at } q_c \end{pmatrix} < \frac{\begin{pmatrix} \text{number of} \\ \text{extinctions in} \\ \text{population} \end{pmatrix} \times \begin{pmatrix} \text{probability frequency of} \\ \text{cooperators among colo-} \\ \text{nizers is greater than } q_u \end{pmatrix}}{\text{number of subpopulations at } q_c}$$

Any empty habitat colonized by more than q_u cooperators will eventually end up at the equilibrium frequency q_c. Thus the numerator on the right-hand side gives the number of q_c subpopulations that are "born" during a particular generation. Dividing this by the number of subpopulations at q_c gives the "birth rate" of these subpopulations. This birth rate depends critically on the way that empty habitats are colonized. If they are typically colonized by people drawn from a single subpopulation, the probability that the frequency of cooperators among colonizers will be greater than q_u is just the proportion of subpopulations that are at q_c (since $q_d < q_u < q_c$). This means that the right-hand side of this inequality is just the probability that a randomly chosen subpopulation will suffer extinction. Since the extinction rate decreases with the frequency of cooperators, it follows that cooperation always increases over time via extinction when colonists are drawn from a single other randomly chosen subpopulation, either mainly cooperators or mainly defectors. If colonists are drawn from more than one subpopulation, the probability that the frequency of cooperators is greater than q_u will be smaller. The more mixing among colonists, the lower the birth rate of cooperative subpopulations, although cooperation could still increase if the effect of cooperation on extinction rates is sufficiently great.

8   On the Relation of Altruism and Self-Interest

Jane J. Mansbridge

> In this, as in all other cases, providence has made our interests and our duties coincide perfectly.
> —Thomas Jefferson, 1819, writing to his overseer of arrangements to prevent miscarriages among his female slaves

We normally see self-interest and altruism as being at opposite poles. Indeed, conceptually we know what we mean by altruism only by contrasting it with self-interest. In practice, however, altruism must coincide with self-interest sufficiently to prevent the extinction of either the altruistic motive or the altruist. This essay argues that while duty and love, the two forms of altruism or unselfish motivation, are valuable in themselves, they must also be sustained by institutions or an environment that provides enough self-interested return to both motivations to prevent actions based on them from being excessively costly.

Conceptually, we distinguish among motivations by opposing them one to another. We know that love or duty is at work only when an action could not possibly have been taken for reasons of self-interest. Empirically, we demonstrate that people are acting for unselfish reasons by devising situations in which they are demonstrably acting against their self-interest.[1]

Yet in practice we often try hard to arrange our lives so that duty (or love) and interest coincide. Eighteenth-century writers—including Jefferson, with his remarks to his overseer on his slaves—often exaggerated the degree of coincidence.[2] Today, in the interests of a misplaced "realism," we often exaggerate in the other direction, claiming that if we can detect any self-interested reason to act in a particular way, that reason provides the only explanation we need. Self-interest does not automatically drive out duty, however, in spite of the conceptual opposition between the two. In

For comments on this essay, I particularly thank Michael Chew, Thomas Cook, Robert Keohane, Roger Myerson, Gregory Pollock, and Cass Sunstein.

my own case, I have a duty to care for my child, and I am made happy by his happiness, and I get simple sensual pleasure from snuggling close to him as I read him a book. I have a principled commitment to work for women's liberation, and I empathize with other women, and I find a way to use some of my work for women as background to a book that advances my academic career. Duty, love (or empathy), and self-interest intermingle in my actions in a way I can rarely sort out. It is because these motives are so frequently intermingled that empirical researchers have to exercise such ingenuity to invent experiments or isolate incidents in which, by pitting duty or love explicitly against self-interest, they can demonstrate that duty or love exist.

This essay looks at the relation between self-interest and altruism in the context of the problem of cooperation, when a war of all against all produces suboptimal group outcomes and cooperative arrangements generate a larger total product. It first points out that there are empathetic and principled as well as self-interested "solutions" to the problem of cooperation. It then argues that self-interested solutions to the problem help sustain empathetic and principled solutions by preventing the extinction of empathetic and principled motives and individuals. This essay examines only one form of the problem of cooperation—a form that as a general problem has been politically salient since the seventeenth century. In the last thirty years it has been codified as the "prisoners' dilemma" (see Appendix A)[3] when two people are involved, or as a "social dilemma" when more are involved. The logic for the one can be generalized to the other in the examples I provide.

In the "rational choice" literature, the usual solutions to the problem of cooperation posed by a prisoners' dilemma require no more than what most people would call self-interest.

The first of these self-interested solutions is the provision of "selective incentives" or side payments, which change the payoffs to the different parties by adding an extra good to the payoffs of anyone who cooperates. If you contribute to a good cause, you receive a valuable copy of the founder's memoirs; if you join the union, you are eligible for its life insurance (Olson 1965). (In a strong version of this solution, the matrix in Appendix A, fig. 8.1, would register an increment of 5 or more for cooperation, thus negating the temptation to defect.)

The second self-interested solution requires the institution of a "sovereign," though the sovereign may for this purpose be diminished to just the smallest amount of external punishment necessary to change the balance of self-interested individual incentives from defection to cooperation. Because I know my will is weak, I may even vote myself at an earlier time for the sanction that I know will at a later time coerce me into doing what is for the good of all.[4] (In the matrix in fig. 8.1, Jane and John each ensure that if they defect, the penalty for defection will be greater than 5, thus negating the temptation to defect.)

A third solution that depends on self-interest works much like the external punishment inflicted by a voluntarily adopted sovereign. In this solution, participants put aside some good as collateral, which they will lose if they do not subsequently cooperate. This collateral is sufficient to make cooperation more rewarding than defection at all later times.[5] (As in the first solution, the penalty for defection will be greater than 5, thus negating the temptation to defect.)

A fourth solution relies on punishment coming from within an interaction that is likely to continue for a long time. In Anatol Rapoport's Tit for Tat strategy,[6] a player first makes a cooperative move and thereafter simply mimics the other player's last move. This strategy punishes defection with defection. No external mechanism is required. The solution, however, requires ongoing interactions and groups (usually two-person groups) in which each actor can monitor the interaction carefully, has the incentive to do so, and can impose sufficient costs through subsequent defection to negate the other's immediate gains.[7] (Unlike the first two solutions, this one does not alter the immediate payoff matrix. Punishment for defection in the first game will come in the second and subsequent games.)

A fifth and related solution, also using a negative sanction for defection, requires that the interaction be voluntary. Those who plan to cooperate can then punish potential defectors by abstaining from interaction whenever they can detect potential defection in advance with sufficient probability to warrant their abstention. (See Frank, chap. 5, this vol. As in the fourth solution, this does not alter the immediate payoff matrix.)

These standard solutions to the prisoners' dilemma are all what I would call self-interested.[8] That is, they change defection to cooperation by relying only on the motive of self-interest. Other solutions derive from love or duty. That is, they require one or more of the interacting parties either to make the other's good their own or to be committed to a principle or course of action that requires cooperation. These two distinct motivations, which I together call the "unselfish" or "altruistic" motivations (see Appendix B), have been variously labeled "sympathy" and "commitment" (Sen), "love" and "duty" (Elster), "empathy" and "morality" (Jencks), "we-feeling" and "conscience" (Dawes, van de Kragt, and Orbell), or "affection" and "principle" (Hume).[9]

In a series of cleverly designed experiments, Dawes and his colleagues (chap. 6, this vol.) demonstrate that a high percentage of American college students can come to act cooperatively and against their own self-interest in prisoners' dilemma–like games. Dawes and his colleagues explicitly distinguish between "we-feeling" and "conscience," demonstrating that both motivations are separately at work. These two sets of motives need not be merely additive. While Dawes, van de Kragt, and Orbell interpret their experiments as distinguishing sharply between "we-feeling" and "conscience," their results are also compatible with their subjects' having a "contingent conscience," that is, acting morally, or more morally, only toward those with whom they have a sense of "we-feeling."[10]

Feelings of sympathy and/or commitment can be thought of as changing the payoff matrix in a prisoners' dilemma by adding to the cooperator's payoff a good derived from knowing that the other has benefited (love) or knowing that one acted morally (duty). (Thus in the matrix in fig. 8.1, the "sucker's payoff" might be 6: 5 from seeing the other get 5, 1 from acting morally.) One might also make a cooperative move in order to avoid the ills of empathetic distress and moral guilt.

Feelings of sympathy, and even of commitment to a principle, however, cannot usually be sustained independently of the actions of others. If others consistently defect, their defection will tend to erode a cooperator's "we-feeling" ("someone who acts like that is not part of 'my' group") or change the content of a cooperator's moral principles ("the rule I follow should not encourage defection"). While the experiments of Dawes, van de Kragt, and Orbell indicate that both sympathy and commitment are at work in the high rates of cooperation their subjects achieve, other experiments, like those of Isaac, McCue, and Plott (1985), indicate that unless cooperation is reciprocated, it diminishes rapidly over time.

The social embeddedness of both empathetic feelings and moral commitment means that they can be undermined by self-interested behavior on the part of others. Even when an unselfish impulse or commitment does not depend in any way on believing that the recipients will repay the favor, it may depend on believing that they deserve the favor.[11] From sympathy or moral obligation one may care for a child whose constant pain keeps him from returning so much as a smile. Yet both motives fade when the child seems willfully evil. A few moral codes require us to behave altruistically to everyone, regardless of desert ("turn the other cheek"), but even the Kantian admonition to treat others as ends in themselves is open to the interpretation that the most moral way to treat defectors ("the willfully selfish") is to change their behavior through a mixture of punishment and reward.

Love and duty are also vulnerable to social cues about appropriate behavior. It is often adaptive to take our cues from the behavior of most people we see around us (Boyd and Richerson, chap. 7, this vol.). If we cooperate but most others consistently defect, we may reasonably think that we have misunderstood the context in which we are operating. At some social point, we are likely to conclude that acting morally when others are immoral is a sign not of virtue but of stupidity. Others may also define inveterate cooperators as suckers rather than saints. When this happens, the cost of cooperation when others defect will include not only material loss but a loss in social approval and self-esteem as well. Moral systems make heroes of those who maintain their moral commitments even at this point, but few systems expect most of humanity to pay the price that heroes pay.

Moral systems therefore usually include not only requirements of extreme moral obligation, like "Be perfect as thy heavenly father is perfect," or some equivalent of the utilitarian command, "Love thy neighbor as thyself" (which nevertheless allows self to count equally with a single other in the moral calculus), but also mediations of these extreme requirements, in which authoritative others, from priests to parents to peers, make clear that in fact much less is required for individuals to consider themselves moral. These authoritative, but not always mutually congruent, determinations of what is required and what is beyond the call of duty take heavily into consideration the self-interest of the moral individual, not generally requiring acts that undermine the most vital aspects of one's own and one's children's interests.[12]

While the ability to follow one's empathetic and moral impulses will have value to most individuals, it will not usually have infinite value. If the costs are very high, many individuals will simply not want to pay the costs. If nice guys always finished last, the cost of niceness to the individual would be intolerable. Social learning would quickly extinguish the behavior.[13]

My point in this essay, then, is that arrangements that generate some self-interest return to unselfish behavior create an "ecological niche" that helps sustain that unselfish behavior. Arrangements that make unselfishness less costly in narrowly self-interested terms increase the degree to which individuals feel they can afford to indulge their feelings of empathy and their moral commitments, as well as their readiness to foster empathy and moral commitment in their children.

Arrangements that either make unselfishness less costly or actually make it pay in narrowly self-interested terms do not negate the content of the empathetic or moral impulses. Although it may be impossible to measure the empathetic or moral component of an act that also benefits oneself, the fact that an act benefits oneself does not mean that empathy or moral commitment is not present.[14]

Many conventions as well as sanctions facilitate the kind of accurate predictions that make cooperative initiatives work to the individual's long-run self-interest whenever interaction is voluntary and cooperation in ongoing interactions produces greater individual benefits than defection.[15] In ongoing interactions, previous cooperation (reputation) communicates the message to potential cooperators that their cooperation will probably be reciprocated. Even the Tit for Tat strategy not only punishes, but punishes in an easily understandable way, thus creating and reinforcing conventions that facilitate predictability. Tit for Tat may also convey empathetic and moral messages, possibly suggesting to human players—only partially correctly, when the opposing player is a computer programmed by a human being—that the other is a being like oneself whose good one can make one's own. The strategy may also suggest that the other subscribes to a moral code very like one's own, thus reinforcing the code itself. Such messages are potentially important, since it seems to be quite easy, at least among college students playing prisoners' dilemma games in the United States, to create a sense of community sufficient to lead most players to cooperate. Experimenters can create a sense of "we-feeling" in a group by simply placing members in it through the toss of a coin.[16]

In initial interactions, or in ongoing interactions in which new and untested issues arise, Robert Frank (chap. 5, this vol.) makes the point that cooperation will benefit from signals that are hard to fake. Blushes, "an honest face," and other subtle but involuntary signals in body language allow potential cooperators to communicate accurately that they can be trusted even when they have had no earlier interaction in which to establish a reputation. Because other cooperators will then use these signals to choose potential cooperators for interaction and shun the defectors, the cooperators' unselfish impulses, which stem genuinely from sympathy, commitment to principles, or a combination of these, can end up working for the cooperators' long-run self-interest.

Frank's work suggests that different societies and subsocieties may maintain different equilibria between cooperation and defection. These equilibria are set not only by the effectiveness of sanctions but also by the degree of empathy and moral obligation inculcated by the society, and by the social system's success in helping its members assess accurately the degree of empathy and moral obligation among potential cooperators. The Victorian world of English "gentle" men and women, for example, fostered certain forms of empathetic unselfishness and prescribed certain forms of honorable behavior within the group. Members of this group were concerned that those brought up to "gentle" behavior not have advantage taken of them by members of a different class or renegades within their class. The novels of Jane Austen and Anthony Trollope, which paint the subtle traits of characters ranging from the superficially trustworthy but ultimately defecting to the superficially unpromising but ultimately trustworthy, can be seen in part as manuals for the momentous and life-altering game of deciding which other people could be trusted to reciprocate a cooperative move and which were likely to defect.

Many forms of complex interdependence, including many market arrangements, require not only a coercive apparatus to enforce contracts but also a considerable leaven of trust.[17] Anything that facilitates accurate judgments about whom to trust therefore has survival value. Small group, tribal, and ethnic solidarity has in several ways often generated enough mutual sympathy and commitment to make complex interdependence work. "In-groups" can increase empathy toward other members of the group by making salient (often through contrast with an out-group) the ways in which members of the group are alike and by promoting mutual contact (often through discouraging contact with others) (Kanter 1972). They can develop conscience through group-wide moral systems (often in the form of "contingent conscience," which enjoins moral action only toward members of the group). They can establish explicit and implicit sanctions for noncooperative behavior within the group, generating among other things the kinds of internalized norms that make individuals feel, consciously or unconsciously, that they will be ostracized if they do not act unselfishly (Hechter 1987). They can establish conventions and reasonable expectations about others' tastes that allow accurate coordination (Hardin 1982). Finally, they can, through habituation, foster the kinds of subtle communications that allow each individual to judge relatively accurately whether or not the other will exploit a cooperative move.[18]

By thus changing the payoffs for cooperation and defection of individuals within the group, all these actions by an in-group make it both more likely that any individual in that group will cooperate initially and also more likely, whenever the interaction is initiated with another in-group member, that the cooperation will be reciprocated. "Landsman!" "Sister!" For those who live largely among strangers, recognizing someone from one's own group translates not only into the simple message, "Here is someone who will understand me and whom I can understand," but also into the message, "Here is someone with whom I can cooperate with a reduced probability of being a sucker." Indeed, if most human beings possess some innate empathy or some innate desire to love, and if not being able to express this empathy or love is a cost, then in-groups, like other arrangements that reduce the costs of unselfish impulses, may provide a relatively protected space in which individuals can act upon these desires.

In international relations, where group sanctions and messages are weak if they exist at all, most cooperative structures have had to build almost exclusively on national self-interest.[19] Uncertainty is reduced and cooperation secured to the degree that all parties are aware both of their self-interest in different interdependent arrangements and of the self-interested mechanisms by which continued adherence is secured on all sides. For this reason, models of interdependence that rely solely on narrow national self-interest may have themselves reduced the chances of nuclear war.

To date, researchers in international relations have been less aware than those in domestic politics of the potential for using sympathy, commitment, and the accurate communication of these motives to build cooperative interdependent arrangements. The primary reason for this neglect is that the motives of sympathy and commitment, and the forms of communication that might lead to accuracy in transmitting these motives, are extremely weak internationally. Even domestic political science, as this volume indicates, has only recently begun to address these issues. Robert Frank's anecdote (in chap. 5, this vol.) about Neville Chamberlain's conclusion after meeting Hitler that "here was a man who could be relied upon when he gave his word," reveals the limitations, particularly in international relations, of judgments about other people's potential cooperation based only on "reading" another's involuntary signals.[20] But in the many situations where stakes are relatively low, or where incremental measures of trustworthiness can be taken, unselfish foundations for cooperation may have an important international role. They make possible, in conjunction with self-interest, a far wider spread of interdependent institutions than self-interest alone can develop.[21]

If the speculations in this essay are correct, one important avenue for future research would be to investigate when self-interest can be used productively in conjunction with unselfishness—to construct an "ecological niche" in which unselfishness is not extinguished—and when self-interest is likely to undermine unselfishness. Robert Frank, as we have seen, indicates how the possibility of a long-term payoff for unselfishness may keep altruists from being extinguished in long-term evolutionary competition. (This is a more direct route than that envisaged by Boyd and Richerson, who rely on group rather than individual selection.) Institutions that apply a small amount of coercion to nonaltruists can also protect cooperators from levels of exploitation that will extinguish either them or their unselfish motives.

The reverse process, however, in which self-interest undermines unselfishness, is illustrated by Richard Titmuss's conclusion (1970/1971) that commercial blood programs drive out voluntary ones. It is illustrated by the many experiments that show intrinsic motivation being undermined by extrinsic reward.[22] It is perhaps also illustrated by the relatively low level of unselfishness displayed in laboratory experiments by economics students, who may have been socialized to believe that selfishness is not only calculatingly rational but also a mark of intelligence.

At least since Hobbes, explaining the world by self-interest alone has tempted those who think of themselves as realists. Hobbes himself, asked why he had just given sixpence to a beggar, answered, true to his belief in self-interest, "I was in pain to consider the miserable condition of the old man; and now my alms, giving him some relief, doth also ease me" (Aubrey 1697/1982:159). Abraham Lincoln, having remarked to a companion that "all men were prompted by selfishness in doing good or evil," and having subsequently run to rescue some trapped piglets for their mother, was asked, "Now, Abe, where does selfishness come in on this little episode?" Lincoln answered, "Why, bless your soul, Ed, that was the very essence of selfishness. I would have had no peace of mind all day had I gone on and left that suffering old sow worrying over those pigs. I did it to get peace of mind, don't you see?"[23]

These kinds of explanations, while charming, obscure as much as they reveal. They may even do actual harm. We seriously underestimate the frequency of altruism when, having designed our lives to make self-interest and altruism coincide, we interpret such coincidences as demonstrating the pervasiveness of self-interest rather than altruism. And because thinking that another has acted unselfishly often leads people to behave unselfishly themselves,[24] underestimating the frequency of altruism can itself undermine unselfish behavior.

Appendix A
The Prisoners' Dilemma

In the prisoners' dilemma a district attorney offers, individually, each of two prisoners release from jail if they give evidence that will convict the other. If one remains silent but the other gives evidence, the prisoner who holds his tongue will receive a heavy jail term but his comrade, who squealed, will be released. If both remain silent, they will both get only a short term in jail. If both give evidence against the other, they will both get moderate terms. For each individual, the best strategy is to give evidence on the other, but if both give evidence they will each be worse off than if they had kept quiet. As game theorists have worked this out, they have arranged the "payoffs" for each move to set off the dilemma starkly. For example, Robert Axelrod uses the payoff matrix in figure 8.1.[25] The numbers represent some form of benefit, say dollars. The payoffs to "John Row" are listed first in each box, the payoffs to "Jane Column" second. If Jane and John both cooperate, they will each get 3, the reward for mutual cooperation. If Jane cooperates but John defects, he will get 5 (the temptation to defect) and she will get 0 (the sucker's payoff). If Jane cooperates but John defects, she will get 0 (the sucker's payoff) and he will get 5 (the temptation to defect). If they both defect, they will each get 1, the punishment for mutual defection. This set of payoffs means that when John thinks about his choices, he first compares the first numbers in the boxes on the left and then compares the first numbers in the boxes on the right. If he thinks Jane will cooperate, he compares 3 (the reward for mutual cooperation) to 5 (the temptation to defect), and chooses 5. If he thinks Jane will defect, he compares 0 (the sucker's payoff) to 1 (the punishment

Jane Column

		Cooperate	Defect
John Row	Cooperate	3, 3 Reward for mutual cooperation	0, 5 Sucker's payoff, and temptation to defect
	Defect	5, 0 Temptation to defect and sucker's payoff	1, 1 Punishment for mutual defection

Fig. 8.1. The prisoners' dilemma.

for mutual defection), and chooses 1. Jane does the same, comparing her payoffs of 3 and 5 if John cooperates, and her payoffs of 0 and 1 if John defects. It is clear that no matter what the other player does, it pays the chooser to defect. But if both defect they will both get less (1) than if both cooperated (3). The individual pursuit of self-interest leads to a worse outcome for both than is possible through cooperation.

Appendix B

By unselfish or altruistic behavior, I mean in this essay behavior promoting another's welfare that is undertaken for a reason *"independent* of its effects on [one's] own welfare."[26] That reason can include both duty and love, both commitment to a moral principle regardless of its effects on the welfare of others, and moral or empathetic concern with the welfare of others.

By suggesting that an individual can compare the utils gained by defecting in a prisoners' dilemma with the utils gained from unselfish empathy and commitment to a principle, this paper does violence in several ways to what it means to act unselfishly. First, the very concepts of "util," "payoff," and "benefit" to the unselfish individual are not conceptually compatible with defining an "unselfish" act as undertaken for a reason *independent* of its effects on one's own welfare. Second, calculating the pleasure an individual gets from others' pleasures suggests that we can conceive of individuals as separate from the other people in their lives. Third, such a calculation sums in a single metric of overall utility empathetic and moral considerations that not only are necessarily defined as independent of utility (the first point) but include within them separate motivations to which we usually assign greater and lesser virtue. For example, this article counts as a "benefit" to the cooperator in a prisoners' dilemma the sense of power in having helped another (sometimes called "impure altruism"), possibly accompanied by a surge of pleasure-giving serotonin in the blood stream.[27] It counts as a benefit on the same metric the pleasure that comes when, having made another's good his own, the cooperator knows that the other has received a benefit ("pure altruism"). The subtleties masked by simply counting both love and duty as benefits to the cooperator emerge in the implicit controversy between Sen (chap. 2, this vol.) and Dawes, van de Kragt, and Orbell (chap. 6, this vol.) on the degree of egoism involved in each motivation. Sen points out that love or sympathy generates a relatively direct emotional pleasure, and argues that because commitment to a principle involves a choice explicitly *against* one's preferences, it cannot be simply egoistic. Dawes et al. reduce the meaning of duty or conscience to egoistic "self-esteem," and argue that love or "we-feeling" is a non-egoistic motivation.[28]

The point of violating the concept of unselfishness by counting unselfish acts as benefits to the actor is to show that even in this dramatically reduced and weakened version the concept of unselfishness helps us make sense of complex forms of interdependence. More is gained, I believe, from introducing the concepts of love and duty into the understanding of cooperation posed by a prisoners' dilemma than from excluding such considerations from that understanding on the grounds that both alone and collectively, under the rubric of "unselfishness," they mean much more than can emerge in this one narrow but powerful exercise. As I indicate elsewhere in this volume, reducing all forms of unselfishness to a single metric is perhaps the least helpful of the several ways of modeling non-self-interested motives. It is required, however, if the language and concepts of prisoners' dilemmas are going to incorporate unselfishness at all.[29]

IV   Citizens

9   Self-Interest in Americans' Political Opinions

David O. Sears and Carolyn L. Funk

The notion that human behavior is governed at least in part by selfish urges plays a role in virtually every psychology and moral philosophy in Western thought. The great thinkers of the Christian era, such as Saint Augustine, denounced the various lusts, of which lust for money and possessions (also known as greed or avarice) was only one, and by no means necessarily the worst; others identified ferocity, pride, or envy. Thomas Hobbes regarded the human being as motivated first and foremost by self-interest. Adam Smith also concluded that hedonistic selfishness was in some contexts the ruling motive of the human species: "every man feels his own pleasures and his own pains more sensibly than those of other people." But he saw self-interest as focused particularly on one motive, "augmentation of fortune." His near contemporary, Jeremy Bentham, argued that people act simply to secure pleasure and avoid pain (including the pleasures and pains of malevolence and benevolence).

From this mixture of antecedents, classical economics has deduced three basic psychological assumptions: the idea of materialistic hedonism, or a simple pleasure-pain principle of human motivation; the idea of egotism, that outcomes to the self are weighed more heavily than outcomes to others; and rationality, that decisions are made on the basis of reasonable calculations limited primarily by the amount of information available.

Theories of self-interest have also been influential in modern psychology. Its formative years were much influenced by Darwin, so accounts of human motivation were dominated by the view that humanity is basically selfish and driven by basic biological needs that ensure species survival. Freud viewed all behavior as motivated principally by such instinctual survival-oriented drives as hunger and procreation, operating according to the pleasure principle. Mainstream academic psychology developed a not

This chapter was prepared while David O. Sears was a John Simon Guggenheim Fellow and a fellow at the Center for Advanced Study in the Behavioral Sciences, Stanford, California. Both authors wish to express their profound appreciation to the staff at the center for their generous help with this project, and are grateful for financial support provided by National Science Foundation grant number BNS87-00864.

dissimilar view, ranging from McDougall's theorizing about human instincts to Hull's and Skinner's ideas of primary drives. Deprivation motivates overt activity, and the organism learns adaptive habits when reinforced with drive reduction. It is perhaps not unfair to say, with Campbell (1975) and the Wallachs (1983), that the dominant modern psychological theories of motivation are fundamentally egoistic and hedonistic.

Self-Interest in Mass Publics

Early studies of mass political behavior suggested that self-interest is a powerful motive in the ordinary citizen's political thinking. Studies of individual voting behavior (e.g., Berelson, Lazarsfeld, and McPhee 1954) emphasized the importance of "position issues," whose motivational appeal was presumed to be "self-interest of a relatively direct kind" (p. 184). *The American Voter* (Campbell et al. 1960) concluded that Americans commonly responded to domestic issues in terms of "primitive self-interest" (p. 205) and "fairly concrete and short-term group interest" (p. 223), rather than ideologically. Neither work, however, actually assessed the effects of self-interest directly.

Others have demonstrated that fluctuations in the strength of the economy explain over-time changes in electoral outcomes fairly well (Kramer 1971; Tufte 1978; Monroe 1979). Their quite plausible interpretation was that individuals were "voting their pocketbooks." Yet this inference of individually self-interested behavior from a pattern of collectively rational aggregate behavior is purely speculative in the absence of individual-level evidence.

Our own research has tested the hypothesis that the individual's self-interest determines his or her policy and candidate preferences. In defining self-interest, we wished to use terms that corresponded to the common-sense, man-in-the-street understanding, and to its usage in intellectual history. We also wanted the definition to be sufficiently restrictive that the self-interest hypothesis would be both verifiable and falsifiable. As a result, we have defined self-interest as the (1) short-to-medium term impact of an issue (or candidacy) on the (2) material well-being of the (3) individual's own personal life (or that of his or her immediate family).

This definition excludes several other possibilities that we feel fall outside the normal connotations of the term and would make its effects much more difficult to assess, such as (1) long-term self-interest, (2) nonmaterial aspects of well-being (e.g., spiritual contentment, self-esteem, social adjustment, social status, or feelings of moral righteousness), and (3) interests that affect the well-being of the individual's group but not that of the specific individual (for a similar definitional analysis, see Barry 1965, chap. 10).

Virtually all of our research has used large-scale public opinion surveys, with national or statewide samples, or in some cases local surveys conducted in Los Angeles County or the city of Los Angeles. Our specific measures of self-interest have varied along two dimensions: retrospective (e.g., having recently lost one's job) versus prospective (e.g., expectations of a tax cut), and objective (the researcher's assessment of the individual's self-interest, e.g., having children in public schools gives one an interest in school funding) versus subjective (e.g., perceiving that one's own finances have been deteriorating gives one an interest in dismissing political incumbents). Contrary to the practice of many researchers, we ordinarily do not regard standard demographic measures as adequate indicators of self-interest, choosing rather to use more proximal measures of the personal impact of an issue on the individual.

Any cross-sectional study poses problems of causal inference. First, we have assumed that any significant correlation of self-interest and policy and/or candidate preference would reflect the causal role of self-interest. This assumption has not been very controversial. Second, most of our research has contrasted the effects of self-interest with those of a small set of "symbolic predispositions," typically, party identification, self-description as a "liberal" or "conservative," and racial tolerance. The importance of this contrast lies in our theory of "symbolic politics," in which political symbols evoke longstanding affective responses rather than rational self-interested calculations (Sears 1975, 1983). These affective responses are presumed to be the residues of earlier-life socialization (not necessarily preadult), which are evoked by relevant political symbols. For example, party identification is likely to be elicited by a partisan election, and racial tolerance by a busing controversy. We selected these particular predispositions because they can be shown to have been relatively stable through most individuals' adult life spans, and so are unlikely to be substantially influenced by the individual's short-term material self-interest in adulthood.

We have used several statistical criteria for assessing the effects of self-interest. A convenient starting point is to ask whether the self-interest index correlates to a statistically significant degree ($p < .05$, two-tailed test) with the political attitude in question. However, because a relatively weak correlation can meet that minimal criterion in large survey samples, we also consider the absolute size of the correlation. From regression equations including self-interest and symbolic predispositions as predictors, we consider the statistical significance and the absolute size of the regression coefficients, as well as the variance explained by the self-interest indicators (taken as a set, or compared to that explained by the relevant symbolic predispositions).

The Minimal Effects of Self-Interest

The results of all our studies are tabulated in table 9.1. The table shows, for each study, the type of self-interest (e.g., "vulnerability to busing"), the number of self-interest measures used, the political attitude that serves as the dependent variable (e.g., "opposition to busing"), the sample area, and the date of survey. It then presents, in order, three statistical indicators: the mean bivariate correlation between self-interest and dependent variables; the proportion of self-interest measures that yielded statistically significant regression coefficients; and the mean standardized regression coefficient for the self-interest terms.[1] The other indicators are referred to in the text. These analyses were taken from previous research reports, rather than being conducted anew for this paper, so the procedures vary somewhat from study to study.

Racial Issues

Our research on the self-interest hypothesis began as an incidental by-product of our work on whites' political resistance to racial change. As the civil rights struggle shifted from the Deep South to the North and West in the late 1960s, one popular hypothesis was that racial threats had finally come to northern whites' doorsteps, thus evoking a self-interested "white backlash." We first tested this thesis in 1969 and 1973 surveys in nearly all-white suburbs of Los Angeles, when the white mayor, Sam Yorty, was challenged by a black city councilman, Tom Bradley. We measured personal racial threat to the respondents' private lives (i.e., self-interest) by asking people how they perceived (1) the dangers from desegregation of their neighborhood; (2) the economic threat they personally felt from blacks; (3) the threat of racial busing to their family; and (4) the fear of personal victimization by black crime. We also asked a series of questions about racial intolerance, which we summed into an index of "symbolic racism" (Sears and Kinder 1971; Kinder and Sears 1981).

Preference for the white candidate was strongly predicted by symbolic racism, and scarcely at all by racial threat. As entry 1 in table 9.1 shows, only 2 of the 18 regression coefficients for racial threat (11 percent) were significant, and their average was a nonsignificant +.04. In contrast, symbolic racism had highly significant effects, accounting for 22.3 percent and 15.3 percent of the variance in candidate preference in the two years.

We then conducted a series of studies focused specifically on whites' opposition to busing. Whites were regarded as self-interested in busing if they had children in the public schools, lived in districts with busing happening or threatened, or lived in all-white neighborhoods. In two national studies, only one of ten self-interested regression coefficients was significant—they averaged just .00 (see entries 2 and 3)—and the self-interest

Table 9.1   Effects of Self-Interest on Public Opinion

Self-Interest	Dependent Variable		Survey			Correlation		Regression			
								Betas: Net Percent Significant	Betas: Mean	No. Tests	
Type	No. Items	Type	No. Items	Sample	Year	Mean	Type*				Source
Racial issues											
1. Racial threat	20	Oppose black mayoral candidate	1	Los Angeles suburbs[a]	1969, 1973	+.21[b]	1	11.1	+.04	(18)	Kinder & Sears 1981
Neighborhood integration	5					+.41[b]	1	0.0	+.06	(5)	
Economic competition	6					+.21[b]	1	25.0	+.02	(4)	
Racial busing	5					+.05[b]	1	0.0	−.01	(5)	
Black violence	4					+.26[b]	1	25.0	+.09	(4)	
2. Vulnerability to busing	5	Opposition to busing	2	national[a]	1972	+.01	4	16.7	+.02	(6)	Sears, Hensler, & Speer 1979
3. Vulnerability to busing	5	Opposition to busing	1	national[a]	1976	NA	4	0.0	−.02	(4)	Sears et al. 1980
4. Vulnerability to busing	24	Opposition to busing	14	national, Calif., Los Angeles[a]	1964–1979	NA	4	21.1	+.03	(52)	Sears & Allen 1984
5. Vulnerability to bilingual education; bilingualism	9	Opposition to bilingual education	7	national[c]	1983	+.02	1	0.0	+.01	(8)	Huddy & Sears 1989
General economic issues											
6. Declining personal finances	2	Presidential performance	3	national	1983	+.04	NA	NA	NA	(6)	Sears & Lau 1983
7. Declining personal finances and vulnerability to inflation	2	Opposition to taxes and spending	18	California	1979	NA	1	0.0	.00	(10)	Sears & Citrin 1985

(Table 9.1—continued)

8. Vulnerability to inflation	2	Presidential performance	4	national	1983	−.03	4	NA	NA	(4) Sears & Lau 1983
Employment										
9. Employment problems	6	Government guaranteed employment	2	national	1976	NA	1	33.3	+.02	(3) Sears et al. 1980
10. Employment problems	4	Guaranteed jobs, presidential performance	5	national	1983	+.04	NA	NA	NA	(8) Sears & Lau 1983
11. Women's role in the workplace	3	Gender equality and feminism	5	national	1984	NA	3	16.7	NA	(6) Sears & Huddy 1990
Energy										
12. Personal impact of energy crisis	4	Proadministration policy support	8	Los Angeles County	1974	NA	3	0.0	.00	(2) Sears et al. 1978
Service recipients										
13. Poor health insurance	3	Support for national health insurance	1	national	1976	NA	1	66.7	+.08	(3) Sears et al. 1980
14. Service recipience	13	Support for taxes and spending	18	California	1979	NA	1	25.0	+.03	(20) Sears & Citrin 1985
15. Service recipience	4	Opposition to Prop. 2½	2	Massachusetts	1980, 1981	NA	4	25.0	+.03	(4) Lau, Coulam, & Sears 1983
16. Women's economic disadvantage	5	Support for women's issues	3	national	1984	NA	3	20.0	NA	(10) Sears & Huddy 1990
Taxes										
17. Federal tax burden	5	Support for tax cuts	4	national	1983	+.10	NA	NA	NA	(16) Sears & Lau 1983
18. State and local tax burden	2	Opposition to taxes and spending	18	California	1979	NA	1	90.0	+.15	(10) Sears & Citrin 1985
19. State and local tax burden	4	Support for Prop. 2½	2	Massachusetts	1980, 1981	NA	4	50.0	+.12	(4) Lau, Coulam, & Sears 1983

Public employment										
20. Public employees	1	Support for taxes and spending	18	California	1979	NA	1	60.0	+.09	(5) Sears & Citrin 1985
21. Public employees	2	Opposition to Prop. 2½	2	Massachusetts	1980, 1981	NA	4	100.0	+.14	(2) Lau, Coulam, & Sears 1983
Crime										
22. Vulnerability to crime	6	Support for law and order policies	5	national	1976	NA	4	33.3	+.03	(3) Sears et al. 1980
War										
23. Relatives and friends in Vietnam service	6	Opposition to Vietnam War	3	national	1968	+.04[d]	3	16.7	+.04	(6) Lau, Brown, & Sears 1978
24. Vulnerability to military draft	7	Opposition to draft; support detente	11	UCLA students	1980	-.08	2	-20.0	-.05	(10) Sears et al. 1983
25. Concern about likely war	3	Opposition to draft; support detente	11	UCLA students	1980	+.20	2	50.0	+.19	(2) Sears et al. 1983
Total	147		168			+.07		22.8	+.04 (188)	

Note: The number of items shown is prior to the development of composite scales. Correlation is Pearson *r* unless otherwise specified. Regression type included only self-interest terms, where possible (type 1); otherwise they included self-interest and some demographics (type 2); self-interest and symbolic predispositions, typically ideology, party identification, and racial attitudes (type 3); or all three (type 4). The standardized regression coefficient (beta) is shown. Net percentage significant is the percentage significant (at least *p* < .05 two-tailed) in the predicted direction minus the percentage significant in the opposite direction.

a. Whites only.
b. Gamma.
c. Non-Hispanics only.
d. Tau – c.

variables did not show any additive or interactive effects (Sears, Hensler, and Speer 1979; Sears et al. 1980). In a later study, eight surveys on busing yielded 24 self-interest coefficients, which averaged +.03 (Sears and Allen 1984; entry 4). Racial intolerance dominated self-interest in all three studies, yielding highly significant regression coefficients of .39 and .31 in the first two, and an average correlation of .26 in the third.

Others who have tested the self-interest hypothesis concerning busing have obtained much the same result (e.g., Bobo 1983, using national data; McConahay 1982, in Louisville; McClendon and Pestello 1983, in Akron; and Gatlin, Giles, and Cataldo 1978, in Florida). Similarly, Kluegel and Smith (1983) and Jessor (1988) have found that whites' self-interest in affirmative action (e.g., perceived personal competition for jobs with blacks) has little effect on attitudes toward racial policies, which instead are best explained by more general attitudes of racial intolerance. Similarly, Anglos' opposition to bilingual education seems to be governed more by racial attitudes than by personal experience with it (indeed those with children in such programs are the most supportive of it; Huddy and Sears 1989; entry 5). These studies of racial issues, then, have almost uniformly yielded little support for the self-interest hypothesis that racial threats to whites' private lives affect their stances on racial policies, and equally uniformly have yielded strong effects of racial intolerance.

Economic Issues

It might be argued that racial conflicts have a complex, profoundly emotional quality that mask or at least complicate the effects of self-interest. Economic issues might therefore be regarded as more appropriate venues for the occurrence of self-interest. Our research in this line began with attitudes toward government-guaranteed full employment and national health insurance (Sears et al. 1980). As entries 9 and 13 in table 9.1 indicate, the self-interest indicators yielded rather small regression coefficients, averaging +.05, although half of them were statistically significant. Green (1988) reports similarly weak self-interest effects on these two issues. Another study focusing on unemployment, inflation, and presidential economic performance yielded eighteen correlations with self-interest, averaging +.02 (Sears and Lau 1983; entries 6, 8, 10, 17). We also found that the personal impact of the 1973–74 energy crisis had no effect whatever on individuals' political attitudes (Sears et al. 1978; entry 12).

A considerably more ambitious study (Sears and Citrin 1985; entries 7, 14, 18, 20) took advantage of three California ballot propositions in 1978–80 that offered, respectively, a massive property tax reduction (Proposition 13 in 1978), a cap on state spending (Proposition 4 in 1979), and a 50 percent reduction in state income taxes (Proposition 9 in 1980). These presented a unique opportunity to study political self-interest, since they offered individual taxpayers large and concrete economic benefits as well as dire threats to public services and public employment, with the intense and focused attention of hotly contested campaigns.

We identified four groups of self-interested respondents: "taxpayers" (those who were homeowners, felt burdened by heavy property and/or income taxes, expected large tax reductions from the propositions, or had high income), the economically discontented (those who had declining family finances or felt hurt by inflation), public employees, and the recipients of various government services. The dependent variables were attitudes toward the three ballot measures and toward size of government and spending on public services, estimates of waste in government, and perceptions of excessive wages for public employees.

The "taxpayers" held quite consistently self-interested political preferences, as shown in table 9.1, entry 18; we will return to this below. The economically discontented, who might have been expected to support tax and spending cuts, did not. Further analyses, not shown in the table, found no evidence for interactions between these types of economic discontent that might reflect "stagflation" (Sears and Citrin 1985:137–39). The public employees and recipients of government services were expected to defend the public sector out of self-interest, but showed only scattered support for it. The regression coefficients averaged +.03 for service recipients (entry 15) and +.09 for public employees (entry 20), though the latter yielded some significant effects to which we will return. Surveys done in Massachusetts before and after the vote on Proposition 2½, another major property-tax-cutting measure, yielded quite similar results in virtually all these respects (Lau, Coulam, and Sears 1983; entries 15, 19, 21).

The rise of the women's movement might have generated self-interested support from women for policy positions benefiting them. However, women have not generally supported women's issues more than have men (Shapiro and Mahajan 1986; Mansbridge 1985). Among women, support for women's issues, gender equality, and feminism and for candidates favorable to women (such as Mondale and Ferraro in 1984) might well have been rooted in special economic interests concerning children, marriage, and work. Our study did show that single mothers were especially supportive of government aid to women, and working women were especially supportive of gender equality (Sears and Huddy 1990; entries 11, 16). But for the most part women responded to these issues as symbolic ones. Feminism and abortion policy proved to be almost pure symbolic issues.

Finally, two studies have examined self-interest among the elderly in programs that do (Social Security and Medicare) or do not (education) especially benefit them. However, Huddy's (1989) literature review finds no greater support for Social Security or Medicare spending among the elderly, and Ponza et al. (1988) actually find less support among them (along with less support for spending on education). The latter also find no great age differences in support for transfer payments either to low-income older people or to (presumably younger) low-income families with children. In both studies, policy preferences are somewhat more closely linked to economic position among older people, but the effects are neither very strong nor very consistent.

In short, these several economic issues yielded somewhat more evidence for self-interested political attitudes than was the case for racial issues, but even here it is unusual.

Crime and War

We have also considered the effects of violence. Analysis of a 1976 national survey tested the hypothesis that support for "law and order" policies would be produced by such self-interest variables as recent victimization by crime and fear of walking in one's neighborhood at night (Sears et al. 1980; entry 22). All told, self-interest explained only 0.4 percent of the variance (compared to 17.1 percent for the usual three symbolic predispositions). Crime would seem to be more a symbolic than a personal issue in politics.

A major source of self-interest in war is vulnerability to combat. However, we found little evidence that those with friends and relatives serving in Vietnam were most opposed to the war there (Lau, Brown, and Sears 1979, entry 23; Mueller 1973 reports similar findings). Moreover, among a representative sample of UCLA undergraduates, in a study conducted during the 1980 confrontations with the USSR over Afghanistan, vulnerability to the draft did not produce increased opposition to registration, draft, or military action toward the Soviet Union (Sears et al. 1983; entry 24). While one possible measure of self-interest, the perceived likelihood of war, was associated with antiwar and antidraft preferences, this proved one of the rare cases in which controls for symbolic predispositions completely eliminated any trace of a self-interest effect.

Pocketbook Voting

Other researchers have focused on the "pocketbook voting" hypothesis that presidential and congressional voting is responsive to the voter's own financial situation. As indicated earlier, Kramer (1971) demonstrated that as aggregate economic indicators go up, so does the incumbent's vote share. His interpretation of this finding as reflecting self-interest was, however, challenged by Kinder and Kiewiet (1979, 1981), who found that people's judgments about how well the nation was doing economically explained their congressional voting better than did their personal finances or employment status.

These findings have led to considerable subsequent research. Correlations between perceived personal finances and presidential vote in all seven National Election Studies (NES) surveys from 1956 to 1980 provide the strongest support for pocketbook voting (Kiewiet 1983).[2] However, personal finances have not related significantly to voting in other contexts. Kiewiet (1983) found that only 7 percent (2 of 26) of the coefficients regressing congressional vote on personal finances were significant. Scattered studies of senatorial and gubernatorial voting in the United States, and of parliamentary voting in Great Britain, West Germany, France, and Italy, yield the same conclusion (Kiewiet and Rivers 1984; Lewis-Beck 1986).

The best study of the effects of unemployment on voting is again Kiewiet's (1983), using the NES series: unemployment was associated with more Democratic voting in 30 of the 36 cases, though the effect was statistically significant in only 20 percent of these instances. Schlozman and Verba's (1979:318) careful examination of the effects of unemployment in the mid-1970s also found a slight (4 percent) shading to the Democrats among the unemployed. On the other hand, other studies have failed to find significant effects on political attitudes of either unemployment or the personal impact of recessions (Feldman 1984; Kinder and Mebane 1983). In sum, unemployment seems consistently to produce a slight tilt toward the Democratic side, particularly in presidential elections.

The personal impact of inflation seems to have had an even weaker political effect. Kiewiet (1983) found that people who said inflation was their most serious personal problem voted significantly more Republican (as predicted), but in only one of five surveys. A number of studies have found no significant political effects of feeling hurt by inflation on presidential job approval or inflation policy (Lau and Sears 1981), support for tax and spending cuts (Sears and Citrin 1985), and judgments of the national severity of inflation (Conover, Feldman, and Knight 1986, 1987).

In most cases, then, these measures of pocketbook motivation do not relate significantly to people's voting behavior. The only real dispute is over the strength of the link to presidential vote. We would agree with Feldman (1984:248), who concludes that "the accumulated evidence very strongly suggests that vote choice and presidential evaluations are at best modestly influenced by *personal* economic considerations."[3]

Information

Economic theories assume that perfect rationality occurs only under conditions of perfect information. That might lead us to expect that self-interest would have stronger effects among the better informed. But available research does not support that view. Sears et al. (1980) found that the better informed were actually the least self-interested in three of four issue areas, but the differences were trivial. Similarly, among better-informed college students, vulnerability to the military draft was associated with greater support for it (Sears et al. 1983). Weatherford (1983) and Conover, Feldman, and Knight (1986, 1987) tested the opposite hypothesis, that the poorly informed would be more self-interested because they could not look beyond the narrow confines of their own personal experiences. But they did not find evaluations of government performance to be any more self-interested among the less informed.

None of these political issues seems, on the surface at least, to be any more or less complex than is usual for mass politics in this country. Given extreme and unusual complexity, information may be more important. Green (1988) investigated attitudes toward a ballot proposition in California limiting rent control which was so confusing (and perhaps even deceptive) that many mistakenly voted against their own real preferences. In this case, renters (the interested parties) voted their own interests considerably more if correctly informed. Aside from this unusual case, greater political information seems not to boost the strength of self-interest very much.

Summary

Clearly averaging over these quite heterogeneous studies cannot be meaningful in any rigorous sense, but a summary statement can perhaps convey a crude approximation of the overall pattern. As shown in table 9.1, we find in our own work that only about 20 to 25 percent of the self-interest terms meet the minimal standard of statistical significance. The average bivariate correlation of +.07 and regression coefficient of +.04 reflect only minor explanatory contributions.

Since ours is a large sample of tests, it is not surprising that the other studies discussed in this section using the same general paradigm have obtained similar findings. Even Kiewiet's (1983) analyses of personal finances and unemployment as determinants of presidential vote yielded minimally significant self-interest terms at about this same rate. Green's (1988) extensive and important new set of studies fits this pattern as well. We would conclude, therefore, that self-interest generally has not been of major importance in explaining the U.S. public's political preferences.

It is possible that even these minimal effects may be exaggerated somewhat. Specifically, some significant findings in the literature may have resulted from item-order artifacts rather than genuine self-interest. An experiment varying the proximity of self-interest to political attitude items induced artificial self-interest effects at high levels of proximity (Sears and Lau 1983). In the National Election Studies series, "pocketbook voting" findings, based on perceived personal finances, have tended to be strongest when the interview schedules presented just such proximal item orderings (though the strength of such artifacts in existing data probably cannot be definitively established; see Sears and Lau 1983; Lewis-Beck 1985; Lau, Sears, and Jessor 1989).

When Does Self-Interest Work?

There are always exceptions to any general principle in the behavioral sciences, and the exceptions usually clarify the principle itself. In our research there have been four cases in which virtually every indicator of self-interest had a statistically significant effect on virtually every relevant dependent variable. What general principles can we extract from these successes, and the more numerous failures, about the necessary conditions for self-interest effects?

Clear, Substantial Costs and Benefits

The strongest and most consistent self-interest effects have been associated with paying taxes. Feeling especially burdened by state and local taxes, and homeownership, and expecting large dollar savings were all substantially related to support for the tax-cutting ballot propositions (Sears and Citrin 1985; Lau, Coulam, and Sears 1983). These self-interest effects were consistent, statistically significant, and of unaccustomed magnitude, as table 9.1 shows. Similar findings have been reported by Hawthorne and Jackson (1987) on support for the tax cuts in the 1978 Tax Revenue Act, on support for the federal tax cuts proposed just prior to the Reagan administration (Lau and Sears 1981), and on acceptance of tax cheating in Norway (Listhaug and Miller 1985). These represent fairly robust and consistent effects of self-interest on political preferences.

Why does self-interest work in these cases? Apparently partly because of the unusual clarity of the personal stakes. This has been shown in several experiments varying the personal tax increases presented as the cost of a particular policy proposal (Green 1988). Greater proposed personal tax increases ($5 versus $50 annually) significantly diminished support for providing shelter for the homeless (from 86 percent to 75 percent) and for building a subway in Los Angeles (from 51 percent to 29 percent). Similar findings emerged from experiments on a ballot proposition designed to clean up California's waterways and on a proposed increase in cigarette taxes (and opposition to the latter was greatest among low-income smokers). Such advertised tax costs did not invariably have a strong effect; they did not affect support for bilingual education, nor did the overall size of an environmental bond issue (as opposed to its personal tax cost) affect support for it (p. 176). Still, self-interest can sometimes be elicited when personal tax increases or reductions are highly salient.

The magnitude of the stakes would seem also to be an important factor. In the tax revolt cases, support for a tax cut was quite specifically linked both to the burden of that particular tax on the individual and to the size of the proposed reduction in his or her own taxes (Sears and Citrin 1985). The dollar benefits to the individual in that case were substantial in absolute terms. We would also speculate that a further helpful condition was that the political remedy was certain—a constitutional amendment that would lock in a reduction in tax assessments and a cap on tax rates.

Ambiguous Severe Threats

In two other cases, threats that were both severe and ambiguous seem to have motivated self-interested political preferences. In both California and Massachusetts, public employees were substantially more opposed to the tax and spending reduction referenda than were other voters. Averaging across eleven different comparisons, public employees were more opposed than other respondents to the three referenda in California by an impressive 24 percent (Sears and Citrin 1985). Similarly, Lau, Coulam, and Sears (1983) found that public employees were more opposed to Proposition 2½ in Massachusetts, both before and after its passage. In both cases the effects held up with all other variables controlled. Public employees' opposition seems to have been based on their desire to prevent job and pay cuts. Their opposition to the spending-cap referendum was correlated with their perceptions that it would cut the number of public employees or their wages ($r = .24$), which was not the case for other citizens ($r = .02$). Green (1988:237) reports similar findings for their opposition to the later income-tax-cutting proposition.

Another set of ambiguous but severe threats seems to have stimulated the operation of self-interest in one particular phase of busing controversies. Surveys of whites in Los Angeles done after a court order mandating school desegregation, but before implementation, found a substantial self-interest basis for whites' opposition to busing (all ten regression coefficients were significant, averaging + .13). However, surveys done prior to any publicity about busing in the community, or after implementation of the court order, yielded the usual crop of generally nonsignificant self-interest effects (only 17 percent of the regression coefficients were significant, averaging + .03; see Sears and Allen 1984; other smaller-sample studies done prior to the court order also obtained nonsignificant results: see Caditz 1976, and Kinder and Sears 1981).

We would speculate that self-interest emerged in these cases because of the combination of uncertainty and severe negative possibilities. The uncertainty, we suspect, allowed for the most threatening sorts of fantasies about one's own possible fate; the imagined threats could reach extraordinary peaks, helped along by the far-ranging rumors that gain circulation in a time of uncertainty and ignorance. All this was no doubt exacerbated in the busing case by the low levels of real contact and reality testing most white Americans have with blacks, and by the fantasies regarding blacks that lurk just below the surface of many white Americans' psyches.

Another example that is perhaps only superficially different has been provided by Green (1988). He has shown that smokers (especially heavy smokers) are considerably more opposed than nonsmokers to bans on smoking in public places and to increases in the cigarette tax. The uncertainties and terrors of cigarette deprivation may seem less cosmic than in the previous examples to readers who have never smoked, but perhaps not to those who are now or have in the past been heavy smokers.

Politicizing Self-Interest

A third category of exceptions consists of events that politicize self-interest. In our research we have but one example, and that arguable: the apparent politicization of economic self-interest by Ronald Reagan over the course of his presidency.

Over the 1956–80 period, there were only modest, marginally significant effects of personal finances on presidential voting in the National Election Studies, as indicated above. By our count (Lau, Sears, and Jessor 1989), the mean correlation of personal finances with vote intention was $+.12$, and with actual vote, $+.11$; the regression coefficients were $+.08$ in each case. In 1980 President Reagan quite explicitly asked Americans to vote on the basis of self-interest: "ask yourself . . . , are you better off today than you were four years ago?" But this explicit appeal to self-interest apparently became salient too late in the 1980 campaign to evoke widespread self-interested voting. Overall, perceived personal finances and presidential vote were only weakly associated ($r = +.08$), and Reagan did not seem to attract more new support toward the end of the campaign from those whose personal finances had been declining (Sears and Lau 1983).

By 1984, the same plea for a self-interested vote was the centerpiece of his presidency and campaign for reelection. The association of personal finances with presidential preference showed a startling increase: the raw correlations jumped to .36 and .33, respectively, and the regression coefficients to .19 and .18. This reflects an increase in the strength of self-interest over his first four-year term of some considerable magnitude. Nevertheless, the fact that self-interest so rarely has a strong and systematic effect suggests that political events and campaigns rarely are successful in mobilizing it, even when they try.

The Narrowness of Self-Interest Effects

The evidence up to this point is that self-interest generally has quite weak effects on political preferences, and that symbolic predispositions have much stronger and indeed overriding effects. Many materialist theorists have suggested that ideology, party preferences, and racial prejudice are themselves mere creatures of real economic interests, as in the class basis of parties in the United Kingdom, Chile, or Italy, or in group conflict analyses of racial prejudice (Bobo 1988; Campbell 1965; Lipset 1981). Self-interest could therefore indirectly influence policy and candidate preferences by shaping more general ideological or partisan preferences.

This indirect influence does not seem likely to be very strong, for several reasons. The many unsuccessful attempts to find cognitively broad ideologies in most Americans (Converse 1964; Kinder and Sears 1985) should make us doubtful that self-interest motivates broad ideological points of view. Moreover, there is fairly good evidence that the affective preferences we have described as symbolic predispositions tend to crystallize and stabilize by the end of early adulthood (though they are scarcely invariant), and so should not be especially susceptible to the vagaries of adult material interests. Nevertheless, it is worth considering the possibility, given the popularity of the theory. As will be seen, even when self-interest has significant effects on policy preferences, they usually prove to be cognitively quite narrow.

Self-Interest and Symbolic Predispositions

To start with, symbolic predispositions are in most instances almost wholly uncorrelated with self-interest. Two examples make the point. Our study of the origins of four policy attitudes (Sears et al. 1980) generated twenty-nine correlations between self-interest indexes and the usual three symbolic predispositions. The largest was .11, and the median a nonsignificant .05. Even our study of the California tax revolt, which yielded several significant self-interest effects, produced similarly null results. We regressed the same set of three symbolic predispositions on our seven basic self-interest indicators, but only 19 percent of the resulting self-interest terms were statistically significant (Sears and Citrin 1985). Both results are typical of our other studies.

Four Specific Cases

But it turns out that self-interest has even narrower cognitive implications, as a review of our several significant effects reveals. First, the public employees' self-interested opposition to the tax revolt extended no further than a narrow defense of their own jobs and salaries. We analyzed their support for the public sector and for the moderate political Left across eleven questions that did not mention the ballot propositions themselves, ranging from the quite general (political ideology and party identification) to the more concrete (desired size of government, levels of spending on public services, or imposition of tuition at public universities). Public employees supported the public sector significantly more than other respondents on just one question: whether or not they thought government workers were overpaid (Sears and Citrin 1985: 156). Similarly, Listhaug and Miller (1985) found that public employees in Norway did not oppose tax evasion any more than did other citizens. In short, public employees were willing to defend their own salaries and jobs, but demonstrated no more general support for the public sector.

During the tax revolt, service recipients did display some self-interested defense of the specific programs from which they personally benefited; for example, people with children in the public schools showed some special support for spending on the schools (Sears and Citrin 1985). But this self-interested thinking was both weak and narrow. These regression coefficients ranged only from + .06 to + .09, and were far outstripped by the effects of symbolic predispositions. The service recipients did not support spending on other domestic programs, nor oppose general tax and spending cuts or otherwise support the public sector more than other respondents. These modest and narrow effects parallel those obtained by Cataldo and Holm (1983) among public school parents on school bond voting.

Third, further analysis of college students' attitudes toward military registration and the draft turned up two limited significant self-interest effects. About twice as many students twenty-one and older were in favor of restricting the draft to eighteen- to twenty-year-olds as were students under twenty-one. Similarly, student deferments were supported by half again as many freshman males, who presumably could benefit from them, as by senior males, who could not. But the younger and older students differed only on these explicitly age-related questions; they did not differ in general support for registration, draft, or military intervention.

Taxpayers again provide one partial exception. The heavily tax-burdened (objectively or subjectively) were markedly more anti–public sector (in opposing service spending, perceiving large amounts of waste in government, and so on) than were others (Sears and Citrin 1985). Being burdened by one kind of tax also transferred to support for cuts in other kinds of taxes; for example, home owners, especially those whose property taxes had been significantly cut by Proposition 13, continued to give unusually high levels of support to the income-tax cuts proposed by Proposition 9 (holding income level constant).

The taxpayers stand out as the sole exception, however. The self-interest effects uncovered in other areas turn out not only to be rather small in absolute terms, or unreliable, but also when present, to be quite specific to the policies most narrowly linked to the self-interest dimension in question. The effects of self-interest usually extend neither to other related policy issues nor to more general policy or ideological questions.

Can Broad Self-Interest Effects Be Induced?

If self-interest effects can be generated by politicizing personal experience (as in the Reagan presidency) or by personalizing political issues (as in our item-order experiment), can they also be made cognitively broader than usual? It would seem to be difficult to do so. Our item proximity experiment did induce several apparent self-interest effects, but they prove to be as narrow and specific as those just described (Sears and Lau 1983). In one case questions about personal financial situations were closely followed by questions on presidential performance. Some self-interest effects were induced, but they were quite specific, occurring only when the time perspective (past versus future) and dimension of performance (economic versus overall) exactly matched. Similarly, item proximity increased the correlation of perceived federal tax burden to closely matching attitudes toward federal tax policy, but not to the more distant association of perceived state/local tax burden with those same federal tax policy items (even those proposing major tax cuts). In short, it would appear that not only are self-interest effects rare, and when they do appear, quite narrow and specific, but attempts to induce them may be successful only in a quite narrow and specific arena.

Why Doesn't Self-Interest Usually Work?

What are the main reasons that self-interest doesn't usually have a major or significant effect on U.S. public opinion? Let us offer two general possibilities.

The Stakes Are Usually Neither Large Nor Clear

One reason, perhaps, is that the stakes are usually small and obscure. Ordinary people simply do not often perceive government as offering them very clear or substantial personal costs or benefits. The California tax revolt would seem to be a splendid exception: local newspapers, for example, ran preelection tables displaying exactly what property or income-tax reductions voters would get if the relevant ballot propositions passed. And the absolute magnitudes of those benefits were impressive.

In contrast, large changes in national economic conditions, such as in the inflation or unemployment rates, may have unpredictable and even mixed effects on individuals, as Kiewiet (1983) has pointed out. The personal costs of unemployment may be intense, but they are concentrated in relatively small groups of disproportionately lower-income and occupational groups, which are both a small subset of the electorate and for other reasons among its least politically active. The immediate short-term costs of inflation to any given individual are difficult to establish. Prices go up, but for some, wages and/or the value of their real property go up much more, so short-term losses may be overshadowed by longer-term gains. And, as Barry (1970/1978) has suggested, when the costs of political actions (or attitudes) are minimal, other motives may take over.

Attributions of Government Responsibility

Personal well-being does fluctuate a good bit, and varies from one person to the next. How much the government is responsible for this variance is not a matter that economists, politicians, or political scientists usually agree on, much less ordinary citizens. An "almost ubiquitous" assumption in the literature on self-interest (Kiewiet and Rivers 1984: 381) is that self-interest will affect political preference only when individuals attribute responsibility for their well-being to the government.

People rarely see government as responsible for their own personal well-being, either for its present state or future prospects. People usually explain why their family's finances have improved or declined in personal (or "privatistic") rather than societal (or "collectivist") terms (Feldman 1982; Kinder and Mebane 1983). Lane observed a number of years ago that Americans "morselize" their personal experiences: "a union demand is a single incident, not part of a more general labor-management conflict; a purchase on the installment plan is a specific debt, not part of a budgetary pattern—either one's own or society's. The items and fragments of life remain itemized and fragmented" (1962: 353). Similarly, Schlozman and Verba (1979) found that the unemployed tend to perceive their unemployment as caused by individual, proximal circumstances, rather than seeing the society at large, or government, as responsible. And Brody and Sniderman (1977) found that people rarely feel government should help them with their personal problems, even the economic ones.

Does self-interest then affect political preferences only in that small subset of individuals who perceive government or society at large as responsible for their personal problems? Feldman (1982) found that perceived family finances affected political attitudes only among those who attributed trends in their own finances to societal, as opposed to personal, causes. Other studies have obtained either similar but not statistically significant differences (Lau and Sears 1981; Kinder and Mebane 1983), or no differences at all (Sears et al. 1980). The evidence seems mixed but mildly supportive of this hypothesis.

Another approach to the same hypothesis has been to look at events that can be unequivocally attributed to government. Some of these have yielded strong self-interest effects: successful tax-cutting propositions ensure that the government cuts taxes (Sears and Citrin 1985; Lau, Coulam, and Sears 1983), and governments are clearly the cause of busing children to racially mixed schools (Sears and Allen 1984). However, other events with unequivocal government responsibility have not produced positive self-interest effects, such as inflation (which is widely perceived as strongly governmentally influenced; see Kiewiet 1983), the Reagan budget and tax cuts, or the 1982 recession (Feldman 1984; Sears and Citrin 1985; Sears and Lau 1983; Conover, Feldman, and Knight 1986, 1987; Kiewiet 1983). In short, the attribution of government responsibility sometimes fosters self-interest effects, and sometimes does not. This attribution may be a necessary but insufficient condition for political self-interest effects.[4]

Americans appear to have a bias toward making internal attributions, that is, toward explaining behavior and events through causes internal to individuals such as motives, ability, personality, or attitudes, rather than through such external causes as social pressure, luck, the difficulties presented by external realities, society—or government. This bias has been described by Langer (1975) as "the illusion of control" and by Sniderman and Brody (1977) as "the ethic of self-reliance." A bias toward internality is often accompanied by the general view that it is a "just world" in which people get the outcomes they deserve (Lerner 1980). If people are responsible for their own outcomes, the rich deserve their wealth, the poor deserve poverty, and accident victims deserve their fates as well. There is clear evidence that Americans value this sense of internal control; for example, Jellison and Green (1981) showed that people most like others who believe in internal control.

This bias toward internality would seem to represent a considerable obstacle to the influence of self-interest on political opinions. If people are predisposed to view their own well-being as caused by their own actions, it will be difficult for them to comprehend the full impact of government actions on their lives and thus adopt rational self-interested preferences.

Critiques

It would perhaps be useful at this point to cite briefly, and respond to, the main criticisms of this research.

Measures and Definitions

One criticism is that it has relied too heavily on objective measures of self-interest, which may be insensitive to self-interest as the individual voter perceives it (e.g., Bobo 1983; Kiewiet 1983). It is true that most (about two-thirds) of our measures have been objective, partly because they yield less ambiguous causal inferences (it is quite unlikely that being a Democrat or Republican will affect one's being a man or having a child in school, but quite possible that it affects one's estimates of the likelihood of war or of personal finances).

However, in actuality, objective and subjective measures of self-interest have had very similar effects in this research whenever parallel measures have been available. Objective home ownership was as closely related to support for the California tax revolt as were subjective feelings of tax burden (Sears and Citrin 1985); neither subjective nor objective measures of vulnerability to busing have much influenced whites' opposition to it (Kinder and Sears 1981; Sears, Hensler, and Speer 1979; Sears et al. 1980); and the objective proportion of Hispanics in one's county increased opposition to bilingual education as much as did subjective estimates of the proportion of Hispanics in the neighborhood (Huddy and Sears 1989). Kiewiet (1983) actually found stronger effects of objective than of subjective measures of unemployment, contrary to his expectation. It is therefore difficult for us to see this as an adequate explanation for the lack of self-interest effects.

Second, our operational definitions of self-interest could be too broad, diluting self-interest by combining people with little real interest with the few genuinely interested parties. We have protected ourselves in most of these studies by examining refined combinations of self-interest variables and interaction effects, and occasionally have mentioned them above (though not exhaustively, for space reasons). In general they have not improved the case for self-interest.

On the other hand, our definition of self-interest may be too narrow. For one thing, political preferences may be influenced by long-term self-interest. For example, young workers' attitudes toward Social Security taxes may be influenced more by their desire for far-distant retirement benefits than by their current tax burdens. We have two responses. Even if that were the case, one would expect short-term self-interest to have a stronger political impact, because it is less remote, more emotionally evocative, and easier to calculate. Yet, as we have seen, short-run self-interest has had little effect. From a more pragmatic point of view, it is difficult to assess long-term self-interest. People's own perceptions of it would seem likely to be influenced by many variables other than self-interest, among them current partisan predispositions. So from a purely tactical point of view, it is not obvious how one could obtain unequivocal empirical tests of long-term self-interest.

Group Interest

Another possibility is that group interest, rather than self-interest, may have the real political clout. A number of sociopsychological theories bear on group interest, focusing variously on such phenomena as social identity, reference groups, group consciousness, or group conflict (see Conover 1987). The link to self-interest lies in the hypothesis that people are more likely to act politically in their own interests when acting collectively rather than individually. That is, self-interest alone may not be very potent, but it can be if linked to a sense of one's group's interests.

So far, most of the relevant empirical work has tested a realistic group-conflict hypothesis, that people's own interests are mobilized when their group is in competition with another group for scarce resources. This suggests that policy and candidate preferences promoting the group's interests have three determinants: perceptions that the two groups have real conflicts of interest; feelings of material interdependence with one's own group; and feelings of in-group solidarity (e.g., Bobo 1983, 1988). A competing view, described as a "symbolic politics" theory, focuses instead on learned antagonisms and prejudices against the rival group (Sears and Kinder 1985).

One pattern of data has emerged from studies of racial conflict in the United States. This pattern appears both in studies of whites' attitudes toward blacks and racial policies (Jessor 1988) and in studies of Anglos' attitudes toward Hispanics and bilingual education (Huddy and Sears 1989). In both cases there was strong evidence for the role of antiminority attitudes, consistent with the symbolic politics view. Promajority solidarity played no role. However, in both cases there was evidence for a limited effect of perceived group conflict. In the case of race, perceived material interdependence with the in-group proved irrelevant, but in the other, Anglos' perception that the education of "people like them" would suffer if special attention were given to Hispanic children contributed to opposition to bilingual education (Huddy and Sears 1989). This reflects limited support for the group-conflict model.

Two other studies focused on the elderly's interests in old-age policies and on women's interests in women's issues (Huddy 1989; Sears and Huddy 1990). Here there was little evidence of any role of antagonistic attitudes toward the rival groups (younger people and men, respectively), nor of any role for in-group solidarity or perceptions of intergroup conflict. But in both cases there was some polarization within the in-group according to economic interests, with less affluent older people and women being particularly supportive of special government aid to the elderly and women, respectively. In short, there is a little evidence that group interest has stronger effects than self-interest, but direct tests of its effects are still in their infancy.

Symbolic Politics

A final alternative is to adopt a wholly different, "symbolic politics," approach to these phenomena (e.g., Sears et al. 1980). At a number of points we have indicated that symbolic predispositions have considerably greater strength than does self-interest in determining policy and candidate preferences; for example, self-interest explained, on the average, 1.7 percent of the variance in policy preferences regarding jobs, health insurance, busing, and crime, whereas three symbolic predispositions explained an average of 14.0 percent, or about eight times as much (Sears et al. 1980). Similarly, Kiewiet (1983) found that party identification exceeded statistical significance in every single case, unlike self-interest, which did so less than a quarter of the time. Why do symbolic predispositions have a stronger effect?[5] We offer two general possibilities (though other plausible ones clearly exist).

Public Regardingness

The first possibility is that people may be socialized to respond to public issues in a principled and public-regarding manner. Perhaps political socialization teaches people to weigh most heavily the collective good when they don their "political hats," and to weigh their private good most heavily only when dealing with their personal affairs (Sears et al. 1980:681). If so, symbolic attitudes might express the adult's sense of the public good, and would be quite deliberately and self-consciously given more weight than private considerations in judgments about public policy. A conservative political ideology may simply reflect the belief that an ordered, predictable, and stable society is best for all, quite aside from one's own interests. This does not necessarily imply that the public-regarding view in question is a particularly noble one. One may wish to prevent the "mongrelization of the race" by voting for genocide, or to eliminate welfare because it simply rewards sloth. Nor would it necessarily rule out all forms of self-interest; for example, de Tocqueville felt that personal and national interests converged in enlightened self-interest.

If this were true, adults should vary in their degree of public regardingness, and self-interest should have a stronger effect among the more privatistic citizens (Wilson and Banfield 1971). One test of this hypothesis (Sears et al. 1980) yielded no such differences, but we would not regard this as a definitive test.

Reflexive Affective Responses to Political Symbols

A second possibility is that cognitive processes favor symbolic predispositions. Political attitudes may reflect mainly the emotions, or affects, previously conditioned to specific symbols. For example, attitudes toward "forced busing" to integrate whites and blacks would depend on affects toward such symbols as "force," "busing," "integration," and "blacks." Presumably this is partly due to the cognitive efficiencies produced by such simplifications. But it can serve political purposes as well. Politicians and journalists constantly condense complexity into simplified symbolic terms to induce constituent and audience concurrence. Moreover, they code political issues and events in familiar symbolic terms that will evoke widespread symbolic predispositions in the citizenry. To do this they use abstract symbols such as "welfare," "crime in the streets," "patriotic," "busing," "Watergate," or "Vietnam." In contrast, it is most difficult to code the rich complexity of private experience into simple symbolic terms. Individual experiences are perhaps too close, too emotionally evocative, to lend themselves to easy generalization. As a result, personal experience may, as Lane says, be "morselized," and so not coded semantically in terms that are readily triggered by political symbols.

If personal experience is morselized and political dialogue is coded into abstract terms, the two should tend to be cognitively compartmentalized. The personal and political worlds would simply be in different cognitive realms. Indeed, as we have seen, even the strongest self-interest motives usually have quite narrow effects on political attitudes. Insofar as people do connect private interests to public life, they make that connection in a highly specific way; no general belief systems connect the two realms, and personal experience rarely gets related to more general symbols.

In short, the dominance of symbolic predispositions may come about because of a general tendency toward reflexive affective responses to political symbols. Political symbols may come semantically coded in ways that make them easy to link to symbolic predispositions, but difficult to connect to the blooming and buzzing confusion that is our daily personal experience.

Conclusion

To summarize, self-interest ordinarily does not have much effect on the mass public's political attitudes. There are occasional exceptions, as when there are quite substantial and clear stakes (especially regarding personal tax burdens) or ambiguous and dangerous threats. But even these conditions only infrequently produce systematic and strong self-interest effects, and then, ones that are quite narrowly specific to the interest in question. The general public thinks about most political issues, most of the time, in a disinterested frame of mind.

10 Justice, Self-Interest, and the Legitimacy of Legal and Political Authority

Tom R. Tyler

Both legal and political authorities recognize that they cannot function effectively relying only on their ability to punish and reward members of the public. To at least some extent, people must willingly comply with the decisions of authorities, whether those authorities are local police officers and judges or national leaders like the president, congressmen, and justices of the Supreme Court.

Knowing that people who view authorities as legitimate are more likely voluntarily to obey their decisions, legal and political authorities have usually been concerned to maintain public support, that is, to maintain legitimacy in the eyes of the public, and to promote a widespread belief that their directives should be obeyed. Concerns about legitimacy lead authorities to be sensitive to any evidence of substantial, widespread dissatisfaction among their constituents.

Like those in positions of authority, social critics are also sensitive to evidence of public dissatisfaction. Their interest, however, is often in further undermining the legitimacy of existing authority and promoting noncompliance with existing rules. Such noncompliance creates political pressure to put new authorities in power, to change existing rules, and, in extreme cases, to change the basic structure of the legal and political systems.

Because public support is a key to the effective functioning of legal and political authorities, both existing authorities and their critics share an interest in understanding the basis on which people judge the legitimacy of authorities.[1] In this chapter I review a series of recent studies that explore this question. These studies contrast two perspectives on legitimacy.

One perspective sees people as evaluating legal and political leaders and institutions according to criteria of self-interest. This perspective, one version of the "public choice" perspective, extends the economic model of

The author thanks Robert MacCoun, Jane Mansbridge, and Susan Scott for comments on drafts of this chapter.

self-interested choice into the political arena. All traditional economic theories see people as acting consistently and in a way that maximizes whatever they value. Public choice versions of economic theory further assume that people seek to maximize their short-term material self-interest (see Laver 1981; Mueller 1979).[2] Public choice theories typically suggest that people's evaluations of legal and political authorities and their policies, as well as people's legal and political behavior, are governed by self-interest calculations (Laver 1981; Mueller 1979). People decide whether to obey the law by comparing the potential gains of disobedience to the potential costs of being caught and punished. They decide whether to vote by weighing the positive gains of voting against its costs. They decide who to vote for by deciding which candidates' policies will benefit them.[3]

A contrasting perspective sees people as evaluating legal and political authorities, and deciding how to act in law and politics, according to normative criteria. In this perspective, the legitimacy of an authority derives from citizens' views that the authority behaves fairly.

Judgements about both distributive and procedural justice can underlie justice-based evaluations and behavior. Judgments about distributive justice compare actual outcomes to a standard of fair or deserved outcomes. Judging a distribution unfair or undeserved generates feelings of relative deprivation (Crosby 1976, 1982) and inequity (Walster, Walster, and Berscheid 1978). Distributive justice theories suggest that even when people receive outcomes from the government that are not in their self-interest, they will not evaluate the government negatively if they feel that the outcomes are fair.

Judgments about procedural justice involve evaluations not of outcomes but of the procedures by which outcome distributions are made. For example, in the studies reported by Thibaut and Walker (1975), people whose cases were handled by the procedurally fairer adversary trial procedure were more satisfied with their trial experience, irrespective of the outcome of their case, than were those whose cases were handled through inquisitorial methods.[4]

I will call "justice models" models that look to conceptions of either procedural or distributive justice for explanations of evaluation and behavior. Justice models assume that individuals are motivated by a desire to receive fair outcomes, arrived at by using fair procedures, and that they evaluate their outcomes against such justice-based criteria as well as against their personal gain and loss. Accordingly, when people go to court, if their case is handled using procedures they view as fair and if they think the outcome is fair, they will evaluate the authorities and institutions they deal with positively, even if they lose.

To contrast the public choice and justice models, imagine a typical civil case—a divorce. Parties to a divorce might care about three different things. The first is winning and securing as many assets as possible for themselves. The second is getting a fair settlement, that is, "having things come out right." The third is having the case resolved through a procedure they view as fair. A fair procedure might include being allowed to participate in the settlement process, being allowed to present their side of the story, and being treated with respect. Public choice theories emphasize winning, theories of distributive justice emphasize fair settlements, and theories of procedural justice emphasize the resolution procedure.

These different models raise two empirical issues. First, are judgments of the justice or injustice of experiences or policies distinct from judgments about the personal gain or loss arising from them? Economic analysts have suggested that ethical judgments are no more than socially appropriate justifications for evaluations and behaviors actually governed by concerns of self-interest. If this is true, then empirical research will not be able to separate concerns about justice from judgments of personal gain and loss. If fairness judgments are only rationalizations for judgments based on outcome favorability, we should be able to predict individuals' fairness judgments by knowing whether or not they benefited from the outcome.

Second, do judgments about justice or injustice exert an influence on legal and political evaluations and behaviors independent of self-interest? People could conceivably distinguish between the justice or injustice of decisions and between policies and their personal consequences, but react to such decisions and policies solely or largely in terms of their personal consequences. The wealthy, for example, may see their own position of advantage as unfair, but may oppose social policies seeking to redistribute wealth because they want to keep their money. In such a case, justice judgments are distinct but unimportant, because the political action results from a judgment about personal gain and loss.[5]

My concern, and the concern of many other researchers in this field, is with the political impact of justice and self-interest judgments. We want to know how these judgments affect people's feelings about the legitimacy of legal and political authorities, and how they affect the way people act in courts and at the ballot box. We have paid less attention to personal satisfaction with outcomes. People who lose their cases in court may indeed be personally unhappy. We want to know, however, whether they translate that unhappiness into negative feelings about their lawyers, the judge, and the court system. When this happens, personal experience has a political impact.[6]

In the area of law, several studies have used these different models to examine peoples' reactions to their everyday dealings with police officers and judges. Some studies have examined the daily interactions between citizens and legal officials (Tyler, in press; Tyler and Folger 1980), others cases in the criminal courts (Tyler, Casper, and Fisher 1989) and civil courts (Lind et al. 1988; MacCoun 1988).

No matter which kind of experience with legal authorities researchers have studied, they have come up with the same results. Peoples' daily interactions with police officers and judges influence their views about the legitimacy of legal authorities, and those views on legitimacy change the degree to which people subsequently follow the law in their daily lives (Tyler, in press; Tyler, Casper, and Fisher 1989a). These studies also suggest that the impact of experience with police officers and judges on evaluations of their legitimacy is primarily determined by peoples' justice-based judgments. Outcome favorability has little or no influence on such evaluations.

The justice-based judgment that has the most effect is the judgment about fair procedures. How legitimate people think the police and judges they have encountered are depends primarily on whether they think their case was resolved using fair procedures. This is true when people have everyday dealings with the police and courts, when they are on trial for felonies, and when they are involved in civil suits.[7]

Studies of public views on the legitimacy of political authorities usually ask general questions about the decisions and policies of political authorities, not questions about personal experiences with those authorities. Surveys, for example, ask whether President Reagan's Social Security policy helps or hurts the respondent, is fair, and was formulated using fair procedures. Analysis of these kinds of general questions reveals that justice-based judgments, particularly about procedures, have more effect than self-interest both on evaluations of the Reagan administration and on views about the legitimacy of government institutions.[8] As with legal authorities, support for political authorities seems to be based primarily on the belief that authorities make decisions and determine policies in a fair way.[9]

Fairness judgments also affect vote choice. In the 1984 presidential election, for example, judgments about the fairness of the procedures by which the two presidential candidates (Mondale and Reagan) made public policy influenced voting choices independently of judgments about the potential benefits of those policies for the individual voter. Vote choice was also influenced by the concerns with economic self-interest which past studies of voting behavior have found important. Here procedural fairness judgments were one of several factors influencing behavior.[10]

These results suggest that issues of procedural justice are important in people's thinking about the legitimacy of legal and political authorities, as well as influencing their law-related and their political behavior. The importance people attach to feeling that decisions are made and policies established according to fair procedures emerges in studies of defendants in misdemeanor court (Tyler 1984, in press), citizen-police encounters (Tyler, in press; Tyler and Folger 1980), civil court cases (Lind et al. 1988; MacCoun 1988), and the political system (Rasinski and Tyler 1988; Tyler, Rasinski, and McGraw 1985). In all of these cases the people who appear in court or deal with the police are more likely to support those authorities and feel that they ought to obey them if they think that the procedures used in those experiences were fair. Americans seem to care a great deal about procedure (Bellah et al. 1985; Easton 1965; Schwartz 1978).

Because legitimacy has a procedural basis, legal authorities can deliver unfavorable outcomes to citizens without harming their legitimacy if those outcomes are delivered through procedures people view as fair. Authorities then have the discretion to act in ways that, although not in the short-term self-interest of citizens, may benefit those citizens in the long run.

In times of scarcity and crisis, for example, authorities have the greatest need of public support, but are least able to give citizens positive outcomes or alter behaviors with material incentives. But the authorities can require sacrifices from the public, and expect their decisions to be accepted, if they decide according to procedures the public views as fair. Authorities can gain public acceptance for their decisions more generally by designing rules that accord with public views on fairness.

Both procedural fairness and a preexisting "reservoir" of legitimacy will sustain authorities through a series of unfair actions, although repeated judgments of unfairness will drain away the reservoir of legitimacy, making it more difficult for the authority to function. A preexisting reservoir of legitimacy also helps authorities by framing the way people interpret their experience. Those with favorable prior views about authorities are more likely at any point to interpret a given experience as fair.

On the negative side, the procedural basis of legitimacy creates the possibility for authorities to exploit the public. They can do so by creating procedures that appear fair but are not. Procedures may encourage people to participate in decisions, for example, when the authorities do not intend to be influenced by citizen views.

Evaluations depend not only on fairness, but also on outcome favorability. In these studies, the small influence of outcomes on evaluations is typically indirect. People see outcomes favorable to themselves as fairer and as more likely to have been arrived at using fair procedures. Thus outcomes influence evaluations through their impact on fairness judgments. The effect of outcomes can be greater on behavior than on evaluations. With some types of behavior, outcomes are as important as fairness issues.

Since people attach such importance to procedural fairness, we must try to understand what they mean by fair procedure. Views about procedural fairness seem to be complex and multidimensional. When citizens deal with legal authorities, for example, several different aspects of procedure independently influence their judgments about whether or not the procedure is fair (Tyler 1988, 1989b).

First, people feel that procedures are fair when they believe they have had an opportunity to participate in the decision. Participation includes having an opportunity to present one's arguments, be listened to, and have one's views considered. Those who feel that they have participated in the decision are much more likely to accept its outcome, whether the outcome benefits them or not.[11] Procedures that allow both sides to state their arguments also expose each side to the other side of the case. Since people are often unaware of the feelings and concerns of the other party to a dispute, the exposure itself is important in generating acceptance of the outcome (Conley 1988).

Second, judgments of procedural fairness depend on judgments about the neutrality of the decision-making process. People believe that decisions should be made by neutral, unbiased, decision makers. They also expect those decision makers to be honest and to make their decisions based on objective information about the case.

Third, procedural fairness is related to interpersonal aspects of the decision-making procedure. People place great weight on being treated politely and having respect shown both for their rights and for themselves as people. When they deal with legal or political authorities, the character of those dealings reflects on their sense of themselves and their standing in the community. Respect from authorities has important implications for self-esteem (Lane 1986) and group identification (Lind and Tyler 1988). People are unlikely to feel attached to groups whose authorities treat them rudely or ignore their rights. The way public officials treat people also communicates information about the likelihood that those people will receive help if they have problems in the future. Hence, that treatment generates feelings of security or insecurity.

Fourth, assessments of procedural fairness are strongly linked to people's judgments about whether the authorities they are dealing with are "motivated" to be fair. Because deciding what motivates someone is even harder than deciding whether a person is honest or biased, we might expect people to avoid making motivational judgments. Instead, motivation seems central to assessments of procedural fairness. Perhaps people think that motives predict future behavior better than characteristics like honesty or bias (Heider 1958). If this is so, inferences about motives may have such a great effect on whether people think a procedure is fair because people want to know how authorities will act toward them in the future.

Finally, judgments of procedural fairness are linked to whether the procedures produce fair outcomes. Because people expect a fair procedure to produce generally fair outcomes, a procedure that consistently produces unfair outcomes will eventually be viewed as unfair.

The criteria of procedural fairness outlined suggest that people are concerned with several aspects of procedures that are unrelated to the dispute or problem they are dealing with. These non-decision-making aspects of procedures are only loosely linked to the formal decision-making structure of the procedure. Hence, they may vary widely within a given formal procedure. Within courtroom trials, for example, people may differ widely in their judgments about the motives of the authorities and the politeness and respect which they are shown. As a consequence, information about the formal procedure used is not a good predictor of whether people will feel fairly treated.

Distinguishing between formal and informal procedures helps us to understand several otherwise puzzling findings in studies of courts. One finding is that in civil cases people often regard informal means of dispute resolution, such as mediation, as fairer than courtroom trials, even though those procedures lack many of the structural safeguards associated with formal trials (Tyler 1989a). Another is that in criminal cases defendants evaluate plea bargaining as a fairer procedure than going to trial (Casper, Tyler, and Fisher 1988; Landis and Goodstein 1986), even though plea bargaining lacks many of the structural features of a trial.

Why might people prefer informal procedures? In some ways informal procedures correspond more closely than the procedures used in formal courtrooms to peoples' feelings about what constitutes a fair procedure. Informal procedures often, for example, offer greater opportunities for direct participation and may allow authorities more opportunity to recognize peoples' interpersonal concerns. People may care more about these issues in determining what is fair than they care about the formal structure of "fair" procedure represented in the courtroom trial.

The same criteria are not used to judge the fairness of all procedures, irrespective of the issues or people involved. In different situations people evaluate the fairness of procedures against different criteria of procedural justice (Barrett-Howard and Tyler 1986; Tyler 1988, 1989b, in press). In the context of a particular type of dispute, however, even different types of people generally agree about the criteria for judging a procedure's fairness (Tyler 1988, 1989b, in press). Among Americans, there seems to be a substantial consensus about what is fair (Merry 1985, 1986; Sanders and Hamilton 1987). As a consequence, it is possible for authorities to maximize their legitimacy in the eyes of everyone they deal with. They need not choose among those they deal with, offending some and pleasing others. Within a particular context everyone involved will agree about how to judge the fairness of the procedures.

These studies, taken together, suggest that public choice, or self-interest, models are insufficient to explain either evaluation or behavior in law and politics. Such models ignore the important role of procedural fairness judgments. Law-related and political evaluations and behaviors have an important normative component, responsive to considerations of justice or injustice. Recognizing this normative component would move political psychologists away from the kinds of answers public choice theorists usually give to issues raised by social dilemmas (Tyler 1986a; Tyler, Rasinski, and Griffin 1986).

Public choice theory has directed attention to evaluations and behaviors that appear irrational when viewed from a self-interest perspective. Voting, for example, is difficult to explain given its low personal gains and high costs (Laver 1981; Mueller 1979). Similarly, most people seem to pay their taxes even when they think they would not get caught if they cheated. Both voting and taxpaying allow people to "free ride" on the contributions of others and not contribute to society. What is surprising is that most people do not do this.

A justice-based perspective focuses the attention of researchers and policymakers instead on normative issues, suggesting that we should study the origin of peoples' schemas for judging which outcomes and procedures are fair. Justice researchers have found that people almost always have a clear opinion about whether a procedure is fair, just as they almost always have strong feelings about whether an outcome is fair. People seem to have well-established frameworks for making justice judgements. While we now have evidence that there is substantial consensus among Americans about what constitutes a fair procedure, we do not yet understand the nature of the socialization process which presumably underlies such effects.

We now see that people have a complex and multidimensional schemata against which they assess the fairness of procedures in legal and political settings. Such inferences respond to issues of participation, neutrality, motivation, interpersonal treatment, and outcome fairness. This complexity of judgment suggests that people not only react to their experiences in justice terms rather than in terms of outcome favorability; their assessments of justice are also largely distinct from issues of outcome favorability. They consider a variety of issues, including subtle inferences about the motives of the authorities. Their judgments also vary by the issue, with different questions being relevant to the fairness of a procedure under different circumstances.[12]

Justice values seem, for example, to be linked to basic political and social values. Rasinski (1987) demonstrates that liberals and conservatives differ both in the degree to which they base their policy evaluations on justice criteria and in the way they define the meaning of justice. Conservatives place greater weight on procedural justice, relative to distributive justice, than do liberals. They also define the meaning of distributive justice more in terms of equity than equality.

Instead of assuming that behavior is primarily responsive to reward and punishment (cf. traditional deterrence theory; Andenaes 1974; Tittle 1980), we should recognize that behavior is deeply affected by the legitimacy of legal authorities and the morality of the law. Creating a moral climate that supports both a law and the authorities promoting it will alter compliance more effectively than will changing people's estimates of the certainty or severity of punishment. Accordingly, those concerned with implementing policy should not focus simply on manipulating penalties and incentives. They should create a normative climate that lets people judge the law and public policies to be fair.

Because the public may not know of all available procedures, or about the consequences of using different procedures, public views about fairness should not be uncritically accepted as the basis for designing formal procedures. Nevertheless, recognizing public concerns about justice helps us understand public discontent with the legal and political systems, design implementation strategies that will more effectively gain public acceptance for new policies, understand how people react to their dealings with police officers, judges, and other legal and political officials, and understand an important basis for public behavior—whether that behavior is rioting or voting.

The studies reviewed here confirm prior evidence that concerns about justice influence peoples' compliance with the law, rioting, and voting behavior (Schwartz and Orleans 1967; Muller and Jukam 1977; Riker and Ordeshook 1973). Issues of justice influence people's reactions to their dealings with legal authorities and their more general evaluations of the political system (Sarat 1977; Harris and Associates 1973). Recognizing that these concerns with justice and morality affect evaluation and behavior may make our public policies more realistic than postulating behavior based solely on self-interest.

V   Legislators

11 Deregulation and the Politics of Ideas in Congress

Paul J. Quirk

In a period of extraordinary policy change from the mid-1970s to the early 1980s, much of the overtly anticompetitive regulatory activity of the United States federal government was reformed or abolished. Stock brokerage commissions, railroad freight rates, interest paid to bank depositors, airline industry routes and fares, trucking industry rates and services, and the services and equipment offered and prices charged by the telecommunications industry, among other things, were largely or entirely freed from government control. The reforms had significant economic consequences. They produced some adverse effects, such as diminished transportation service for certain communities and a trend toward monopolization of some markets. But for the most part, prices fell, services improved, and the pace of innovation increased in the deregulated industries.

Whatever the economic effects, the adoption of procompetitive deregulation had important lessons for political analysis. In some cases, like banking and stock brokerage, reform was facilitated by economic developments that led segments of the regulated industry or other well-organized interests to demand policy change; to a great extent it represented the ordinary workings of interest-group politics. In several other cases, however, especially airlines, trucking, and (in the crucial initial phases of policy change) telecommunications, deregulation occurred without benefit of significant interest-group support. Indeed, as Martha Derthick and I pointed out in *The Politics of Deregulation*,[1] the political

This chapter is derived primarily from the author's previous work in Martha Derthick and Paul J. Quirk, *The Politics of Deregulation* (Washington, D.C.: Brookings Institution, 1985), chap. 4; and Paul J. Quirk, "In Defense of the Politics of Ideas," *Journal of Politics* 50 (February 1988): 31–41. It incorporates, with minor revisions, passages from both those works. Documentation of quotations and further evidence about the cases are provided in the original study. The general direction of the argument is a product of the author's collaboration with Martha Derthick, who, along with Jane Mansbridge and Stella Herriges Quirk, also provided helpful comments on an earlier draft.

success of deregulation required in each case that a diffuse, unorganized interest in reform (primarily consumers) defeat an intense, well-organized opposition (the regulated industry and its labor unions)—while at the same time overcoming the normal tendency of government organizations to protect their jurisdictions. Instead of interest-group politics, deregulation demonstrated the importance of what Derthick and I called the politics of ideas. It also revealed the inadequacy of self-interest theories of politics.

In this chapter, I describe and explain the response of the United States Congress to the issues posed by deregulation. I argue that despite the expectations of self-interest theorists and some others to the contrary, Congress has a rather robust capacity to serve general interests and respond to ideas. I identify the principal sources of this capacity. Finally, I discuss some broader implications of the analysis for the study of public policy-making.

Self-Interest Theories: Capture and Reelection

Economic or self-interest theories of politics generally begin by assuming that political actors pursue only self-referential objectives, like reelection or individual economic welfare, and end by concluding that narrow, well-organized interests dominate public policy-making. Two such theories, the capture theory of regulation and the electoral theory of Congress, apply to the congressional response to deregulation.

The capture theory of regulation is stated in an article by economist George Stigler.[2] As the premise of his analysis, notorious for its radical debunking of regulatory politics, Stigler assumed self-interested behavior by both politicians and their constituents. Representatives and political parties, in his view, seek electoral success and the perquisites of office. They do not act on their own views about the merits of policies or therefore respond to preaching; rather they in effect sell political power to any group that purchases policies with votes and resources. A group's ability to offer the requisite payment is the sole basis of an effective political demand.

For their part, constituents are assumed to seek only their individual economic welfare. Their efforts to learn about policy issues or express their preferences, through voting or lobbying organizations, are determined by the individual costs and returns, just as in a private market. Unfortunately, any large group of constituents—especially an inclusive group like consumers or taxpayers—faces prohibitive obstacles to generating an effective demand. On most issues members of such a group will have low per capita stakes, high costs of organization and information, and strong incentives for free riding. The principal demands come from narrow interests, such as industries and cohesive occupational groups, that have high stakes, low information costs, and the organization to pursue their collective interests. For an issue of regulatory policy, the dominant group is normally the regulated industry itself, which usually has more at stake than any other affected group.

"As a rule," Stigler concluded, "regulation is acquired by the industry and is designed and operated primarily for its benefit." [3] Rather than benefiting the public, regulation transfers wealth to the industry by protecting it from competition. The principal exception Stigler recognized is that a more powerful industry may obtain regulation of a weaker rival for the purpose of hampering it. Apart from that case, Stigler considered the logic of self-interest to be largely inescapable: to blame a regulatory agency for serving industry, he quipped, is like blaming the Great Atlantic and Pacific Tea Company for selling groceries.

In this unvarnished form, the capture theory was massively inaccurate in its predictions. It failed to account for the existence of many regulatory programs that the regulated industries had strongly resisted (and rival industries had not sponsored); for the tendency even among programs that benefit regulated industries to also benefit certain consumers; and most dramatically, for the wave of consumer, environmental, and civil rights regulation that was well under way when Stigler's article was published in 1971.

Recognizing such discrepancies, economic theorists sympathetic with Stigler's effort have proposed amendments. Peltzman points out that a regulated industry often must share the benefits of regulation with other producers (such as suppliers) or even consumers (say, rural telephone users) with sufficient stakes, organization, and political resources to make effective demands. [4] Giving up even more of Stigler's position, Noll and Owen argue that general interests are occasionally effective in the political process. [5] They attribute this efficacy largely to the activity of entrepreneurial leaders, who, for "political or personal motives," promote policies that elicit widespread support and are designed to serve general interests. Evidently viewing such behavior as marginal and episodic, Noll and Owen appeal to it only as a residual form of explanation. Other economists have abandoned Stigler's assumptions entirely or have given up explaining the relative power of different interests. [6]

The electoral theory of Congress, developed by David Mayhew and Morris Fiorina, [7] is broadly compatible with the capture theory—although it includes a more refined analysis of the political process and a more qualified view of the dominance of interest groups. Like the capture theory, it starts with the premise that members of Congress seek only reelection. It proceeds by identifying the activities that best serve that objective.

In regard to legislation, the theory suggests, members of Congress earn electoral rewards mainly by servicing organized interest groups and seeking concentrated benefits, like defense contracts or public works projects, for their constituencies. These activities bestow benefits on groups that are capable of recognizing the effort and rewarding it with support. In contrast, members of Congress gain little support by trying to advance broad interests or to implement an ideology. Few voters in congressional elections make their decisions on the basis of broad policy issues or ideologies; apart from issues of exceptional salience, few are even aware of their congressman's positions.

The electoral theorists argue that the main objective guiding the development of Congress's institutional structure has been to help members obtain credit for distributing benefits to interest groups and geographic areas. The standing committees recruit members largely by self-selection and yet have substantial autonomy in policy-making. Such committees give control over programs to the legislators whose constituencies they most affect and thus are ideal vehicles for congressional response to narrow interests.

In short, Congress has an exceedingly limited capacity to serve broad or diffuse interests of the nation as a whole; its central impulse is instead to distribute particularized benefits to specific localities and organized groups. Unlike Stigler's theory, however, the electoral theory of Congress acknowledges certain means by which that impulse is sometimes overcome. Presidents, who are elected nationally, and congressional party leaders, who are concerned with their parties' national reputations, have incentives to pursue general interests. Provided they have sufficient control of Congress, presidents and party leaders can moderate the tendency toward particularism. In certain critical areas of policy, such as the budget and taxes, Congress has given committees unusual authority and special institutional incentives to impose some discipline on the granting of special-interest benefits. And even ordinary members of Congress respond to broadly based interests when the public is aroused. Generally speaking, however, the theory holds that narrow interests are in control.

Taken together, the capture theory of regulation and the electoral theory of Congress have several implications about the prospects for reforming anticompetitive regulatory programs. Deregulation should occur primarily if a regulated industry, perhaps responding to changed economic circumstances, asks for it. It may also occur if some other well-organized group—like potential competitors or business users of a regulated service—stands to gain from deregulation and has sufficient resources and intensity to overcome the regulated industry. Finally, it may occur if the general public demands deregulation and is highly attentive to the issue. In the absence of such favorable circumstances, deregulation should not be possible. Congress in particular should be an institutional bulwark against reform. And within Congress, the committees with jurisdiction should be the main outposts of resistance.

Congress and Deregulation

In the deregulation of airlines, trucking, and telecommunications, none of these expectations was borne out. The regulated industries and their labor unions opposed reform strenuously (even though not always to the bitter end). There was no interest-group support remotely comparable to the opposition. And the general public was largely oblivious to the debates. Yet Congress, led for the most part by the committees, endorsed reform.

Airlines

When Sen. Edward Kennedy first advocated deregulating the airline industry in 1975, the certificated airlines opposed the notion intensely and unanimously. United Airlines predicted that "carrier profits would surely vanish." Some groups peripheral to the industry, like charter operators and commuter airlines, had particular restrictions they wanted relaxed, but they did not form a cohesive coalition and were no match, economically or politically, for the certificated airlines. The public, a Harris poll found, approved of airline regulation by a wide margin.

Importantly, reforms that the Civil Aeronautics Board (CAB) adopted administratively throughout the period of the debate tended to undermine the industry's position and helped cause its resistance gradually to deteriorate. Yet when the Senate and House committees drafted bills in late 1977 and early 1978, the preponderance of the industry still opposed deregulation. The industry was defeated. Both committees reported bills providing for substantial deregulation, and both bills were strengthened in floor debate. In the end, industry resistance collapsed, enabling the conference committee to abolish economic regulation of the airlines.

Telecommunications

After the Federal Communications Commission (FCC) started to admit new competitors to parts of the telecommunications industry in the early 1970s, the American Telephone and Telegraph Company (AT&T), attacking these "experiments in economics," embarked on a campaign with the independent telephone companies and the industry's unions to block competition by legislation. Deploying the company's massive political resources with such intensity that it was widely criticized as overbearing, AT&T tried to push an anticompetitive bill through Congress—recruiting over two hundred House and Senate cosponsors in 1975 and 1976. The principal interest groups supporting competition, the competitors themselves, were vastly outweighed by AT&T; in fact the new long-distance carriers had no lobbying organization until they formed one to fight the AT&T bill. The public, according to polls, was satisfied with the traditional monopoly.

The communications subcommittees in both Houses dismissed the anticompetitive AT&T bill and instead, with virtually no dissent, set about drafting bills to endorse the FCC's procompetitive policies. As it happened, disagreement on difficult subsidiary issues (in particular, whether to break up AT&T, which of the former monopoly's operations to deregulate, and how to control the restructuring of telephone rates) prevented the passage of legislation. But the subcommittees' response provided a political foundation for court decisions and further FCC rulings that over several years gave competition essentially unlimited scope in the industry.

Trucking

"If we are serious about defeating deregulation, then now is the time to prove our strength," the American Trucking Association (ATA) warned its members just before Senate committee markups on trucking deregulation in 1980. The Teamsters Union also urgently wished to defeat it. Interest-group support for deregulation was again negligible: Although a few segments of the trucking industry (contract carriers, private carriers, and owner-operators) wanted additional leeway for their particular operations, they were indifferent, at best, to wide-ranging deregulation. Nor did the public demand deregulation of the trucking industry; only a small part of the public even knew that it was regulated.

Handing the industry and the Teamsters a sharp defeat, the Senate Commerce Committee reported a bill that, said the ATA, "cuts the heart out of regulation." The Senate passed it without change. However, the House Surface Transportation Subcommittee (part of the client-oriented Public Works Committee) was far more deferential to the industry and was inclined to oppose deregulation. Eventually, the House subcommittee leaders struck a compromise with the reformers. Though moderated in some respects, the resulting bill was still highly deregulatory and led to a substantial restructuring of the industry.

Sources of Congressional Support

Despite the expectations of the relevant self-interest theories, Congress largely supported procompetitive deregulation. This support reflected both some attractive features of the reform proposals and some dispositions and capacities of the institution and its members. As Derthick and I explain in detail,[8] procompetitive deregulation was in several respects an unusually compelling policy proposal. The reform proposals had strong backing in economic theory and evidence and, accordingly, the virtually unanimous endorsement of economists. The economist's rationale of relying on competition to reduce prices and improve efficiency was comprehensible and convincing to laymen. The proposals fit well into ideological agendas at both ends of the political spectrum: Deregulation appealed to conservatives because it would reduce government control and liberate markets; and it appealed to liberals because it would attack business privilege and benefit consumers. With the exception of telecommunications (the only case where purported cross-subsidies were in fact substantial), reform was relatively free of divisive distributive effects among social groups, geographic regions, or economic sectors; the only clear losers were to be regulated industries and their labor.[9] Finally, even though deregulation was never in itself a salient issue to the general public, it had connections that could be used in political rhetoric with two of the public's major concerns—big government and especially inflation.

All of these attributes of the reform proposals and advocacy helped compensate for the intense interest-group opposition. They were able to do so, however, only because Congress also was able to respond to claims on behalf of general interests. As the evidence in these cases demonstrates, there are at least three important sources of that capacity. In part, though not exclusively, they involve motivation other than self-interest.

The Electoral Efficacy of Broadly Based Interests.

To the extent that members of Congress seek reelection, they have a stronger incentive than is often acknowledged to respond to the interests and beliefs of the general public. That incentive is strong enough to affect legislative decisions not only in a handful of exceptionally visible policy conflicts, but even in relatively routine conflicts of which only a small fraction of the electorate is directly aware.

As we have seen, there was hardly any overt public demand for procompetitive reform in the airline, trucking, or telecommunications industries. There was, however, a demand for actions that in some way addressed public concerns about inflation and intrusive government. So reform advocates stressed the links between deregulation measures and those concerns. "It is a rare opportunity for the Senate," Senator Howard Cannon pointed out as he opened floor debate on the trucking bill, "to be able to do something more than merely pay lip service to reducing Government regulation and do something concrete to fight inflation." Largely by drawing such connections, advocates of deregulation helped create electoral incentives to support reform.

Such incentives evidently existed even in the case of trucking—the industry farthest removed from the personal concerns of most voters. A number of congressional aides and other informed observers were asked in interviews, around the time of congressional action, whether members of Congress risked the loss of any electoral support if they opposed deregulation of the trucking industry. The observers generally did perceive such risks and attributed them to the voters' agitation about inflation, big government, or excessive regulation. Significantly, these observers did not claim that the electoral risks of opposing deregulation were equivalent to the risks of offending interest groups by supporting it. The risks of supporting deregulation were considered greater. But, in the estimate of one deregulation advocate, the diffuse support balanced the interest-group opposition sufficiently to make the electoral calculation, overall, "a close call."

That members of Congress actually perceived diffuse electoral pressures to support deregulation is illustrated by an episode in the House Surface Transportation Subcommittee. At one point chairman James Howard, an opponent of deregulation, floated the idea of introducing a bill that provided for total deregulation and then modifying it (drastically, he presumed) by amendments in the subcommittee. (He hoped this procedure would force the Carter administration to support weakening amendments, taking some of the heat off of deregulation opponents in the House.) The subcommittee members, however, especially the Republicans, vetoed the strategy. Even though most of them were also sympathetic to the trucking industry and were willing to approve a weak bill, they refused to be put in the position of having to vote openly for amendments restoring regulation.

More important, despite intense and one-sided interest-group pressure to oppose deregulation, majorities in the Senate Commerce Committee and on the Senate floor supported it. They would probably not have done so if there had been no diffuse pressure in favor of deregulation and supporting deregulation had seemed an unmitigated loss in electoral terms.

Why would a member of Congress worry about how voters in the district will react to a relatively obscure issue like trucking deregulation? After all, survey research shows that few voters in congressional elections make their decisions on the basis of even the most salient policy issues, or even know the candidates' positions. Conceivably, members of Congress simply overestimate the voters' concern with issues. More likely, however, they have learned from experience and observation that the voters' response to a policy issue affects a member's prospects for reelection a good deal more often than the prevalence of explicit issue voting would lead one to suppose.

Without detectable issue voting, the voter's response to an issue may have electoral consequences in two principal ways. First, if a member of Congress or a challenger uses an issue effectively in campaign rhetoric, the effect on the voters' images of the candidates and voting decisions may persist long after most of them have forgotten the specific issue. (Indeed, an issue can provide the basis for an effective campaign claim without even being explicitly mentioned.) According to some of the staff of senators who ran for reelection in 1980, the issue of trucking deregulation received occasional mention in the senate campaigns. To take only one example, one senator included his support for trucking deregulation in a list he often recited of things he had done to fight inflation. Such use of the issue implies at least the perception of an electoral reward.

Second, a relatively small group of opinion leaders may share most of the public's moods and concerns, pay close attention to debates in Congress, and influence voters' images of congressional candidates accordingly, yet without transmitting much information about issues. Newspapers throughout the country editorialized almost uniformly in favor of deregulation. Members of Congress probably assumed that many opinion leaders, and because of them some voters, would respond favorably to support for deregulation.

To account for electoral incentives that could influence decisions on legislation, these implicit forms of issue voting need not affect a large proportion of the electorate. They must merely have an effect on the vote in the same order of magnitude as the effect of the interest-group response at stake in a given decision. Considering the large number of legislative decisions that affect interest groups and the relatively small number of swing voters, an issue-voting effect sufficient to influence those decisions is likely to involve a tiny fraction of the vote—too small for detection in survey research. One part of the explanation of Congress's response to deregulation, then, is that the electoral incentives of members of Congress are considerably less skewed in favor of narrow interests than the economic theorists have supposed.

The Role of Members' Beliefs.

Contrary to the economic theories, however, members of Congress do not act almost solely on the basis of electoral calculations. To a great extent they act on their judgments about the merits of issues and conceptions of the public interest.

That they do so (and are presumed by other participants to do so) was again especially evident in the Senate debate on the trucking bill. To begin with, policy advocates—particularly reformers—invested heavily in efforts to persuade senators on the merits. In a close collaboration among the White House, the Department of Transportation, and the Senate Commerce Committee staff, they assiduously gathered evidence, polished arguments, worked out rebuttals to industry claims, planned and sponsored new research, and presented the resulting flood of information—along with summaries and oral briefings—to the Commerce Committee, other senators, and their staffs. Much of the research was designed specifically to answer questions senators had raised.

Accordingly, participants in the conflict saw the members' judgments of the merits as a major influence in their decisions. Even though, as we have seen, senators had some electoral grounds to support deregulation, at least in the trucking case they were widely presumed to have, on balance, even stronger grounds to oppose it. Participants sympathetic to reform often described the choice facing a senator as one of whether to stand up to the interest-group pressures, decide on the merits, and support deregulation or rather bow to those pressures, minimize electoral risk, and oppose deregulation. They showered praise for courage and independence on senators who supported reform. Such senators, not surprisingly, felt they deserved the praise: "I know I'm going to take heat for this, but damn it, it's right," one told another senator during the vote. Senators who opposed trucking deregulation also professed to be acting out of conviction, of course, but did not make a comparable pitch for moral credit.

Finally, the pattern of roll-call votes in the Senate suggests that support for trucking deregulation was associated with willingness to discount electoral costs. Senators who were up for reelection in 1980, the year of the debate, were substantially less likely to vote for trucking deregulation than those who were up for reelection in 1982 or 1984 or who had announced their retirement from the Senate (see table 11.1). For example, in the most closely contested floor vote (in which the Senate rejected an industry effort to restore regulation of processed foods), senators up for reelection opposed deregulation by about two to one (19 to 8) while those not up for reelection supported it two to one (40 to 21). The same pattern appeared in varying degrees on the two other substantive amendments and on final passage, and was evident within each party. The lesser support for deregulation from senators more immediately at risk suggests that such support was considered to be, on balance, more harmful than beneficial to a senator's electoral prospects—an inference that should apply even to senators up for reelection in later years. (In a few years, the electoral effects presumably would diminish, perhaps sharply, but not disappear, and they certainly would not change directions. If anything, interest groups will have a longer memory than the general public.) Yet more than a majority of senators, including some up for reelection, supported deregulation in crucial votes.

The notion that members of Congress have opinions about public policy and that those opinions are a principal source of their legislative decisions was taken for granted by nearly all academic and other analysts of Congress until quite recently—when some academic analysts began to posit reelection as the objective of all or most legislative decisions.

The reelection assumption could hold for any of three reasons. First, members of Congress could want only to hold office and obtain any ben-

Table 11.1   Senate Voting on Amendments to and Passage of the Motor Carrier Reform Bill in 1980, by Reelection Status and Party

Reelection Status and Party	Processed Foods Amendment[a]		Entry Standard Amendment[b]		Small-Community Entry Amendment[c]		Final Passage	
	For	Against	For	Against	For	Against	For	Against
Running	8	19	10	16	7	19	18	8
	(30)	(70)	(38)	(62)	(27)	(73)	(69)	(31)
Democrat	4	16	5	14	3	16	11	8
	(20)	(80)	(26)	(74)	(16)	(84)	(58)	(42)
Republican	4	3	5	2	4	3	7	0
	(57)	(43)	(71)	(29)	(57)	(43)	(100)	(0)
Not running	40	21	46	18	30	33	52	12
	(66)	(34)	(72)	(28)	(48)	(52)	(81)	(19)
Democrat	18	14	19	14	13	19	23	10
	(56)	(44)	(58)	(42)	(41)	(59)	(70)	(30)
Republican	22	7	27	4	17	14	29	2
	(76)	(24)	(87)	(13)	(55)	(45)	(94)	(6)
Total	48	40	56	34	37	52	70	20
	(55)	(45)	(62)	(38)	(42)	(58)	(78)	(22)

Source: Derthick and Quirk, *The Politics of Deregulation,* p. 134. Authors' calculations based on voting data from *Congressional Quarterly Weekly Report,* vol. 38 (April 19, 1980), p. 1062. The voting data include those who were paired for and against each measure. Votes on amendments, all three of which were defeated, are coded so that a vote "for" indicates support for deregulation. Numbers in parentheses are percentages of the raw totals in each category.
a. Offered by Ernest F. Hollings, Democrat of South Carolina; would have eliminated an expanded agricultural exemption.
b. Offered by Warren G. Magnuson, Democrat of Washington; would have imposed a more restrictive test on applications for entry.
c. Offered by Harrison H. Schmitt, Republican of New Mexico; would have eliminated the requirement to meet a test of public convenience and necessity as it applied to applications to provide service to small communities.

fits that come automatically with doing so. The principal benefit cannot be money income; many members of Congress could earn much more in private life. Rather, this condition would require a specific and peculiar set of tastes for other benefits. Members of Congress would have to want a career of debating public issues, but not one of defending their own convictions about those issues; a sense of participation in policy-making, but not discretion and genuine power; the approval of voters, but not that of congressional colleagues or other elites; and the achievement of getting and keeping office, but no achievement beyond that. It is far more plausible that for many members the opportunities to defend their convictions, exercise power, win respect among the political elite, and make a contribution to the nation's well-being are among the main reasons for wanting the job.

Second, members of Congress could have concerns beyond reelection but be forced to set them aside to stay in office. This notion lacks support, however, in the politics of congressional elections. Reelection depends mainly on campaigns and party fortunes. In view of the large number of significant issues decided in each Congress, the large differences in issue positions even among members with similar districts, and the exceedingly high rate of reelection of congressional incumbents, few issues can pose a substantial threat to a typical member's reelection. The members usually have considerable leeway. It is sometimes urged that many members appear electorally secure only because they bend every effort (and every principle) to achieve security. But the fact that most members are returned to office in no way suggests that a specific pattern of roll-call votes is the basis of their success.

Finally, single-minded reelection seeking could also result if, although members of Congress had concerns beyond holding office and, objectively speaking, had considerable leeway to pursue those concerns, they nevertheless had too strong an aversion to risk to take any unnecessary chances with reelection. In the heat of a reelection campaign, members of Congress are undoubtedly anxious about their prospects. But to suppose that such anxiety pervades members' legislative decisions throughout their terms and regardless of their electoral strength runs against what we know of human decision-making generally and politicians specifically. Cognitive psychology suggests that individuals tend to discount rather than exaggerate low-probability risks. And politicians, however safe their seats eventually become, all chose to start out in what they knew was a risky career.

In the end, there is no compelling ground for assuming that reelection is even the single most important motive in legislative decisions. The goal of reelection undoubtedly often governs a member of Congress's decisions on those occasions when his policy beliefs and electoral interests are in conflict and the electoral stakes are significant. But for most members such occasions may be relatively infrequent, and the latitude to act on the merits far more typical.

The Incentives of Committee Leadership.

The leaders of congressional committees and subcommittees, instead of being reliable protectors of committee clients as the electoral theory's view of committees would imply, actually have special incentives and more inclination than other members to act on behalf of general interests.

Partisan and ideological differences among such leaders often obscure their common tendency to serve general interests. That tendency emerged clearly in these cases, however, because of an unusual configuration of conflicting pressures. On the one hand, the interest groups associated respectively with the Republican and Democratic parties—the regulated industries and their labor unions—strongly opposed deregulation. On the other hand, the ideological principles associated respectively with the Republican and Democratic parties—free market conservatism and liberal consumerism, as well as ideologically neutral policy analysis—favored deregulation. Regardless of party or ideology, therefore, those members who were more inclined to deny narrowly based interests and serve broadly based ones tended to support deregulation.

In each of the three cases of deregulation, in both parties and in both houses the leaders of the committees or subcommittees with jurisdiction almost uniformly supported reform. The airline deregulation bill was cosponsored in the Senate by Aviation Subcommittee chairman Howard Cannon and ranking minority member James B. Pearson. After some initial partisan maneuvering, it was cosponsored in the House subcommittee by chairman Glenn Anderson, ranking member Gene Snyder, and other members of both parties.

In telecommunications, support for procompetitive reform held through a succession of committee leaders over three Congresses. Led by chairman Ernest F. Hollings, the Senate subcommittee in 1977 held hearings designed largely to defend the FCC's procompetitive policies against the criticisms leveled by AT&T. For the next six years, subcommittee and full Commerce Committee leaders of both parties—Democrats Cannon and Hollings, and Republicans Bob Packwood, Barry Goldwater, and Harrison H. Schmitt—proposed a series of bills endorsing competition. House subcommittee chairman Lionel Van Deerlin and ranking member Louis Frey worked to kill AT&T's anticompetitive bill, held hearings to defend competition, and attempted a massive procompetitive "rewrite" of the entire communications act. Subsequently, Van Deerlin sponsored procompetitive bills with James M. Collins, Frey's successor as ranking member. Van Deerlin's successor, Timothy E. Wirth, who had been an early advocate of telecommunications competition, took the same view as chairman.

In trucking deregulation, the Senate bill was again sponsored by Howard Cannon, then chairman of the full Commerce Committee, and ranking minority member Bob Packwood; they worked in concert to push a highly procompetitive measure through the Senate. As mentioned earlier, the leadership of the House Surface Transportation Subcommittee was the only exception to the pattern of support. In the clientelist tradition of the full Public Works Committee, subcommittee chairman James Howard, ranking minority member Bud Schuster, and full committee ranking member William Harsha were closely tied to the trucking industry. Yet although they tried to resist deregulation, even they were unwilling to oppose it in open confrontation with the reformers. Rather, they ended up sponsoring a compromise and even demanding a share of the credit for deregulation.

Despite the political benefits available to committee leaders in their relationships with interest groups, they have strong moral, electoral, and institutional incentives to lead their committees to respond effectively to general interests. The circumstances of committee leadership accentuate the same incentives that induce general-interest responses from other legislators. Committee leaders know that their decisions on legislation have major consequences for public policy and the condition of American society. To some extent this encourages greater concern for the public effects of those decisions and a greater disposition to decide on the merits.

With respect to reelection, committee leaders know that their role in the legislative process (which may include introducing the bills, presiding over the committee proceedings, leading the floor debates, and lending their names to the final products) is exceptionally visible and that they are personally identified with the legislation their committees produce. Senator Cannon, for example, observed in an interview that his role in airline and trucking deregulation had gained him a reputation, useful in his home state of Nevada, as an opponent of excessive regulation. Committee leaders are also relatively immune to electoral retaliation by interest groups, which would take a large risk in opposing a committee leader in an election campaign. Thus committee leaders have electoral incentives stronger than those of other members to appeal to the beliefs and interests of the general public.

Institutional inducements for responding to general interests, supplied by Congress itself and the Washington community, are also enhanced for those in positions of leadership. A leader is likely to be more concerned than other members about his prestige in Washington circles. He will want to have a reputation for effective leadership and his committee to have a reputation for significant contributions to public policy. Such reputations are earned mainly by skillful promotion of innovative and responsible legislation, not by dedicated service to special interests.

To be sure, when a committee has a political alliance with an interest group, committee leaders are usually central figures in the arrangement. But when there are pressures or opportunities to pursue broader objectives, the leaders often respond. In addition, they sometimes create these opportunities. The responsiveness of committee leaders to general interests undermines the electoral theory's view of the committee system as mainly a device to deliver benefits to narrow groups.

Conclusion

The response of Congress to deregulation and procompetitive reform in the airline, trucking, and telecommunications industries reflects three influences that the economic theories overlook or explicitly deny. First, members of Congress have electoral incentives shaped not only by interest-group demands but, even on issues of low or moderate salience, by the beliefs and preferences of the general public. The fact that such incentives are important implies of course that members of Congress do pursue reelection and, in that respect, is consistent with the self-interest assumption. But the existence of diffuse electoral incentives also implies that voters are concerned with the general consequences of policy choices and thus that they are not self-interested in any strict sense. As the economic theorists have pointed out, voters who sought to enhance their individual economic welfare (and not the welfare of large groups to which they belong) would attend only to issues in which they had exceedingly high per capita stakes.[10] Members of Congress would not have expected such voters to respond to deregulation on the basis of general concerns about inflation, big government, or excessive regulation.

Second, members of Congress do not pursue reelection exclusively. Contrary to the self-interest assumption, many act on judgments about the merits of policy issues or, more generally, conceptions of the public interest. They do so because to act in that manner is one of the major satisfactions of holding office and because, under many circumstances, it causes very slight additional risk of electoral defeat.

Finally, congressional committee and subcommittee leaders, that is, the principal issue-by-issue leaders of the contemporary Congress, have even stronger incentives and a greater inclination to serve general interests than other members. These incentives involve a combination of self-interested and non-self-interested motivations. Compared with other members, they are likely to feel a stronger sense of duty to serve general interests. They can also obtain greater electoral rewards by appealing to broad segments of the electorate and will face less threat of retaliation from interest groups. And they can earn respect in the Washington community for their leadership.

As a result of this combination of motivations and influences, Congress has the capacity to defeat narrow, well-organized interests and vindicate diffuse, unorganized interests. Put differently, it can act on beliefs and values presumed to express general interests.

One might object that Congress has such a capacity only occasionally, when it enacts "landmark reforms" (so named for their infrequency), that it creates or maintains special-interest benefits far more frequently, and that serving narrow interests is therefore its characteristic mode of policy-making. Undoubtedly, the defeats suffered by powerful, well-organized interests in the deregulation cases were unusual. They were expected by few, if any, informed observers.

The objection, nevertheless, is unwarranted. In focusing merely on the frequency of actions that provide special-interest benefits, it overlooks the disproportionate magnitude of the occasional general-interest reforms, the frequency with which Congress refuses to grant special-interest benefits or deters potential recipients from even asking for them, and the degree to which policies that may look like deference to interest groups arise from widespread beliefs about the workings of markets or the requirements of equity. In addition, a group's ability to preserve special benefits often results in large part from obstacles in Congress to policy change of any kind—the advantage of the status quo—rather than superior resources or political efficacy. Instead of current group power, existing benefits may reflect mainly the past power of interest groups or even the past beliefs of the general public.

Although Congress defers to narrow interests far more often than one would wish—perhaps even enough to suggest a need for structural reform—such deference is by no means consistent or complete. To the contrary, if one looks at the outcomes of congressional policy-making in relation to the actual and potential demand for special-interest benefits, the deference appears quite limited. Congress has established regulatory programs to limit competition, for example, in only a handful of major industries. Some of those were natural monopolies that only later become potentially competitive; most of the others were infrastructure industries first regulated during the Depression, when even economists had abandoned faith in free markets. Most industries, evidently anticipating failure, have not sought direct regulatory restrictions on pricing or entry. Similarly, Congress has either denied or managed to deter requests for trade protection from most industries exposed to import competition, preserving a generally liberal trade policy since the 1930s. The trade bills, criticized as protectionist, that Congress has debated under the pressure of unprecedented trade deficits in recent years have sought to modify that policy at the margins. Until the Reagan administration, Congress had disciplined federal budget policy well enough to reduce the national debt in relation to national income in most periods other than wartime. The legislature's most promiscuous granting of benefits, historically, has perhaps been the creation of special provisions in the tax code. But even before the Tax Reform Act of 1986, Congress limited such provisions sufficiently to keep general tax rates in a supportable range. Moreover, surveys indicated that most of the special provisions had widespread public support.

In short, the capacity of Congress to respond to general interests and to act on ideas about those interests is not limited to rare episodes like the abolition of an anticompetitive regulatory program or the adoption of a major tax reform bill. Though often overridden by special-interest politics, this tendency is regularly a prominent feature of congressional policy-making.

The strength of this capacity has two broad implications for political analysis. On the one hand, it implies that policy debates are less dominated by distributive conflict, and policy outcomes less distorted by narrow functional and geographic interests, than the capture and electoral theories would predict. As a result, it also implies a greater likelihood of responsible, effective public policy and suggests a more sanguine view of the effects of government intervention. A capacity to act on ideas about general interests also points to possibilities for improving policy-making through collective learning—suggesting, for example, that the Depression-era mistake of sacrificing competition to achieve stability may not be repeated, de novo, on a massive scale.

On the other hand, this congressional capacity is reason to look for important sources of policy failure other than excessive regard for special interests. Instead of resulting from the political advantages of narrow groups with respect to organization, information costs, and the like, important failures are likely to reflect other barriers to effective, responsible policy-making. Such barriers include, among others, cognitive biases and limitations that affect both public and elite understanding of policy issues, institutional weaknesses with respect to information gathering or deliberation, and the difficulties of conducting negotiations and achieving constructive outcomes in the conflictual environment of public policy-making. Policy-making may be shaped by ideas about the public interest, but they may not be *good* ideas. The obstacles to a deliberate, informed politics of ideas are more serious threats to the nation's well-being—and more worthy of researchers' attention—than the potential for exploitation and waste that arises in the politics of self-interest.

12 Congress and Public Spirit: A Commentary

Steven Kelman

Among the institutions involved in the political process in the United States, Congress, according to the common view, is the one least likely to address policy alternatives in terms of what would be good for the nation as a whole. Members of Congress, it is noted, represent constituencies considerably smaller than the entire country. A local orientation is strengthened further because members usually need it for reelection and because jobs that foster such an orientation attract people who already find it congenial; Samuel Huntington's statistics show that the proportion of congressional leaders still living in their hometown is much higher than that of executive branch leaders or corporate executives.[1] The devolution of much formal authority in Congress to committees also means that disproportionate power over the results of the process goes to an often unrepresentative subset of the membership as a whole, since members often seek committee assignments that allow them to shape programs to help their districts. (Members representing rice-growing districts are likely to try to get onto the agriculture subcommittee dealing with the price supports for rice.) The committee selection process thus discourages examination of bills from a wider range of considerations. The lack of party discipline in the United States political system contributes to the same result, because developing a single position for an entire party encourages a broad examination.

Some in the pluralist tradition in political science would not be troubled by all this, believing as they do that good public policy results from a weighted sum of the number and intensity of local self-interests. I disagree. Even an idealized version of aggregating self-interests can be expected to produce public policies that meet only the utilitarian ethical test of maximizing overall net benefits. While maximizing overall net benefits, policies from an idealized version of this process might still violate people's rights or treat people unjustly.[2] I believe instead that a significant dose of public spirit—an old-fashioned term by which I mean the inclination to make an honest effort to achieve good public policy—is required for both achieving good public policy and allowing the policy-making process to serve as a school to build in people the inclination to take the concerns of others into account in our everyday lives outside of politics.[3]

In looking at why members of Congress might engage in public-spirited behavior, it makes sense to start with what motivates people to take up a political career in the first place. Professional participants in the political process receive rewards and bear costs far more significant than those of individual citizens, most of whose participation in politics is quite casual. For rewards, politicians get fame, deference, adulation, and a feeling of power over establishing policy with the force of law. They bear the costs of working long hours, much of it away from their families, for salaries that are relatively low for work with this degree of responsibility and demands on time. Their jobs are insecure and stressful. This diversity of rewards and punishments ensures that the motivations of professional participants in government will be more complex than any dichotomy between public spirit and self-interest implies. Furthermore, motivations vary from person to person. While Harold Lasswell claimed forty years ago that political men above all seek power, more recent scholarship reveals many different motivations that vary with the personality and the structural position of the legislator.[4] People enter politics not necessarily because they want power more than most, but, for example, because their families were politically active—just as the children of artists tend to become artists.[5] "The search for the jugular of power," notes Robert Lane, "may very likely lead to the world of finance, journalism, or industry instead of politics."[6]

Two motivations are relatively distinctive in persons in elective office. One is the desire for attention and adulation. Politicians seem to want, more than the average, to be liked. They crave media attention. And while people can gain similar attention through careers in the entertainment industry, aptitudes for the two worlds may be of limited transferability (the career of Pres. Ronald Reagan notwithstanding). As Alexander Hamilton pointed out in the *Federalist Papers,* the desire for adulation and attention need not work against public spirit but rather encourage it. People driven by personal self-interest are not likely to get far in the estimation of others, who have no reason to value the self-interest of another. But the person who seeks the admiration of others both depends on them and recognizes their importance. Although such admiration can be achieved by advocating the demands of a narrow group, rather than seeking the good of society as a whole, this tendency is often countered by the interest of the national media in exposing such behavior. A second distinct motive is the desire to participate in formulating good public policy, which work in the public sector can provide. People so motivated are "seeking power," but less power over individuals than the power to do good.

The sparse literature on the topic of why people enter careers in government is not very enlightening, both because researchers often rely on the self-reports of respondents and because of the tendency of biographers to psychoanalyze their subjects. However, the literature at least suggests that public spirit is an important reason many people go into politics. The largest group in James David Barber's sample of Connecticut legislators, for example, falls into the category he calls "lawmakers," who derive satisfaction from producing good legislation.

Vocational guidance tests provide an unconventional source of insight here. These tests help young people determine what careers might be appropriate for them, through a battery of questions to reveal interests and inclinations. The most highly regarded of such tests does not include "politician," but it does include "public administrator." The kinds of people who choose "public administrator" are also likely to choose the occupations of rehabilitation counselor, YMCA general secretary, social worker, and minister.[7]

Moving from individual motivation to the effects of institutions, we may conclude that although many features of Congress as an institution encourage attention to the particular interests of constituents or campaign contributors, other features of the institution promote public spirit.

First, American opinion is divided on the normative question of whether congressmen should vote their own best judgment or the opinion of the majority in the district. When citizens have been asked how they believed congressmen should behave in instances of such a conflict, anywhere from one-third to more than half of the population (depending on the wording of the survey) has reported that representatives should vote their own judgment.[8]

Second, congressional staffs are having a growing impact on the development of policy initiatives and the substance of particular bills. Staff people tend to be interested both in issues and in making a difference on policy. Not having to face reelection themselves, they are not as concerned as members of Congress with the district or with campaign contributions (although no wise staffer ignores the concerns of the boss). Like journalists for national media, they tend to regard themselves as representatives for poorly organized groups or, more generally, as trying to do the right thing.

Third, as Arthur Maass emphasizes in *Congress and the Common Good*, committee members do not enjoy the unconditional deference of the body as a whole. They must pay attention to whether proposals they are considering are acceptable to the wider range of members. Deference to committee proposals can be withdrawn if committees exploit their privileged position to advance their district's narrow concerns.[9] The growing practice of multiple committee referral further reduces the danger that a single committee will consider bills from only a single, narrow point of view.

Fourth, constituency interests and the interests of campaign contributors may pull in opposite directions. Certainly, lobbyists try to show members how their district would be affected by legislation in which the lobbyists are interested. But demonstrating commonality between constituency interests and the interests of campaign contributors is frequently difficult or impossible. The competing pressures create room for members' independent judgment.

Finally, members of Congress are under the eye not only of their own constituents and political action committees, but also of their colleagues and the media. Spending a great deal of time together, members of Congress can be expected to care about the regard of their peers. More instrumentally, the more their colleagues respect them, the more influence they are likely to have over floor votes and over the results of legislation. And members tend to respect colleagues who are well informed and able to argue on the merits. The journalists who followed the daily lives of Senators Edmund Muskie and John Culver emphasize how important a political asset in Congress is the ability to make a credible and convincing argument. "Real power" in the Senate, Muskie is quoted as saying, "comes from doing your work and knowing what you're talking about. . . . The most important thing in the Senate is credibility."[10] "When a Senator makes a speech," writes Elizabeth Drew in her book on Culver, "he is far more likely to command the attention and respect of his colleagues if he seems to know actually what he is talking about."[11] Along similar lines, a group of freshmen congressmen discussing their experiences for political scientists "made frequent allusions to the importance of knowledge and expertise" in determining "who wielded real power in committee and in the House."[12] Knowing how to advance your constituents' interests or showing special devotion to the interests of a favored lobby does not garner the same kind of respect. The national media are also likely to regard devotion to the interests of one's own constituency or political action committees as a craven bow to "special interests." Since the 1970s more features of the congressional process have become public. Committee mark-up sessions are now public. More floor votes are now recorded. These reforms mean that the behavior of members of Congress is now more accessible not only to constituents (and, perhaps, especially to lobbyists) but also to the media.

Richard Fenno noted more than a decade ago that members of Congress have different goals. Some seek mainly assurances of reelection; others influence within Congress; still others to formulate good public policy.[13] These considerations balance out differently for different issues. Although few members vote against their constituency on matters of overriding concern to the district, such bills constitute only a small proportion of the bills before Congress. Although congressmen try to get discretionary government funds for public works and government buildings in their districts, these funds too make up only a modest proportion of the federal budget. "The question of where a few thousand office workers will be located is usually secondary," notes R. Douglas Arnold, "to the issue of exactly what they will do."[14] And lobbyists tend to be most effective on technical, low-visibility issues. While these "technical" issues may have a great impact on policy, and the distinction I am making may thus seem like the one in the family where one spouse makes the "important" decisions about whether we should give aid to Nicaragua and the other the "unimportant" ones about what the family should eat for dinner, the broad outlines of policy often remain open to genuine debate on the direction of good public policy.

One study measuring the effect of "the district" on the votes of congressmen has found a long-term decline in the influence of constituency interests on voting behavior beginning around the time of the New Deal.[15] Nor have the big increases in government spending since the 1950s been in federal grants to localities, which provide visible constituency benefits, but rather in general transfer programs that do not allow members to demonstrate that they have gotten something special for the district.[16] In addition, the tendency since the beginning of the 1970s has been to decrease dramatically the use of "categorical grants" to localities and to increase the use of "formula grants." As R. Douglas Arnold points out, this direction is exactly the opposite of a prediction generated by assuming that members will single-mindedly seek reelection by bringing goodies to their districts for which they can claim credit. Localities must *apply* for categorical grants, and members can therefore take credit for helping their districts get them. Formula grants, by contrast, are allocated automatically. They are generally not even tied to specific projects, where congressmen can be present at the opening ceremonies and cut a ribbon. Yet it is the formula grants that are increasing, not the categorical ones. This shift is the result of a debate on the merits of federal versus local control.[17]

Similarly, in recent years Congress has occasionally voted to deprive itself of the opportunity to provide visible constituency benefits, by granting formal authority to the executive branch or by legislating automatic formulas. In trade policy, Congress has given up the opportunity to save constituents in trouble from foreign imports by giving tariff power to the executive branch. And when Congress indexed Social Security benefits in 1972 it denied itself the chance each year to vote politically visible benefit increases. Both of these instances share a common theme. If Congress legislated in these areas, the members would face intense constituency pressures—to protect threatened industries or to legislate large Social Security increases. Yet in each case the policies resulting from such pressures would go against what most congressmen believe to be good public policy—free trade and moderate benefit increases. So, like dieters who padlock the refrigerator door, members of Congress voted to deprive themselves of power and the chance to provide visible constituency benefits—in order to bring about good public policy.

Nor are the most sought-after committees in Congress those that dispense benefits to constituents, such as Public Works, or those that help members procure a stable of eager campaign workers, such as Post Office and Civil Service. They are, rather, the committees that deal with broad issues of national policy.[18] And in a 1977 survey of members of the House, the most common problem members cited about their work-load pressures was that "constituent demands detract from other functions."[19] Congressmen appear to look after their constituency in order to remain around for the important thing—participation in making public policy.

Perhaps we should draw our conclusions on the overall importance of public spirit versus self-interest in Congress by looking at the broad sweep of legislative change during the past twenty years. Self-interest cannot account, except through the grossest of contortions, for the vast increases in spending for the poor that occurred in the 1960s and early 1970s. The poor were not an electoral majority, nor were they well organized into interest groups. Lobbies of social workers and other providers of services to the poor hardly rank among Washington's great power players. Similarly, health, safety, and environmental legislation during the late 1960s and 1970s were adopted against the wishes of well-organized producers, and for the benefit of poorly organized consumers and environmentalists. (Much of the organization of environmentalists into interest groups followed environmental legislation, rather than preceding it.)

The self-interest model of politics does equally poorly in accounting for rollbacks in government programs during the late 1970s and 1980s. And as Paul Quirk (chap. 11, this vol.) demonstrates, in the late 1970s the greatest victories for industry deregulation were won in exactly those industries, such as trucking and airlines, where well-organized producers benefited from regulation; the consumers who would benefit from the deregulation occurred in areas such as environmental policy, where well-organized producers supported it.[20] The pattern of deregulation in short was exactly the opposite of that predicted by the self-interest model.

We may conclude that, as a general rule, the more important a policy is, the less important will be the role of self-interest in determining that policy. Self-interest does a great job explaining the location of a new federal building in Missoula. It fails with regard to the major policy upheavals in the United States of the past decades.

VI   Constitutional Interpretation

13 Political Self-Interest in Constitutional Law

Cass R. Sunstein

Efforts to understand political behavior as a reflection of self-interest, narrowly defined, are likely to run into serious obstacles in the context of constitutionalism. Indeed, most of the recent academic qualifications of self-interest theories played a large role in the decisions of the framers and ratifiers about the content of the United States Constitution. Collective action and coordination problems provided a significant impetus behind a number of constitutional provisions, most notably the rejection of state autonomy in favor of national control of interstate commerce. Constitutional provisions often reflect aspirations, or higher-order beliefs and preferences, rather than the sorts of first-order preferences reflected in self-interested decisions.[1] The Bill of Rights can itself be understood in these terms. The framers' frequent references to deliberation and to the long-term view presage the problems posed for rational choice theory by individual myopia and weakness of the will. One function of constitutionalism is to overcome precisely these problems by creating mechanisms to ensure deliberation in government.

Antidiscrimination provisions are responsive to the existence of the interest-induced preferences and beliefs on the part of the beneficiaries of existing injustice, and adaptive preferences on the part of its victims. Sometimes both preferences and beliefs reflect an effort to reduce cognitive dissonance by adjusting to a seemingly intractable status quo, or by adapting to the deeply and sometimes irrationally held view that the world is in fact just.[2] Constitutional norms of equality can be understood as an effort to counteract such phenomena. More generally, constitutionalism represents a form of precommitment on the part of the citizenry at large, in which people ensure that their considered judgments will be chartered in law.[3]

Despite these considerations, a number of recent observers have ex-

Some of this essay is revised from parts of Cass Sunstein, "Naked Preferences and the Constitution," *Columbia Law Review* 84 (1984):1689. © 1984 by the directors of the Columbia Law Review Association, Inc. All rights reserved. Reprinted by permission.

plored the possibility that the constitutional system of the United States is a self-conscious outgrowth of a model of government that takes self-interest, narrowly conceived, as the fundamental motivating force behind political behavior.[4] Many such efforts derive from interest-group pluralism, which treats politics as a self-interested struggle among private groups.[5] There are significant differences among competing forms of pluralism. Sometimes pluralist approaches attempt to describe U.S. politics; sometimes they are frankly normative, arguing that a proper democracy will, above all, reflect numbers and intensities of preferences. For some, the fact of interest-group struggle provides a reason for severe constraints on the operation of the public sphere;[6] for others, the interest-group struggle creates a largely well-functioning market, one with which it will be counterproductive to interfere.[7]

The unifying pluralist claim, however, is that laws should be understood as a kind of commodity, subject to forces of supply and demand. Various groups in society compete for loyalty and support from the citizenry. Once the relevant groups are organized and aligned, they exert pressure on political representatives, also self-interested, who respond in a marketlike manner to the pressures thus imposed. This process of aggregating and trading off "interests" ultimately produces political equilibrium.

The descriptive force of pluralist conceptions of politics is a subject of considerable dispute.[8] In the view of some, governmental outcomes reflect factors other than legislative and constituent self-interest, unless the concept of self-interest is understood so capaciously as to be trivialized. The normative appeal of interest-group pluralism is also highly questionable. A conception of politics that takes the existing distribution of wealth, existing entitlements, and existing preferences as static and exogenous to politics is unlikely to have much appeal.[9] In this essay, however, I explore a different set of questions. To what extent does current constitutional law accept or reject pluralist conceptions of politics? Is it possible to find, in existing legal doctrines, an approach that operates as an endorsement of or as a coherent alternative to pluralism? In short: What conception of politics emerges from judge-made public law?

In General

Judicial interpretation of many of the most important provisions of the Constitution—the commerce, privileges and immunities, equal protection, due process, contract, and eminent domain clauses—reflects a striking commonality. Although the clauses have different historical roots and were originally directed at different problems, they appear to be united by a common theme and to share a concern with a single underlying evil: the distribution of resources or opportunities to one group rather than another solely on the ground that those favored have exercised the raw political power to obtain what they want. I call this underlying evil a naked preference.

The privileges and immunities clause, for example, prohibits a state from preferring its citizens over outsiders unless the preference is supported by reasons independent of protectionism. The commerce clause allows states to discriminate against commerce from out of state only if that discrimination is a means of promoting some goal unrelated to helping self-interested insiders. The due process and equal protection clauses permit a state to enact laws treating two classes of people differently only if there is a plausible connection between the distinction in the law and a legitimate public purpose. The contract clause allows government to break or modify a contract, whether between private parties or involving the government, only if the changes are intended to promote a general public goal and do not reflect mere interest-group power. The eminent domain clause protects private property against self-interested private groups by both demanding that a "public use" be shown to justify a taking of private property and distinguishing between permissible exercises of the police power and prohibited takings.

The prohibition of naked preferences derives from the notion that government action must be responsive to something other than private pressure, and the associated idea that politics is not the reconciling of given "interests" but instead the product of some form of deliberation about the public good. In the ethos of civic republicanism that played an important role at the time of the framing of the Constitution,[10] citizens' entitlements and preferences were not seen as purely private, or as exogenous to the process of government. In that tradition, deliberating about, selecting, and shaping preferences were among the most important tasks of the governmental process. Both the hostility to the exercise of arbitrary power on the part of the king and the republican belief in deliberative democracy provided important motivations here.

The prohibition of naked preferences conforms closely to the original Madisonian belief in deliberative government. In recent years, Madison's approach to the problem of factions has often been thought to presage pluralist approaches and indeed to anticipate the insights of modern public choice theory.[11] There is a kernel of truth in this claim, but in fact Madison attempted to counter factionalism largely by increasing the likelihood of deliberation in government, not by ensuring an equilibrium among self-interested groups.[12] Both the basic constitutional structure and many individual rights are designed to promote this purpose. The division of national powers into three coequal branches, the system of bicameralism, the forms of representation, and the electoral college were intended to promote deliberation by government officials.[13] The protection of private contract and property was associated with similar ideas.[14]

As it operates in current constitutional law, the prohibition of naked preferences—like Madison's approach to the problem of factionalism—is focused on the motivations of legislators, not of their constituents. The prohibition therefore embodies a particular conception of representation. Under that conception, the task of legislators is not to respond to private pressure but instead to select values through deliberation and debate—a conception with clear roots in the founding period.

The notion that governmental action must be grounded in something other than an exercise of raw political power is of course at odds with pluralism. Naked preferences are common fare in the pluralist conception; interest-group politics invites them. The prohibition of naked preferences, recognized and enforced[15] as it is by the courts, stands as a repudiation of theories positing that the judicial role is only to police the processes of representation to ensure that all affected interest groups may participate. In this respect, the prohibition of naked preferences reflects a distinctly substantive value and cannot easily be captured in procedural terms. Above all, it presupposes that constitutional courts will serve as critics of the pluralist vision, not as adherents striving only to "clear the channels" in preparation for the ensuing political struggle.[16]

The Basic Framework

If naked preferences are a legitimate basis for government action, it is sufficient that a particular group has been able to assemble the political power to obtain what it seeks. Might makes right. A legislature might protect in-state industries from outside competition simply because they have exerted pressure; it might ban the sale of margarine because of lobbying from the butter industry; it might discriminate on the basis of race because of the power of the white majority. If naked preferences are forbidden, however, and the state is forced to invoke some public value to justify its conduct, government behavior becomes constrained.

The nature and extent of the constraint will depend on two considerations, one relating to ends and the other to means. The first involves the content of the public values that courts will accept as a legitimate basis for government action. The constraint would be strengthened if, for example, the government were barred from relying on disfavored ideas about women or members of minority groups, on the ground that reliance on such ideas is illegitimate and ought to be excluded from the category of public values.

The second consideration relates to the devices developed to ensure that public values do in fact account for legislation. If courts are willing to hypothesize a public value as the basis for government action and do not require a close fit between the public value and the measure under review, all or almost all government action will be upheld. By contrast, if courts require a good reason to believe that a naked preference was not at work, many statutes will be invalidated.

Let us assume that the content of public values is subject to no limitations and that courts do not carefully scrutinize either the process or the outcome to ensure that a public value was at work. These assumptions generate a "weak version" of the prohibition of naked preferences. This version has two main features. First, all ends are permissible except those based only and totally on political power. Second, scrutiny of the relationship between means and ends is deferential. Courts will adopt a strong presumption that almost all legislative outcomes can be justified by reference to some public value.

The weak version of the prohibition of naked preferences places only a trivial constraint on government action, for it is nearly always possible to justify an action on grounds other than the raw exercise of political power. For example, the Court has upheld a statute prohibiting opticians, but not ophthalmologists, from selling eyeglasses on the ground that the prohibition protected consumers from fraud and deception.[17] In the circumstances of the case, the justification looked specious. The statute was far more plausibly understood as a reflection of the political power of well-organized ophthalmologists.[18] But because the weak version requires some justification that goes beyond raw political power, it cannot be dismissed as a purely formal constraint. It forces those who seek to obtain government assistance to invoke some public value as a basis for assistance. In so doing, even the weak version invokes familiar constitutional themes. By requiring that some public value justify the exercise of governmental power, it acts as a check on the tyranny of factionalism—a core Madisonian evil. The weak version also reflects the idea that the role of government is to engage in a form of deliberation about governing values rather than to implement or trade off preexisting private interests. On this view, the fact that a majority is in favor of a particular measure is not, standing alone, a sufficient reason for it—though, under the weak version, it will be a rare case in which a public-regarding justification cannot be provided for measures that majorities favor.

Under many constitutional provisions, courts review statutes for "rationality," understood as a requirement that the state provide some public reason to justify the imposition of a burden or the selective grant of a benefit. Rationality review is characterized by extremely deferential means-ends scrutiny. The Supreme Court demands only the weakest link between a public value and the measure in question, and it is sometimes willing to hypothesize legitimate ends not realistically attributable to the enacting legislature. As a result, few statutes fail rationality review.

The constitutional text, read in light of its history, unambiguously provides a few—but only a few—of the elements of a more robust set of constraints. Under the privileges and immunities and commerce clauses, a preference for in-staters at the expense of out-of-staters is impermissible. Under the equal protection clause, the same is true for discrimination against blacks. As a constitutional matter, both out-of-staters and blacks are entitled to special protection from discrimination; discrimination against either group cannot be understood as a public value.

Even within this narrow area of protectionism and discrimination against blacks, however, the Constitution is ambiguous, leaving considerable room for judicial interpretation. What if a state justifies discrimination against out-of-staters on the ground that they have been the main factor contributing to in-state unemployment, or discrimination against blacks on the ground that, when blacks are jailed with whites, the likelihood of violence is dramatically increased? Outside these areas, the judicial inquiry is even more open-ended. To be sure, certain constitutional provisions give some guidance. For example, it may be possible to derive from the equal protection clause a general principle by which to judge all classifications. But in giving content to that principle, there will always be room for discretion. In such cases, how do courts enforce the prohibition of naked preferences?

In answering this question, two devices have been of special importance under all six clauses. These devices, which are logically independent, have been the key elements in strengthening and supplementing the constraint imposed by the weak version of the prohibition.

Heightened Scrutiny

The first device involves careful judicial review of governmental claims that a public value is being served by the measure under review. When courts apply "heightened scrutiny," they examine with much more than the usual suspicion a government's argument that a public value motivates its actions. Courts applying heightened scrutiny will not conclude that a public value is at work simply because some connection can be hypothesized between a measure and some public value. Courts will scrutinize the means-ends connection to ensure that it is sufficiently close, and sometimes even inspect the process to ensure that it functions as a form of deliberation rather than as a response to self-interested private groups.

In many cases, courts have carefully examined means-ends connections and scrutinized the legislative process itself, looking for genuine deliberation rather than political pressure.[19] If the connection between the public

end and the statutory means is weak, or if there is little evidence of legislative deliberation, there is reason to believe that the public justification is
a fraud, disguising the actual basis for decision. If so, the measure will
probably be invalidated.

Theory of Impermissible Ends

A second device in a more rigorous version of the prohibition on naked
preferences—typified by doctrines developed under the due process and
equal protection clauses—consists of judicial formulation of a normative
theory designed to distinguish between legitimate and illegitimate bases
for government action. The courts attempt to root this normative theory
in the text or history of the Constitution. In this view, a number of ends
are illegitimate even if they are not exercises of raw political power in the
ordinary sense. The theory of impermissible ends supplements the procedural requirements of heightened scrutiny with a substantive constraint.

The strong version could of course accommodate a wide range of normative theories of government. Modern equal protection doctrine reflects
the development of one such theory: courts have come not to recognize
as public values government ends that involve the subordination of
women, aliens, illegitimates, and members of racial minority groups. For
example, states have attempted to justify classifications based on gender
on the ground that women participate less frequently or less ably in the
labor market. Although justifications of this sort would qualify as public
values under the weak version, good reasons, grounded in constitutional
antidiscrimination principles, can be advanced for prohibiting government to invoke them. We may make some sense of the reasons that the
courts have disqualified certain justifications by suggesting that those justifications are based on values that merely reflect past and present relations
of unequal power. A full-fledged constitutional theory based on this insight would, however, have to be quite elaborate, and only the most preliminary of steps, taken up below, can be found in current law.

In short, a number of constitutional provisions call for rationality review, which consists of a deferential examination of whether a statutory
burden can be justified by reference to some public value. Because the category of public values is so large, excluding only raw political power, and
because courts will not look carefully at the relationship between statutory
means and statutory ends, rationality review is extremely deferential. In a
few areas, where courts apply "heightened scrutiny" to the connection between means and ends, and where the constitutional text is used as the
basis for developing a category of impermissible ends, invalidation is far
more frequent. But in both the weak and strong versions of the prohibition of naked preferences, the courts have decisively rejected pluralist conceptions of politics. In no modern case has the Supreme Court suggested

that interest-group compromise, standing by itself, is a permissible basis for legislation.

Illustrations: Naked Preferences and the Clauses

In this section I explore how the prohibition of naked preferences operates under the different clauses. There have of course been significant changes over time, and there are significant differences among the various clauses.

Dormant Commerce Clause

The commerce clause is both an authorization to Congress and a prohibition on certain state actions burdening interstate commerce. Under this more controversial, so-called dormant commerce clause, the central evil is protectionism: measures that citizens of one state enact in order to benefit themselves at the expense of out-of-staters. A simple illustration is a California statute that forbids out-of-staters from competing with California liquor sellers; such a statute would be flatly unconstitutional.

The prohibition of protectionism rests on a familiar idea. When states discriminate against people outside their boundaries, the ordinary avenues of political redress are unavailable to the burdened class, which does not have access to the state legislature. By contrast, when regulation imposes burdens on in-staters as well as out-of-staters, the political safeguard is more reliable. If a state imposes safety regulations on everyone who engages in construction work within its borders, in-staters will be affected in (roughly) the same way as out-of-staters, and should represent the interests of out-of-staters adequately in the political process. Such regulations would in all likelihood raise no serious constitutional question.

Current doctrine under the dormant commerce clause has a simple structure. The perception of protectionism as the core prohibited end is reflected in a three-part doctrinal framework. First, courts impose a rule or strong presumption of invalidity against measures that discriminate on their face against interstate commerce; such measures are almost always unconstitutional. Second, courts employ heightened scrutiny—by asking whether there are less restrictive alternatives and by making sure the questioned means are necessary to achieve the desired ends—whenever the burdens fall disproportionately on interstate commerce, the benefits accrue mostly to in-staters, or both. Third, when there is no discrimination between in- and out-of-staters, courts review measures deferentially; statutes that discriminate neither on their face nor in effect are almost automatically upheld. To a large extent, all three parts of the doctrinal framework attempt to filter out naked preferences for in-staters over out-of-staters.

Privileges and Immunities Clause

There is a substantial overlap between the privileges and immunities clause and the dormant commerce clause. Both clauses are aimed at discrimination against out-of-staters. Both focus on the theme of political representation, justifying an active judicial posture when discrimination alerts courts to the likelihood that unrepresented persons have been harmed by self-interested private groups. Above all, the privileges and immunities clause protects against state laws that deny to outsiders benefits granted to those who live within the state. Despite some minor differences, the commerce and privileges and immunities clauses are aimed at substantially identical evils.

Equal Protection Clause

The equal protection clause is not concerned solely with the special case of discrimination between in-staters and out-of-staters; its prohibition is far broader. Indeed, in many respects the clause may be understood as a generalization of the central concerns of the dormant commerce and privileges and immunities clauses, applying to all classifications their prohibition of naked preferences at the behest of in-staters.

Disadvantaged groups, impermissible ends, and heightened scrutiny. Discrimination against blacks, the central evil at which the equal protection clause was aimed, is the equal protection analogue of discrimination against out-of-staters under the commerce and privileges and immunities clauses. The doctrinal framework for addressing this central evil is formally almost identical under the three clauses. When a statute discriminates on its face against blacks, the Court applies a strong presumption of invalidity. The presumption is nearly irrebuttable: it can be overcome only by showing a legitimate and "compelling" government interest and an extremely close connection between that compelling interest and the particular discriminatory means the government has chosen to promote it.

One reason for heightened scrutiny is a belief that when a statute discriminates on its face against members of racial minority groups, a naked preference is almost certainly at work. Here, as under the dormant commerce and privileges and immunities clauses, a familiar idea—the relative political powerlessness of members of minority groups—helps account for that belief. The central notion here is that the ordinary avenues of political redress are much less likely to be available to minorities, and the danger that such statutes will result from an exercise of (what is seen as) raw political power is correspondingly increased. The equal protection context differs from that of the commerce clause in that minorities have formal access to power; the doctrinal protection is based on the functional rather than literal absence of a political remedy. By contrast, when discrimination is worked against whites—as in affirmative action legislation—there is good reason to suppose that the government motivation will be entirely different. As a result, the same degree of scrutiny is not applied.[20]

Current equal protection doctrine also goes beyond the use of heightened scrutiny to identify a number of ends as impermissible. These prohibited ends involve a wide range of justifications that do not involve the exercise of raw political power in the ordinary sense. The point becomes clearest in cases involving judicial scrutiny of classifications drawn on the basis of gender, alienage, and legitimacy. For example, when a statute provides that the spouses of male workers automatically qualify for Social Security benefits, but that spouses of female workers must show dependency, the classification hardly reflects an exercise of raw political power, narrowly understood, but instead embodies certain conceptions about the nature of female participation in the labor market. The Court's willingness to invalidate such statutes cannot be explained only as an enforcement of the minimal requirement that classifications rest on something other than raw power.

In the equal protection context, the Court has ruled that a wide range of legislative judgments about certain social groups are impermissible bases for differential treatment. The strong version of equal protection goes far beyond the minimal requirement that classifications must rest on something other than raw power; it embodies a complex and perhaps not entirely coherent normative framework. In part, the framework is the logical outgrowth of a theory that prohibits government from treating one person differently from another solely on the ground that it is desirable to do so. But the framework also reflects changing conceptions about the social subordination of the relevant groups. Such conceptions have made justifications involving the inability of women to compete in the job market, or the punishment of adultery through harming those born out of wedlock, seem increasingly intolerable—not public values at all.

Although the Court has not provided a clear rationale for its decisions here, the central ideas seem to be that the relevant groups are politically weak and that the traditional justifications for differential treatment both reflect and perpetuate existing relations of unequal power. In this respect, the Court's skeptical attitude toward such justifications reflects a willingness to scrutinize values that are apparently public and in any case widely shared to see whether they are in fact the product of political power.

Unlike in the dormant commerce clause context, however, and in an exceptionally controversial set of decisions, the Court has concluded that discriminatory effects on members of disadvantaged groups raise no constitutional problem except insofar as those effects reveal that the state has acted as a result of a discriminatory purpose.[21] This conclusion has substantially narrowed the constitutional antidiscrimination principle. It requires plaintiffs to allege and prove an impermissible motivation—a difficult burden—and thus insulates from serious constitutional scrutiny the enormously wide range of enactments that have disproportionate discriminatory effects on blacks and women. But if some of the Court's constitutional rulings are based on a principle that forbids the use of justifications based on purported public values in order to subordinate disadvantaged groups, legislative and judicial innovations, grounded in constitutional norms, might well be expected in the future. Such innovations would call into question discriminatory practices even if discriminatory purpose cannot be established.

Rationality review. The equal protection clause also calls on courts to assess classifications for "rationality" even if traditionally disadvantaged groups are not involved. Here, as elsewhere, the exercise of political power, standing alone, is an insufficient basis for classifications; but here, as elsewhere, rationality review is highly deferential and almost always results in the validation of statutory classifications.[22]

Due Process Clause

Similar considerations apply to constitutional tests under the due process clause. As it has come to be interpreted, the due process clause requires the government to come forward with a public value by which to justify the imposition of a burden on citizens. In the early part of the twentieth century, this norm was enforced quite aggressively, as courts invalidated a wide range of redistributive measures, treating them as naked transfers of wealth.[23] Since the New Deal, however, many justifications, including those that are redistributive in character, count as permissible exercises of the police power and are not regarded as simple reflections of the power of self-interested private groups. The police power is properly used to safeguard the interests of groups or subgroups of workers, consumers, and victims of discrimination. The Court has allowed a wide range of justification to count as public values, and it has applied limited scrutiny to most social and economic regulation. Even though it remains necessary to be able to point to some public value by which to justify legislative burdens, statutes are rarely invalidated under the due process clause.

An important exception to the usual rule of deference is the Court's protection of certain "fundamental rights," most notably privacy; here heightened scrutiny is applied.[24] It is under this rationale that the Court has invalidated laws restricting access to and use of contraceptives, interfering with familial intimacy, and (of course) regulating abortions. Some of these decisions might have been understood in terms of sex discrimination as well as privacy. Laws that restrict reproductive rights tend both to reflect and to perpetuate the social subordination of women—a fact to which the Court could not have been entirely blind. But whatever the rationale, the Court has applied heightened scrutiny to legislative intrusions on some rights thought to be central to bodily integrity, self-definition, or intimate association.

Contract Clause

The contract clause prohibits states from passing any "Law impairing the Obligations of Contracts." The clause was enacted in response to a perception that contracts were entitled to special protection from government manipulation, especially in the context of debtor relief legislation. The contract clause produced a series of early cases invalidating legislation on the ground that governmentally enacted changes in contractual obligations reflected only simple self-interest on the part of the benefited classes.

In the modern period, the prohibition of the contract clause has become far more lenient. The contract clause cases thus provide another example of an area in which the weak version of the prohibition of naked preferences offers little barrier to government action. No normative theory has developed to constrain the category of public values; no impermissible ends have been enumerated; courts rarely apply heightened scrutiny. Judicial scrutiny is now highly deferential—in general, identical to what we have seen under most applications of the equal protection and due process clauses. Scrutiny is heightened only when there is a particular basis for suspicion about the reasons for government action—as, for example, when the government impairs a contractual obligation in an agreement to which the government was itself a party.

Eminent Domain Clause

The eminent domain clause prohibits the taking of "private property . . . for public use, without just compensation." Two aspects of eminent domain doctrine are centrally concerned with the prohibition of naked preferences. First, eminent domain doctrine requires that a taking be for a "public use." The public use requirement is designed to ensure that legislation is for a plausibly public purpose and is not an effort to help a particular private group solely because of its political power.[25] Second, eminent domain doctrine draws a distinction between an impermissible taking and a legitimate exercise of the police power. In deciding whether legislative action falls legitimately within the police power, the courts consider whether the legislature is attempting to promote a general public good rather than simply transferring wealth to a self-interested private actor.[26] In both areas, however, courts are quite deferential to the legislature.

The Prohibition of Naked Preferences Revisited

This short survey should suffice to show the wide range of settings in which constitutional doctrines reject pluralist conceptions of politics. We are also in a position to examine some variations in the basic prohibition of naked preferences under the several clauses. Under the due process, contract, and eminent domain clauses, the Court has generally adopted the prohibition in close to its weakest form. Raw political power is not a legitimate basis for government action, but no other normative theory limits the ends that the government may pursue. For practical purposes, the line between public value and naked preference is quite thin, since attempts to protect particular groups are usually justifiable as responsive to some public value. Heightened scrutiny is applied under the contract clause only when a state abrogates a contract to which it is a party.

Of all these provisions, the equal protection clause has the most complex structure. As under the due process clause, rationality review reflects the weak version of the prohibition. Paralleling the prohibition of protectionism under the commerce and privileges and immunities clauses, discrimination against members of racial minority groups triggers a strong presumption of invalidity. But modern equal protection doctrine also reflects a theory that prohibits discrimination against women, aliens, illegitimates, and others, even in cases in which the weak version of the prohibition of naked preferences has not been violated. In part, these results are responsive to the perceived powerlessness of the various groups and to a resulting fear that a naked preference is at work. The cases go further than this, however, by prohibiting measures that are plausibly justified by reference to what would count—if majority sentiment is the criterion—as a public value. Perhaps the Court's approach can be attributed to changing social perceptions of the role and status of such groups; perhaps it is traceable to a perception that the relevant values in fact reflect existing relations of unequal power; perhaps it can be justified on other grounds. But there is no doubt that it assimilates several forms of discrimination to the prohibition of naked preferences, identifying certain government ends as impermissible.

An important question raised by these developments involves the reasons for the shift from a strong to a weak version of the basic prohibition and—under several clauses—the more recent shift to a different kind of strong version. The due process, eminent domain, and contract clauses in particular reflect an almost identical shift from a pre-New Deal conception of impermissible government ends to modern rationality review. A central reason for this shift is the declining centrality of private property to modern constitutional adjudication. Under all three clauses, courts have come to see the existing distribution of entitlements and wealth not as natural and inviolate, but as the result of conscious government choice. The governmental decision to allow the existing distribution to stand is itself a choice requiring justification. As a result, efforts to alter an existing distribution in favor of an alternative appear not be naked wealth transfers, but legitimate efforts to promote the public good.[27]

The abandonment of private property as a touchstone for judicial inquiry has left something of a vacuum in constitutional adjudication. Under the contract, eminent domain, and due process clauses, private property served an important ordering function. The pre-New Deal decisions under these clauses illustrate the point. In these decisions, a large category of legislative ends, usually including the redistribution of wealth or entitlements, did not qualify as public values. In the modern era, the vacuum left by the decline of private property has been filled only by a crudely conceived right of "privacy" developed under the due process clause.

A strong version of the prohibition has reemerged in recent years, primarily under the equal protection clause. That strong version substitutes for the touchstone of property a new conception based on an amalgam of three principal features: a theory of impermissible motivations for treating one group differently from another; a rough guess about the groups that are likely to be subordinated or otherwise mistreated in the pluralist process; and (occasionally) an effort to inspect the legislative process in order to ensure that the relevant values are genuinely public, in the sense that they are the product of broad deliberation rather than interest-group struggle.

All of these elements amount to an attack on the premises of interest-group pluralism. The last one in particular embodies a perception that even if the political process is open and available to all, particular exercises of government power should be inspected to ensure that a public value, defined in both procedural and substantive terms, is at work. In this respect, the rise of equal protection scrutiny may be understood as comparable not to the aggressive judicial role preceding the New Deal, but to the subsequent understanding that the existing social order should be regarded not as natural but as the product of public choices. As such, it must be subjected to critical scrutiny. An understanding of this sort holds out the promise (or threat) of a highly intrusive judicial role. But whether the various developments discussed in this essay will coalesce into a coherent substitute for the property-based rationale of previous constitutional doctrines remains to be seen.

Conclusion

Many provisions of the Constitution are aimed at a single evil: the distribution of resources to one person or group rather than another on the sole ground that those benefited have exercised political power in order to obtain government assistance. This understanding straightforwardly rejects interest-group pluralism, which sees the political process as precisely this sort of unprincipled warfare for scarce social resources. Under all of the clauses, such warfare is constitutionally impermissible. To be sure, the prohibition does not always result in invalidation. But the cases are strikingly unanimous in their vision of the prohibited end. In this respect, they reflect a sharp critique of interest-group pluralism, rather than an attempt to improve it through ensuring the representation of all private interests.

This prohibition derives from a conception of politics having roots in both republican thought and the writings of James Madison. It places a high premium on political deliberation, and it envisions deliberative processes as a constraint on governmental outcomes. Constitutional doctrines thus reject self-interest as a sufficient basis for legislative behavior. Nor would it be plausible to explain judicial behavior under these clauses as a function of judicial self-interest. The category of influences on federal judges is too open-ended and diffuse to permit attribution of judicial outcomes simply to the self-interest of the judges.

All this raises a number of questions. We have seen that for the most part, the prohibition of naked preferences is only weakly enforced. Courts give the legislature the benefit of every doubt, finding public values in cases in which naked self-interest is quite plausibly at work. Some observers have suggested that courts ought to approach such measures more aggressively.[28] Moreover, some of the equal protection cases carry the seeds of a substantive theory that treats some public values as a mask for private power. This development remains, however, in a highly tentative state. Perhaps the prohibition of naked preferences will eventually be used as the basis for a constitutional theory striking at measures that subordinate various social groups.

However these problems are resolved, there can be no question that current legal doctrines conspicuously reject interest-group pluralism as a constitutional creed. They point instead to a conception of politics that demands a measure of deliberation from government representatives, deliberation that has some autonomy from private pressures. In judge-made constitutional law, as in the founding period, self-interest is an inadequate basis for the distribution of social benefits or the imposition of social burdens.

VII   International Relations

14 Empathy and International Regimes

Robert O. Keohane

Of the two major schools of thought on international relations in the United States, idealists have traditionally called for international cooperation in the interests of humanity as a whole. Idealism has a long history in Anglo-American thinking on foreign affairs and has been particularly prominent in American foreign policy (Osgood 1953; Wolfers and Martin 1956). Since World War II, however, idealism has clearly been subordinate to a contrasting Realist emphasis on self-interest. Indeed, much of my own work has deliberately adopted Realist assumptions of egoism, as well as rationality, in order to demonstrate that there are possibilities for cooperation even on Realist premises.

Writers who by and large accept the Realist tradition sometimes admit that not all international behavior can be explained egoistically. Hans J. Morgenthau, for instance, declares that the ultimate goals of foreign policy may derive from legal and ethical principles. His distinctive argument is not that ideals are unimportant in determining goals, but that foreign policy analysis can ignore ideals because power is a necessary means: "the immediate aim is power" (1948, 1966: 25; see also 84–85). The flaw in this contention, which has often been pointed out, is that power is by no means homogeneous, so that the "search for power" takes many different forms, whose characteristics depend in part on the ultimate goals of the actor (Wolfers 1962: 81–102), as well as on the particular contexts within which attempts at exerting influence take place (Baldwin 1979). In discussing these goals, Arnold Wolfers argued that states sometimes pursue policies of "self-abnegation." For Wolfers, self-abnegation "is the goal of those who place a higher value on such ends as international solidarity, lawfulness, rectitude, or peace than they place even on national security and self-preservation" (1962: 93). Wolfers regards pursuit of self-abnegation as rare but not impossible (p. 94):

This essay has been adapted from Robert O. Keohane, *After Hegemony: Cooperation and Discord in the World Political Economy* (Princeton: Princeton University Press, 1984), pp. 120–32.

Cases in which self-abnegation goals have precedence over national self-preservation may be rare in an era in which nationalism and the ethics of patriotism continue unabated. This does not preclude the possibility, however, that where influential groups of participants in the decision-making process place high value on a universal cause such as peace, pressures exerted by these groups may affect the cause of foreign policy. It may lead to a more modest interpretation of the national interest, to more concern for the interests of other nations, to more concessions for the sake of peace, or to more restraint in the use of power and violence. Whether the nation will profit or suffer in the end from the success of such "internationalist," "humanitarian," or "pacifist" pressures depends on the circumstances of the case; whichever it does, the abnegation goals will have proved themselves a reality.

Wolfers is particularly concerned with military and security issues, in which the price of self-abnegation may be national independence. It is not surprising that policies of self-abnegation are rarely followed when threats to independence are severe. But if tendencies toward self-abnegation occasionally appear even when the costs of failure are so high, such policies may be more plausible when the stakes are lower, as in the world political economy. Wolfers's argument suggests, at a minimum, that we should not assume the universal validity of egoistic models. To reveal the inadequacy of the logic that derives the necessity of discord from fragmentation of power, it is sometimes useful to adopt the egoistic assumption (Keohane 1984). It is also, however, illuminating to relax this premise.

To relax the assumption of egoism by drawing a sharp distinction between egoism and altruism, however, would confuse the issue. Egoism can be farsighted as well as myopic. Altruism is difficult to identify clearly, since apparently altruistic behavior can always be reinterpreted as egoistic: the "altruist" may be seen as *preferring* to sacrifice herself rather than to violate a principle or see someone else suffer. Thus it is often impossible to determine whether to classify a given action as one of farsighted egoism or altruism. This difficulty is instructive, for it reflects the fact that the very idea of self-interest is so elastic. Rather than argue about egoism versus altruism, we need to ask how people and organizations define self-interest. What beliefs and values do they take into account?

⟶ The crucial issue here is how actors see their own interests relative to those of others. To what extent are their interests independent of those of others, and to what extent are they interdependent with others' welfare? Four different situations can be imagined.

1. Actors may be *indifferent* to the welfare of others. This would be the situation in a purely Hobbesian world in which exchanges took place between entities that would never have anything to do with each other again.

But for the same reasons that single-play Prisoners' Dilemma is not a good representation of world politics, this is a deficient image of reality. Relationships among states are ongoing and persistent.

2. Actors may be interested in the welfare of others only insofar as the others can take action that affects them. In such a situation, we will refer to interests as being *instrumentally interdependent*. Egoists in iterated Prisoners' Dilemma have instrumentally interdependent interests: each takes into account the effect of her actions on those of the other players, not because she cares about their welfare per se but because they may retaliate against her own defection.

3. Actors may be interested in the welfare of others not only for instrumental reasons, but because improvements in others' welfare improve their own, and vice versa, whatever the other actor does. In this case, interests are *situationally interdependent*. As the world economy has become more tightly knit together since the end of World War II, situational interdependence has increased. It is bad for the U.S. economy for Europe or Japan to undergo a severe recession, reducing demand for American goods. Brazil's prosperity is important to the United States, even apart from what might happen politically as a result of economic collapse, because a bankrupt Brazil could not pay its debts to American banks. Close-knit trade and financial networks in the contemporary world, reflecting the growth of economic interdependence, can directly transmit welfare effects, good or bad, from one society to another. They therefore make the interests of even egoistically inclined actors situationally interdependent, *regardless* of any actions that any of them may take.

4. Finally, actors may be interested in the welfare of others for their own sake, even if this has no effect on their own material well-being or security. Public and private agencies in wealthy countries send relief to victims of disaster and provide considerable amounts of foreign aid. Much governmental aid can be explained on narrowly self-interested grounds, but this explanation may not be convincing in accounting for programs of small countries such as Holland or Sweden, and it seems largely irrelevant to activities of voluntary agencies such as Oxfam or CARE. We will label this *empathetic interdependence*.[1]

The distinction between myopic and farsighted self-interest presupposes instrumental or situational interdependence. The farsightedness of an egoistic actor depends on the number and range of issues that she treats as potentially related to her behavior on a given question. The myopic actor takes into account only the immediate issue, whereas the farsighted one also assesses the effects of the decision facing her on other interests she may have. Both, however, only consider their own welfare in making these calculations.[2] Raising the question of empathy takes us beyond this distinction to a deeper question of values.

To speak of empathy in world politics may seem to put one beyond the Realist pale. Yet, in a world of high mobility, instantaneous communication, and extensive transnational relations of various kinds (Keohane and Nye 1972), it is not obvious that solidaristic relationships coincide with national boundaries. Paul Taylor has pointed out that feelings of community in Europe may on occasion prevail over utilitarian considerations: "the calculation of advantage from cooperation in relation to particular interests may be secondary to a preference for cooperation with a particular partner or partners" (1980: 373). Furthermore, public opinion research in Europe has shown that, when asked about intra-European relations, a large proportion of people display policy preferences that deviate from what one would expect on the basis of narrow self-interest. In response to a poll taken in 1977, for instance, over 70 percent of respondents in each of the nine European Community countries declared that if another member of the Community were in serious economic trouble, its partners should help it; and a plurality of respondents even said that their own representatives to the European Parliament should put European interests ahead of national ones (Inglehart and Rubier 1978: 78, 82–84). These responses may reflect a mixture of instrumental, situational, and empathetic interdependence. But, along with recent work questioning the moral significance of boundaries in world politics (Beitz 1979a, 1979b), they suggest the possibility that, in limited ways, interests could be interpreted empathetically. In such situations, self-interests would by no means have disappeared. Rather, they would have been redefined so as to depend on the welfare of others being realized as well.

What I have called "egoism" refers to conceptions of interests as independent or only instrumentally or situationally interdependent. Relaxing the assumption of egoism means entertaining the possibility that governments and other actors in world politics may redefine their interests so that they are empathetically dependent on those of others. The consequences for cooperation could be far-reaching. Governments that regard themselves as empathetically interdependent will be more inclined than egoists to reach for greater joint gains—solutions to international problems that lead to larger overall value—even at the expense of direct gains to themselves. They will be so inclined because they will also benefit vicariously from the gains achieved by others. Shared interests will therefore be greater. The set of possible agreements regarded as mutually beneficial will be at least as large as it is for egoists, and probably larger.

Egoism and Empathy as Competing Explanations

Empathetic explanations of behavior in world politics are limited to relatively small spheres of activity: situations in which actions do not have obvious explanations in terms of more narrowly defined self-interest. The presumption in a self-help system is that empathy will play a subordinate role. Even when behavior appears to be motivated by empathy, it may be possible to construct an alternative, and plausible, explanation for it on the premise of egoism. Examination of these competing accounts may suggest some of the strengths and limitations of egoistic and empathetic interpretations of behavior associated with international regimes.

I will now consider two patterns of behavior that seem difficult to explain on egoistic grounds: the moralistic overlay of rules in world politics, and the existence of exchange relationships that, at least for a substantial period of time, are unbalanced. I seek first to account for these phenomena through the use of rational-egoist models. In both cases, a line of argument can be constructed using such models to account for the behavior in question. This suggests the power of the premise of egoism, since even where action seems at first glance to be motivated by empathy, it can be reinterpreted as egoistic. Yet in neither case is the egoistic account entirely satisfactory. It should be clear that I have no intention of debunking explanations resting on the assumption of self-interest; rather, I wish to see how far they can legitimately run, and whether there are some phenomena, even at the margins of political economy, that are accounted for more adequately on the basis of empathetic interdependence.

Treating Rules as Moral Obligations

From a Realist perspective, it is remarkable how moralistic governments often are in discussing their obligations and those of others. The rules of international regimes are often discussed not merely as convenient devices for altering transaction costs and reducing uncertainty, but as principles and rules that create obligations. Leaders of governments proclaim their adherence to these principles and rules; furthermore, they argue that other governments are morally obligated to keep their agreements as well. International regimes can be valuable for purely egoistic states. But why do normative connotations, involving an intertwining of moral codes with international law, develop? As H. L. A. Hart (1961: 226) emphasizes, law need not be based on a system of morality, but can be maintained by calculations of long-term self-interest or for other reasons. If rational egoism were a sufficient explanation for international regimes, how could one explain the moralistic overlay of world politics?

A fairly straightforward argument on egoist grounds can be constructed in response. Even rules regarded as having no moral validity may be obeyed by egoists, since to violate them would damage not only a mutually beneficial set of arrangements but also the violator's reputation, and thus her ability to make future agreements. Now notice how much more effective these rules and principles can be if they do have moral content!

Members of the group will suffer from less uncertainty about others' behavior, because defecting from agreements will be morally proscribed and therefore more damaging to a rule-violator's reputation than if the regime were regarded merely as a convenient device to facilitate the coordination of behavior. Since there will be less uncertainty, members of the group will be better able to make mutually beneficial agreements than they would have been if no moral code existed. In a discussion of cooperation that begins with the example of Prisoners' Dilemma, a philosopher has concluded that "prudence is not enough, that the rational calculation of long-term self-interest is not sufficient in itself (necessarily) to lead men to make mutually beneficial agreements or, once made, to keep them" (Mackie 1977: 119–20). He concludes that "the main moral is the practical value of the notion of obligation, or an invisible and indeed fictitious tie or bond, whether this takes the form of a general requirement to keep whatever agreements one makes or of various specific duties like those of military honour or of loyalty to comrades or to an organization" (p. 119).

Morality may therefore "pay" for the group as a whole. It may also pay for the individual government. Adhering to a moral code may identify an actor as a political cooperator, part of a cluster of players with whom mutually beneficial agreements can be made, as in Robert Axelrod's model (1981, 1984). That is, publicly accepting a set of principles as morally binding may perform a labeling function. If the code were too passive—turn the other cheek—the moralist could be exploited by the egoist, but if the code prescribes reciprocity in a "tit-for-tat" manner, it may be a valuable label for its adherents. Each egoistic government could privately dismiss moral scruples, but if a moral code based on reciprocity were widely professed, it would be advantageous for even those governments to behave as if they believed it. Vice would pay homage to virtue.

Thus we could account for the existence of professed moral principles in world politics on purely self-interested grounds. Perhaps rules would not really be regarded as moral obligations, but they would be treated publicly as if they were. However neat this explanation, though, it is probably too cynical. For representative governments such as those that rule the major market-economy countries, it is difficult to separate "real" from "public" motivations. Moralists such as Woodrow Wilson and Jimmy Carter sometimes gain high office; indeed, their moralism may appeal to the electorate. Furthermore, even officials without strong moral principles have to defend their policies, and it is often convenient to do so in moral terms. This requirement may lead them, in order to avoid cognitive dissonance, to take on some of the beliefs that they profess. The act of piety may engender piety itself, as in Pascal's famous wager.[3]

Unbalanced Exchange

International regimes sometimes seem to facilitate unbalanced material exchanges in which, at a given time, one side provides much more in the way of tangible resources than the other. These apparently one-sided exchanges may involve resources provided in the present—such as aid or access to markets—as did the Marshall Plan, many of the trade arrangements characteristic of the 1950s, and some contemporary foreign aid. They may also involve promises to provide such resources in the future.

Unbalanced exchanges seem prima facie to contradict rational-egoist premises. Yet the theorist of egoism has a powerful response, which is to reinterpret them as, by definition, balanced exchanges. Each observable material flow is assumed to have an intangible counterpart. Often such an interpretation is justified, as in European and Japanese deference after World War II in exchange for American aid, reflecting the "influence effect" of the latter (Hirschman 1945/1980). The United States sent material goods to Europe that were of greater value than those received. In return, the U.S. gained influence—the basis for what Klaus Knorr (1975: 25) calls "patronal leadership," or hegemonic leadership. The reverse flow of influence, resulting from deference by the client, suggests that a patron-client relationship can often be reconceptualized as an exchange relationship in which intangible as well as tangible flows of benefits take place.

This response rests on the assumption that reciprocity is the underlying principle of a self-help system: when we observe a flow of resources in one direction, there must be a reciprocal flow in the other. Before accepting this premise, however, it may be worthwhile to probe more deeply into the concept of reciprocity and its implications for international relations.

Norms of reciprocity seem to be virtually universal as elements of culture, making "two interrelated minimal demands: (1) people should help those who have helped them, and (2) people should not injure those who have helped them" (Gouldner 1960: 171). But reciprocity takes different forms in different societies, or for the same relationships in the same society. In his discussion of "stone-age economics," Marshall Sahlins makes a useful distinction among what he calls "negative," "balanced," and "generalized" reciprocity (1972, chap. 5, esp. pp. 185–220).

Negative reciprocity refers to attempts to maximize utility at the expense of others, through fraud and violence if necessary. At the limit, it corresponds to aggressive war in world politics. Negative reciprocity reflects a strategy that is not well adapted to situations in which each actor's welfare depends, at least in part, on securing the voluntary cooperation of others over a protracted period of time. Indeed, Sahlins finds (consistent with our argument about international regimes) that elaborate institutional arrangements develop among primitive peoples with the function of achieving "a social suppression of negative reciprocity" (p. 201).

Balanced reciprocity is characterized by simultaneous direct exchange of equally valued goods (pp. 194–95). Balanced reciprocity is closer than negative reciprocity to exchange relationships in the world political economy, since it is based on realization of mutual gains from trade. But the characterization of balanced reciprocity as *simultaneous* distinguishes it rather sharply from patterns of exchange facilitated by international regimes. Indeed, this distinction helps us clarify further the role played by regimes. International regimes can be thought of in part as arrangements that facilitate *nonsimultaneous* exchange. In purely simultaneous exchange, neither party has to accept obligations, rules, or principles, since the exchange is balanced at every moment. There is never a "debt" or a "credit." An extreme example is provided by the settlement between Iran and the United States in 1981, in which American diplomats held hostage by Iran were liberated in return for the release of Iranian financial assets in the United States. Elaborate arrangements were made, involving Algeria and Britain, to ensure that neither side could double-cross the other by withholding its part of the bargain after receiving what it wanted. In the complete absence of an international regime linking the United States with the revolutionary government of Iran, laborious negotiations were necessary to set up an ad hoc arrangement to permit balanced reciprocity that benefited both sides.

This sort of perfectly balanced reciprocity provides an unsatisfactory basis for long-term relationships. Sahlins comments that among primitive tribes "a measure of imbalance sustains the trade partnership, compelling as it does another meeting" (p. 201). In the world political economy, international regimes make temporary imbalances feasible, since they create incentives (in the form partly of obligations) to repay debts. Thus regimes perform functions similar to those of credit markets, and it is not surprising that much of their activity is devoted to providing information that facilitates agreement. This is true of contemporary investigations of "country risk" undertaken by banks that want to know their borrowers; and it was true of the medieval European Bourses, which provided information in the form of merchants' newsletters and exchanges of information at fairs.[4] Like international regimes, furthermore, credit markets depend on institutional reputation, which cannot be created in a short period of time, or through promises or argument alone, but is based on past performance. As Walter Bagehot said, "every banker knows that if he has to *prove* that he is worthy of credit, however good may be his arguments, in fact his credit is gone. . . . Credit is a power which may grow, but cannot be constructed" (1873/1962: 33). The reputations of international organizations and governments grow over a substantial period of time; they can be quickly destroyed, but not so rapidly rebuilt.

Credit arrangements, like insurance contracts, provide for exchanges that are expected to benefit both parties in the long run, but not to be balanced at any given time. The principle of ultimate symmetry of benefits, however, is maintained. In Sahlin's third type of reciprocity, "generalized reciprocity," this constraint is lifted. Generalized reciprocity characterizes certain sustained one-way flows of transactions, which Sahlins terms "putatively altruistic." No obligations are specified in return for the transfer of resources; the expectation of reciprocity is indefinite. Receipt of a gift only creates "a diffuse obligation to reciprocate when necessary to the donor and/or possible for the recipient. . . . Failure to reciprocate does not cause the giver of stuff to stop giving: the goods move one way, in favor of the have-not, for a very long period" (pp. 193–94).

Within primitive societies, generalized or near-generalized reciprocity is limited to relatively close kinship and residential groups. We should therefore be cautious about assuming that whenever we see an apparently onesided flow of benefits in world politics, it should be considered a true example of generalized reciprocity, especially since the egoistic explanation for this phenomenon is so powerful. What Sahlin's categories do, however, is to broaden our conception of reciprocity and therefore call attention to the fact that apparently unbalanced exchanges can be interpreted in a variety of ways. They may be regarded as balanced by the exchange of intangible for tangible benefits; they may involve credit or insurance, in which current benefits are exchanged for future ones; or they may be cases of "generalized reciprocity," without specified reciprocal obligations.

Insofar as apparently unbalanced exchanges can be reinterpreted as balanced, they can be accounted for by instrumental self-interest. Regimes play an important role in exchanges such as these: institutionalizing deference, as in America's period of hegemony, or providing information that facilitates credit or insurance agreements. Generalized reciprocity, by contrast, reflects either situational or empathetic interdependence of interests. One gives unrequited gifts either because doing so will help oneself, regardless of reciprocity, or because one cares about the recipient's welfare.

The notion of generalized reciprocity does not substitute for an egoistic interpretation of unbalanced exchanges, but it may supplement such an interpretation by helping us to broaden our notions both of self-interest and of reciprocity. For instance, an interpretation of the Marshall Plan and other U.S. measures toward Europe after 1947 as generalized reciprocity would clearly not be adequate alone, since in times of crisis, such as Suez, the United States did require deference. Nevertheless, ascribing some weight to situational or empathetic interdependence is plausible in view of the widespread perception in America that U.S. welfare depended on a prosperous and democratic Europe, and in view of the close personal ties that many American statesmen had with Europeans. Furthermore, a difficulty with the pure egoistic-exchange view is that it would be hard now, much less in 1947 or 1956, to determine whether the United States extracted "enough" deference to compensate for its aid. It seems best to view the Marhsall Plan as a combination of an exchange relationship—material benefits in return for present and future deference—and generalized reciprocity based on situational and empathetic interdependence.

In short, I have argued here that if governments' definitions of self-interest incorporate empathy, they will be more able than otherwise to construct international regimes, since shared interests will be greater. Empathy is more fragile and elusive than bounded rationality: actions that may lend themselves to explanations based on empathy can also be interpreted in ways consistent with egoistic theories. Yet the behavior of actual nations has led me to question the solidity of the assumption of self-interest on which rational-egoist models rely. Since the notion of self-interest is so elastic, we have to examine what this premise means, rather than simply take it for granted. A complete analysis of regimes would have to show how international regimes could change as a result not of shifts in the allegedly objective interests of states, or in the power distributions and institutional conditions facing governments, but of changes in how people think about their interests, including the possibility that they may be interested in the welfare of others, both from empathy and from principle.

VIII Modeling

15   Dual Utilities and Rational Choice

Howard Margolis

Nobody is puzzled when a colleague says of a piece of legislation, "I would be personally better off without it, but in terms of the public interest I hope it passes." It would be hard to make sense of such remarks, which all of us have heard and most of us have made, unless people have a sense of social preferences distinct from their sense of private preferences. Further, social preferences apparently can command some share of our resources. No one has been able to make much sense of such commonplace acts as contributing to charity or public television, or helping a stranger in distress, or simply bothering to vote, other than in terms of social motivation or something functionally equivalent.

Readers who follow the rational choice literature will be aware of various formulations which work as well as postulating social preferences to account for contributing or voting, but on the whole work no better. We can say a person votes because he likes to vote, or feels good about voting, or wants to look like a good citizen, or feels a duty to be a good citizen. Most often, all these reasons are just ways of saying that the person is behaving, on this occasion, *as if* moved by social rather than narrowly self-interested preferences. So if the citizen does not vote, rational choice explains his abstinence as a natural response to the microscopic significance of one vote; if he does vote, then any of the possibilities mentioned seems to serve about equally well to patch things up.

We might have a theory with real analytical bite, however, if we could specify something about *when* a person acts as if moved by social preferences, and how such motivation might interact with private preferences.

The three sections of this paper give (1) an informal summary of the dual-utilities model I developed in my *Selfishness, Altruism, and Rationality* (Margolis 1982/1984); (2) an illustration of how the model works in the context of a puzzle that arises in accounting for rational voting even when

The author is indebted for comments to Bob Chirinko, Jane Mansbridge, and Norman Schofield, and to a seminar organized by Jon Elster.

actors might be socially motivated; and (3) a description of two more conventional contexts in which models of choice arise which turn out to be mathematically identical to that of the dual-utilities model.

In all three sections, the paper emphasizes the *irreducibly* dual character of the preferences postulated, and seeks to suggest why there may be nothing conceptually wrong or unreasonable in that duality, and much that is empirically plausible.

1

We want a rule, or set of rules, that will determine when a marginal bit of resources will be allocated to satisfy social, rather than private, preferences. The choice could concern time, material resources, or the favor of other actors, but for simplicity I will just speak of the "marginal dollar." We want some procedure that will govern the *balance* or *equilibrium* between spending on social and private preferences. Translated into a person's subjective sense of things, we want a specification that could capture a person's sense that he is doing his fair share, so that he feels neither selfish nor exploited in the way he allocates between spending on his private interests and spending on what he takes to be social interests.

Here is a particularly simple pair of rules that might provide all we need (Margolis 1982/1984: 39). Rule 1 concerns the *value ratio;* rule 2 concerns the *participation ratio.*

Rule 1. Other things equal, the more social utility I can get with a marginal dollar relative to the private utility I can get, the more likely I will be to allocate the dollar to my social preferences.

Rule 2. Other things equal (in particular, even if the marginal value ratio of rule 1 is unchanged), the larger the ratio of my social spending to my private spending, the less likely I am to allocate yet another dollar that way.

So we have a pair of rules, of which the first can be seen as favoring social spending, the second as restraining it. Economists, especially, are tempted to read rule 2 as merely an addendum to rule 1 which postulates diminishing marginal utility. But that is a mistaken reading, and the parenthetical clause is intended to preempt that misreading. What rule 2 says is illustrated by the following: Suppose that in a certain context a person would allocate a dollar to her social preferences only if the social value were at least twice as great as the private value she could obtain with that dollar. And suppose she does spend that dollar on her social preferences. Rule 2 says that if we now give her another dollar to spend, then a social value to private value ratio of 2 would no longer be enough to get her to spend the dollar on social preferences. The value ratio would now have to be more than 2. And this has nothing to do, one way or the other, with any assumption about declining marginal utility.

A seesaw diagram lets us picture how the pair of rules would operate: in fact, two different but equivalent seesaw diagrams work, and it may help to look at the balancing problem both ways (see figs. 14.1 and 14.2).

Let G' be the value of a marginal dollar if spent on social preferences. Let S' be the corresponding value if the dollar is spent on private preferences. The G here stands for "group interest"; S here stands for "self-interest." So G'/S' will give us the value ratio needed to implement rule 1. It is the ratio between the value of group-interested, social use of the dollar versus self-interested, private use of the dollar. The bigger that ratio is, other things equal, the more likely the dollar will be spent on group interest (G-spending). The smaller it is, the more likely the dollar will be spent on self-interest (S-spending).

Now we need to define the weight (W) needed to handle rule 2. Specifically, W must govern how far the person favors self-interest over group-interest. According to rule 2, W must vary such that the larger the participation ratio, the larger the value of W must be. Mathematically, $W = f(g/s)$, where g is the amount spent on G-utility, and s is the amount spent on S-utility. Rule 2 then requires $W' > 0$. Equilibrium occurs when $G' = WS'$.

Consider a sample citizen (call her Ellie Smith).[1] From rules 1 and 2, she will allocate the dollar to social G-spending if $WS' < G'$, allocate it to self-interest if $WS' > G'$, and be in balance (in equilibrium, and so not moved to shift the balance of her spending one way or the other) when $WS' = G'$. Alternatively, we can write the same equilibrium condition as $W = G'/S'$, which has the virtue of emphasizing the intuition that grounds the model (the balancing of the conflicting pressures from the value ratio in rule 1 and the participation ratio, which governs W, in rule 2).

In the first seesaw diagram (fig. 14.1), the value ratio (G'/S') is on the right and the weight (W) is on the left. As Ellie uses resources, or as things happen to Ellie or to Ellie's society, G', S', and W all change. If the seesaw is tilted down to the right, then she would allocate a marginal dollar to

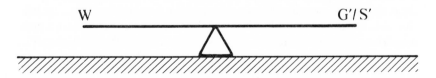

Fig. 14.1. Seesaw.

Fig. 14.2. Off-center seesaw.

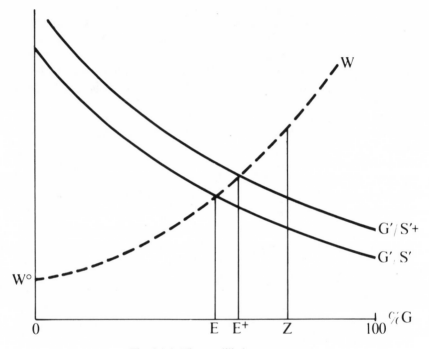

Fig. 14.3. The equilibrium process.

G-spending, and the converse if the seesaw is tilted to the left. She is in equilibrium, feels she has done her fair share, feels neither selfish nor exploited when the seesaw is in balance.

A second seesaw diagram may give a better picture of the dynamics of the situation. Here (fig. 14.2) *S'* is on the left, *G'* on the right, and *W* is the fulcrum. As you will remember from playground days, the heavier person does not necessarily tilt the seesaw her way. How the allocation goes depends on how far the fulcrum favors *S'* over *G'*. The farther to the right the fulcrum is, the greater the leverage given to *S'*. If Ellie allocates the dollar to *G*-spending, that pushes *W* even more to the right (rule 2), increasing the leverage of *S*-spending in allocating the next dollar.

Figure 14.3 shows how the equilibrium process would work. Along the vertical axis we have scales for both the weight (W) and the value ratio (G'/S'). On the horizontal axis, we have the fraction of Ellie's resources that have been allocated to G-spending. So at the origin Ellie is spending nothing at all socially, and on the right she is spending 100 percent of her resources socially with nothing left for her private interest. Consider the particularly simple case where diminishing marginal utility always holds. For that usual case, G'/S' must decline as we move to the right in the diagram. For Ellie is spending less on herself, so S' (marginal utility of private spending) must be increasing. G' correspondingly will be decreasing or perceptibly constant (since if Ellie is one person in a large society, G' would not ordinarily be noticeably affected by the spending of any single person). Whether the decline in G' is perceptible or not, the value ratio (G'/S') must be getting smaller. Hence the curve for G'/S' is downward sloping, as shown.

The rising curve measures W. We can set $W = 1$ when the share of Ellie's resources allocated to G-spending is zero (so the participation ratio is zero). But from rule 2, W must increase as the participation ratio increases. Equilibrium occurs at the point labeled E, where $W = G'/S'$.

Suppose Ellie found herself at Z, where $W > G'/S'$. By shifting resources to favor her private interests, she could restore herself to equilibrium. For that would move her left in the figure, decreasing W and increasing G'/S', reaching equilibrium at E.

Alternatively, suppose Ellie's wealth increases. Then for any fraction of wealth allocated to G-spending, the amount left for S-spending will be larger, hence S' smaller. For Ellie as one citizen in a large society, G' would ordinarily be sensibly constant. So the increase in Ellie's wealth would shift her value ratio upward (the dashed line, $G'/S' +$, in fig. 14.3), and her equilibrium allocation would therefore shift to the right, to $E +$. So an almost immediate implication of the dual-utilities model is that, other things equal, as wealth increases, the share of resources spent on what an individual takes to be social spending increases. In the language of economics, social spending turns out to be a superior good, though in another sense Ellie is also becoming more selfish: W is increasing.

Although I cannot go much further here with the detailed articulation of the model, one point that is especially important is that for actual spending (in contrast to the abstract G- and S-spending considered so far) there will rarely be pure G- or S-spending. Almost any way Ellie might use a dollar would yield some S-utility and also some G-utility. Of course in many contexts one or the other can be ignored as too small to warrant explicit attention. But for a large class of cases both elements are essential. If a person contributes to public television, he is doing what he presumably thinks is something socially useful, but the station will also send him some private gift (a coffee mug, t-shirt, or whatever). A man may volunteer time and money to what he takes to be a good social or political cause. But doing that might also be good for business, or get him invited to a party he'd enjoy attending. And so on.

The "dual-utilities" logic emphasizes the essentially mixed character of the motivation that governs most real choices (Margolis 1982/1984): 25, 51–55). Social motivation is not treated merely as an escape hatch, to be used when the usual self-interested assumptions get into trouble; nor does allowing for social motivation involve "shifting moral gears" or any more schizophrenic mental feats. Ellie is not strictly selfish most of the time, then abruptly a social paragon on certain other occasions. She is moved all the time by social as well as private motivation, and her spending is allocated in a way that (following the logic of the rationality assumptions that underlie the model) seeks to exploit complementaries in her spending opportunities, so that spending can yield a favorable return to social interests with as little loss as possible to self-interest, and the converse.

In more recent work (Margolis 1987), and in common with many other theorists in the past few years, I've become much more aware of the need to augment the mechanical calculus of rational choice with allowance for how flesh-and-blood cognition and perception actually work. Allowing for cognition as well as calculation would require some change in our conception of the operation of equilibrium-seeking process. But the essentials of the model would remain as I have sketched them.

2

To rational choice scholars, what looks particularly suspicious about this dual-utilities model is the claim that people have *irreducibly* distinct social and private preferences. There is no grand maximand, where social value is traded off against private value. We have an equilibrium condition ($W = G'/S'$) that looks something like the usual first-order optimizing condition. But nothing is specified which the equilibrium condition is the first-order condition *of.* This seems bizarre to almost anyone well drilled in rational choice formalisms, where the process routinely turns on deriving an equilibrium condition from a specified maximand. But here, although resources allocated to S-spending are used to maximize S-utility in the usual way, and resources allocated to G-spending are used to maximize G-utility in a straightforward analogue of the usual way, no grand maximand governs the allocation *between* G- and S-spending. The model could be called a model of "dual rationality," if we want to distinguish it from the standard notion of rational choice (Margolis 1982/1984: 14–16).

What counts, of course, is how the model works empirically, not how we label it.

We can give an account of how the model works by thinking of conflicting Darwinian selection pressures at the level of individuals and groups (Margolis 1982/1984, chap. 3). If there were selection at only one level or the other, then we would have a maximum problem (with respect to fitness of individuals or of the group). But if both factors were significant, then we would get some compromise between individual and group motivation that isn't *maximizing* anything—just as the final score of a football game doesn't maximize anything, even though it emerges as the interaction of two teams, each trying to maximize its probability of winning.[2]

In this section I try to take a step or two toward making the dual-utilities idea less counter intuitive, or at least try to set up a clearer target for critics. The discussion uses a particularly familiar concrete context— that of voting.

The expected value to self-interest of one vote could hardly amount to as much as a penny when that vote is one among many millions (Margolis 1982/1984: 82–86). Noticing the low payoff to self-interest yields the notorious "paradox of rational voting." But would allowing for social (not just self-interested) motivation resolve the paradox? If Ellie were voting out of social concern, she might reasonably see a large social gain (easily $1 billion or more) from the election of a particular presidential candidate. For $1 billion is a small number compared to the trillion-dollar federal budget a president shapes, smaller still compared to the GNP his policies influence, and trivial compared to the costs should a president blunder into a nuclear war.

Hence if Ellie were to attach a numerical value to the advantage to the country of electing what she judges to be the better president, that number could easily be in the billions.[3] Ellie's one vote would provide only a tiny increment (one part in tens of millions) to the probability that Ellie's candidate actually wins. But since the social value is very large, the expected value of her vote can still be perfectly respectable (say $10 or more) compared to the cost of voting.

So there seems to be no great puzzle about how to account for rational voting if Ellie were moved by social, not only by self-interested, motivation. Yet the puzzle returns when we carry the analysis one step farther.

Suppose it were possible to show that Ellie doesn't attach a value of anything like $1 billion to the outcome? Then she could not be acting rationally (consistently) if she acted as if she did. There may be realistic levels of social valuation large enough to make a vote rational. But such values apparently aren't Ellie's values in the sense relevant for the standard sort of rational actor analysis. What counts for that purpose is the personal sacrifice Ellie would make to promote those values. What the presidential election is worth to Ellie is just what she would give up to secure the result she takes to be socially valuable.

So from that standard point of view, consider how much of a private reward Ellie would require to make her prefer an election outcome in which her presidential candidate loses. Before an election, we might ask Ellie how much money in her own pocket it would take to make her hope for the defeat of the candidate she favors. The dollar amounts you will find if you ask people about this will rarely exceed $10,000. And that is far too small to make Ellie's vote rational when discounted by any reasonable estimate of the effect of her vote on the election (Margolis 1977).

So, on this argument, if Ellie is rational, and if she reports she would begin to hope her candidate would lose if some rich rascal were to give her $10,000 in that event, then in terms of her preferences the election is worth no more than $10,000. The point is not that Ellie is insincere if she says that the social value is vastly larger than $10,000. But in terms of what that large social value is worth to Ellie—in terms of what Ellie would personally give up to obtain that large gain for society—the smaller number ($10,000, not $1 billion) is alone relevant. When that smaller number is further discounted for the effect of one vote on the probable outcome, what is left of the value of Ellie's vote could hardly be enough to explain her bothering to vote.

But this argument, though perfectly sound in the context of the standard model of rational choice, does not work if the way human beings actually behave fits the dual-utilities model. Rather, I want to claim that this Ellie argument is just another of the empirically somehow-crazy inferences that can be deduced from the standard model when that model is used in the context of social choice (Margolis 1982/1984: 17–25).

The key point is that under the standard model, a rational actor maximizes some single index of preference (not necessarily called a utility function). Mathematically, all the actual work is done by an equilibrium condition derived from that index. But the equilibrium condition is grounded in that ultimate single preference function. In contrast, for the dual-utilities model the equilibrium condition arises directly from the pair of rules introduced in section 1. Even if a sufficiently complicated mathematical function could be devised with the property that, when differentiated, it yields $W = G'/S'$ as its first-order condition, it would only be a mathematical freak, having no useful role to play in the logic of the model (Margolis 1982/1984: 41–44). For someone well entrenched in the habits of mind that come with working with the standard model, it will be hard to make sense of the dual-utility argument. Rather, well-entrenched intuitions will tell you that the dual model as I have presented it must be incomplete (the dual-utility functions are really components of some overall, or total, or authentic, maximand, but I've neglected to spell it out). If the problem is incompleteness (so there really is a single maximand hidden somewhere), then the Ellie argument just sketched shows that social motivation can't account for voting after all. And (standard intuitions will tell you), if there really isn't any single ultimate maximand, the case is even simpler—you don't need to take the proposal seriously; it must be wrong.

Given the habits of mind that yield strong intuitions of this sort (note well, I haven't said strong *arguments,* for just the point I will be making is that while the intuitions are strong, there is no strong argument to be made in their support), then the dual-utilities argument will look like a proof that 2 + 2 = 5: you know there is something wrong with it, even if you haven't put your finger on just where the error lies.

Yet we have all experienced situations in which strong intuitions turned out to have been mistaken. Here the strong intuition can't be merely that the dual-utilities model isn't what has been usually understood to be a rational choice model. That complaint is correct but scientifically trivial. As I have repeatedly emphasized, on the dual-utilities view there is no single maximand for an actor, but two maximands inside the actor which are balanced in the way I've described. Whether this makes sense is not itself a technical question, but an empirical one. For the point (everyone can agree) is to model how actual people behave. If it turns out that we don't behave in a way that fits the familiar notion of rational choice, then the obvious step is to broaden our notion of rational choice, not religiously affirm adherence to a class of models that doesn't work. The intuition that the dual-utilities approach must be empirically wrong, not merely that it violates the usual assumptions (as indeed it does), is the intuition I think can't be backed by good arguments.

In the dual-utilities model there indeed is no grand utility function of which the G- and S- functions are ultimately components. To suppose there must be is simply a logical error. Alternatives to a single utility function have been explored not only in my own book, but also by Sen (chap. 3, this vol.) in a way akin to and antedating my own, and by other well-known scholars in a set of papers put together by Elster (1986). There seems to be no logical bar to exploring the possibility that social and private preferences are irreducibly distinct, not merely aspects of an individual's single *authentic* (ultimate, overall) scale of preferences.

The contrast between the dual-utilities model and the standard model is not that one allows for social motivation and the other can't (Hirshleifer 1985; Mueller 1986). Rather, as a technical issue, it concerns the (debatable and, in my view, empirically wrong) presumption that if the model is workable, a well-specified single maximand ought to lie behind its equilibrium condition. My argument is that the reason for the wider applicability of the dual-utilities approach lies precisely in the contrast between a (standard) model, where social versus private preferences must trade off in a person's overall "authentic" utility function, and the dual-utilities model, where the balancing comes by way of the seesaw mechanism sketched in section 1.

In the standard model, a person maximizes utility by choosing an allocation such that the utility of the last dollar allocated to social utility just equals that of the last dollar allocated to private utility. Hence (setting aside here the question of how accurate a hypothetical answer can be taken to be), asking Ellie how much money in her own pocket it would take to get her to prefer the election outcome she thinks socially perverse would give us logically certain knowledge about the actual value to Ellie of the social gain she expects from electing one candidate over another. That is correct if the standard model is correct.

But in the dual-utilities model that logic does not hold. Equilibrium is determined by a condition that, however much it may look like a usual first-order equilibrium condition for maximizing utility, in fact works on an entirely different principle. As mentioned in section 1, its roots lie in competing Darwinian pressures favoring group versus self-interested behavior. The outcome is a kind of pragmatic compromise between those competing pressures. Hence it makes no more sense (empirically or mathematically) to try to cram that compromise into the standard maximizing framework than to insist on treating the outcome of a sporting competition, or the bargaining result between labor and management, as a maximizing process. Each side can be treated in terms of rational maximizing. But the total process can't be. In the dual-utilities context, the marginal allocation is *not* one that balances marginal returns to some hypothesized grand preference function across self-interested and group-interested spending opportunities. Instead it is the allocation that brings the individual as close as feasible to a "fair-share" balance—feeling neither selfish nor exploited—between spending to satisfy private versus spending to satisfy social preferences.

In the "Ellie" context, even if Ellie would truly give up no more than $10,000 to guarantee her presidential choice, she can also rationally judge the social value of that choice to be very much more than she personally is willing to pay. There are simply two distinct questions: (1) about Ellie's social judgment, and (2) about how large a share of her personal resources she would spend to support that judgment in a context where she has the power, if she is willing to make a large enough sacrifice, personally to determine the social outcome.

Suppose (as is reasonable) that Ellie in fact would ordinarily devote only a small share of her resources to social G-preferences, but that the cost of voting still will be very small as a fraction of her total G-spending. Then how much of her personal resources she would sacrifice is irrelevant to the voting context. No choice remotely on that scale is at stake. In terms of the seesaw diagrams of section 1, any shift in S' or G' or W contingent on whether or how Ellie votes would be very small.

But in the Ellie thought experiment, Ellie is asked how much it would take to make her truly prefer the "wrong" social choice, so that if her vote were decisive she would vote against the candidate she thinks would be best for the country. Ellie, in other words, is being asked about her personal willingness to sacrifice for what she takes to be the common good. Why should it be puzzling that Ellie's response to this question about personal sacrifice is not the same as her response to a question about social value?

The two questions—about Ellie's judgment of the social value, and about how much Ellie would personally sacrifice to gain that value—must be connected. But they are not the same question. To take the answer to the question about personal sacrifice as the answer to the question about the importance of the issue for the country is not a necessary condition for rational choice. Rather, it's a mistake.

Applying the "fair share" rules: as the price Ellie must pay for voting her social preference gets larger (hence the share of her resources required gets larger), her reluctance to sacrifice that much must grow, to the point at which she eventually takes the money offered for changing her vote. Somewhere between the amount she would pay out of pure self-interest (the S-value of the election) and the vastly larger social value (the G-value), she will feel that she personally is being asked to do too much.

It would be embarrassing for the dual-utilities model if in fact a voter who feels strongly about a presidential election would actually prefer $10,000 in her own pocket to what she takes to be the clearly better social outcome, in a situation where the actual outcome somehow will be determined by whatever she prefers. If we found that to be the case, it would not of itself prove the model is formally wrong. But it would at least raise gross questions about whether the balancing between private and social spending is not so overwhelmingly in favor of private spending that we can treat it as negligible.

However, from the pragmatic evidence we have about what happens when people face choices between large private sacrifices and social gains they judge very important (behavior in time of war, for example), it is apparent that sacrifice of self-interest in such contexts frequently—even routinely, though not universally—is very much greater than we notice in everyday situations, and often far greater than the individuals themselves could anticipate.

A good way to think about social G-utilities is by analogy with a board member of a public service organization who holds sole responsibility for choices on some component of the organization's budget (Margolis 1982/

1984:156f.). Suppose Ellie were asked to organize a reception for the organization's major contributors and as part of that task decided to spend $500 on floral arrangements. What would Ellie say if we asked what the floral arrangements were worth to *her*, and claimed that Ellie would be irrational to allocate that $500 unless the value to her (allowing of course for her altruistic interest in the organization) is at least $500. Her reaction would probably be that the $500 reflects her view of how some money entrusted to her to be spent for the organization could best be spent. It is what (she judges) the spending is worth to the organization, which will almost automatically be far more than she sees it as worth to herself, even allowing for her altruistic interest in the organization.

Similarly, under the dual-utilities model, resources allocated to G-spending are used to obtain social benefits, and it would be odd to try to think of them as private value to the individual. If we put the question only in private terms, we shouldn't be surprised to get an answer that understates the actual willingness to spend (Margolis 1982/1984:168–70). But the more essential point is that under the dual-utilities setup, the resources Ellie spends for voting ordinarily come from resources allocated to her social preferences (Margolis 1982/1984:92–94), just as Ellie's spending on the flowers comes from resources allocated (this time by an outside agency, not by an internal brain process) to spending for the organization.

In general, we make judgments (I argue in Margolis 1987) by a process of anchor-and-adjust, starting from patterns of response that are already in our cognitive repertoire. But in the Ellie thought experiment, there is nothing familiar to anchor on which is anywhere near the hypothetical situation in which Ellie's vote decides a presidential election. So she can be expected to anchor unconsciously on something far removed (on a situation in which her choice does not decide for all of society), and the adjustment is then likely to fall far short. That prospect is aggravated when we frame the question in terms of what her candidate's success is worth to Ellie, rather than in terms of some balancing between what that success is worth to Ellie and what (in Ellie's own view) it is worth to society. If we could actually put Ellie in the situation, she might be surprised at her willingness to spend for a social cause when her choice alone determines what happens.

3

In the example of Ellie and the flowers, Ellie would probably feel herself bound to treat the $500 as the organization's money, not her own, so the example doesn't show that a person must ordinarily have the divided preferences required by the dual-utilities model. That empirical claim is essential to the dual-utilities argument, but it is not seriously tested by the flowers example. Rather, the example only illustrates how the standard trade-off argument would be misleading if preferences, in fact, have the dual character I've sketched.

I have also mentioned several examples of situations (sports competitions, bargaining) where results emerge from the interaction of two entities, each of which can be modeled as a utility-maximizing rational actor, but where the overall outcome can't be treated effectively in those terms. Let me conclude with a couple of further examples which are closer to the dual-utilities structure, and which give rise to an equilibrium condition mathematically identical to the dual-utilities setup.

Consider a country that must impose restraints on overseas investment. To allocate the quota of exportable capital, the country adopts *rule A*—other things equal, overseas investment by a firm ought to be easier to the extent that the investment would yield a higher rate of return than investment at home.

Yet for political or equity reasons, the country also wishes to avoid allocating all the overseas investment it can tolerate to one or a few firms that happen to face the most favorable opportunities at the moment. So a second principle is adopted: *rule B*—other things equal, the more a firm has already been allowed to invest overseas, the more difficult it ought to be for it to export even more capital.

If you compare rules A and B here with rules 1 and 2 at the beginning of this chapter, you will see that the parallel is exact. The G' and S' of the dual-utilities setup would here be reinterpreted as rate of return on overseas and domestic investment, respectively. The weighting function takes a mathematically identical form [$W = f(g/s)$, $W' > 0$], but now g and s are, respectively, overseas and domestic investment. The equilibrium condition is, as before, $W = G'/S'$, and the whole discussion of figures 14.1–14.3 then carries over into this mainstream economics example.

For this case (Margolis 1982/1984:43), although the mathematical setup comes out identical to that of the dual-utilities model, we are unlikely to think of the firm as having dual preferences. Each firm would ordinarily prefer to be free to invest wherever it wants. We would interpret each firm's choices as maximizing subject to a government-imposed constraint. So here the same formal structure proposed to account for individual choice has a perfectly conventional interpretation. No economist would see anything bizarre in the situation, or suppose that the way to deal with the problem would be to reformulate the framework in terms of some overall, ultimate firm maximand, within which the analogues of G' and S' (here, they would be rate of return on overseas versus domestic investment) were subsumed. Although an individual firm would see the situation as maximizing subject to a constraint, in its observed behavior the firm would choose *as if* it held dual preferences.

Indeed, situations could even arise in which the dual structure is the actual preference structure of the firm. Suppose the firm wants to ward off pressure for government controls or unfavorable publicity. Then it could plausibly, that is, without condemning its management as unreasonable or irrational, choose to adopt an investment policy governed by rules A and B. A sufficiently zealous proponent of canonical notions of rational choice might even interpret the dual-utilities setup as the pragmatic outcome from trying to produce a species capable of large-scale, open-ended co-operation, given the constraints on what is feasible for that metaphorical rational actor, Ms. Evolution.

A final example unambiguously involves the unconstrained preferences of a single individual. Suppose Ellie has two children, one of whom could gain more from her financial help than the other. This child (G) might be handicapped, so he needs more help; he might be exceptionally talented, so he can make better use of whatever help he gets; or as a struggling artist he might have less income than his otherwise equally deserving business-man brother (S). Thinking of G's greater gain from her help, Ellie might wish to use almost all her spare resources to help G. However, Ellie also feels she ought to treat both children equally. She might resolve her difficulty by adopting versions of rules 1 and 2 of section 1 (or, equivalently, rules A and B of the investment example): (1') Other things equal, the larger the value to G of a marginal dollar compared to the value of that marginal dollar to S, the more likely the dollar should to G. (2') Other things equal, the more Ellie has already given more to G than to S, the less likely it is that the next dollar will be spent to further help G.

We would once again get the mathematical structure of the dual-utilities model. Now G' and S' are the marginal values of dollars to help son G and son S, respectively; g and s are the amounts she has spent on G and S; and the weighting function, W, tells Ellie how big the marginal value ratio (G'/S') has to be to warrant allocating still more to G over S. Once again, figures 14.1–14.3 are readily reinterpreted to cover Ellie and her children.

But there is no ambiguity about whether the structure represents the authentic preference structure of a single individual. Some such structure no doubt captures the essentials of choice for many parents.

These examples show that formally equivalent analogues of the dual-utilities model either easily could exist or in fact do exist in actual societies. They are not examples that look especially bizarre, or that look in any plausible sense irrational. To conclude with a more general point: we now have thirty years of post-Downs (1957) efforts to account for voting within the standard model of rational choice. The record is coming to look like one of the psychologists' *umwelt* experiments. Put a starving chicken, then a starving dog, on one side of a wide glass wall, with food visible on the other side. Each animal starts out by trying to bang through the wall. Eventually the dog seems to catch on and, after some searching, finds its way around the wall. The unfortunate chicken starves to death, banging its head against the wall. To me it seems about time to consider alternatives to the standard model. But I observe that the chicken is still hard at work.

Far more is at stake here than accounting for why a citizen might spend the modest resources (the bit of time) required to vote. *How* a person votes can't be plausibly assumed to be independent of why she is motivated to vote in the first place. So although the cost of voting is ordinarily very small for any individual, and far from enormous even for the whole electorate, the social consequences of how people vote are enormous. Even more important: the same pattern of argument can be extended to social choice generally. The argument (I would argue) works not only for the special context of voting, or for contexts involving only very modest conflicts, but for the entire range of human choices that involve both private and social motivation.

16   Expanding the Range of
Formal Modeling

Jane J. Mansbridge

A critical task for those engaged in the formal modeling of behavior is to accommodate motives other than self-interest without losing the very advantages that a simplified model offers for advancing human thought. Models help us think by making it possible to reduce complexity with a few assumptions, then draw out the implications of those assumptions, creating a new kind of complexity we could not capture if we tried to account at the outset for all aspects of reality. If we accept this need for relative simplicity, we can accommodate motives other than self-interest in three ways: by extending the range of single motives we model, by modeling the relations between two or more motives in new ways, and most importantly, by trying out models based on different single motives in different contexts. This chapter discusses these three ways of expanding the range of formal modeling, then addresses the problems inherent in disentangling human motivation.

Extending the Range of Motives,
in and outside "Self-Interest"

Some scholars reject models that take account of motives other than self-interest. George Stigler explains political behavior as almost entirely self-interested. He contends that deviations from narrow self-interest are generally confined to one's "family, plus a close circle of associates." Dennis Mueller argues even more forcefully that "the only assumption essential to a descriptive and predictive science of human behavior is egoism."[1]

Within the group that insists on self-interest, some, who recognize that a great deal of observed behavior cannot be accounted for by self-interest, are nevertheless so wedded to the concept that they are prepared to salvage it by sacrificing the modeler's other stock-in-trade—rationality. Mueller,

For comments on this essay, I particularly thank Max Bezerman, John Kingdon, Dennis Mueller, Douglas Nelson, and Eugene Silberberg.

for example, proposes to explain behavior that cannot be explained by rational self-interest as an irrational by-product of habitual conditioning. To explain the fact that "most of us choose the cooperative strategy most of the time," he turns to the principles of "behaviorist psychology," arguing that we act out behavior to which we have been conditioned in the past. Thus when the data do not fit the model of self-interested and rational economic man, Mueller suggests that "we retain the egoistic portion of rational egoism, and drop, or better modify the rationality assumption, at least in the strong form in which this assumption is usually employed" (1986: 5).

The tone of these discussions sometimes suggests that self-interest appeals to modelers not just because of its simplicity, but also because it ensures that they will appear tough-minded. Mueller describes the behaviorist principles to which he appeals as familiar to "anyone who has ever trained a dog," and contends that *homo economicus* "bears a close resemblance to Skinner's rat." "Man," he proclaims, "is basically base" (1986: 6, 8, 15).

While some formal modelers join Mueller in insisting on the assumption of self-interest, many, whom I have dubbed "inclusive" modelers, will work with any set of goals so long as actors follow certain rules of consistency and maximization in pursuing those goals.[2] If, through love, I have made your good my own, inclusive modelers are happy to create a model in which I maximize your good. If, through duty, I have become a utilitarian and count other people's good exactly equal to my own, inclusive modelers are happy to model my pursuing the greatest good for the greatest number.

Yet even for many inclusive modelers, an elegant model requires a single motive or goal.[3] They can incorporate some other considerations by assuming that rational actors attain their goals under constraints, which usually involve cognitive limitations or biases (people cannot collect or take in much information except at a cost; people act differently faced with negative and positive risks; Quattrone and Tversky 1988). When Western scholars assume only one motive, they almost always assume that people are self-interested. They do not live in a culture like the one Charlotte Perkins Gilman imagined, where the dominant concern was effective child rearing, experience offered more instances of concern for others than of self-interest, and it might seem more natural to model altruistic motives than self-interested ones.[4]

Even within Western culture, however, some scholars in the field of formal modeling have reached out, first to define self-interest less narrowly, to include interests distinct from or even antithetical to monetary reward, then to include in their models forms of self-interest that are hard to distinguish from altruism, and finally, to model forms of altruism itself.

The first, and critical, path involves defining self-interest in ways that deviate from monetary or material reward. Dennis Mueller takes a long step down this path by admitting "ethically conditioned" behavior into the category of "selfish" behavior. Others introduce into their models forms of self-interest that compete with material reward. Robert Frank, for example, postulates that people desire high rank as much as or more than money, and explains top earners' choices of a relatively egalitarian pay scale by their willingness to trade material payoff for high status.[5] Carol Heimer and Arthur Stinchcombe (1980) model the human desire for play as it is traded off against other goods in games of love. Howard Margolis postulates a strong motive not to feel exploited or look like a sucker, and predicts a much higher rate of cooperative behavior when this interest is met.[6]

In a very small step along the spectrum, others have modeled forms of self-interest that are hard to distinguish from altruism. Postulating a human desire for sociability, Carol Uhlaner has modeled citizens participating in politics in order to be close to others.[7] Postulating a human desire for long-run praise, Albert Hirschman (1973/1981) has suggested modeling what he calls "obituary-improving activities." It might be possible to model politicians seeking reelection primarily to prove to themselves how many people admire them.[8] Or we could postulate a desire to see oneself as the active cause of benefits to others (sometimes considered "impure altruism," sometimes a form of desiring power)[9] and model individuals seeking conditions in which giving vent to that desire produces the least personal harm and the greatest return.

As we get closer to altruism itself, some have modeled acting for the public good as a kind of "consumption" that "yields utility in the form of the warm glow of moral rectitude."[10] Within this typology we could even postulate love for others as an innate need, pursued for its own sake.[11] Not being able to express this empathy and love would be a cost, although expressing it in a way that diminished self-esteem would also be a cost. We could then model individuals as searching, among the available people and communities to love, for those least likely to return harm and most likely to return good.

Finally, with what might seem only a semantic shift, some have modeled "pure altruism," motivated by either love or duty. Some assume that individuals make the good of others in their family so much their own that the boundary between individuals and family members disappears, and for many purposes it makes sense to consider the family the "actor" in the model.[12] On the assumption that some actors make the good of several others their own, Gary Becker (1976) models the way they allocate benefits among these others according to specific rules of fairness and efficiency. Taking up Kristin Monroe's conclusion that some actors see themselves as "at one with all humanity," William Riker has suggested that one could model the emergence of actions congruent with this motivation under appropriate conditions and constraints.[13]

Because the study of non-self-interested motives—whether benevolent or malevolent—has not been central to the social sciences, modeling such motives will usually require finding out more about them. Although citizens probably turn out to vote largely because they feel that citizens *should* vote,[14] for example, no empirical political scientist has investigated the content of this commitment to voting. We do not know what normative explanations people give for going to the polls. We do not know in what part their decisions to turn out derive from commitments to democracy, to the established order, or to an efficacious self-image. When people explain this "irrational" act by saying, "What if everyone didn't vote?" we do not know to what degree they are indulging in a form of "magical thinking," which implicitly assumes that if I abstain I will cause others to do the same,[15] or to what degree their words reveal a commitment to some concept of fairness, or to an implicit Kantian ethic. As in this case, sensitive modeling will often require prior empirical investigation of the relevant motivation.[16]

The point of "economic" thinking ought not to be to postulate one set of motives rather than another, but, having determined through empirical investigation that one or another set of tastes or values seems to prevail in a given context, to see how actors possessing those tastes or values respond to changes in constraints.

Modeling More Than One Motive: Indifference Curves and Ratios

The most traditional method of adding more than one motive to a model is to assume a single goal of maximizing "utility," and turn motives other than narrow self-interest into desires for different kinds of consumption goods, revealed to be valued by the process of choice itself. These goods can then be modeled as goods the actor trades off against one another in the familiar pattern of indifference curves. In this kind of model, if I were an idealistic legislator elected by a southern conservative constituency, I might choose between voting for civil rights and pursuing reelection the way I might choose between apples and oranges. If I were fairly sure of reelection, I would vote for civil rights. If I felt extremely deprived in the realm of civil rights (I felt intensely about a certain issue), I might risk not being reelected. If I felt sufficiently strongly, I might give up all chance of reelection in order to cast an important vote for civil rights.[17] Indifference curves help model trade-offs between reelection and following one's ideas of good policy, with data like Quirk's or Kalt and Zupan's showing legislators voting more on the basis of principles the further they stand from their next election.[18]

Less traditional ways of modeling the choice process do not assume a single grand utility function into which all else fits. Margolis (chap. 15, this vol.) thus postulates a chooser with two distinct utilities, social and personal. The actor makes cost-benefit calculations within each utility, but adjusts the ratio between the two utilities according to rules that are not simply cost-benefit rules.

One might modify and generalize Margolis's idea by introducing into the modeling scheme the concept of identity, and postulating several competing but separate utilities, within which one makes relatively easy cost-benefit calculations, but between which adjustments either follow specific rules, as in Margolis's scheme, or are merely "sticky," or costly to adjust, because they are deeply connected with personal identity. For example, in my present identity I might implicitly allocate one-fourth of my self to my family, one-fourth to my research, one-fourth to collective responsibilities both academic and political, one-eighth to teaching, and one-eighth to my friends. It would be a fairly simple matter to assume, given my present identity, a relatively fixed allocation of time in each of these categories, so that I felt it legitimate to take time for one good within a category only from another good within the same category, making implicit cost-benefit calculations only among within-category goods. Changing the time allocation among categories would require an identity shift, more or less painful depending on the speed of the change and the nature of the external or internal demands that induced the shift. (As my son grew up, my time for research might expand, perhaps causing little pain but deeply affecting my identity.)

While this way of formulating relations between categories might illuminate only individual behavior,[19] it might also be possible to model, say, legislative trade-offs between reelection and ideas of good public policy in the way Margolis proposes, with specific rules applying to the shift from one relatively inviolable category to another.

Deploying Different Single Motives in Different Contexts

For years social psychologists have been developing data that predict the contexts in which people are more or less likely to behave self-interestedly.[20] These experiments assume more than one motivation. To keep some advantages of a single-motive model while taking account of other motives, we could assume that individuals had only one motive at a time, but that this motive varied from one social context to another. We could then compare the predictive capacities of different models in different contexts. In studying politics, say, we might ask in which contexts models based solely on self-interest best predicted the behavior of Congress, the executive, the bureaucracy, and the citizenry. In a more complex world, we could allow for interactions between context and motivation.

Presuming that "there is no hope for ever stating a refutable proposition if any behavior at all can be postulated,"[21] the point of looking at context is to predict when different forms of self-interest and altruism will prevail.

Whenever self-interest and altruism are not congruent but opposed,[22] we might expect narrow self-interest to predict behavior most accurately when the rewards for acting in one's narrow self-interest were high and the costs low. The trade-off between narrow self-interest and altruism can take on several shapes, depending on the stakes involved, and on whether altruism acts like a luxury good or whether a basic core of self-interest acts like a fixed constraint.

In many prisoners' dilemma games, raising the monetary stakes seems to reduce the participants' level of cooperation.[23] Some interpret this result by saying simply that increasing the "stakes" increases the effect of self-interest.[24] But experimenters producing this result have raised only the monetary stakes (the return to self-interest), not also the moral stakes or the stakes in group solidarity. Assuming that the stakes of duty or love in these games are not affected, the pattern we see may result simply from the benefits of self-interested behavior being increased, while its costs (in duty or love) remain the same. The situation might also work interactively. Raising the monetary stakes might raise not only the benefits accruing to self-interest behavior but also the benefits accruing to behavior prompted by duty or love, if participants felt more virtuous or loving when they withstood greater temptations. In this case, the two goods to be traded off against one another, monetary reward and feelings of duty or love, would not be independent. Rather, increases in the first would generate increases in the second. But judging by the results of prisoners' dilemma games played by students in the United States, when communication with other participants is prohibited and the monetary stakes are raised, the moral or group solidarity benefits gained by resisting temptation do not increase at as fast a rate as the direct benefits gained by succumbing to temptation. We might therefore say that as the monetary stakes alone increase, the benefits of altruism increase more slowly than its costs. We cannot choose between the static and the interactive model without having an independent measure of the stakes in duty or love.

In some contexts, altruism seems to function like a luxury good, being chosen with proportionately greater frequency as resources rise. Albert Hirschman suggests that "obituary-improving activities" are luxuries.

They occur with greater frequency as income rises, and respond in a non-linear manner to other costs as well, occurring more frequently, for example, in a president's second term than in his first (Hirschman 1973/ 1981). Michael Taylor (1987: 111) also suggests that we think of departures from egoism as luxuries.

Several bits of evidence seem to support the analysis of altruism as a "luxury good." The authors of *The Federalist*, along with other eighteenth-century writers, believed that representatives with enough independent income to be above financial need were more likely than others to take a disinterested approach to legislation. Freed from the necessity of securing their livelihoods, they could be expected to turn to promoting the public good (Wood 1987: 84–89). Today, U.S. senators seem more likely to vote their convictions regarding deregulation and strip-mining when they are not coming up soon for reelection. Again, they predictably turn to the "superior" good when they have a low probability of jeopardizing the good necessary for their continued legislative existence.[25]

These behaviors might be modeled better in an extreme version of the luxury model, in which achieving or maintaining necessities acts as a constraint on one's capacity to pursue luxuries the way information costs or cognitive bias may act as constraints. The pattern of trade-offs differs from the luxury model in that the "constraint" is relatively fixed. In this pattern actors assure themselves first of basic necessities in their lives, like a "reasonable style of life" for citizens and their children, or reelection for politicians. The necessities having been secured, resources are freed for "luxuries" like public-spirited action. The same pattern could be modeled as a hierarchy of needs, with actors filling material needs first and, at some absolute or relative plateau, turning to other forms of self-fulfillment.[26]

The "luxury" approach to altruism does not, however, fit all cases. Oliner and Oliner's study of European rescuers of Jews found little difference in income or other resources (except having a cellar in the house) between rescuers and nonrescuers.[27] Woody Guthrie (1943/1968: 265) reports that early in his career as a migrant worker he learned that when he arrived in a strange town he had better luck asking for a job or handout in a poor neighborhood than in a rich one. While the poor may use close friendship circles and the informal sanctions possible in such circles to pool their collective resources against bad times, neither a reciprocity nor a luxury model fits the relatively free giving of small amounts to strangers in the poor communities that Guthrie describes.[28] Studies of giving to charity as a percentage of one's income reveal that poor people give away at least as high a percentage of their income as the rich (Jencks 1987). Finally, even extremely high stakes do not rule out altruistic behavior. Although more people will try to save another when the risk is low rather than high, a "luxury" model does not easily explain those soldiers who throw themselves on grenades to save their comrades.

The costs to self-interested behavior depend in part on the contexts in which institutional roles, collective social norms, and personal identity interact strongly and clearly to denigrate self-interest. Understanding institutional roles, for example, leads us to expect senators to vote for what they regard as the common good more often on general committees like Appropriations than on specific committees like Agriculture. William Muir (1982) contends that instituting a "third reading" in the California legislature increased the legislators' appeal to general principle as opposed to self-interest in their wording of their bills, and perhaps in their motivations as well. Institutional roles affect attitudes and behavior even after leaving the role. J. S. Mill (1861/1977) argued for democracy in part on the grounds that taking responsibility for others by voting, holding a small parish office, or taking jury duty would give citizens an enduring "largeness of view" and an increased concern for others.

Investigating context also requires discriminating among issues, on some of which both external and internal sanctions are more likely to be invoked against self-interested behavior. We might therefore expect senators to vote for what they regard as the common good more often when issues involve "rights" or "justice" rather than commercial advantage, and when the common good conflicts with their own economic interest (an "illegitimate" consideration) rather than with their chances of reelection (a "legitimate" consideration).

We know that some contexts generate severe external sanctions against narrowly self-interested behavior. The interaction of internal sanctions and context, however, is relatively uncharted territory. We do not yet know why and in what contexts people vote, give money to causes, or make great sacrifices to promote ends that they see as good. We do not yet know how internal sanctions are tied to identity, although it is clear that in some contexts political actors act public-spiritedly on the grounds that they "couldn't live with themselves" or "would be letting themselves down" if they did otherwise.

Disentangling Motivations

Several economists looking at political life have recently advocated paying attention to the interaction of motivation and context.[29] Doing so, however, generates problems even beyond the necessary practical ones of working closely with specific cases and pooling talents across disciplines. Partly because people often try to make self-interest, duty, and love coincide, these motivations are often heavily entangled.

John Kingdon, writing only of the legislative arena, spells out a few points of entanglement. First, electoral processes weed out candidates whose policy views are wholly unlike those of the majority of constituents or influential elites. Most of the time legislators' conclusions regarding good public policy accord with those of most of their constituents. Thus, "most of the time, legislators take *both* the expedient and the principled course at once." [30] That entanglement makes interpreting motivations in, say, the 1986 tax reform act or industry deregulation extremely difficult.

Second, people need arguments to persuade others. Even when each of two opposing sides is motivated by self-interest, they both must appeal through argument and evidence to a set of decisive actors in the middle. As a consequence, "people in and around government spend a lot of time, money, and energy on ideas. They hire analysts; they marshall arguments and collect evidence in support of those arguments; they argue and persuade. . . . And once they are committed to this world of talk, they end up being constrained by it." [31]

Third, people persuade themselves in the process of deliberation. "Ideas become part of one's self, and therefore part of one's self-interest" (Kingdon 1988:17). Even in principle, ideas and self-interest are inseparable, because people need to attach meaning to their behavior. Their need for meaning is not simply rationalization or a cloak for self-interested motives. "The point is that without meaning, people do not behave in the same way as they do if they can find meaning in their actions" (p. 17).

Both individuals and groups, even "interest groups," often find it hard to decide what is in their interest, partly because "even if they are motivated to behave in their own self-interest, they are implicitly choosing among concepts of the self" (p. 20). Thus, while self-interest has its objective components, it is also in part constructed, through public and private deliberation. [32] Legislators, and to a lesser degree citizens, worry about precedents and consequences (pp. 18–19), about what is really going on and whether they have their facts right. While the legislators' roles in the larger structure and their narrow self-interest undoubtedly constrain what they see and how they understand what they see, their institutional roles and their identities as competent professionals sometimes make them recognize facts and agree with arguments that do not bolster that self-interest narrowly conceived. In such situations, disentangling even what people think is in their interest is not an easy job.

Resisting the Seductions of Self-Interest

None of these considerations makes life easier for the modeler. The power of an elegant model derives from its ability to explain much with little. Once a modeler admits into the scheme more than one motive, let alone a tangle of mixed and possibly indecipherable motives, the question becomes where to stop. This is a genuine problem, and I do not mean to slight it here.

As Gary Becker and others have demonstrated, however, dropping the assumption of self-interest narrowly conceived can enhance both prediction and insight without sacrificing elegance. This volume has demonstrated over and over that self-interest narrowly conceived fails to predict well in many arenas of human life. One possible and useful response is to forgo prediction and simply explore, for their heuristic value, the consequences that would ensue if actors *were* motivated only by self-interest narrowly conceived.[33] The other possible response is to retain a concern for prediction and, in appropriate contexts, expand the conception of self-interest or add to it other motives, including those of duty and love.

IX   Alternatives to Self-Interest, Malevolent and Benevolent

17 The Secret History of Self-Interest

Stephen Holmes

> What is to be gained by overturning the table, by hurling cups upon the floor, by dashing oneself against pillars, tearing the hair, and smiting the thigh and the breast?
>
> —Seneca, "On Anger"

George Stigler exhorts us to admire "the granite of self-interest" upon which the palace of economics is built. Throughout most of *Wealth of Nations*, he writes, Adam Smith took a hard line, explaining the endurance of colonialism, primogeniture, and slavery by invoking the self-interest of the principal actors involved. Slavery panders to the pride of slaveholders, and *therefore* serves their self-interest. (This is Stigler's paraphrase of Smith.) Unfortunately, Stigler continues, Smith failed to turn "the jaundiced eye of a master economist" upon political life. In thinking about politics, he was not hard but soft. He ascribed excessive influence to emotion and prejudice, and, shockingly, spied "failures of self-interest in guiding people's behaviour." If Smith had only been as tough-minded as Stigler and his colleagues, he would have recognized that every "alleged failure" of self-interest was "non-existent or of negligible magnitude."[1]

Today this attitude toward self-interest is widespread among economists and the social scientists most influenced by them. But it was rare or unheard-of in the eighteenth century. Throughout Smith's great economic treatise, significantly, interest was *contrasted* with pride.[2] Although Britain would benefit from relinquishing its dominion over the American colonies, it was unlikely to do so: "Such sacrifices, though they might frequently be agreeable to the *interest*, are always mortifying to the *pride* of every nation."[3] Because it is an unnatural means of enriching one child while beggaring his siblings, primogeniture is against "the real *interest* of a numerous family" even though it supports "the *pride* of family distinction."[4] Landowners retain their slaves because they are driven by a natural

For comments on an earlier draft of this essay, the author thanks Albert Hirschman, Jane Mansbridge, James Moore, Nancy Maull, Richard Posner, Judith Shklar, and Bernard Yack.

inclination to bully and preside—even when such gratuitous domineering entails economic deprivation.[5]

Smith repeatedly states that self-interest, however robust, is merely one motive among others. He also assumes that people are sometimes rational, sometimes not. The majority of every class is usually governed by common prudence; yet Europe's landed nobility destroyed itself by a most imprudent vanity.[6] In other words, Smith concedes, indeed he stresses, the massive historical importance of self-destructive and noncalculating behavior. Under certain conditions, we must appeal to motives other than interest to understand not this or that scattered event, but the drift of social and political change. His ideas about motivation, in other words, are distinct from, and perhaps more interesting than, those of his purported successors. In explaining human action, he routinely invokes the distinction (common at the time) between "interests, born of calculation, and passions, based on impulse."[7] This opposition is fundamental—and not merely for those seeking to master the vocabulary of *Wealth of Nations*.

The concept of self-interest was one of the most striking coinages of modern European thought. In phrases such as "special interests" and "interest groups," it continues to play an important role in the self-description of contemporary societies. To study its origins and development is to learn something essential about the prism through which we have come to interpret our lives. Unfortunately, for a variety of reasons, the evolution of the concept of self-interest has remained shrouded in obscurity. To dispel the clouds, to disclose some remarkable aspects of the idea's history, we must focus sharply on the all-important contrast between calculating interest and noncalculating passion.

This essay has three objectives. First and foremost, I want to document the incredible finesse with which Smith and his contemporaries analyzed the human psyche. A brief historical survey is meant to suggest the pitiful impoverishment that befell us, sometime in the nineteenth century, when Marxism and liberal economics conspired to assert the supremacy of interest and thus to extinguish an older and subtler tradition of moral psychology. Second, I hope to explain how the increasingly positive attitude toward self-interest, typical of a broad range of seventeenth- and eighteenth-century theorists, was motivated not only by discontent with the aristocratic ideal of glory, but also by disenchantment with the Christian dogma of original sin. And third, I want to suggest that the postulate of *universal* self-interest, although logically incompatible with insight into the rich variety of human motives, first rose to cultural prominence because of its unmistakably egalitarian and democratic implications.

Consider, first of all, some intriguing psychological assumptions Smith borrowed from David Hume.

Against Simplicity

The hypothesis of universal self-interest has provoked its fair share of protest and disgruntlement. Moralists bridle at what they consider an implied slur on human nature—a denial of the sincerity of self-sacrifice, for example. But the most persuasive complaint about the idea has a different source. The decision to group together sharply dissimilar motives under the single category of "calculating self-interest" is said to involve an undesirable *loss of information* about rudimentary psychological and behavioral processes. This is the essence of Macaulay's mocking remark that to discover self-interest behind an action is to say, with tautological banality, that "a man had rather do what he had rather do."[8]

As economists will explain, of course, the hypothesis of universal self-interest is theory not description. A deliberate simplification enables us to construct mathematically tractable models of human behavior. This is an important consideration. But social scientists who choose to see maximizing behavior everywhere they look should also admit that they are discarding an important dimension of Smith's thought—for *he* obviously shared with Hume a prevalent eighteenth-century worry about the uninformative character of the self-interest postulate.

Hume himself was echoing Shaftesbury, Hutcheson, and others when he denounced the false "love of simplicity"[9] underlying motivational reductionism. To say that patriots and misers, cowards and heroes all aim exclusively at "their own happiness and welfare"[10] illustrates only how little we learn about behavior by adducing self-interest. We can always *say* that the altruist includes the welfare of others in his own utility function. But when the motivational reductionist traces all action to self-love or the rational pursuit of personal advantage, he "makes use of a different language from the rest of his countrymen, and calls things not by their proper names."[11] Theorists are free to indulge in such linguistic idiosyncrasy, of course. If they make no distinctions, then, naturally enough, everything will be the same. But why jettison well-entrenched and useful contrasts between, say, interested and disinterested or calculating and noncalculating behavior? A generic concept such as the maximization of personal utility (referring to "the" aim of all human choice) swallows up such distinctions. Is there anything wrong with that? Hume thinks so. The very idea of interest-driven behavior is meaningless, he argues, unless we can identify some behavior that is *not* interest-driven. The idea of calculating action loses all content if it can no longer be opposed to action that is *not* calculating. An accurate account of social action calls for a fine-grained mapping of rival motivations.[12] Ultimately, descriptions and explanations will be more straightforward if we adhere to common usage and frankly acknowledge the reality of disinterested impulses and noncalculating styles of conduct.[13] Smith emphatically agrees.

Hume also denies that moral judgment is a pliant tool of our self-interest, narrowly understood. Conclusive evidence for this claim he finds in the praise we commonly bestow upon actions from which we cannot conceivably profit. A miser admires the niggardliness of a fellow miser in a purely disinterested fashion, perhaps from an aesthetic appreciation of penny-pinching, certainly not from any expectation of personal advantage.[14] Sometimes we praise the moral quality of actions that harm us. Although moral assessments and commitments affect behavior in important ways, they cannot be boiled down to underlying interests. Furthermore, benevolence exists. A disinterested preference for the happiness of others also has significant behavioral effects.[15] Normally, a person will not step briskly upon "another's gouty toes,"[16] even if he finds it inconvenient to go around them.

Against Dichotomy

But fellow feeling and humanity are by no means the only disinterested emotions discussed by Hume. Mankind is also moved by "disinterested resentment,"[17] for example. Indeed, Hume's rich account of the motivations vying with rational self-interest reveals the second most important aspect of his theory. He denies the completeness of binary schemes, such as egoism/altruism or selfishness/benevolence, just as vigorously as he does the hypothesis of universal self-interest. Such simplifying dichotomies, too, obscure the range and diversity of human motives.

Hume identifies a wide array of violent emotions, all of them distinct, he believes, from both self-interest and social benevolence. In general, such emotions prove destructive to the community as well as to the individual.[18] They include principally "the disagreeable passions, fear, anger, dejection, grief, melancholy, anxiety, &c." Unlike self-interest, these sentiments provoke immediate psychophysical outbursts or paralysis, without any intervening calculation of costs and benefits. Interest induces strategic or instrumental action. Passion hurls us willy-nilly into consummatory or expressive acts. The "darker passions of enmity and resentment" are disinterested in an emphatic sense: they motivate self-destructive behavior.[19] Violent passions can take possession of an individual's soul, poison his existence, and ruin his simplest pleasures.[20] Such self-destructive impulses are motivationally coequal with benevolence and self-interest.

In the *Theory of Moral Sentiments*, Smith, too, replaces the egoism/altruism dichotomy with a trichotomy of social/selfish/unsocial passions.[21] Self-interest, on this scheme, is located somewhere between disinterested benevolence and disinterested malevolence, between virtue and vice.[22] Unsocial passions—such as envy and anger—tear the breast, blur the mind, interfere with purposive conduct, and make rational comparison of alternatives next to impossible. Hume, as well, stresses the sheer immediacy of malevolent impulses: "there are mental passions by which we are impelled immediately to seek particular objects, such as . . . vengeance *without any regard to interest.*"[23] Because the hot-blooded pursuit of revenge can plunge people to their deaths, the contrast between the selfish and the vengeful (or the selfish and the unsocial) is just as sharp as the more conventional contrast between the selfish and the social.[24]

Selfless Cruelty

A surreptitiously moralized dichotomy between (good) altruism and (bad) egoism makes it difficult to conceptualize something so elementary, not to say elemental, as *selfless cruelty*. It is manifestly easier to be cruel when you act in the name of others, or in the name of an ideal, or even for the benefit of your victim, than when you act for your own sake. Blood revenge for a humiliation suffered by one's ascriptive group, even at the risk of one's own life, is a pertinent example. Think, also, of those Catholic zealots in medieval France, described by Montesquieu, who rushed onto the scaffold where a Jew was about to be executed for having blasphemed the Virgin Mary: they subdued the public executioner and used their knives to peel off the sinner's skin.[25] They were not acting from egoistic motives, but for the common good—as they saw it. Neither bargain hunting nor gentle benevolence was involved. Neither acquisitive egosim, nor loving altruism. Nonselfish, but nonetheless murderous, behavior abounds in history. It is not marginal, but massively important. And that is the way it appeared to those living in the wake of Europe's religious civil wars.

If our concepts precommit us to the idea that whenever people overcome selfishness they necessarily act in a morally admirable manner, then our vision of political behavior is bound to be blurred. A moralized selfish/selfless scheme blinds us in precisely this manner. Thus, any vocabulary lacking the category "selfless cruelty" is historically impoverished. It also provides an inadequate guide to the thought of the keenest observers of early modern Europe.

Interest in Hume

Many seventeenth- and eighteenth-century writers were obsessed with mankind's irrational psychological compulsion toward *factionalism.*[26] A faction is a third alternative between the individual and the community. Not accidentally, Hume's "Of Parties in General," devoted entirely to this subject, is one of the best eighteenth-century sources for understanding how the concept of self-interest was used during this phase in its long career.[27] Hume explains what self-interest is by explaining what self-interest is not. Factions are not mere interest groups. They can enlist behavior that is simultaneously selfless and unspeakably vicious toward others. People may suppress their personal interests and even cease to weigh the consequences of their actions because of a natural "propensity" to fall into factions.[28] This joining instinct is a universal characteristic of mankind and one that can easily vanquish the natural propensity to truck and barter. Not even intense selfishness can prevent a person, in the right circumstances, from kindling in "the common blaze."[29]

Factions are deplorable, Hume believed, because they make communitywide cooperation impossible. Narrow group loyalties often prevent citizens from coming to each other's assistance.[30] The mutual hostility of subgroups is a perverse but direct result of (selective) identification with other human beings.[31] To repeat: Hume draws a sharp contrast between the inborn tendency to identify emotionally with an exclusive subgroup and strategic rationality in general, particularly the calculating pursuit of personal advantage.

Murderously factional conflicts often have astonishingly trivial origins, for example, "the difference between the colour of one livery and another in horse races."[32] Onlookers at the hippodrome in ancient Constantinople witnessed races between rival charioteers who were outfitted in blue and green. Identifying psychologically with one side or the other, rival factions engaged in deadly attacks on one another. But why? Self-interest was not a decisive factor. One-shot rioting and mayhem, fueled by spontaneous enmity, is not calculating at all. It reflects instead something like "an original propensity"[33] or primordial need: when you observe a conflict, you tend to identify yourself emotionally with one party or the other. (Every sports fan experiences something of this kind.) The universal human proclivity to fall into factions presumably results from this deep-rooted psychological impulse.

Hume does not stop here, of course. He is not content with explaining the formation of factions by invoking the universal human tendency to form factions. Instead, he provides a bold typology for the various motives which lead individuals to cluster and divide into hostile groupings. At first, he does not even mention this compulsion to identify with a group in a situation of conflict (he returns to it later), and instead presents a tripartite scheme, distinguishing between *interest-driven, affection-driven,* and *principle-driven* behavior.[34] On this basis, he then distinguishes between factions based on economic interest, factions based on affection for a person, and factions based on abstract principles—such as a theological dogma or the divine character of royalty. If we wanted to generalize, we could say that Hume here identifies three independent factors that exert causal force upon human action: interests, passions, and norms.

Several things should be said about this three-part scheme. First, according to Hume, factions based on interest can be very dangerous. There is no insinuation whatsoever that interested behavior is always harmless. But Hume obviously considers interests far less dangerous than a number of more violent and volatile passions.[35] Second, he assumes that a person's motives are always mixed. Interests, passions, and norms conspire together to shape every human action. Nevertheless, sometimes one motive predominates and sometimes others. We can therefore speak meaningfully of largely principle-driven, largely interest-driven, and largely affection-driven behavior. Third, within a single group, such as a religious sect or movement, Hume tends to correlate different motives with different roles—so that leaders and elites are ordinarily motivated by interest while followers are usually motivated by principle or affection.[36] Fourth, by distinguishing motives in this way, Hume makes it possible to analyze the causal interconnections between them. To use his example, a man may be a royalist from principle, but when he receives a sinecure from the king his ardor for his principles may suddenly redouble.[37]

Fifth, and even more interesting, Hume explains how animosity among hostile factions is able to sustain itself even though it runs counter to every party's present interest.[38] Originally, he says, two groups may be divided by competition over a scarce resource or over some principle. With the passage of time, however, the original bone of contention vanishes but the animosity does not. Why? The answer Hume offers is simple. Certain emotional patterns become so etched or ossified in the human mind that they do not readily adapt to altered circumstances. What was initially an interest-based or principle-based enmity can thus become a habitual or inherited one. Resentments, grudges, and hatreds are bequeathed from generation to generation, without requiring further stimulus from new conflicts of interest. Hume thus supplements his original list. Alongside interest and principles, he places affections. And he particularly stresses *inherited animosity,* a perverse form of affection which is disinterested, unprincipled, and wholly irrational.

Another politically important form of affection is identification with a leader. This is what Hume calls an "imaginary interest," whereby individuals attach themselves psychologically to a leader whom they will never meet and from whom they can expect no material benefits.[39] Quasi-erotic fixation on prominent individuals may sometimes inspire acts of personal foolhardiness or courage. But it usually has less dramatic effects. For instance, it allows devotees to live national events vicariously, to feel involved in large affairs. Psychological attachment to the great, Hume also notes, can sometimes arise from spite: if we hate our neighbor sufficiently, we may express our loathing by identifying with *his* hero's most conspicuous enemy or rival.

Admittedly, "men are much governed by interest." Nevertheless, "even interest itself, and all human affairs, are governed by *opinion*."[40] In other words, Hume never doubts the causal efficacy of disinterested ideas. Yet he professes mock bafflement at factions based on differences of religious dogma. Can the opinions that rule the world really be as nonsensical as those promoted by Christian sects? Hume mentions Morocco where racial wars are based on a "pleasant difference" (of skin color) which Europeans scorn.[41] But how much more absurd were Europe's religious civil wars, terrifying struggles not provoked by a clash of sentiment but based on a difference in a few phrases that one party accepts without understanding and the other rejects in the same manner. Despite the philosopher's perplexity, people are fiercely attached to their principles—even to unintelligible or preposterous ones. The bloody conflicts about the meaning of the Eucharist, which originally split the reform churches, cannot be traced to conflicts of interest in a narrow sense. Why one sect is driven to persecute another so ferociously seems impossible to explain on a rational-actor model. Why *did* Europe drown itself in blood? Once again, Hume's answer is succinct. Human beings are emotionally flustered and embroiled. They do not think about what they are doing. Their minds are clouded by childish myths and unspeakable fears. As a result, they often fail to grasp their private advantage or to act upon it when they do.

Individuals are not always clear-eyed about their interests. But they *are* always impatient of being contradicted. We long mightily and involuntarily to find our own beliefs mirrored in those around us. We grab anyone by the lapels who crosses our path and hammer the unlucky party into agreement because our minds are shocked by contrariness and fortified by consensus. This compulsive intolerance is not a symptom of arrogance but of insecurity. We do not compare alternatives in such situations, but clutch desperately at straws. And what we seek is not a strategic ally in the pursuit of power or plenty but symbolic comfort from a fellow believer. This primitive need explains why we are so "keen" in controversy, something neither self-interest nor even vanity could explain.[42]

After parties have been formed in any of these ways (from material interest, inheritance, emotional identification with a leader, or compulsive attachment to an idea), new adherents can be won by the independent motive of imitativeness.[43] This is Hume's theory of *l'homme copie*. A contemporary of Hume (and thus of Rousseau) gave the following variation on the opening to the *Social Contract:* Man is born original, but everywhere he is a mere copy.[44] Behavior is contagious and some people copy others, not because it is in their interest to do so, but because imitation comes naturally.[45] (One might argue that it is easier to discover what is fashionable or what other people are doing than to identify one's own interests. But this way of speaking makes imitation sound too much like the strategic reaction to a scarcity of information. Hume has something much more instinctual in mind here—the spontaneous internalization of observed patterns—presumably, say, the way Texans learn to lope.)

Finally, some people have nothing to do when they rise in the morning. They fall into factions from propinquity and from the lack of a better idea.[46] In a civil war when two factions have an exactly equal chance of winning, moreover, individuals who habitually act according to rational self-interest are at a loss what to do. They cannot choose the side more likely to benefit them in the long run, since the winner is perfectly incalculable. As a consequence, in situations such as these, self-interest falls silent and individuals must be moved to action by some other motive such as affection, principle, habit, or imitation.[47]

As this brief exposition should have made clear, Hume puts forward an unprudish, unhysterical, and humorous view of men and morals. His essay on factionalism testifies beautifully to the subtlety of eighteenth-century moral psychology. Hume does not view self-interest as the hard rock on which all social life is built. He clarifies the nature of self-interested and rational behavior by contrasting it with disinterested and irrational behavior. Compulsive and impulsive reactions as well as spontaneous sympathies and antipathies provide a foil for "calculating self-interest," giving sharp contours to that idea. For Hume, and many others, "interest" is a useless category unless it is reserved for one motive contending with others. He rejects imperialistic attempts to explain *all* behavior by invoking the rational pursuit of personal advantage. Motivational reductionism is unattractive, among other reasons, because it robs "calculating self-interest" of the specificity it acquires when viewed against a backdrop of selfless urges and thoughtless acts.

Passions and Interests

In *The Passions and the Interests,* Albert Hirschman explores the Humean contrast between calm and violent passions in a broad intellectual context.[48] Briefly, the main thesis of this highly original book is that the idea of self-interest was popularized, and self-interestedness itself morally endorsed, by a variety of seventeenth- and eighteenth-century thinkers. They looked favorably upon interest because they saw it as a relatively peaceful and harmless alternative to the violent passion for glory which had long inspired the military, aristocratic, and landed ruling classes of Europe. To understand what the advocates of self-interest were for, one must understand what they were against—what they were up against. Some of the most intractable difficulties they faced resulted from the upper-class obsession with glory, with an ideal that often had bloody and destructive consequences, that had painful or even fatal externalities for the bystanders of glorious escapades.

The notion that self-interest was a *relatively* harmless and even beneficial passion was, according to Hirschman, a new and untraditional idea, contradicting the old association of avarice with sin.[49] But even though it eased the transition to commercial society, even though it eventually became—if we want to speak this way—the cornerstone of bourgeois ideology, its earliest advocates and defenders were not necessarily members of the "rising" middle class. Rather they were randomly distributed participants in the old order, weary of the destruction caused by glory, bent on reform, and hopeful that the mild passion for money-making, although admittedly ignoble and uncouth, could defeat and bury the violent passions that so ruinously stoked the endless cycles of civil butchery. Commerce is "low," but it is not the cruelest fate individuals and groups can inflict on each other. Interests are ignoble, but they also raise the comfort level of social interaction. The self-interested agent is "cool and deliberate."[50] He is reliable, predictable, calculable, and susceptible to influence by others.[51] An individual who is flushed with a hot passion or in the grip of some abstract principle is more obstinate, less amenable to compromise, and less prone to cooperation than any rational seeker of private advantage. It is much easier to defend oneself against enemies fretting about their interests than against opponents swollen by selfless emotions and inspiring ideals.[52]

Interest was originally viewed as an alternative to various dangerous and unpredictable motivations. Here lies the crux of Hirschman's argument. If we fail to perceive this implicit contrast, we will be at a loss to explain the relatively positive attitude toward economic interests displayed by obviously humane writers during the seventeenth and eighteenth centuries. If we ignore the irrational and destructive antonyms of self-interest, we may even stumble into the kind of error popularized by R. H. Tawney, who interpreted every affirmation of calculating self-interest as a mean-spirited repudiation of brotherly love.[53]

For all its suggestiveness—which I have only touched on in this brief synopsis—Hirschman's account of the history of "self-interest" has three shortcomings: (1) it focuses too heavily on the pursuit of glory, slighting other irrational motivations with which interest was contrasted; (2) it neglects the extent to which religion, particularly the idea of original sin, helped provoke new and more favorable attitudes toward self-interest; and (3) it mentions, but leaves undeveloped, the egalitarian implications of the postulate of *universal* self-interest. I return to the second and third points below. But first it will be useful to round out Hirschman's analysis of the antonyms of interest-driven behavior.[54] Following Hume's lead, we can

construct a fuller list of the irrational motivations to which seventeenth-
and eighteenth-century thinkers contrasted the calculating pursuit of private advantage. Here is Hume's catalog again: the intolerant adherence to
abstract principle, inherited animosity, love of imitation, psychological
identification with a leader, and psychological identification with a group.
To these motives, he also adds the craving for approval, anger, envy, fear,
grief, shame, depression, melancholy, and anxiety.[55]

Smith, too, surveys a number of "disinterested" passions.[56] Among
them are envy,[57] malice, the longing for revenge, parochial loyalty, eager-
ness to conform, the urge to act as befits one's station, irrational avarice,
zealotry, caprice, aversion to change, sheer habit, the instinct to imitate
others, and the need to be told what to do. This last impulse is worth
stressing. Irrational "obsequiousness" toward the rich and powerful is the
flip side of *libido dominandi*. It, too, is a lamentable but natural "disposition" of the human soul.[58] We bend the knee unthinkingly, without knowing why. Superstitious submissiveness toward the great has enormous social consequences. Yet it is not a product of calculation. The unsocial
passions in general make reasoning difficult. As motivational forces, they
are just as "hard" as self-interest. But individuals in the thrall of unsocial
passions do *not* act from rational self-interest—not, at least, as the founder
of modern economics understood that basic idea.

The urge to better one's condition is a forceful and persistent motive—
a steady drip that gradually sculpts a hollow into the stone. But it remains
one motive among others. Even those early modern theorists who emphasized man's natural proclivity for self-preservation admitted that this impulse was less than all powerful. The survival instinct vied with a whole
range of self-destructive passions. According to Francis Bacon, in fact,
"there is no passion in the minde of man, so weake, but it Mates, and
Masters, the Feare of *Death*." And he listed the following emotions, all of
which, in his view, could trump the desire for self-preservation: revenge,
love, honor, shame, grief, fear, pity, and boredom.[59] This list overlaps remarkably with those advanced later by Hume and Smith. Intoxicated or
stunned by such mental states, individuals will ignore the foreseeable consequences of their acts. Emotionally excited or overwrought, they will sacrifice not only their interests but even their lives. When these motives control behavior, the longing for self-preservation does not.

Passions and norms often drive people to neglect their own advantage.
Impulses, compulsions, and social taboos often propel behavior directly,
without the benefit of calculation or reasoning. The question is: where did
Hume and Smith learn to appreciate this short-circuiting of strategic rationality? Direct observation and the study of political history gave them
ample occasion to ponder the foibles and follies of mankind. But they were
also well acquainted with a rich body of literature, including Bacon's *Es-*

says, devoted to the analysis of noncalculating motives and self-destructive behavior. The study of emotionalism and irrationality, in fact, stretches back to antiquity.[60] Scholars now seem to be agreed that "Stoic philosophy" was "the primary influence on Smith's ethical thought."[61] That is a very useful piece of information, for the stoics were centrally concerned with perturbations and disorders of the soul. A passionate man, they believed, was mentally deranged and unable to pursue his own best interests (or, for that matter, any goal) in a coherent fashion.[62] However personal advantage is defined, its methodical pursuit can be derailed by irrationality on the one hand and by disinterestedness on the other.[63]

In stoic psychology, the most impressive example of an irrational passion was *malice,* the "pleasure derived from a neighbor's evil which brings no advantage to oneself."[64] Today we might say that the malicious individual includes the welfare of others as a (negative) argument in his own utility function. But to the stoics, and to those influenced by them, this would have seemed a perverse way to talk. They were too impressed by the stark diversity of human motivations to sympathize with a reductionist approach, however justified methodologically. Thoughtfulness and thoughtlessness are obviously different. Self-preserving and self-destructive behavior are equally so. Distinctions such as these dominated stoic and neostoic psychology. The stoics described anger, for example, as "giving no thought to itself if only it can hurt another."[65] Cruelty can be heroically selfless, they observed. An individual sometimes cuts off his nose to spite his face. But this merely demonstrates how demented passion-driven conduct can be.[66] Only a diseased soul would pine for patently useless things or fear obviously harmless ones. Passion-driven behavior is unreasoning. Therefore, they concluded, rational choice is impossible until the individual has achieved a state of "apathy."[67] Tranquillity of mind, in turn, presupposes a strenuous process of mental self-discipline. The rational pursuit of utility, far from being universal, is a rare moral achievement, possible only for those who have undergone an arduous dispositional training.

The Principal Antonyms of Self-Interest

Stoic emphasis on both the *variety* of human motives and the *rarity* of rational goal-seeking continued to exert an influence on psychological theories up through the eighteenth century. Rational and self-interested behavior was repeatedly contrasted with irrational and self-destructive behavior. To exploit Hirschman's thesis fully, indeed, we need only provide a more systematic survey of the motives typically contrasted with the calculating pursuit of private advantage. After consulting many seventeenth- and eighteenth-century works, in both England and France, I have managed to compile a list of the twenty-four most frequently discussed antonyms of self-interest. Disinterested benevolence and malevolence are opposed to the rational pursuit of personal advantage and, of course, opposed to each other as well. With this in mind, I have attempted to organize the following catalog of antonyms in pairs. They are all opposed to the rational pursuit of private advantage. But each one is opposed to a rival irrational motive as well.

According to numerous writers of the seventeenth and eighteenth centuries, including Smith and Hume, deviations from calculating self-interest can be explained by the following:

1. Animosity, enmity, and hatred
2. Affection, attachment, and love

3. The relish of telling people what to do
4. The relish of being told what to do

5. Excessive pride, megalomania, the passion for superiority, and the desire to eclipse others
6. Self-deprecation, dejection, spiritlessness, and a failure to take an interest in oneself

7. The love of spewing vilifications on others
8. Extreme touchiness about social slights

9. Primordial inertness or the desire not to work
10. Primordial restlessness or the desire to do something, anything—to be where the action is

11. The need for consensus
12. The relish of conflict—it clarifies life—and the spirit of contradiction

13. The hatred of change
14. The love of change

15. The hatred of uncertainty
16. The love of uncertainty[68]

17. Instinctual imitativeness—monkey see, monkey do
18. The desire to be different

19. The obsessive desire to follow rules
20. The obsessive desire to break rules

21. Identification with the victors
22. Identification with the victims

23. Envy for merited or unmerited success
24. Pity for undeserved misfortune

These impulsive or compulsive motives are all described as noncalculating and disinterested. They dictate responses "immediately," without the intervention of common prudence. They provoke behavior that is expressive or consummatory, not instrumental or strategic. To be sure, even the most irrational emotional outbursts can be *used* to gain a strategic advantage. Thomas Schelling, an expert on bluffing,[69] could easily explain to Seneca what is to be gained by overturning the table, hurling cups onto the floor, dashing oneself against pillars, and so forth. But the possibility of using an emotion rationally does not imply that emotion is intrinsically rational. Indeed, we can sometimes treat emotions strategically, as instruments to achieve our ends, because passions are usually spontaneous and involuntary.[70] If passions never drove us uncontrollably into committing imprudent and thoughtless acts, neighbors could not be so easily intimidated by shrewdly timed displays of frenzy or rage.

My roster of the principal antonyms of self-interest, in any case, remains awkward in several respects. It gives insufficient prominence to habit or inherited patterns of response. It omits anger (which classical authors considered a premier example of irrational passion). Vengefulness and malice, too, are poorly represented. I have also excluded identification with a group, partly because of an uncertainty about the "contrary" motivation with which it should be paired. (Is the passion for membership opposed to the xenophobic hatred of rival groups or to antisocial withdrawal into hermetic isolation?) And so on.

Moreover, I have accentuated negative and morally neutral motivations. I have done this, in part, because the list is already too long. Emphasizing the negative also helps corroborate Hirschman's thesis that self-interest was embraced because of the disagreeable alternatives. In any case, benevolence, romantic love,[71] patriotism, noble moral principles, and devotion to justice[72] are mentioned frequently by others. There is no need to go on flattering human nature. People sink below self-interest just as often as they soar above it—perhaps more often. In evaluating attitudes toward interest-driven behavior, we should never forget that "Disinterestedness is often created by Laziness, Pride, or Fear; and then it is no virtue."[73] The person who overcomes selfishness, as I said at the outset, is not necessarily a moral hero.

Even in its present and truncated form, however, our checklist retains considerable interest. Unfortunately, it is not yet a catalogue raisonné. I cannot now undertake a point-by-point commentary on each irrational urge inventoried above. I will have to let the twenty-four antonyms stand as if chiseled on a tablet. Even in their unglossed state, they provide striking evidence for the complexity of seventeenth- and eighteenth-century theories of motivation. If I have convincingly suggested this complexity, I have achieved one of the main objectives of this essay.

I now explore two other questions mentioned at the outset. I focus first on religion and then on the norm of equality. In both cases, there are some powerful but neglected forces that have also profoundly affected the way the concept of self-interest has evolved.

Religion and Self-Interest

The interest/glory polarity loomed large in seventeenth-century political theory.[74] Students of the conflict between the commercial ethic and the chivalric ethic, however, should also keep the biblical ethic in mind. For one thing, Christian hostility toward pridefulness and glory-seeking helped pave the way for secular and "bourgeois" attacks on aristocratic sentiments and ideals.[75]

Hirschman emphasizes the labeling of avarice as a sin. But Christianity's role in the shaping of modern attitudes toward self-interest was not exhausted in its doomed attempt to shore up the usury taboo. Hume, for example, saw Christianity as a moral provocation. He conceived commercial self-interest as a peaceful alternative to hot-gospeling and sectarian zealotry. Enthusiasm was just as socially undesirable, and just as incompatible with a calculating temperament, as the nobility's addiction to glory.[76]

Within Christian culture, moreover, the flesh was often described as the root of moral depravity.[77] The prison-house of concupiscence was a principal sign of our fallen condition. Self-love itself was sometimes considered a sin.[78] Attentiveness to oneself can mean forgetfulness of God. Augustine even identified self-love with the hatred of God. Conversely, he coupled love of God with contempt for oneself.[79] This way of thinking is what Hume was referring to when he complained that Christianity often "represents . . . man to himself in such despicable colours, that he appears unworthy in his own eyes."[80] According to Voltaire, too, the Augustinian tradition had taught men to hate themselves and hold worldly pursuits in disdain.[81] For both Hume and Voltaire, the "rehabilitation" of self-love was inseparable from the attack on Christian severity and asceticism. At the very least, their hostility to religious self-abnegation helped reinforce their relatively welcoming attitude toward self-interest.[82]

Marx writes of "the spiritual egoism of Christianity,"[83] assuming that an obsession with one's personal salvation is fundamentally selfish and antisocial. But this diagnosis may well underestimate the sincerity of

Christian "self-denial."[84] Self-mortification means striving to be "dead to self."[85] One must love God for *His* sake, not in order to go to heaven, but from astonishment at His glory and revulsion at the thought of His being blasphemed. Marx is partly right, nonetheless. Devotion to the glory of God sometimes required neglect of others as well as neglect of self. In the mystical tradition, the pious Christian was encouraged not only to feel "loathing" and "horror" for himself but also to turn away from "all earthly creatures."[86] This is precisely what Hume has in mind when he writes that "self-denial" and other "monkish virtues" are contrary to *both* private advantage *and* the public good.[87]

John Stuart Mill elaborates on this point with his claim that the distinction between active and passive characters is much more fundamental than the distinction between egoistic and altruistic motives. Religion, he believes, generally favors "the inactive character, as being more in harmony with the submission due to the divine will."[88] If you can get a person interested in himself, it takes little more than a gentle nudge to get him interested in others as well.[89] The large step is not from egoism to altruism, but from religiously induced "absence of desire" to a willingness to bestir oneself in the world at all.[90] Voltaire, for the same reason, insists that self-love assists human beings in loving others.[91] This coupling of selfishness and benevolence may seem counterintuitive today. But it made perfect sense in a cultural context where hatred of the world was a widely acclaimed moral ideal.

Significantly, the entry under "self-interest" in Diderot's *Encyclopédie* is an attack, in the spirit of Voltaire, on Augustinian misanthropy.[92] Nicole and Pascal are justly famous for having anticipated Smith's theory of the invisible hand. A society based on cupidity and self-love can be orderly and productive even if it is sinful.[93] But this "modern" aspect of their thinking is entirely neglected in the article on *Intérêt*. Here, the Jansenists are attacked for striving to make people ashamed of their natural and healthy self-love. Despite what severe theologians suggest, it is a good thing to want to preserve yourself. Self-love is nothing more shameful than a steady desire for well-being and an attachment to life. A natural result of our physical makeup, the self-love with which human beings come into the world is, in fact, *morally neutral*—neither good nor bad.[94] At birth, the human being is a blank slate. Depending on how it is transformed through education, primitive self-love will become just or unjust, a virtue or a vice. In its primal state, however, it cannot be classified in either way.[95] This argument, too, sheds important light on the modern "rehabilitation" of self-interest. Those who defended the idea of an inborn but morally neutral self-love were not celebrating avarice. They were attacking the idea of original sin—a form of guilt no one could possibly understand.

Interest and Equality

The story I have told so far, while accurate enough, is clearly one-sided. Smith often contrasted self-interest with a variety of social and unsocial passions. But he also suggested, at least occasionally, that self-interest was *the* fundamental motivation spurring all human endeavor.[96] Thus, present-day economists who lay claim to Smith's legacy have not simply projected contemporary views back into *Wealth of Nations*. By selective citation, they can adduce Smith's own words in their defense. The confusing oscillation between an exclusive and an inclusive conception of self-interest was characteristic of Smith, in fact, and of other eighteenth-century theorists as well.

Hirschman has already drawn attention to a seeming contradiction in the evolution of the concept of self-interest, in what he calls its semantic drift.[97] On the one hand, the concept became, in the course of the seventeenth and eighteenth centuries, progressively more narrow and specialized: having first meant any rational style of behavior, it came to refer exclusively to money-making. On the other hand, during the same period, the concept broadened to the point of becoming a tautology. Everything that anyone did became explainable as a consequence of interest. (This is the development that provoked Macaulay's criticism of James Mill.) But which is it? Did the concept become broader or narrower?

Both. The idea of self-interest simultaneously expanded and contracted. To explain this paradoxical development, we must penetrate even deeper into the secret history of the concept. Sometimes two seemingly contrary tactics were pursued for the same reason.[98] By claiming that *all* actions were motivated by self-interest, theorists friendly to commercial society made it impossible to discredit money-making by smearing it as self-interested. But they also made the rational pursuit of economic gain seem relatively harmless by an opposite tack—by distinguishing interest from a variety of malevolent passions. So interest was identified both as one motive among others *and* as the basic motor of all human action. Smith, like many of his contemporaries, alternated dizzyingly between these two claims.

I have already explored at length the "narrowing strategy," the decision to contrast rational self-interest with various irrational motivations. I now look at the *political rationale* behind the "broadening strategy," the decision to identify rational self-interest with human motivation in general. Republican theorists in particular were prone to assert that it is "impossible for any Man to act upon any other Motive than his own Interest . . . in the larger Sense of the Word."[99] It is not difficult to see why. Self-interest is a profoundly egalitarian and democratic idea. Only a few have hereditary privileges, but everyone has interests. To acknowledge the legitimacy of interests is to say that all citizens, no matter what their socially ascribed status, have concerns that are worthy of attention. Far from being mean-spirited and selfish, the "rehabilitation" of interest made it morally obligatory, for the first time, to attend to "the interests of the excluded."[100]

At the end of the sixteenth century, Richard Hooker summarized traditional thinking with his claim that the common people are motivated by self-interest, while religious and political elites are motivated by virtue and devotion to the common good.[101] Viewed in this context, the postulate of universal self-interest appears as a subversive doctrine, designed to remove all flattering obscurity about the motives of kings, aristocrats, and priests. It allowed republican theorists to declare, disrespectfully, that "the interest of the few is not the profit of mankind."[102] The exaggerated tendency to trace all action to self-interest was, to some extent, a by-product of modern egalitarianism. To say that *all* individuals were motivated by self-interest was to universalize the status of the common man.

Not just virtue, but self-interest, too, was an essential ingredient in modern republican ideology.[103] The king and the nobility, of course, benefited most from the self-obliviousness of canon fodder: "Tyranny being nothing else but the Government of one Man, or of a few Men, over many, against their Inclination and Interest."[104] The notion that it is always noble to transcend self-interest was also useful to the tax collector. Republican writers simply asked rulers to explain what advantages the average citizen might reap from paying taxes and dying in dynastic wars.

As it gradually spread into common usage, the concept of self-interest accustomed people to discovering *conflicts of interest* in every sector of social life. Particular attention was paid to a discrepancy between the interests of citizens and the interests of wielders of power—a gap formerly papered over by uplifting rhetoric about the public good. Smith is an excellent example. Rather than associating the notion of private interest with some sort of preestablished harmony, he uses it to stress the semipermanent character of conflicts of interest—particularly the conflict of interest between merchants and the rest of the community.[105] He was fundamentally opposed to those medieval *Harmonielehren* that pictured society as a large organic body, differentiated by a divinely ordained division of labor. Conflicts of interests were much more significant than such mythology allowed. Thus, despite the apparent inconsistency it entailed, Smith was drawn to broaden and universalize the idea of self-interest. The postulate of *universal* self-interest helped him demolish the old illusion that harmony was a natural product of hierarchy and subordination.

Unless we see interests, we cannot see conflicts of interest. Thus, the principal modern theorists of self-interest can be said to have laid the anthropological foundations for democracy.[106] Assuming, for the sake of argument, that all men were driven by the rational pursuit of private advantage, they clearly posed—for the first time—the problem that modern democratic institutions were eventually designed to resolve: how to make the interests of rulers coincide with the interests of the ruled.[107] Elections, of course, turned out to be the most effective mechanism for ensuring this desirable result. Republican theorists instructed citizens "to choose Representatives, whose Interests are at present the same with your own, and likely to continue the same."[108] Democratic institutions were said to provide "the means by which identity of interest may be insured between the representatives and the community at large."[109] Indeed, the very perfection of government was defined as the "identity of interest between the trustees and the community for whom they hold their power in trust."[110] Elections are necessary because a "governing class not accountable to the people are sure, in the main, to sacrifice the people to the pursuit of separate interests and inclinations of their own."[111] These and similar statements imply that the question answered by modern democratic procedures cannot even be formulated until the universality of self-interest is assumed.

One may speak, as Hirschman does, about a "rehabilitation" of self-interest in modern culture. But there was never any blanket endorsement of the idea. The concept of "sinister interest"[112] never disappeared. In Smith's words, every man should be free to follow his own interests in his own way, but only "as long as he does not violate the laws of justice."[113] Every individual has *many* given interests, some good, some bad.[114] The norm of justice must be invoked to discriminate between interests that should be satisfied and those that should not be. In Smith's view, for example, the interests of monopolists are invariably unjust. The classical formulation of this distinction between just and unjust interests is found in section 57 of the *Second Treatise*. There, Locke argues that law enlarges freedom, and not merely by restricting the behavior of criminals for the sake of honest men. Rather, "Law, in its true Notion, is not so much the Limitation as the direction of a free and intelligent agent to his *proper Interest*, and prescribes no further than is for the general Good of those under that Law."[115] Proper interests are those that are compatible with "the general Good" of all.

A further relevant consideration is this: Writers in the Enlightenment tradition were ardent debunkers and unmaskers. Without wishing to imply that self-interest was the motive behind all human actions, they were naturally fond of exposing self-interested motives wrapped in rhetoric about the common good.[116] Exposés of this sort, repeated endlessly, eventually convey the impression that mercenary motives lurk behind every human act, however decked out in the robes of decency and benevolence. But this is a false impression. We must not misinterpret polemical skirmishes as psychological generalizations. The idea of *universal* self-interest, as it was used at the time of Adam Smith, had a political rationale. It suggested that citizens should distrust every expression of disinterestedness on the part of authorities. Such distrust was not merely cynical. It was also, at least potentially, democratic.

Conclusion

It is plainly contradictory to say that rational self-interest is a universal motivation underlying all human action and to contrast, at the same time, private interest to a whole series of rival motivations (envy, anger, vengefulness, and so forth). Here lies a profound paradox—and a key for unlocking the "secret history" of self-interest. Self-interest was initially defined in opposition to noncalculating and self-destructive motivations. But a commitment to equality and a relish of exposé encouraged some influential modern theorists (some of the time) to overemphasize its exclusiveness and universality. As a result, this singularly cool and deliberate passion was conceived simultaneously in two contrary ways: as one impulse vying with others and as the fundamental motor propelling all human effort. This "contradiction" cannot be dissolved, but it can, as I have tried to show, be more or less adequately explained.

The second conception, the notion that interest is the principal driving force behind all behavior, has had an astonishingly triumphant career. In some quarters, "the granite of self-interest" has now been blessed as the rock of ages. The consistency, rigor, and explanatory success of this reductionist approach may be genuinely admirable. But, as Hume would have said, a methodological commitment to the maximization hypothesis has some empirical disadvantages. It obscures the *actual* motives of individual revenge-seekers, for example. It classifies delirious self-hatred and frantic self-torture as subvarieties of methodical self-interest—an odd use of language, to say the least. It also encourages a simplistic approach to the enduring problems posed by ethnic and religious factions. Selfless cruelty exists and has large-scale social effects. Fortunately, we may still consult the account of human motivation advanced by Smith and Hume themselves. They provide a clearer perspective on the irrational and mutually destructive behavior we read about every day. Their analysis of the human psyche is rich, not parsimonious. Ultimately, their attentiveness to the microfoundations of human irrationality makes social behavior easier not harder to understand.

18   Mothering versus Contract

Virginia Held

Contemporary society is in the grip of contractual thinking. Realities are interpreted in contractual terms, and goals are formulated in terms of rational contracts. The leading current conceptions of rationality begin with assumptions that human beings are independent, self-interested or mutually disinterested, individuals; they then typically argue that it is often rational for human beings to enter into contractual relationships with each other.

On the side of description, assumptions characteristic of a contractual view of human relations underlie the dominant attempts to view social realities through the lenses of the social sciences.[1] They also underlie the principles upon which most persons in contemporary Western society claim their most powerful institutions to be founded. We are told that modern democratic states rest on a social contract,[2] that their economies should be thought of as a free market where producers and consumers, employers and employees make contractual agreements.[3] And we should even, it is suggested, interpret our culture as a free market of ideas.[4]

On the side of prescription, leading theories of justice and equality, such as those of Rawls, Nozick, and Dworkin, suggest what social arrangements should be like to more fully reflect the requirements of contractual rationality.[5] And various philosophers claim that even morality itself is best understood in contractual terms.[6] The vast domain of rational choice theory, supposedly applicable to the whole range of human activity and experience, makes the same basic assumptions about individuals, contractual relations, and rationality, as are by now familiar in the social contract tradition.[7] And contractual solutions are increasingly suggested for problems which arise in areas not hitherto thought of in contractual terms,

This chapter was adapted from "Non-contractual Society: A Feminist View," in Marsha Hanen and Kai Nielsen, eds., *Science, Morality, and Feminist Theory* (Calgary, Alberta: University of Calgary Press, 1987), 111–37.

such as in dealing with unruly patients in treatment contexts, in controlling inmates in prisons, and even in bringing up children.

When subjected to examination, the assumptions and conceptions of contractual thinking seem highly questionable. As descriptions of reality they can be seriously misleading. Actual societies are the results of war, exploitation, racism, and patriarchy far more than of social contracts. Economic and political realities are the outcomes of economic strength triumphing over economic weakness more than of a free market. And rather than a free market of ideas, we have a culture in which the loudspeakers that are the mass media drown out the soft voices of free expression. As expressions of normative concern, moreover, contractual theories hold out an impoverished view of human aspiration.

To see contractual relations between self-interested or mutually disinterested individuals as constituting a paradigm of human relations is to take a certain historically specific conception of "economic man" as representative of humanity. And it is, many feminists are beginning to agree, to overlook or to discount in very fundamental ways the experience of women.

I try in this paper to look at society from a thoroughly different point of view than that of economic man. I take the point of view of women, and especially of mothers, as the basis for trying to rethink society and its possible goals. Certainly there is no single point of view of women; the perspectives of women are potentially as diverse as those of men. But since the perspectives of women have all been to a large extent discounted, across the spectrum, I do not try to deal here with diversity among such views, but rather to give voice to one possible feminist outlook.

The social contract tradition and bourgeois conceptions of rationality have already been criticized for some time from Marxian and other Continental perspectives. These perspectives, however, usually leave out the perspective of mothers as fully as do those they criticize, so I do not try to deal here with these alternatives either. I try instead to imagine what society would look like, for both descriptive and prescriptive purposes, if we replaced the paradigm of "economic man" and substituted for it the paradigm of mother and child. I try to explore how society and our goals for it might appear if, instead of thinking of human relations as contractual, we thought of them as *like* relations between mothers and children. What would social relations look like? What would society look like if we would take the relation between mother and child as not just one relation among many, but as the *primary* social relation? And what sorts of aspirations might we have for such a society?

On the face of it, it seems plausible to take the relation between mother and child as *the* primary social relation, since before there could have been any self-sufficient, independent men in a hypothetical state of nature, there would have had to have been mothers, and the children these men would have had to have been. And the argument could be developed in terms of a conceptual as well as a casual primacy. However, let me anticipate a likely reaction and say before I begin this exploration that I doubt that the view I am going to present is the one we should end up with. I doubt that we should take any one relation as paradigmatic for all the others. And I doubt that morality should be based on any one type of human relation. In my book *Rights and Goods* I argue for different moral approaches for different contexts and try to map out which approaches are suitable for which contexts.[8] Perhaps this book will turn out to be a mere stage in my thinking, and I will eventually suppose that relations between mothers and children should be thought of as primary, and as the sort of human relation all other human relations should resemble or reflect. But I am inclined at this point to think that we will continue to need conceptions of different types of relations for different domains, such as the domains of law, of economic activity, and of the family.

To think of relations between mothers and children as paradigmatic, however, may be an important stage to go through in reconstructing a view of human relationships that will be adequate from a feminist point of view. Since the image of rational economic man in contractual relations is pervasive in this society, and expanding constantly, it may be a useful endeavor to try to see everything in this different way, as if the primary social relation is that between mother and child, and as if all the others could and should be made over in the image of this one, or be embedded in a framework of such relations. In any case, if we pay attention to this neglected relation between mother and child, perhaps we can put a stop to the imperialism of the model of economic man, and assert with conviction that at least there are some or perhaps many domains where this model is definitely not appropriate. And perhaps we can show that morality must be as relevant to, and moral theory as appropriately based on, the context of mothering as the context of contracting. To the extent that some of our relations should be seen as contractual, we should recognize how essentially limited rather than general such relations are. And to the extent that some of morality should be understood in terms of what rational contractors would agree to, we should recognize that such a morality can only be suitable for a particular domain of human relations, and should not be supposed to be a model for morality in general.

Rational choice theorists point out that their theories are formulated for just those situations where individuals do seek to maximize their own interests and are uninterested in each others' interests. Their theories, they suggest, are not intended to deal with people in love. But the questions I am trying to raise in this paper have do to with how we ought to treat, conceptually, a great variety of human relations. Of course we *can*, theo-

290 / Chapter Eighteen

retically, treat them *as* contractual, but *should* we do so? Is it plausible to do so? And when we ask these questions we can see that of course it is not only in special cases that persons can be and perhaps should be and often are bound together in social ties of a noncontractual kind.

To see society in terms of family rather than marketplace relationships is not new. Feudal conceptions, for instance, drew analogies between monarchs and the heads of households. But these were views based on relations between patriarchal fathers and their wives and children, not views of society seen in terms of mothering. To explore the latter is not to suggest a return to precontractual society, but to consider what further progress is needed.

Since it is the practice of mothering with which I am concerned in what follows, rather than with women in the biological sense, I use the term *mothering person* rather than *mother*. A mothering person can be male or female. So I speak of mothering persons in the same gender-neutral way that various writers now try to speak of "rational contractors." If men feel uncomfortable being referred to as, or even more so in being, "mothering persons," this may possibly mirror the discomfort many mothers feel adapting to the norms and practices, and language, of "economic man."

It is important to emphasize that I look at the practice of mothering not as it has in fact existed in any patriarchal society, but in terms of what the characteristic features of this practice would be without patriarchal domination. In method this may be comparable to what has been done in developing a concept of rational contracting. This concept of course developed while large segments of society were in fact still feudal, and of course actual human beings are not in fact fully rational. These realities have not prevented the contractual relation from being taken as paradigmatic.

Furthermore, it may well be that the concept of the mother/child relation that I develop is somewhat historically specific. But perhaps no concept can avoid being that. My aim is only to have the conception I try to develop capable of being considered an alternative to the conception of economic man in contractual relations, that is, of being no more historically limited, and contextually dependent, than that. To the extent that the mother/child relation is an idealization, I hope it will not be more severely idealized than the relation between rational contractors that it is to replace; for the purposes of my exploration, it does not need to be less of an idealization.

Women and Family

A first point to note in trying to imagine society from the point of view of women is that the contractual model was hardly ever applied, as either description or ideal, to women or to relations within the family. The family was imagined to be "outside" the polis and "outside" the market in a "private" domain. This private domain was contrasted with the public domain, and with what, by the time of Hobbes and Locke, was thought of as the contractual domain of citizen and state and tradesman and market. Although women have always worked, and although both women and children were later pressed into work in factories, they were still thought of as outside the domain in which the contractual models of "equal men" were developed. Women were not expected to demand equal rights either in the public domain or at home. Women were not expected to be "economic men." And children were simply excluded from the realm of what was being interpreted in contractual terms as distinctively human.

The clearest example of the extraordinary bias to which such views can lead can be seen in the writings of Rousseau. Moral principles were to be applied to men and to women in ways thoroughly inconsistent with each other. Rousseau argued that in the polity no man should surrender his freedom. He thought that government could be based on a social contract in which citizens under law will be as free as in the state of nature because they will give the law to themselves.[9] But, he argued, within the household, the man must rule and the woman must submit to this rule.[10] Rousseau maintained that women must be trained from the beginning to serve and to submit to men. Since the essence of being fully human was for Rousseau being free from submission to the will of another, women were to be denied the essential condition for being fully human. And he thought that if women were accorded equality with men in the household (which was the only domain to be open to them), this would bring about the dissolution of society. Human society, Rousseau thought, was incompatible with extending the principles of contractual society to women and the family.

The contrast, in this view, is total: complete freedom and equality in the exclusively male polity; absolute male authority and female submission in the household. And Rousseau seems not to have considered the implications of such a view. If one really believes that two persons in a household, with ties of affection and time for discussion, can never reach decisions by consensus, or by taking turns at deciding, but must always have one person in full authority to have the final word, what hope could there possibly be for the larger democratic, participatory, consensual political life Rousseau so eloquently advocated? On the other hand, if decisions in the political realm *can* be arrived at in such a way that the will of no man needs to be overpowered, as Rousseau thought, why cannot such concern for avoiding coercion be extended to relations between men and women in the family?

One way in which the dominant patterns of thought have managed to overlook such inconsistencies has been to see women as primarily mothers, and mothering as a primarily biological function. Then it has been supposed that while contracting is a specifically human activity, women are engaged in an activity which is not specifically human. Women have accordingly been thought to be closer to nature than men, to be enmeshed in a biological function involving processes more like those in which other animals are involved than like the rational contracting of distinctively human "economic man." The total or relative exclusion of women from the domain of voluntary contracting has then been thought to be either inevitable or appropriate.

The view that women are more governed by biology than are men is still prevalent. It is as questionable as many other traditional misinterpretations of women's experience. Human mothering is an extremely different activity from the mothering engaged in by other animals. It is as different from the mothering of other animals as is the work and speech of men different from the "work" and "speech" of other animals. Since humans are also animals, one should not exaggerate the differences between humans and other animals. But to whatever extent it is appropriate to recognize a difference between "man" and other animals, so would it be appropriate to recognize a comparable difference between human mothering and the mothering of other animals.

Human mothering shapes language and culture, and forms human social personhood. Human mothering develops morality, it does not merely transmit techniques of survival; impressive as the latter can be, they do not have built into them the aims of morality. Human mothering teaches consideration for others based on moral concern; it does not merely follow and bring the child to follow instinctive tendency. Human mothering creates autonomous persons; it does not merely propagate a species. It can be fully as creative an activity as most other human activities; to create *new* persons, and new types of *persons,* is surely as creative as to make new objects, products, or institutions. Human mothering is no more "natural" than any other human activity. It may include many dull and repetitive tasks, as does farming, industrial production, banking, and work in a laboratory. But degree of dullness has nothing to do with degree of "naturalness." In sum, human mothering is as different from animal mothering as humans are from animals.

On a variety of grounds there are good reasons to have mothering become an activity performed by men as well as by women.[11] We may wish to continue to use the term *mothering* to designate the activity, in recognition of the fact that it has been overwhelmingly women who have engaged in this activity,[12] and because for the foreseeable future it is the point of view of women, including women engaged in mothering, which should be called on to provide a contrast with the point of view of men. A time may come when a term such as *the nurturing of children* would be preferable to *mothering*.[13]

Clearly, the view that contractual relations are a model for human relations generally is especially unsuitable for considering the relations between mothering persons and children. It stretches credulity even further than most philosophers can tolerate to imagine babies as little rational calculators contracting with their mothers for care. Of course the fundamental contracts have always been thought of as hypothetical rather than real. But one can not imagine hypothetical babies contracting either. And mothering persons, in their care of children, demonstrate hardly any of the "trucking" or trading instinct claimed by Adam Smith to be the *most* characteristic aspect of human nature.[14] If the epitome of what it is to be human is thought to be a disposition to be a rational contractor, human persons creating other human persons through the processes of human mothering are overlooked. And human children developing human personhood are not recognized as engaged in a most obviously human activity.

David Hume, whom some admire for having moral views more compatible with "women's moral sense" than most philosophers have had,[15] had the following to say about the passion of avarice: "Avarice, or the desire of gain, is a universal passion which operates at all times, in all places, and upon all persons."[16] Surely we can note that in the relation between mothering person and child, not only as it should be but often enough as it is, avarice is hard to find. One can uncover very many emotions in the relation, but the avarice that fuels the model of "economic man" with his rational interest is not prominent among them.

There is an exchange in Charlotte Perkins Gilman's *Herland* that illustrates the contrast between the motives ascribed to rational economic man building contractual society and those central to the practice of mothering. Herland is an imaginary society composed entirely of women. They reproduce by parthenogenesis, and there are only mothers and daughters in the society. Everything is arranged to benefit the next generation, and the society has existed peacefully for hundreds of years, with a high level of technological advancement but without any conception of a "survival of the fittest" ethic. Three young men from twentieth-century America manage to get to Herland. They acknowledge that in Herland there are no wars, no kings, no priests, no aristocracies, that the women are all like sisters to each other and work together not by competition but by united action. But they argue that things are much better at home. In one exchange they try to explain how important it is to have competition. One of them expounds on the advantages of competition, how it develops fine qualities, saying that "without it there would be 'no stimulus to industry.'"[17] He says competition is necessary to provide an incentive to work; "competition," he explains, "is the motor power" of society.

The women of Herland are genuinely curious and good-naturedly skeptical, as they so often are in Gilman's novel. "Do you mean," they ask, "that no mother would work for her children without the stimulus of competition?" In Herland, the entire, industrious society works on the strong motivation of making the society better for the children. As one woman explains, "the children in this country are the one center and focus of all our thoughts. Every step of our advance is always considered in its effects on them. . . . You see, we are *Mothers*."[18]

Of course, this is an idealized picture of mothering. But I am contrasting it with an idealized picture of rationally contracting. Quite probably we would not want a society devoted entirely to mothering. But then we might not want a society devoted entirely to better bargains either. In developing these suggestions, it is instructive to see what is most seriously overlooked by a contractual view of society, and to see how important what is overlooked is.

Family and Society

In recent years, many feminists have demanded that the principles of justice and freedom and equality on which it is claimed that democracy rests be extended to women and the family. They have demanded that women be treated as equals in the polity, in the workplace, and, finally, at home. They have demanded, in short, to be accorded full rights to enter freely the contractual relations of modern society. They have asked that these be extended to take in the family.

But some feminists have also asked whether the arguments should perhaps, instead, run the other way. Instead of importing into the household principles derived from the marketplace, perhaps we should export to the wider society the relations suitable for mothering persons and children. This approach suggests that just as relations between persons within the family should be based on concern and caring, rather than on egoistic or nontuistic contracts, so various relations in the wider society should be characterized by more care and concern and openness and trust and human feeling than are the contractual bargains that have developed so far in political and economic life, or even than are aspired to in contractarian prescriptions. Then, the household instead of the marketplace might provide a model for society. Of course what we would mean by the household would not be the patriarchal household which was, before the rise of contractual thinking, also thought of as a model of society. We would now mean the relations between mothering persons and children *without* the patriarch. We would take our conception of the postpatriarchal family as a model.

The model of the social contract was certainly an improvement over that of political patriarchy. Locke's prescriptions for political order are so clearly better than Filmer's that almost no one still reads the arguments made by philosophers such as Filmer, whose views were completely dominant until replaced by those of contractualists like Locke. Filmer thought that political authority should be based on correct inheritance: God gave the world to Adam, and authority to govern was transferred from Adam through the ancient patriarchs to the legitimate monarchs of any historical period. Democracy, to Filmer, was dangerous nonsense. Of course no feminist would wish to go back to such views as Filmer's, nor to those of Aristotle if interpreted as holding that the polity should be a version on a grander scale of the patriarchal household. But to consider whether we should generalize the relation between mothering person and child to any regions beyond the home is to consider generalizing a quite different relation from that which has existed within the patriarchal household, even between mothers and children within patriarchal society. It is to explore what relations between mothering persons and children should be in nonpatriarchal societies, and to consider how a transformed household might contribute to a transformed society.

These questions lead us to focus on the family as a social institution of the utmost importance. The family is a set of relations creating human persons. Societies are composed of families. And a family is a small society. The family is undergoing profound change at the present time, and the attendant upheavals in the personal lives of many persons hold out the promise of remarkable social change, quite possibly for the better.

The family is only beginning to receive the central attention from feminists that it deserves, partly because feminist theory is still in such exploratory stages, trying to understand all at once the multiplicity of forces—social, economic, political, legal, psychological, sexual, biological, and cultural—that affect women. Multiple causes shape the sex/gender structures within which human females and males develop feminine and masculine characteristics and come to occupy the roles that existing societies designate as female and male. We need to understand empirically how this happens. We also need normative theories of the family. Jane Flax, surveying recent feminist writing on the family, writes that to develop alternatives to the oppressive relations that now prevail, we need to think through "what kinds of child care are best for parents and children; what family structures are best for persons at various stages of the life cycle . . . ; how the state and political processes should affect families; and how work and the organization of production should be transformed to support whatever family forms are preferred."[19] It is an enormous task, but recent years have provided more new thought on these subjects than have many previous decades.[20]

The major question remains: what are the possibilities of remaking society by remaking what have been thought of as "personal" relations? Societies are composed of persons in relation to one another. The "personal" relations among persons are the most affective and influential in many ways. But the extent to which they are central to wider social relations, or could possibly provide a model for social and political relations of a kind that has been thought of as "public," remains an open question.

Western liberal democratic thought has been built on the concept of the "individual" seen as a theoretically isolatable entity. This entity can assert interests, have rights, and enter into contractual relations with other entities. But this individual is not seen as related to other individuals in inextricable or intrinsic ways. This individual is assumed to be motivated primarily by a desire to pursue his own interests, though he can recognize the need to agree to contractual restraints on the ways everyone may pursue their interests. To the extent that groups have been dealt with at all, they have been treated *as* individuals.

The difficulties of developing trust and cooperation and society itself on the sands of self-interested individuals pursuing their own gain are extreme.[21] Contractual society is society perpetually in danger of breaking down. Perhaps what are needed for even adequate levels of social cohesion are persons tied together by relations of concern and caring and empathy and trust rather than merely by contracts it may be in their interests to disregard. Any enforcement mechanisms put in place to keep persons to their contracts will be as subject to disintegration as the contracts themselves; at some point contracts must be embedded in social relations that are noncontractual.

The relation between mothering person and child, hardly understandable in contractual terms, may be a more fundamental human relation, and a more promising one on which to build our recommendations for the future, than is any relation between rational contractors. Perhaps we should look to the relation between mothering person and child for suggestions of how better to describe such society as we now have. And perhaps we should look to it especially for a view of a future more fit for our children than a global battleground for rational, egoistic entities trying, somehow, to restrain their antagonisms by fragile contracts.

The Marxian view of the relations between human beings is in various ways more satisfactory than the contractual one and more capable of accounting for social relations in general. However, the Marxian view of our history, split into classes and driven by economic forces, is hardly more capable of encompassing, and does not lend itself to reflecting, the experience of the relation between mothering person and child either. So I continue to develop here the contrast between the relation between mothering person and child on the one hand, and the contractual exchanges of "economic man" on the other.

The Mother/Child Relation

Let us examine in more detail the relation between mothering person and child. First, it is to a large extent not voluntary and, for this reason among others, not contractual. The ties that bind mothering person and child are affectional and solicitous on the one hand, and emotional and dependent on the other. The degree to which bearing and caring for children has been voluntary for most mothers throughout most of history has been extremely limited; it is still quite limited for most mothering persons. The relation *should* be voluntary for the mothering person but it cannot possibly be voluntary for the young child, and it can only become, gradually, slightly more voluntary.

A woman can have decided voluntarily to have a child, but once that decision has been made, she will never again be unaffected by the fact that she has brought this particular child into existence. And even if the decision to have a child is voluntary, the decision to have this particular child, for either parent, cannot be. Technological developments can continue to reduce the uncertainties of childbirth, but unpredictable aspects are likely to remain great for most parents. Unlike that contract where buyer and seller can know what is being exchanged, and which is void if the participants cannot know what they are agreeing to, a parent cannot know what a particular child will be like. And children are totally unable to choose their parents and, for many years, any of their caretakers.

The recognition of how limited are the aspects of voluntariness in the relation between mothering person and child may help us gain a closer approximation to reality in our understanding of most human relations, especially at a global level, than we can gain from imagining the purely voluntary trades entered into by rational economic contractors to be characteristic of human relations in other domains.

Society may impose certain reciprocal obligations: on parents to care for children when the children are young, and on children to care for parents when the parents are old. But if there is any element of a bargain in the relation between mothering person and child, it is very different from the bargain supposedly characteristic of the marketplace. If a parent thinks "I'll take care of you now so you'll take care of me when I'm old," it must be based, unlike the contracts of political and economic bargains, on enormous trust and on a virtual absence of enforcement.[22] And few mothering persons have any such exchange in mind when they engage in the activities of mothering. At least the bargain would only be resorted to when the callousness or poverty of the society made the plight of the old person desperate. This is demonstrated in survey after survey; old persons certainly hope not to have to be a burden on their children.[23] And they prefer social arrangements that will allow them to refuse to cash in on any such bargain. So the intention and goal of mothering is to give of one's care without obtaining a return of a self-interested kind. The emotional satisfaction of a mothering person is a satisfaction in the well-being and happiness of another human being, and a satisfaction in the health of the relation between the two persons, not the gain that results from an egoistic bargain. The motive behind the activity of mothering is thus entirely different from that behind a market transaction. And so is, perhaps even more clearly, the motive behind the child's project of growth and development.

Second, the relations between mothering parent and child are largely permanent and nonreplaceable. The market makes of everything, even human labor and artistic expression and sexual desire, a commodity to be bought and sold, with one unit of economic value replaceable by any other of equivalent value. To the extent that political life reflects these aspects of the market, politicians are replaceable and political influence is bought and sold. Though rights may be thought of as outside the economic market, in contractual thinking they are seen as inside the wider market of the social contract, and can be traded against each other. But the ties between parents and children are permanent ties, however strained or slack they become at times. And no person within a family should be a commodity to any other. Although various persons may participate in mothering a given child, and a given person may mother many children, still no child and no mothering person is to the other a merely replaceable commodity. Acknowledging the character of permanent and irreplaceable relations makes it possible to ask which of our relations—for instance, our relations with our society's cultural productions—should be conceived more in these terms, and which more in terms of the marketplace.

Third, the relation between mothering parent and child provides insight into our understandings of equality. It shows us unmistakably that equality is not equivalent to having equal legal rights. All feminists are committed to equality and to equal rights in contexts where rights are what are appropriately at issue. But in many contexts, concerns other than rights are more salient and appropriate. And the equality that is at issue in the relation between mothering person and child is the equal consideration of persons, not a legal or contractual notion or equal rights.

Parents and children should not have equal rights in the sense that what they are entitled to decide or to do or to have should be the same. A family of several children, an adult or two, and an aged parent should not, for instance, make its decisions by majority vote in most cases.[24] But every member of a family is worthy of equal respect and consideration. Each person in a Western postindustrial family is as important a person as any other.

In the past, the interests of children have sometimes been thought in some sense to count for more, justifying "sacrificing for the children." Certainly the interests of mothers have often counted for less than those of either fathers or children. Increasingly we may come to think that the interests of all should count equally. But we should recognize that this claim is appropriately invoked only if the issue should be thought of as one of interest. Often, it should not. Much of the time we can see that calculations of interest, and of equal interests, are as out of place as are determinations of equal rights. The rights and interests of individuals seen as separate entities, and the equality between these rights and interests, should not exhaust our moral concerns. Shared joy, mutual affection, bonds of trust and hope, harmony, love, and cooperation cannot be broken down into individual benefits and burdens. These are relations *between* persons, and goals we ought to share. And although their intensity may be lower, some relations between persons at the level of a community or society determine the character of that society—whether the relations between its members are trusting and mutually supportive, or suspicious and hostile. To focus only on contractual relations and on the gains and losses of individuals obscures these often more important relational aspects of societies.

Fourth, the relation between mothering parent and child makes it clear that we do not fulfill our obligations by merely leaving people alone. An infant left alone will starve. A two-year-old left alone will quickly hurt herself. The "Robinson Crusoe" tradition, which assumes that people can fend for themselves and provide through their own initiatives and efforts what they need, is false in the case of infants and children. Recognizing this necessary dependence can lead us to see vividly how unsatisfactory are those prevalent political views according to which we fulfill our obligations and even express our respect for others merely by refraining from interference. The fact of dependency may itself provide a reason for certain rights, leading us to acknowledge that not only our children but also our fellow citizens and fellow inhabitants of the globe have moral rights to what they need to live. We ought to acknowledge that all persons have rights to the food, shelter, and medical care that are the necessary conditions of living and growing, and that when the resources exist for honoring such rights there are few excuses for not doing so.[25]

Fifth, the relation between mothering parent and child provides an understanding of privacy very different from the liberal view. We come to see that to be in a position where others are *not* making demands on us is a rare luxury, not a normal state. To be a mothering person is to be subjected to the continual demands and needs of others. And to be a child is to be subjected to the continual demands and expectations of others. Both mothering persons and children need to extricate themselves from the thick and heavy social fabric in which they are entwined in order to enjoy any pockets of privacy at all.

Here the picture we form of our individuality and the concept we form of a "self" is entirely different from the one we get if we start with the self-sufficient individual of the "state of nature." If we begin with the picture of rational contractor entering into agreements with others, the "natural" condition is seen as one of individuality and privacy, and the problem is the building of society and government. From the point of view of the relation between mothering person and child, on the other hand, the problem is the reverse. The starting condition is an enveloping tie, and the problem is individuating oneself. The task is to carve out a gradually increasing measure of privacy in ways appropriate to a constantly shifting interdependency. For the child, the problem is to become gradually more independent. For the mothering person, the problem is to free oneself from an all-consuming involvement. For both, the progression is from society to greater individuality rather than from self-sufficient individuality to contractual ties. A new concept of the self, built on these insights into development and individuation, would greatly affect our conceptualizations of what we now think of as the "impersonal" and "public" domain of politics, as distinct from the "personal" and "private" sphere of the family.

Sixth, the relation between mothering parent and child provides an understanding of power different from the prevailing understanding of power as something that can be wielded by one person over another, as a means by which one person can bend another to his will. One ideal had been to equalize power so that agreements can be forged and conflicts defused. But the relation between mothering parent and child affords a different understanding of power. The superior power of the mothering person over the child is relatively useless for most of what the mothering person aims to achieve in bringing up the child. The mothering person seeks to *empower* the child to act responsibly. She wants neither to "wield" power nor to defend herself against the power "wielded" by the child. When the child is physically weakest, as in infancy and illness, the child can "command" the greatest amount of attention and care from the mothering person because of the seriousness of the child's needs.

The mothering person's stance is characteristically one of caring, of vulnerability to the needs and pains of the child, and fearing the loss of the child before the child is ready for independence. It is not characteristically a stance of domination. The child's project is one of developing, of gaining ever greater control over his or her own life, of relying on the mothering person rather than of submitting to superior strength. In a degenerate form the relation may become one of domination and submission, but this is not as it should be. In the usual and normatively sanctioned relation between mothering parent and child, the conceptions of power with which we are familiar, from Hobbes and Locke to Hegel and Marx, are of little use for understanding the aspects of power involved in the relation.[26] The power of a mothering person to empower others, to foster transformative growth, is a different sort of power than that of a stronger sword or dominant will. And the power of a child to call forth tenderness and care is perhaps more different still.

Hobbes thought we could build society on the equal vulnerability of every man to the sword of his fellows. And the vulnerability of men may bring them to seek peace and to covenant against violence. We can hope for whatever progress can be made in curbing the murderous conflicts, tempered by truces and treaties, to which this has led, though our expectations under current conditions must realistically be very modest.

But let us speculate about a different vulnerability and a different development. Mothering persons are vulnerable to the demands and needs of children. We do not know if this is instinctive or innate, or not. Some claim that the experiences of carrying a child, of laboring and suffering to give birth, of suckling, inevitably cause mothers to be especially sensitive to the cries and needs of a child. Others claim that fathers, placed in the position of being the only persons capable of responding to the needs of a child, develop similar responsiveness. Whatever the truth, one can admit that no one can become a mothering person without becoming sensitive to the needs of relatively helpless or less powerful others. And to become thus sensitive is to become vulnerable. If the vulnerability is chosen, so much the better. Mothering persons become in this way vulnerable to the claims of morality.

It is not, however, the morality of following abstract, universal rules so much as the morality of being responsive to the needs of actual, particular others in relations with us. The traditional view, reasserted in the psychological studies of Lawrence Kohlberg, that women are less likely than men to be guided by the highest forms of morality, would be plausible only if morality were no more than the abstract and rational rules of pure and perfect principle.[27] For traditional morality, increasingly recognizable as developed from a male point of view, there seems to be either the pure principle of the rational lawgiver or the self-interest of the individual contractor. There is the unreal universality of *all*, or the real *self* of individual interest.

Both views, however, lose sight of acting *for* particular others in actual contexts. Mothering persons cannot lose sight of the particularity of the child being mothered or of the actuality of the circumstances in which the activity is taking place. Mothering persons may tend to resist harming or sacrificing those particular others for the sake of abstract principles or total faith; on the other hand, it is for the sake of *others,* or for the sake of relationships between persons, rather than to further their own interests, that such resistance is presented by mothering persons. Morality, for mothering persons, must guide us in our relations with actual, particular children, enabling them to develop their own lives and commitments. For mothering persons, morality can never seem adequate if it offers no more than ideal rules for hypothetical situations: morality must connect with the actual context of real, particular others in need. At the same time, morality, for mothering persons, cannot possibly be a mere bargain between rational contractors. That morality in this context could not be based on self-interest or mutual disinterest directly is obvious; that a contractual escape is unavailable or inappropriate is clear enough.

The morality that could offer guidance for those engaged in mothering might be a superior morality to those available at present. It would be a morality based on caring and concern for actual human others, and it would have to recognize the limitations of both egoism and perfect justice.[28] When we turned to the social and political theories that would be compatible with such a view of morality, we would see that they would have to differ not only from the patriarchal models of precontractual conceptions, but also from the contractual models that so dominate current thinking. Contractual relations would not be ruled out, but they would cease to seem paradigmatic of human relations, and the regions within which they could be thought justified would be greatly reduced.

The Child's Perspective

What about the point of view of the child? A most salient characteristic of the relation between mothering person and child is the child's relative powerlessness. The child cannot possibly rely on the Hobbesian safeguard of the equal vulnerability of the caretaker. Not even when the caretaker is asleep is she vulnerable to the sword of the small child, and it will be years, if ever, before the child can match the caretaker in even physical strength, let alone social and economic and psychological power. Whatever claims the child makes against a mothering person must be based on something else than superior strength, and the child should come to trust the restraint of one who could but does not wish to cause the child harm.

The child in relation to the mothering person is permanently in the best possible position from which to recognize that right is *not* equivalent to might, that power, including the power to teach and enforce a given morality, is not equivalent to morality itself. Becoming a person is not so much learning a morality that is being taught as it is developing the ability to decide for oneself what morality requires of one. Children characteristically go beyond the mothering persons in their lives, becoming autonomous beings. They do not characteristically then respond to the mothering persons they leave behind with proposals for better bargains for themselves now that they have the power to enforce their terms. The relation between mothering person and child is such that disparities of power are given. Though the positions may reverse themselves, unequal power is almost everpresent. But it is often also irrelevant to the relation.

When young men are invited to enter the public realm of contractual relations they are encouraged to forget their past lack of power and to assume a position of equality or superiority. But we should probably none of us ever forget what it is like to lack power. Taking the relation between child and mothering person as the primary social relation might encourage us to remember the point of view of those who cannot rely on the power of arms to uphold their moral claims. It might remind us of the distinction between the morality that, as developed autonomous persons, we come to construct for ourselves, and the moral injunctions which those with superior force can hold us to.

Models for Society

There are good reasons to believe that a society resting on no more than bargains between self-interested or mutually disinterested individuals will not be able to withstand the forces of egoism and dissolution pulling such societies apart. Although there may be some limited domains in which rational contracts are the appropriate form of social relations, as a foundation for the fundamental ties which ought to bind human beings together, they are clearly inadequate. Perhaps we can learn from a nonpatriarchal household better than from further searching in the marketplace what the sources might be for justifiable trust, cooperation, and caring.

On the first occasion when I spoke about considering the relation between mothering person and child as the primary social relation, a young man in the audience asked: but in society, by which he meant society outside the family, who are the mothers and who are the children? While meant as a hostile question, it is actually a very good question. The very difficulty so many persons have in imagining an answer may indicate how distorted are the traditional contractual conceptions. Such persons can imagine human society on the model of "economic man," society built on a contract between rationally self-interested persons, because these are the theories they have been brought up with. But they cannot imagine society resembling a group of persons tied together by ongoing relations of caring and trust between persons in positions such as those of mothers and children where, as adults, we would sometimes be one and sometimes the other. Suppose now we ask: In the relation between mothering person and child, who are the contractors? Where is the rational self-interest? The model of "economic man" makes no sense in this context. Anyone in the social contract tradition who has noticed the relation of mothering person and child at all has supposed it to belong to some domain outside the realm of the "free market" and outside the "public" realm of politics and the law. Such theorists have supposed the context of mothering to be of much less significance for human history and of much less relevance for moral theory than the realms of trade and government, or they have imagined mothers and children as somehow outside human society altogether in a region labeled "nature," and engaged wholly in "reproduction." But mothering is at the heart of human society.

If the dynamic relation between mothering person and child is taken as the primary social relation, then it is the model of "economic man" that can be seen to be deficient as a model for society and morality, and unsuitable for all but a special context. A domain such as law, if built on no more than contractual foundations, can then be recognized as one limited domain among others; law protects some moral rights when people are too immoral or weak to respect them without the force of law. But it is hardly a majestic edifice that can serve as a model for morality. Neither can the domain of politics, if built on no more than self-interest or mutual disinterest, provide us with a model with which to understand and improve society and morality. And neither, even more clearly, can the market itself.

When we explore the implications of these speculations we may come to realize that instead of seeing the family as an anomalous island in a sea of rational contracts composing economic and political and social life, perhaps it is instead "economic man" who belongs on a relatively small island surrounded by social ties of a less hostile, cold, and precarious kind.

Notes

Chapter 1

1. See Glaucon and Thrasymachus in the *Republic*, 358 E-359B, 359–61, 338C ff.; Aristotle, *Politics* iii. 1280b10, 1280b29; Antiphon, "On Truth," in *Oxyrhynchus Papyri*, xi, no. 1364, pp. 92–104, cited in Gough, 1936. These ideas, expressed by different thinkers, do not seem to have been set forth as a coherent theory. Nor is it absolutely necessary that they be connected by self-interest as we understand it (that is, association for self-defense undoubtedly includes the defense of one's family). Considerable controversy has developed over the role of self-interest in Greek thought, Havelock claiming that "a basic split between the moral or ideal and the expedient or selfish did not develop until Christian other-worldly influences had begun to affect the vocabulary and the mind of the West" (1957/1964: 391). See Mabbott (1937/1971) and Vlastos (1971) on the kind of individual happiness that Socrates thought acting justly promotes, Adkins (1963, 1972) on friendship as no more than "cooperation to meet the harsh demands of Homeric life," and Dover (1974: 180–83), Pearson (1962: 87–88), and Connor (1971, *passim*) on the common Greek assertion that *arete* consists in doing the things of the polis in such a way as to benefit one's friends and harm one's foes (*Meno* 71e2 ff.; see also *Republic* 331e).

It is Havelock (1957/1964) who suggests that the group he calls the "Elder Sophists," particularly Protagoras, were building "an edifice of democratic theory" (p. 158).

2. *Ad Gebhardum Liber*, c. 1085, excerpted in Lewis 1954: 165. For other theorists, see Gough 1936.

3. For the "masterlesse men," who live in "perpetuall war, of every man against his neighbor," see Hobbes 1651, chap. 21. For the times, see Walzer 1967.

4. Gough 1936: 40, 42, 43, 58, 59, 61, 65, 69 for descriptions of the state of nature in early contract theories from the end of the thirteenth century to the end of the sixteenth century.

5. Hobbes 1651, chap. 13: "because there be some, that taking pleasure in contemplating their own power in the acts of conquest, which they pursue farther than their security requires; if others, that otherwise would be glad to be at ease within modest bounds, should not by invasion increase their power, they would not be able, long time, by standing only on their defence, to subsist." Hobbes also

makes it clear in both the passage on felicity consisting not in the repose of a mind satisfied and in the passage on the general inclination of mankind being a perpetual and restless desire for power after power (chap. 11) that the cause of this unending quest is not that human beings cannot be content with moderation, but that they need to assure the moderate amount they may want by continually acquiring more power. Hobbes's point here either undermines or makes more complex the implicit analogy he draws between his view of human nature and the discoveries of Renaissance physics, which replaced the Aristotelian *telos* with unending motion.

6. See Taylor 1976, 1987 and Hardin 1982. Both Taylor and Hampton 1986 reconstruct and critique parts of Hobbes's logic in this respect.

7. John Bramhall, *The Catching of Leviathan* (1658), cited in Skinner 1966: 316.

8. See Gough 1936 and Skinner 1966 for those, including Spinoza, who adopted the analysis from self-interest.

9. Joseph Lee, *A vindication of a regulated enclosure* (1656), p. 9, quoted in Appleby 1978: 62.

10. "L'interest seul ne peut jamais manquer"; in le Duc de Rohan, *De l'interest des princes et estates de la Chrestianité* (Paris, 1638; translated into English 1640). The common reference to the French proverb "interest will not lie" appeared first in Herle, *Wisdom's Tripos* (London, 1655). References and discussion in Gunn 1969: 36–44, and Gunn 1968.

11. Lee, *Vindication,* pp. 22–23, quoted in Appleby 1978: 62.

12. "A memorial concerning the coyn of England" (1695), in Abbot Payson Usher, ed., *Two Manuscripts by Charles Davenant* (Baltimore, 1942), 20–21, cited in Appleby 1978: 187. For the naturalness of self-interest, and also its compatibility with concern for the public good, see Appleby 1978, *passim.* Gunn 1969 also stresses throughout his survey of the seventeenth century that many writers saw no conflict between private and public interest. A Leveller pamphlet could speak on page 8 of "that law of nature and common prudence which enjoins every man to preserve himself, and to seek his own good," and on page 9 of "that law that obliges every commoner according to his ability, and opportunity to seek the good of that politic body of which he is a member" (Gunn 1969: 22). In the eighteenth century, writers such as Shaftesbury, Butler, Hutcheson, and Maxwell insisted on the harmony of self-interest and social interest. Alexander Pope concluded, "Thus God and Nature link'd the gen'ral frame,/And bade Self-love and Social be the same" ("An Essay on Man," Epistle III, lines 317–18, in Pope 1733/ 1966). See Myers 1983 for commentary.

13. Gunn 1969: 1, 84. The idea that the public interest is no more than the aggregate of individual goods played the same antimonarchical political role. See Ireton (1648), Durie (1642), Locke (1689), and Paine (1786) in Gunn 1969: 13, 15, 293, 336.

14. The Putney Debates in Woodhouse 1957: 59; see also p. 67. Colonel Rainborough, a déclassé aristocrat among the yeoman Levellers, had the structural role of "marginal man" which Mannheim 1936/1966 suggests facilitates having ideas that foreshadow the future.

15. Heinberg 1926: 59, citing Gierke, "On the History of the Majority Principle" (1913).

16. Kishlansky (1977), in a path-breaking work, documents the transition of Parliament in mid-seventeenth century from a primarily consensual institution, committed to reasoned debate among men uncommitted to predetermined positions, to an adversary institution accepting as inevitable the conflicting interests of its members. Zuckerman (1970) and Lockridge and Krieder (1966) document a similar change in New England town meetings during the late seventeenth century.

17. Kishlansky (1986) documents this major, and previously unnoticed, change in methods of parliamentary selection in the mid-seventeenth century.

18. Locke 1689/1955: 57; *Second Treatise,* in Locke 1689/1965: 376. Note that Kendall (1965) sees in Locke also a "latent premise," compatible with the older view of majority rule, in which "the people always wills that which is right" (p. 139).

In economic policy Locke (1691/1923: 5) also recommended accepting the inevitable: "it will be impossible, by any contrivance of law, to hinder men, skilled in the power they have over their own goods," from buying money at whatever rate they think necessary to procure it.

19. Hirschman 1977. See Holmes, chap. 16, this vol.

20. Shaftesbury and Bishop Butler in Hirschman 1977: 46. See Holmes, chap. 16, this vol.

21. Helvetius, *De l'esprit* (Paris, 1758), cited in Hirschman 1977: 43.

22. Ibid., cited in Hirschman 1977: 28. Lovejoy 1961: 45 also gives examples of what one might call "the French science of politics" from Vauvenargues, *Réflexions et maximes* (1746): "If it is true that one cannot eliminate vice, the science of those who govern consists in making it contribute to the common good;" and Helvetius, *Poésies* (1781): "Le grand art de régner, L'Art du Législateur,/Veut que chaque mortel qui sous ses lois s'enchaîne,/En suivant le penchant ou son plaisir l'entraîne,/Ne puisse faire un pas qu'il ne marche à la fois/Vers le bonheur public, le chef-d'oeuvre des lois."

23. This formulation is hinted at in Hume 1739–40/1888, book 3, 535. Later, see "Eternal Peace," in Kant 1795/1949: 452–53. For problems with this theory, see Mansbridge, chap. 8, this vol. On Hume's later argument against the philosophers, from Epicurus to Hobbes, who attempted to "explain every affection to be self-love," see Hume 1751/1975; for the derivation of Hume's argument from Hutcheson, see Selby-Bigge 1893/1975.

24. See Kramnick 1982 for a summary of the literature on both strands in the framers' thought.

25. Wood 1969: 612, 606. See pp. 53–70 ("The Public Good" and "The Need for Virtue") for the ideals of 1776, and pp. 606–15 ("The End of Classical Politics") for the ideals of 1787. As Wood points out, the legitimation of self-interest came hand in hand with the legitimation of conflict: "[By 1787] the people were thought to be composed of various interests in opposition to one another. . . . The people were not an order organically held together by their unity of interest but rather an agglomeration of hostile individuals" (p. 607).

26. George Washington to John Bannister, 1778, cited in Diggins 1984: 23.

27. Madison, 10 *Federalist,* in Madison, Hamilton, and Jay 1788/1987: 125, 126, 124, 127, 126. Madison lodged virtue in both the representatives and the

people. "No theoretical checks, no form of government," he argued, "can render us secure. To suppose that any form of government will secure liberty or happiness without any virtue in the people, is a chimerical idea" (Debate on the Adoption of the Federal Constitution, June 20, 1788, in the Convention of Virginia, in Eliot n.d.: 537).

Wood (1969: 610, 611) cites Noah Webster (1785) and James Wilson (1790–91) to confirm the basis in self-interest of what he calls the "American science of politics." Webster makes the best case for Wood's argument, as Webster denied that "disinterested public spirit . . . [as a] general principle ever did or ever can exist in human society. The real principle that is predominant in every individual is self-interest. . . . In a democracy, where offices and preferment are at the disposal of the people, an ambitious man must court the people, by his condescension, by public acts of beneficence, and by pretentions to the public good. In order to retain any emoluments, which he holds by the choice of the people, his conduct must be agreeable to them, and apparently, if not really for their interests. This conduct springs from self-love, but takes the name of *virtue* or *public spirit*" (1785: 24n.). Yet even Webster saw no contradiction between self- and public interest: "Self interest, both in morals and politics, is and ought to be the ruling principle of mankind; but this principle must operate in perfect conformity to social and political obligations. Narrow views and illiberal prejudices may for a time produce a selfish system of politics . . . , but a few years experience will correct our ideas of self-interest, and convince us that a selfishness which excludes others from a participation of benefits, is, in all cases, self-ruin" (p. 48n.).

James Wilson makes a less convincing case for Wood's contention. Wilson put forward four principles of good government: first, to elect the "wisest and best" to office; second, to "communicate to the operations of government as great a share as possible of the good, and as small a share as possible of the bad propensities of our nature"; third, to "increase, encourage, and strengthen those good propensities, and to lessen, discourage and correct those bad ones"; and fourth, to "introduce, into the very form of government, such particular checks and controls, as to make it advantageous even for bad men to act for the public good" ("Lectures on Law," in Wilson 1790–91: 290). Wood (1969: 612) correctly cites the last of Wilson's principles as evidence for the new American science of politics. That principle should be seen, however, in the immediate context of Wilson's first three principles and the larger content of his lectures, which stress the natural sociality of humankind, explicitly deny that self-interest predominates in human motivation, and vehemently attack the "perversion," the "preposterous zeal," and the "narrow and hideous representation of these philosophers" who argue that "the only natural principles of man are selfishness" (1790–91: 227–29).

Half a century later, Alexis de Tocqueville would argue, as Webster did, that when public offices are elective, those who aspire to them must attend to the demands of the electorate: "Men learn at such times to think of their fellow-men from ambitious motives, and they find it, in a manner, their interest to be forgetful of self" (*Democracy in America*, 1835–40, cited in Diggins 1984: 246). Diggins thinks that "Tocqueville's view would have bewildered the *Federalist* authors, who could foresee no individual or faction acting disinterestedly" (p. 246). My own analysis argues for greater commonality between the authors of the *Federalist*, their contemporaries, and de Tocqueville on this issue. Alexander Hamilton, for example, seems to have paralleled de Tocqueville in thinking to generate virtuous action among representatives by balancing the temptations to avarice (one form of self-interest) with the reelection motive (deriving from vanity, ambition, and the love of fame—not so obviously, in his view, forms of self-interest). Hamilton, 72 *Federalist,* in Madison, Hamilton, and Jay 1788/1987: 414. See Hirschman 1977: 29.

In a recent article, Wood warns against interpreting Madison as a forerunner of twentieth-century pluralists: "He did not see public policy or the common good emerging naturally from the give-and-take of hosts of competing interests. Instead he hoped that these clashing interests and parties in an enlarged national republic would neutralize themselves and thereby allow liberally educated, rational men, 'whose enlightened views and virtuous sentiments render them superior to local prejudices, and to schemes of injustice,' to promote the public good in a disinterested manner" (Wood 1987: 92, citing 10 *Federalist*). In this refinement of his earlier position, Wood argues that "if either side in the debate therefore stood for the liberal, pluralistic, interest-ridden future of American politics, it was the Antifederalists" (p. 93; see also p. 102).

28. See Kolm 1983 for Smith's perception of the "dual" nature of humankind, and Holmes 1988a on the many motives, beyond the two of benevolence and self-interest, that Smith perceived and took into account. Smith's predecessor, Sir James Steuart, rejected the idea that self-interest was "the universal spring of human actions," and argued that "you must not prefer your own interest to that of your country" (1767/1966, 1: 143, 144). Nevertheless, he asserted that the "principle of self-interest" is the "only motive which a statesman should make use of, to engage a free people to concur in the plans which he lays down for their government." Otherwise, he explained, "the statesman would be bewildered," for "every one might consider the interest of his country in a different light, and many might join in the ruin of it, by endeavoring to promote its advantages" (pp. 143–44). Compare, more recently, Barry 1965: 63–65.

29. Bentley (1908) was the first, but in a Progressive atmosphere based on the assault on interests and a belief in the common good, his book "fell so far outside the conventional language of political science that the profession scarcely noticed it" (Rogers 1987: 185). By the 1930s, however, New Deal intellectuals were turning against the Progressives' "exalted moral tone" (Hofstadter 1955: 316) toward what would become a "hard-boiled, pragmatic, realist" political science based on conflicting self-interests (Rogers 1987: 204ff.).

30. MacIver 1947: 416: "We should never imply that the people are a unity on any matter of policy. The people are always divided." Sorauf 1957: 625: "It seems clear that no interest motivates all citizens." Truman 1959: 51: "We do not have to account for a totally inclusive interest, because one does not exist."

31. See Schumpeter 1942 and Downs 1957 for the descriptive theory of adversary democracy, Mansbridge 1980/1983 for its normative foundations. (The word *adversary* derives from Mansbridge 1980/1983.)

32. Mansbridge 1980/1983 spells out the fully developed descriptive and normative theory of adversary democracy, including (pp. 17, 30) the adversary rationale for majority rule. Descriptive theorists cannot, of course, avoid normative

implications. Downs, for example, while seeing his theory as only descriptive, incorporates norms into his description. His model includes the condition, among others, that "each voter may cast one and only one vote in each election." (p. 24). He regards this and similar conditions "merely as descriptions of society's actual rules. But exactly the same conditions can be derived from certain ethical precepts," for example, the precept of political equality, that "Control over governmental decisions is shared so that the preferences of no one citizen are weighted more heavily than the preferences of any other one citizen" (p. 32). His model also assumes two limits for self-interest: "(1) that the actor will not perform illegal acts, such as taking bribes . . . and (2) he will not try to benefit himself at the expense of any member of his own party team." "Although these limits are unrealistic," he comments, "without them our analysis would have to be extended beyond the purview of this study" (p. 30).

33. Gray v. Sanders, 372 U.S. 368 (1963) marks an important early point in this evolution. See Rogowski 1981 and Still 1981; also Reich 1988: 129–31. The Supreme Court works incrementally, rather than on the basis of any explicit theory of democracy. Thus, while this line of cases implies a theory of adversary democracy, other cases suggest the Court's repudiation of such a theory (Sunstein, chap. 13, this vol.).

34. See Purcell 1973 and Reich 1988: 10, 127. In philosophy, Isaiah Berlin (1958/1969) warned of the totalitarian dangers of synthetic rather than pluralist approaches in philosophy.

35. For example, Vidich and Bensman's (1968) conflictual interpretation of consensus mechanisms in a small town in upstate New York. For the role of Marxist theory, see Orren 1988: 22–23; for the role of Freud, see Krebs 1970: 260.

36. "The ruling ideas of each age have ever been the ideas of the ruling class" (Marx and Engels 1848/1954: 52). "Wherever there is an ascendant class, a large portion of the morality of the country emanates from its class interests" (Mill 1859/1947: 6).

37. Downs 1957: 27, citing in support of this "self-interest axiom" John C. Calhoun, "Disquisition on Government." Calhoun's larger argument does not in fact support the implications of the two sentences (Calhoun 1853/1953: 5) that Downs quotes in isolation. Calhoun assumed "as an incontestable fact, that man is so constituted as to be a social being" (p. 3), but that "his direct or individual affections are stronger than his sympathetic or social feelings" (p. 4). Noting "this two-fold constitution" of human nature (p. 5), Calhoun argued that "to enlist the individual on the side of the social feelings to promote the good of the whole, is the greatest possible achievement of the science of government" (p. 70). Calhoun saw his proposal for a concurrent majority (in my terms replacing adversary with unitary democracy) as having along with its "political" goals the important "moral" goal of making citizens' characters less self-interested (p. 49).

38. Downs 1957: 28. Downs adds in a footnote that "Schumpeter's profound analysis of democracy forms the inspiration and foundation for our whole thesis" (n. 11, p. 29).

39. Tullock 1976. Tullock did not, however, present the evidence for his assertion. See below for the critical distinction between rational choice theories that

insist on self-interest and "inclusive" rational choice theories that do not require such an assumption.

40. Mayhew 1974 and Fiorina 1974. See also Fiorina 1977. For Fiorina, re-election is a subset of a larger category: "I assume that most people most of the time act in their own self-interest" (1977: 38).

41. See discussion in Mansbridge 1988, citing Mayhew 1974: 52, 61, 132–33, 141, 143–44, 146–47, esp. n. 133, and Fiorina 1974: 31, 35. Mayhew took the reinterpretive route, Fiorina that of reasonable prediction.

42. Tullock 1979: 31, 33. See Kelman 1988: 234. Kuhn (1970: 19) tells us that in the natural sciences, the triumph of a new paradigm is associated with "the formation of specialized journals, the foundation of specialists' societies, and the claim for a special place in the curriculum." The Public Choice Society was begun in 1963 and the journal *Public Choice* in 1964. Few political science departments now feel their faculty complete without one or more members who work in the rational choice (public choice) tradition.

43. Wilson 1962 and 1973. See also Etzioni 1961. Wilson continued to emphasize solidarity and purposive incentives (or to use Sen's words in this volume, the motives of "sympathy" and "commitment") in his writing on crime (e.g., 1983), where he countered the rational choice emphasis on deterrence (self-interest) with an emphasis on potential criminals' attitudes toward the well-being of others (sympathy) and internalized conscience (commitment).

44. Banfield and Wilson 1964. See also Wilson and Banfield 1971 and Banfield and Wilson 1963. Banfield's earlier (1958) study of "amoral familism" in southern Italy had contrasted a self- or family-interested style in rural Italy with a more public-regarding style in other countries.

45. Wilson was a student of Banfield, and Banfield may have been inoculated against his political science training by a stint in government administration.

46. Kingdon 1988; Sinclair 1983; Smith and Deering 1984; Bessette 1979.

47. Drew 1983: 249; Drew 1979; Asbell 1978.

48. Mansbridge 1986. Like many other analyses of social movements, this work relied heavily on insights originally derived from Mancur Olson (1965), an early economist in the rational choice field. Almost all the analyses that used Olson's work pointed out, as I did, that social movements, relying primarily on purposive and solidary incentives, fall into a category of organizations that Olson himself purposely omitted from his analysis. See, for example, Fireman and Gamson 1979; Oberschall 1973; Jenckins 1981; Frolich, Oppenheimer, and Young 1971; and Douglas and Wildavsky 1982. For a review of the literature, see Knoke and Wright-Isak 1982. Conover and Gray (1983) indicate that in their sample of thirty-six right-wing and liberal movement activists, every member gave personal principles or ideology as the primary motive in joining the organization.

49. Downs 1957: 21. Milton Friedman (1953: 40–42) had made the same argument. Dennis Mueller (1979: 5) phrased the point this way: "The use of simplified models of political behavior is justified so long as they outperform the competitors in explaining political behavior." This zero-sum approach in which one winning model outperforms all competitors across the board is, I will argue, less useful than an approach in which different models each work best in a specific context.

50. Ferejohn and Fiorina 1974, 1975; Strom 1975; Stephens 1975; Mayer and Good 1975; Beck 1975; Tullock 1975; Goodin and Roberts 1975; For comment, see Fiorina 1986.

51. See literature review in Schwartz 1987.

52. Ledyard 1984; see Fiorina 1986.

53. Barry 1970, commenting on Riker and Ordeshook 1968.

54. Stigler 1971; Becker 1976.

55. Sen 1977a: 328–29. See also Sen 1987.

56. See also Harsanyi 1955 for the "dual structure" (Sen's words) of "ethical preferences" and "subjective preferences."

57. Hirschman 1985; Schelling 1960, 1978a, 1978b; Elster 1986; McPherson 1984; Frank 1988, 1985; Kau and Rubin 1982; Kalt and Zupan 1984: 279. Kalt and Zupan conclude (p. 298) by arguing for looking at context to "predict the conditions (for example, types of issues, institutional settings, economic contexts) under which ideological shirking is likely to be an important political phenomenon." See also Kalt and Zupan, forthcoming.

58. A typical question (Kahneman, Knetch, and Thaler 1986a: 730) ran as follows: "Question 2A. A small photocopying shop has one employee who has worked in the shop for six months and earns $9 per hour. Business continues to be satisfactory, but a factory in the area has closed and unemployment has increased. Other small shops have now hired reliable workers at $7 an hour to perform jobs similar to those done by the photocopy shop employee. The owner of the photocopying shop reduces the employee's wage to $7." Acceptable 17%; unfair 83% ($N = 98$). "Question 2B. A small photocopying shop has one employee [as in Question 2A]. . . . The current employee leaves, and the owner decides to pay a replacement $7 an hour." Acceptable 73%; unfair 27% ($N = 125$).

59. Kahneman, Knetch, and Thaler 1986a: 735. See also Thaler 1985. The conclusion regarding implicit commitment is my own.

60. Cf. Arrow 1973 and Okun 1981.

61. Isaac, McCue, and Plott 1985 on extinguishing; Marwell and Ames 1981 on high payoffs and economics students. The "high" stakes, which reduced the average number contributing from 40–60 percent of the total to 28–35 percent, amounted to $33.25 per subject. The economics students were first-semester economics graduate students, whose socialization to the profession would have had to come primarily in their undergraduate years. Dawes and Thaler 1988 point out that Marwell and Ames's finding regarding economics students requires replication.

62. Sears and Funk, chap. 9, this vol.; Lau, Brown, and Sears 1978; and Russett and Hanson 1975. See Orren 1988 for a summary. Kinder and Kiewiet's 1979 and 1981 work on "socio-tropic" voting pointed out that we can predict votes for incumbents for president or members of Congress better by how well the voter says the country did economically in the past year than by how well the voter says he or she personally did economically in the past year. Respondents may altruistically be giving the country's well-being more weight than their own well-being in deciding how to vote, but they may also simply be concluding that the country's economic experience in the past year is a better indicator of their own future well-

being than is their individual economic experience during the past year (cf. Weatherford 1983).

63. Hoffman 1987. Some scholars (e.g., Rushton 1982) suggest that empathetic reactions are totally learned, while others (e.g., Hoffman) suggest that the disposition to empathize has some innate roots. Citing MacLean 1973 and others, Krebs (1971, 1982) argues that "there is good reason to believe that biological evolution has promoted the development of empathetic affective reactions in humans (and other mammals), and that these reactions may mediate altruistic behavior" (1982: 454). He points out that "the signs of distress in other members of a species are noxious to observers," and that "the evolution of the brain permits highly evolved animals to 'see' (i.e., role-take) 'with feeling' (i.e., empathy)."

While newborn humans and animals seem to experience what Eisenberg and Strayer (1987: 7) call "personal distress" in the presence of another's pain, that distress may not translate into "empathy" (feeling *with,* sharing the perceived emotion of another), "sympathy" (feeling *for,* feeling concern or sorrow), behavior that avoids the stimulus, or, finally, "prosocial" behavior. Anthropologist Ronald Cohen (1972) argues that although giving is ubiquitous across cultures, "empathy and sympathy as human qualities are not ubiquitously stressed outside of the great religious traditions (e.g., Hinduism, Buddhism, Judaism, Christianity, and Islam)" (p. 54). Interpersonal relations in European cultures, he notes, are particularly high in affect and empathy, perhaps because technological advances protect their members from many harsh emotional experiences like the death of loved ones, and perhaps because of the Europeans' relatively long nuclear family bond.

Just as context affects when personal distress translates into empathy, so it also affects when empathetic dispositions translate into prosocial behavior. Summarizing the literature, Rushton (1982) and Eisenberg and Miller (1987) conclude that among adults, measures of individual empathy correlate positively (though not exactly) with measures of prosocial behavior, while among children the results are mixed. Krebs (1982: 264) and Oliner and Oliner (1988: 177) point out that prosocial behavior requires not only the impulse to do good, but a conviction, deriving from a larger sense of personal efficacy, that one's attempt to do good will have an effect.

64. Radke-Yarrow, Zahn-Waxler, and Chapman 1983. For an overview of this field, see articles in Staub et al. 1984; Eisenberg and Strayer 1987; and Zahn-Waxler, Cummings, and Iannotti 1986. In the field of education, researchers have revived Morton Deutsch's work from the 1950s (summarized in Deutsch 1973) and amassed evidence that self-oriented, competitive study produces less mastery of facts and inferences in many situations than does "cooperative learning," in which students help one another. Slavin 1983 indicates that cooperative learning works best when learning is assessed individually and the group is rewarded on the basis of the collective aggregate performance. See also Johnson et al. 1984.

65. McClintock 1981, 1987 on menstrual synchrony; Frank 1985 and Madsen 1985, 1986, citing McGuire, Raleigh, and Brammer 1982 on serotonin.

66. Axelrod 1984. See also Kreps et al. 1982 on how, if a player thinks another player might act irrationally (cooperatively), it can make sense to cooperate even in a finite number of plays. Michael Taylor (1987, 1988) has evolved a theory of

"conditional cooperation" from the sanctions, which go far beyond tit for tat, available to a small and ongoing community.

67. At the 1988 American Political Science Association, nine papers took up this issue, including Monroe 1988a; Weatherford 1988; Kingdon 1988; Conlan, Beam, and Wrightson 1988; and papers by Margolis, Quirk, Sunstein, Frank, and Mansbridge collected in this volume. See also Bessette, forthcoming.

68. Monroe 1987, 1988b. Uhlaner 1986, 1988. Monroe 1988a suggests, on the basis of a small pilot project, that the conviction that one cannot act otherwise, springing from a perception of self as one with all humanity, plays a key role in exceptionally altruistic behavior. For a similar point, see Oliner and Oliner 1988, esp. pp. 156–57, 164–69. See also Conover 1988. As Conover points out, the traditional male devaluation of altruistic concerns as typically feminine has opened up an important role for women's scholarship on these issues.

69. Barber 1984; Pitkin 1981, 1984; Pitkin and Shumer 1982. Schwartz (1988), unlike more "participatory" theorists, emphasizes the potential for education and preference transformation in the process of electing representatives.

70. See, e.g., Tronto 1988, and essays and references in Hanen and Nielsen 1987, Kittay and Meyers 1987.

71. E.g., Rawls 1971 on the maximin rule for choice under uncertainty, Taylor 1987 on the state, and selections in Gambetta 1988 on trust.

72. I am endebted to Don Herzog for much of this formulation.

73. See Frank, chap. 5, this vol., n. 1; Holmes, chap. 16, this vol., n. 12; and Mansbridge, chap. 15, this vol., first page and accompanying note. Michael Sandel (conversation with the author), however, makes the point that certain goods and virtues are diminished by, and so do not survive the translation into, maximizing language. That language not only misses the claim of a person who relies on divine grace, but also tarnishes such a claim in a world in which maximizing is identified with the exercise of human intelligence.

74. Buchanan 1986: 11–12. Brennan and Buchanan (1981 and 1988) explicitly distance themselves from the claims of George Stigler and others that self-interested motivation either accurately describes most of reality or results in accurate predictions. They suggest instead that *homo economicus* is an abstraction whose value lies in allowing analysts to compare alternative socioeconomic arrangements ("constitutions") on both the narrow question of the degree to which they function as "invisible hands" converting private interest into public interest (1981) and the broader question of the incentive structures embodied in various institutional forms (1988).

In his 1986 speech, Buchanan argued that we should structure rules and institutions to reduce the need to rely on good motivations, or as he put it, to reduce "the differential impact of self-interested and other-directed behavior." While this may in some circumstances be a useful goal, if institutions that reduce the need to rely on good motivations also reduce the rewards accruing to those motivations and the ability to practice them, the benefits of such institutions may well be outweighed by their costs.

75. On transforming preferences, Offe and Wiesenthal 1980, Elkin 1987. On elections, Schwartz 1988. On the potential for ill, Holmes, chap. 17, this vol. On ritual and symbols, Johnson, 1988. On identity, Beck 1974, Touraine 1984/1988,

Flacks 1988. On deliberative arenas, Mansbridge 1988. On the components of deliberation, Fisher and Ury 1981/1983, Bessette 1982.

76. Carter Braxton (1776), criticizing institutions based purely on civic virtue, cited in Wood 1969: 96.

Chapter 2

1. F. Y. Edgeworth, *Mathematical Psychics: An Essay on the Application of Mathematics to the Moral Sciences* (London, 1881), 16.

2. Ibid., 104. In fact, he went on to make some interesting remarks on the results of "impure" egoism, admitting an element of sympathy for each other. The remarks have been investigated and analyzed by David Collard, "Edgeworth's Propositions on Altruism," *Economic Journal 85* (1975).

3. Edgeworth, 52.

4. Ibid., 52–53.

5. H. Spencer, *The Data of Ethics* (London, 1879; extended ed., 1887), 238.

6. See, especially, K. J. Arrow and F. H. Hahn, *General Competitive Analysis* (San Francisco, 1971).

7. Edgeworth, 56.

8. Ibid., 82.

9. If a person's actions today affect his well-being in the future, then under this approach his future interests must be defined in terms of the way they are *assessed today*. In general, there is no reason to presume that the future interests as assessed today will coincide with those interests as assessed in the future. This adds an additional dimension to the problem, and I am grateful to Derek Parfit for convincing me of the conceptual importance of this question.

10. J. Butler, *Fifteen Sermons Preached at the Rolls Chapel* (London, 1726); see also T. Nagel, *The Possibility of Altruism* (Oxford, 1970), 81.

11. See H. S. Houthakker, "Revealed Preference and the Utility Function," *Economica 17* (1950); P. A. Samuelson, "The Problem of Integrability in Utility Theory," *Economica 17* (1950).

12. For the main analytical results, see M. K. Richter, "Rational Choice," *Preference, Utility and Demand Theory,* ed. J. S. Chipman et al. (New York, 1971).

13. A. K. Sen, "Behaviour and the Concept of Preference," *Economica 40* (1973). See also S. Körner's important recent study, *Experience and Conduct* (Cambridge, 1971). Also T. Schwartz, "Von Wright's Theory of Human Welfare: A Critique," in L. A. Hahn and P. A. Schilpp, ed., *The Philosophy of Georg Henrik von Wright* (Lasalle, Ill., 1986); T. Majumdar, "The Concept of Man in Political Economy and Economics," mimeo, Jawaharlal Nehru University, New Delhi, 1976; and F. Schick, "Rationality and Sociality," mimeo, Rutgers University, Philosophy of Science Association, 1976.

14. See T. Scitovsky, *The Joyless Economy: An Inquiry into Human Satisfaction and Consumer Dissatisfaction* (London and New York, 1976). See also the general critique of the assumption of "rational" consumer behavior by J. Kornai, *Anti-Equilibrium* (Amsterdam and London, 1971), chap. 11; and the literature on "psychological choice models," in particular, D. McFadden, "Economic Applica-

tions of Psychological Choice Models," presented at the Third World Econometric Congress, August 1975.

15. See H. Liebenstein, "Allocative Efficiency vs. x-Efficiency," *American Economic Review 56* (1966). Also critiques of the traditional assumption of profit maximization in *business* behavior, particularly W. Baumol, *Business Behavior, Value and Growth* (New York, 1959); R. Marris, *The Economic Theory of Managerial Capitalism* (London, 1964); O. Williamson, *The Economics of Discretionary Behavior* (Chicago, 1967); and A. Silberston, "Price Behaviour of Firms," *Economic Journal 80* (1970), reprinted in Royal Economic Society, *Surveys of Applied Economics,* vol. 1 (London, 1973).

16. On the required conditions of consistency for viewing choice in terms of a binary relation, see A. K. Sen, "Choice Functions and Revealed Preference," *Review of Economic Studies 38* (1971); H. G. Herzberger, "Ordinal Preference and Rational Choice," *Econometrica 41* (1973); K. Suzumura, "Rational Choice and Revealed Preference," *Review of Economic Studies 43* (1976); S. Kanger, "Choice Based on Preference," mimeo, Uppsala University, 1976.

17. P. A. Samuelson, *The Foundation of Economics* (Cambridge, Mass., 1955), 90.

18. Ibid., 91.

19. The recent philosophical critiques of rational behavior theory include, among others, M. Hollis and E. J. Nell, *Rational Economic Man* (Cambridge, 1975); S. Wong, "On the Consistency and Completeness of Paul Samuelson's Programme in the Theory of Consumer Behaviour," Ph.D. diss., Cambridge University, 1975. See also the pragmatic criticisms of Kornai, *Anti-Equilibrium,* chap. 11.

20. See A. K. Sen, "Labour Allocation in a Co-operative Enterprise," *Review of Economic Studies 33* (1966); S. G. Winter, Jr., "A Simple Remark on the Second Optimality Theorem of Welfare Economics," *Journal of Economic Theory I* (1969); Collard, "Edgeworth's Propositions"; G. C. Archibald and D. Donaldson, "Nonpaternalism and Basic Theorems of Welfare Economics," *Canadian Journal of Economics 9* (1976).

21. G. B. Shaw, *Three Plays for Puritans* (Harmondsworth, 1966), 94.

22. See A. K. Sen, "Behaviour and the Concept of Preference, " *Economica 40* (1973); and Schick, "Rationality and Sociality."

23. See J. S. Duesenberry, *Income, Saving and the Theory of Consumer Behavior* (Cambridge, Mass., 1949); S. J. Prais and H. S. Houthakker, *The Analysis of Family Budgets* (Cambridge, 1955); W. Gaertner, "A Dynamic Model of Interdependent Consumer Behaviour," mimeo, Bielefeld University, 1973; R. A. Pollak, "Interdependent Preferences," *American Economic Review 66* (1976).

24. See E. Lindahl, *Die Gerechtigkeit der Besteuerung* (Lund, 1919), translated in R. A. Musgrave and A. Peacock, *Classics in the Theory of Public Finance* (London, 1967); P. A. Samuelson, "The Pure Theory of Public Expenditure," *Review of Economic Studies 21* (1954); R. Musgrave, *The Theory of Public Finance* (New York, 1959); L. Johansen, *Public Economics* (Amsterdam, 1966); D. K. Foley, "Lindahl's Solution and the Core of an Economy with Public Goods," *Econometrica 38* (1970); E. Malinvaud, "Prices for Individual Consumption, Quantity Indicators for Collective Consumption," *Review of Economic Studies 39* (1972).

25. T. Groves and J. Ledyard, "Optimal Allocation of Public Goods: A Solu-

tion to the 'Free Rider Problem,'" Discussion Paper No. 144, Center for Mathematical Studies in Economics and Management Science, Northwestern University, 1975; J. Green and J. J. Laffont, "On the Revelation of Preference for Public Goods," Technical Report No. 140, Institute for Mathematical Studies in the Social Sciences, Stanford University, 1974. See also J. Dreze and D. de la Vallee Poussin, "A Tatonnenment Process for Public Goods," *Review of Economic Studies* 38 (1971); E. Malinvaud, "A Planning Approach to the Public Goods Problem," *Swedish Journal of Economics* 73 (1971); V. L. Smith, "Incentive Compatible Experimental Processes for the Provision of Public Goods," mimeo, Econometric Society Summer Meeting, Madison, 1976.

26. See J. Ledyard and D. J. Roberts, "On the Incentive Problem for Public Goods," Discussion Paper No. 116, CMSEMS, Northwestern University, 1974. See also L. Hurwicz, "On Informationally Decentralized Systems," in R. Radner and B. McGuire, *Decisions and Organizations* (Amsterdam, 1972).

27. See Theorem 4.2 in Groves and Ledyard, "Optimal Allocation of Public Goods."

28. L. Johansen, "The Theory of Public Goods: Misplaced Emphasis," Institute of Economics, University of Oslo, 1976. See also J. J. Laffont, "Macroeconomic Constraints, Economic Efficiency and Ethics," mimeo, Harvard University, 1974; P. Bohm, "Estimating Demand for Public Goods: An Experiment," *European Economic Review* 3 (1972).

29. A. Gibbard, "Manipulation of Voting Schemes: A General Result," *Econometrica* 41 (1973); M. A. Satterthwaite, "Strategy-proofness and Arrow's Conditions," *Journal of Economic Theory* 10 (1975); D. Schmeidler and H. Sonnenschein, "The Possibility of Non-manipulable Social Choice Functions," CMSEMS, Northwestern University, 1974; B. Dutta and P. K. Pattanaik, "On Nicely Consistent Voting Systems," Delhi School of Economics, 1975; P. K. Pattanaik, "Strategic Voting without Collusion under Binary and Democratic Group Decision Rules," *Review of Economic Studies* 42 (1975); B. Peleg. "Consistent Voting Systems," Institute of Mathematics, Hebrew University, Jerusalem, 1976; A. Gibbard, "Social Decision, Strategic Behavior, and Best Outcomes: An Impossibility Result," Discussion Paper No. 224, CMSEMS, Northwestern University, 1976.

30. See A. K. Sen, *Collective Choice and Social Welfare* (Edinburgh and San Francisco, 1970), 195.

31. See Ragnar Frisch's discussion of the need for "a realistic theoretical foundation for social policy" in his "Samarbeid mellom Politikere og Økonometrikere om Formuleringen av Politiske Preferenser" (Socialøkonomen, 1971). (I am grateful to Leif Johansen for translating the relevant portions of the paper for me.) See also J. A. Mirrlees, "The Economics of Charitable Contributions," Econometric Society European meeting, Oslo, 1973.

32. See A. Fox, *Beyond Contract: Work, Power and Trust Relations* (London, 1974); H. G. Nutzinger, "The Firm as a Social Institution: The Failure of a Contractarian Viewpoint," Working Paper No. 52, Alfred Weber Institute, University of Heidelberg, 1976.

33. Cf. "Nor . . . should we forget the extent to which conventional theory ignores how and why work is organized within the firm and establishment in the

way it is, what may be called the 'social relations' of the production process," R. A. Gordon, "Rigor and Relevance in a Changing Institutional Setting," Presidential Address, *American Economic Review* 66 (1976). See also R. Dahrendorf, *Class and Class Conflict in Industrial Society* (Stanford, 1959); O. E. Williamson, "The Evolution of Hierarchy: An Essay on the Organization of Work," Fels Discussion Paper No. 91, University of Pennsylvania, 1976; and S. A. Marglin, "What Do Bosses Do? The Origins and Functions of Hierarchy in Capitalist Production," *Review of Radical Political Economics* 6 (1974).

34. "The Decision of the Central Committee of the Chinese Communist Party concerning the Great Proletarian Cultural Revolution," adopted on 8 August 1966, reproduced in Joan Robinson, *The Cultural Revolution in China* (Harmondsworth, 1969). See also A. K. Sen, *On Economic Inequality* (Oxford, 1973); and C. Riskin, "Maoism and Motivation: A Discussion of Work Motivation in China," *Bulletin of Concerned Asian Scholars*, 1973.

35. See Williamson, "Evolution of Hierarchy," for a critical analysis of the recent literature in this area.

36. J. Harsanyi, "Cardinal Welfare, Individualistic Ethics, and Interpersonal Comparisons of Utility," *Journal of Political Economy* 63 (1955): 315.

37. Ibid., 315–16.

38. Note that for Harsanyi, "an individual's preferences satisfy this requirement of impersonality if they indicate what social situation he would choose if he did not know what his general position would be in the new situation chosen (and in any of its alternatives) but rather had an equal chance of obtaining any of the social positions existing in this situation, from the highest down to the lowest" (p. 316).

39. A. K. Sen, "Choice, Orderings and Morality," in S. Körner, ed., *Practical Reason* (Oxford, 1974). See also J. Watkins' rejoinder and my reply in the same volume; and R. C. Jeffrey, "Preferences among Preferences," *Journal of Philosophy* 71 (1974); K. Binmore, "An Example in Group Preference," *Journal of Economic Theory* 10 (1975); and B. A. Weisbrod, "Comparing Utility Functions in Efficiency Terms," *American Economic Review* 67 (1977).

40. This presupposes some "independence" among the different elements influencing the level of overall welfare, implying some "separability." See W. M. Gorman, "Tricks with Utility Functions," in M. Artis and A. R. Nobay, eds., *Essays in Economic Analysis* (Cambridge, 1975).

41. See n. 16 above.

42. This result and some related ones emerged in discussions with Ken Binmore in 1975, but a projected joint paper reporting them is still, alas, unwritten. More work on this is currently being done also by R. Nader-Ispahani.

43. See Sen, "Choice, Orderings and Morality"; and also Sen, "Liberty, Unanimity and Rights," *Economica* 43 (1976). Note also the relevance of this structure in analyzing the incompleteness of the conception of liberty in terms of the ability to do what one *actually wishes*. Cf. "If I find that I am able to do little or nothing of what I wish, I need only contract or extinguish my wishes, and I am made free. If the tyrant (or 'hidden persuader') manages to condition his subjects (or customers) into losing their original wishes and embrace ('internalize') the form of life he has invented for them, he will, on this definition, have succeeded in liberating

them." I. Berlin, "Two Concepts of Liberty," in *Four Essays on Liberty* (Oxford, 1969), 139–40.

44. See R. D. Luce and H. Raiffa, *Games and Decisions* (New York, 1958); A. Rapoport and A. M. Chammah, *Prisoner's Dilemma: A Study in Conflict and Co-operation* (Ann Arbor, 1965); W. G. Runciman and A. K. Sen, "Games, Justice and the General Will," *Mind* 74 (1965); N. Howard, *Paradoxes of Rationality* (Cambridge, Mass., 1971).

45. See Runciman and Sen, "Games, Justice, and the General Will."

46. See, for example, L. B. Lave, "An Empirical Approach to the Prisoner's Dilemma Game," *Quarterly Journal of Economics* 76 (1962), and Rapoport and Chammah, *Prisoner's Dilemma*.

47. Rapoport and Chammah, *Prisoner's Dilemma*, 29.

48. Sen, "Choice, Orderings and Morality." See also K. Baier, 'Rationality and Morality," and A. K. Sen, "Rationality and Morality: A Reply," *Erkenntnis* 11 (1977) 197–223: 225–32; K. Baier, *The Moral Point of View* (Ithaca, 1958); and Fred Schick's analysis, "Rationality and Sociality."

49. On the nature of "consequentialism" and problems engendered by it, see B. Williams, "A Critique of Utilitarianism," in J. J. C. Smart and B. Williams, *Utilitarianism: For and Against* (Cambridge, 1973).

50. H. Sidgwick, *The Method of Ethics* (London, 1874; 7th ed., 1907), 418–19. See also Nagel's forceful exposition of the thesis that "altruism itself depends on a recognition of the reality of other persons, and on the equivalent capacity to regard oneself as merely one individual among many" (*Possibility of Altruism*, I).

Chapter 3

1. The second part of this sentence adds something to the first. I might take account of other people's interest only in the choice between two actions that serve my interest equally well.

2. Indeed, sometimes the motivating force seems to be the desire to give, and to be known as giving, *more than other donors*. I was first struck by this motivation in the Art Institute of Chicago, where the size of the plaques honoring the donors is carefully adjusted to the size of the donation. What looks like altruistic behavior toward the public may in fact spring from emulation and envy of other donors.

3. Actually, we might observe differences in behavior when both institutions and motivations are similar, namely, when the situation has multiple equilibria. History and accidents will then determine which of them is realized.

4. In addition there is the view that altruistic motivations can be explained in terms of "selfish genes," e.g., because it pays a gene to have its bearer sacrifice itself for the sake of close relatives who are also bearers of the gene.

5. Love is not the true converse of spite. A spiteful person acts to frustrate other people's desires because their frustration makes him feel good. Their suffering is instrumental to his welfare. The true converse of this attitude is the person who helps others because he likes to see happy faces around him.

6. This need not be true. A person may help his grandchild, to whom he feels indifferent, in order to give (nonselfish) pleasure to his child. But that presupposes that the child derives pleasure from the selfish pleasure of the grandchild.

7. When a small child buys a gift for her parents, they are often more touched by the act of giving than pleased by the gift—but they are touched only because they know the child was trying to please them rather than to touch them.

8. One might need only one selfish person, and all others could get all their pleasure from watching him and each other.

9. I am referring here to societies in which parents cannot disinherit their children.

10. Many, no doubt, would most like to have their cake and eat it too: to be well known as an anonymous donor.

11. And even when income redistribution is in the interest of the donors, it need not be motivated by that interest.

12. I am assuming, for simplicity, that we have no intrinsic pleasure just in being together.

13. For long-term self-interest to induce the firm to pay out wages, it must not be too myopic. In fact, a myopic firm will be doubly tempted to defect. In the first place a myopic bargainer is a disadvantage. By his impatience he will be forced to concede more than he would otherwise have done. If the workers are less impatient, they may claim and get high wages. The combination of high wages and myopia may then, in the second place, induce the firm to defect at the end of the first period.

Chapter 4

1. Thomas Hobbes (1651), chaps. 13 and 14.

2. See W. D. Hamilton, "The Genetical Evolution of Social Behavior," *Journal of Theoretical Biology* 7 (1964): 1–52, for a full analysis of altruism among relatives.

3. Robert Trivers, "The Evolution of Reciprocal Altruism," *Quarterly Review of Biology* 46 (1971): 35–57.

4. See Donald Campbell, "On the Conflicts between Biological and Social Evolution and between Psychology and Moral Tradition," *American Psychologist* 30 (1975): 1103–26. My entire argument in this section has been heavily influenced by Campbell's analysis.

Chapter 5

1. There are almost as many definitions of rationality as there are people who have written on the subject. Many authors (for example, Harsanyi 1977) define it as the use of efficient means in the pursuit of a given end (no matter how self-destructive that end might be). By this standard, it might be possible to call even the bloodiest family feud rational (if the participants' overwhelming motive was merely to avenge the latest provocation). Here, by contrast, I use the terms *rational behavior* and *self-interested behavior* to mean the same thing. Needless to say, nothing of importance turns on this choice of definitions.

2. In purely material terms, of course, her payoffs remain the same. And since, in biological theories of behavior, these are the only payoffs that matter, her aversion to cheating does not make her dilemma any less real.

3. Trivers discusses the role of self-deception as a device for deceiving others—to hide "the truth from the conscious mind the better to hide it from others" (1985: 415–16). And a large body of research in the psychological literature demonstrates that self-deception is indeed widespread. The difficulty is that if everyone had limitless capacities for self-deception, no one could solve commitment problems via the mechanism outlined in this essay. There is advantage in self-deception only up to a point. Once it becomes sufficiently widespread, it becomes self-defeating. The only stable equilibrium is one in which at least some people have less then perfect capacity for self-deception.

4. In very recent times, of course, there has been a negative relationship between income and family size. But if sentiments were forged by natural selection, the relationship that matters is the one that existed during most of evolutionary history. And that relationship was undisputedly positive: periods of famine were frequent and individuals with greater material resources saw many more of their children reach adulthood. Moreover, most early societies were polygynous—their most wealthy members usually claimed several wives, leaving many of the poor with none.

5. Elsewhere (Frank 1987) I describe the details of a model that allows this feature.

6. Akerlof 1983 makes a similar point.

7. Gauthier 1985 also notes that predispositions to behave in non-self-interested ways can be advantageous, but does not focus on how they are achieved or how others discern them.

8. In fairness I must note that among economists and other behavioral scientists, there are many who recognize the limitations of the strict self-interest model. See, in particular, Schelling 1978b; Akerlof 1983; Hirshleifer 1984; Sen, chap. 2, this vol.; and Arrow 1975. See also Leibenstein 1976; Scitovsky 1976; Harsanyi 1980; Phelps 1975; Collard 1978; Margolis 1982; and Rubin and Paul 1979.

9. I develop these particular claims at length elsewhere (Frank 1985).

10. See Kahneman, Knetsch, and Thaler 1986b, for an extended discussion of the role of fairness in economic transactions.

11. A recent *New Yorker* cartoon suggested a way of curtailing the waiter's risk. It portrayed a solitary diner in the midst of his meal. On the table was a plate with a few coins on it and a small placard reading, "Your tip so far."

Chapter 6

1. Note that social dilemmas do not involve a conflict between "short-term" self-interest and "long-term" self-interest. A dominating strategy, such as driving a car during a pollution alert, is always in the individual's interests.

2. We point out that this strategy can be reframed in repeated symmetric dilemma games in a manner totally unrelated to reciprocity: defect only if behind. That yields cooperation on trial 1, defection immediately after another player's first defection, and cooperation immediately following any trial on which that player subsequently switched to cooperation (at which point, after all but two trials on which the players received identical payoffs for the same choices and two in which they received different payoffs discrepant in opposite directions, they

would have accumulated the same total payoffs). Thus, a player or program insisting on equity in such symmetric repeated games—the type in Axelrods's tournament—would make precisely the same choices as would a player using Tit for Tat.

3. We point out, as does Blarney 1976, that the process is probabilistic, and hence self-sacrificial altruistic characteristics that decrease the probability of survival per se may actually enhance inclusive fitness if they simultaneously enhance the probability of being selected as a desirable mate. And despite "just so" evolutionary stories of rape and pillage, throughout most of human history mates have been chosen—when not by individuals themselves, by genetically related relatives.

4. For example, Kramer and Brewer (1986) have shown that they can create a group identity between subjects by simply having the magnitude of their payoffs determined by the same coin flip. Wit and Wilke (1988) have replicated this result through the simple procedure of paying subjects in a group on the basis of the same coin toss versus individual tosses.

5. Percentages are simply equal to one-ninth the number of people who opted to give away the $5; the analyses are based on these simple numbers, one characterizing each group. The significance levels are determined by standard ANOVA procedures, given equal cell size and no a priori reason to believe these numbers violate the normality assumption (which is sufficient justification for the reported levels, but not necessary given the equal cell sizes). The actual experiments involved four additional conditions not presented here.

Chapter 8

1. See Dawes, van de Kragt, and Orbell, chap. 6, this vol. The absence of persuasive indicators that "public-regarding" individuals paid a significant price for their attitudes was an important criticism of Banfield and Wilson's (1964; Wilson and Banfield 1971) "ethos theory" (I thank Michele White for this point).

2. The epilogue is from *Jefferson's Farm Book* (Jefferson 1774–1826/1953: 43). The absolutism of Jefferson's language, rather chilling in this context, might be rhetoric aimed at the overseer (but see Jefferson's letter to John W. Eppes, 1820, in Jefferson 1774–1826/1953: 46: "I consider a woman who brings a child every two years as more profitable than the best man of the farm. What she produces is an addition to the capital, while his labors disappear in mere consumption"). In a letter to William Burwell (1805), Jefferson wrote disapprovingly that for many slaveholders in his day, "interest is morality." He added, however, "interest is really going over to the side of morality. The value of the slave is every day lessening; his burden on his master daily increasing. Interest is therefore preparing the disposition to be just; and this will be goaded from time to time by the insurrectionary spirit of the slaves" (p. 20, capitalization and spelling modernized). Such sentiments are consonant with the belief that in the long run Providence will make interest and duty coincide, but in the short run the two may often conflict.

Joseph Butler (1726/1897, 1: 181) also concluded, with many of his contemporaries (see chap. 1, n. 12, above), that self-interest and the social interest "do indeed perfectly coincide; and to aim at public and private good are so far from being inconsistent, that they do mutually promote each other."

3. See Appendix A for a description of the prisoners' dilemma. The prisoners'

dilemma was developed by game theorists around 1950 (Luce and Raiffa 1957; Hardin 1982: 24–25). Luce, Raiffa, Hardin, Rapoport (1960), and Axelrod (1984) use the punctuation "prisoner's dilemma." I follow Michael Taylor's (1987) punctuation, addressing the dilemma from the collective viewpoint.

4. This solution, whose democratic version was first suggested by Hardin (1968: 1247), combines categories 1 and 3 in Dawes, van de Kragt, and Orbell, chap. 6, this vol.

5. Schelling 1960/1963; H. Becker 1960, citing Schelling; Hardin 1982.

6. See Axelrod 1984.

7. As I have described it, the ultimate goal of all the cooperation problems is increasing the size of the group pie. Game theorists see the goal as increasing the individual's long-run payoff. Most evolutionary biologists see the goal in comparative terms, most defining comparative success purely as relative individual success, and some noting that success in an iterated prisoners' dilemma depends on dyads or groups whose members interact cooperatively, outproducing other groups whose members interact conflictually (Pollock 1988). In absolute terms, of course, if the accumulated payoff for cooperation over time is greater than the payoff for defection, it would pay even members of an isolated dyad to cooperate.

8. The list is illustrative rather than complete.

9. See Sen (chap. 2), Elster (chap. 3), Jencks (chap. 4), Dawes, van de Kragt, and Orbell (chap. 6), and Holmes (chap. 17, p. 272), this vol.; also J. Wilson 1962, "solidary" and "purposive." See Rawls 1971: 269 for commitment to a cooperative principle solving the prisoners' dilemma, and Taylor 1987 for altruism as a solution, both in itself and as the basis for "starter" groups and "entrepreneurs" who encourage conditional altruism in others.

10. I am endebted to Thomas Cook for the phrase "contingent conscience." Dawes points out (pers. comm.) that in the current state of experimentation, "contingent conscience" defies falsification. The experiments of Dawes, van de Kragt, and Orbell indicate that rhetoric is not sufficient to activate contingent conscience. If nothing other than "we-feeling" activates contingent conscience, then it becomes impossible to distinguish from in-group concern.

11. Hoffman 1982 indicates that the later stages of empathy in human development are both more likely to result in actual help for others and more contingent on cognitive determinations of questions like desert.

Cognitive determinations play a central role in transforming the content of moral principles away from indiscriminate cooperation. In what has been called the "samaritan's dilemma" (Buchanan 1975), purely cooperative behavior encourages the responses of exploitation and parasitism (Bernheim and Stark 1988), which a moral person might not want to encourage. Axelrod (1984: 136–38), for example, suggests replacing the Golden Rule, (which he interprets as "always cooperate") with a forgiving form of Tit for Tat, on the grounds that while pure Tit for Tat will prolong feuds, the rule "always cooperate" will give defectors the incentive to hurt "other innocent bystanders with whom the successful exploiters will interact later." Following this and similar arguments, a logic based on 100 percent altruism could generate a principled moral code that was far from 100 percent altruistic.

12. On supererogation, or acts beyond the call of duty, see Fishkin 1982; Heyd

1982; Feinberg 1970; Urmson 1958; and Mill 1865/1968. Thinking of the larger "moral system" as mediated to make extreme preachings supererogatory suggests that "Social System Preaching" should not be set at "100% Altruism," as Campbell (1975: 1118) has it (particularly if altruism is defined as counting others as all and self as nothing), but somewhere farther down his scale toward "Selfishness." Where the preaching of each cultural group and subgroup falls on this scale will be the contingent result of social negotiation.

Taking mediation and supererogation into account suggests that most social system preaching does not require acts of altruism that seriously undermine one's comparative ability to propagate. Even risking one's life in war, the extreme and unusual case, can entail propagatory benefits for the survivors, through rape in enemy territory (Brownmiller 1975/1976) and the marital benefits of social prestige in one's own.

13. If some altruistic behaviors greatly inhibited reproduction and if specific genes promoted those behaviors directly or indirectly without offsetting benefits, one would expect those genes eventually to disappear. A genetic approach, however, is not required for my argument in this chapter.

14. Hoffman 1981 cites the beginnings of research on the physiological correlates of certain forms of empathy. Until we have more accurate measurement of this sort, however, it will remain necessary to define unselfish behavior operationally as behavior that helps another while hurting oneself.

15. M. Taylor 1987; Hardin 1982; Axelrod 1984.

16. Tajfel 1984; Brewer and Kramer 1986.

17. Hirsch 1976. Lukmann, in Gambetta 1988, distinguishes between the "confidence" produced by what I have called "self-interested" solutions and the "trust" produced by unselfish solutions.

18. Such communications must, to be effective, stay ahead of learning and genetic mechanisms that facilitate not only selfish behavior but the more difficult to detect "sincere hypocrisy" (Alexander 1975; Campbell 1975: 1112, 1119; see Frank, chap. 5, this vol., on mimicry).

19. Note that even in models of international relations predicated on "self-interest," individual actors are often presumed to be acting in the nation's interest.

20. There is some evidence, however, that Hitler considered himself "tricked" by Chamberlain at Munich, and that he later felt that by postponing war with Britain he had given that country time to arm.

21. See Keohane chap. 14, this vol. It is conceivable that near-universal agreement on certain moral principles could help promote the complex structures of interdependence that the modern world requires. John Rawls (1971), for example, attempted to establish a potentially universal foundation for judgments about justice. But the operational test of the universalism of Rawls's theory is actual concurrence. In the United States at least, a package of equal opportunity plus basic needs seems in practice to garner more approval than Rawls's "difference principle," while at the same time arguably meeting the demands of the original position (Oppenheimer, Frolich, and Eavy 1986, 1987).

22. Deci 1971, 1972; Deci et al. 1981.

23. *Springfield* [Ill.] *Monitor,* quoted in *The Outlook* 56 (1897): 1059.

24. Krebs 1970. Rushton 1982: 436.

25. This figure and the ensuing discussion are adapted from Axelrod 1984: 8. Axelrod points out that the definition of a prisoner's dilemma requires that the four outcomes be ranked in the following order: temptation to defect, reward for mutual cooperation, payoff for mutual defection, and sucker's payoff. It also requires that the players cannot get out of the dilemma by taking turns defecting on one another; therefore the reward for mutual cooperation must be greater than the average of the temptation to defect and the sucker's payoff. He further points out that two self-interested choosers playing the game once will both defect (this is their "dominant" choice). Axelrod addresses himself to the question of what, in these circumstances, are "the precise conditions that are necessary and sufficient for cooperation to emerge" (p. 11).

26. Jencks, chap. 4, this vol., emphasis in original. See also Rushton 1987: 427; Monroe 1988a: 1; and Collard 1978: 7.

27. Arrow 1975. For helping as a form of power, see D. Winter 1973. For the correlation of serotonin and exercising influence, including helping another, see Madsen 1985, 1986.

28. I consider both love and duty non-self-interested because they are both ways in which individuals make the welfare of others their own. Sen gives commitment the sole claim to pure non-egoism, on the grounds that "behavior based on sympathy is in an important sense egoistic, for one is oneself pleased at others' pleasure and pained at others' pain, and the pursuit of one's own utility may thus be helped by sympathetic action" (p. 31 this vol.). Dawes, van de Kragt, and Orbell give "we-feeling" the sole claim to non-egoism, on the grounds that behavior based on conscience is in an important sense egoistic, for it rests on "internal side payments, in the form of good or bad feelings," like "self-esteem," instilled by social training. They thus place the effects of conscience in the same category with other "consequences *accruing to the individual,*" or "egoistic incentives" (pp. 98, 99 this vol.).

This implicit debate between Sen and Dawes, van de Kragt, and Orbell on the competing claims to unselfishness of love and duty has a parallel in the more visible recent philosophical debate, in feminist theory and elsewhere, on whether duty has a higher moral status than love, or vice versa (e.g., Blum 1980; Herman 1983; Baron 1984).

29. Hardin (1982: 14) strongly objects to what he calls "a modified theory of collective action," in which variables like avoiding a feeling of guilt and cultivating a feeling of goodness are "summed in as additional costs and benefits of contributing or not contributing to a collective action." He objects primarily on the grounds that "the results are too flimsy to be worth the effort, since most of the relevant behavior may be explained already by the narrowest assessment of costs and benefits, and the host of motivations underlying the additional elements of behavior to be explained is sure to be far more crudely measured than the narrowest cost-benefit motivation."

The first part of Hardin's objection may be met by the 85 percent cooperation rates in the experiments of Dawes, van de Kragt, and Orbell, in chap. 6, this vol. These rates suggest that in some not unusual circumstances "most" of the relevant behavior cannot be explained by "the narrowest assessment of costs and benefits." These experiments also suggest an answer to the second part of the objection, for they succeed to some extent in separating out conscience from we-feeling, and in measuring the strength of these motives, as distinct from self-interest, through the numbers of subjects engaging in each form of behavior.

Chapter 9

1. For nonstatistical readers, a mean correlation of .00 indicates no relationship between self-interest and attitude, and .40 indicates a rather strong one, comparable to the relationship between race and income in the United States. The regression equation includes other variables, including symbolic predispositions such as party identification and ideology, in the calculations. The regression coefficient, therefore, is the result when the effects of symbolic predispositions have been, in essence, "subtracted." We report correlation and standardized regression coefficients primarily because they are intuitively interpretable. Some researchers would contend that relying on either is inappropriate because they reflect both the strength of the effect and the amount of error. However, over a large number of cases, they yield a fairly accurate approximation of the strength of self-interest effects.

2. However, it would appear that only four of the fourteen relevant terms, or 29 percent, are statistically significant if the customary two-tailed, $p < .05$, criterion is used.

3. It may be somewhat stronger for that minority who, for whatever reason, feel that economic problems are especially important: Young et al. 1987 found that respondents who designated economic problems as the most important for the country *and* for themselves were most likely to link their presidential preferences to the employment and government benefit experiences of themselves and their friends.

4. Kramer 1983 has contended that self-interest effects are relatively rare in cross-sectional survey studies precisely because government is responsible for relatively little of the variance in individuals' material well-being, and such studies are poorly equipped to distinguish governmentally induced changes from all others. This does not seem to us to rescue the self-interest hypothesis. As indicated above, personal economic changes unequivocally induced by government sometimes breed a self-interested response, but more often not. People who do attribute responsibility for changes in personal well-being to government do not always behave self-interestedly. People's perceptions of government-induced changes in their well-being have been used as self-interest indicators (e.g., Lewis-Beck 1986), but this leaves the analysis quite vulnerable to simultaneity problems. Finally, the assertion that individuals' well-being is not much influenced by government (and not all economists would agree) might help explain why they so rarely behave self-interestedly.

5. Our procedures in this regard have been rather conservative, including only those predispositions most unarguably stable over time, and often measured quite modestly with a single item. We have tried only once to milk these symbolic predispositions for every last jot of predictability, and then were successful in explaining a healthy 29.1 percent of the variance in whites' opposition to busing with two symbolic predispositions (racial intolerance and political conservatism), self-interest (which had trivial effects), and three demographic variables (all with weak

effects; see Sears, Hensler, and Speer 1979). It seems likely that with improved measurement, this level of explanation could be achieved in many other cases.

Chapter 10

1. The interest of authorities and their critics is not simply instrumental. Both groups are also interested in their legitimacy in the eyes of the public for intrinsic reasons. Judges, for example, have personal values that lead them to want to exercise authority in an appropriate, reasonable, and just way, in addition to their concern with securing public compliance.

2. The second aspect of an economic approach is a theory of human judgment. Since the work of Von Neumann and Morgenstern (1947), the primary theory of judgment and behavior underlying economic models has been the familiar subjective expected utility model. According to that model, behavior is governed by calculations involving the multiplicative combination of probabilistic judgments and values (Feather 1964; Luce and Raiffa 1957; Luce and Suppes 1965; Savage 1954). A number of writers have suggested modifications to the subjective expected utility model, recognizing that people utilize a variety of heuristics and shortcuts to simplify decision making (Kahneman, Slovic, and Tversky 1982; Simon 1957, 1979, 1985). These shortcuts often lead to satisfactory, but not optimal, decisions.

Both the original and revised versions of subjective expected utility theory assume that people use their past experience to develop expectations about the future consequences of their possible actions. Those expectations, in turn, shape their behavior (Downs 1957). Such models employ a concept of utility similar to psychological models of learning. Like recent learning models, they suggest that people use past experience to predict future behavior and that such future predictions shape current behavior (Bandura 1972; Lea 1978). The validity of this second aspect of the economic approach is not an issue here. The model suggested here expands the equation underlying the subjective expected utility model to include terms reflecting peoples' concerns with fairness.

3. It is, of course, possible to broaden the concept of self-interest to include the possibility that people find it personally rewarding to behave morally and to help others. Some public choice theorists do broaden self-interest in this way. This discussion focuses on the narrower definition of self-interest that has dominated public choice theories.

4. It is important to distinguish between objective and subjective criteria when discussing the "fairness" of procedures such as the adversary or the inquisitorial trial procedures. This discussion will be about procedures that those involved judge to be fair, that is, subjective fairness. It is also possible to develop objective criteria against which to evaluate the fairness of procedures. Efforts of that type will not be discussed here.

5. Although the two issues outlined are distinct conceptually, they are not distinct empirically. Justice judgments can only exercise an independent influence on political evaluations and behaviors to the extent that they are different than judgments of self-interest. In other words, if the correlation between justice judgments and judgments of self-interest is 1.0, justice judgments cannot exercise any influence. To the extent that there is some independence between these two types

of judgment, the possibility exists that justice judgments will exercise some independent influence. The second question is whether, to that extent, such an influence does occur. Suppose, for example, that the correlation between justice judgments and judgments of self-interest is 0.0. In that situation, any influence of justice judgments would be independent of issues of self-interest. In that situation, how much of a justice influence would be found?

6. This discussion assumes that experience-based judgments influence views about the legitimacy of legal authorities. It is important to recognize, however, that this assumption represents a simplified causal model. Panel studies that have examined views about the legitimacy of legal authorities prior to and following personal experiences with particular police officers and judges have found that prior views about the legitimacy of the authorities influence peoples' interpretation of their experiences (see Tyler, Casper, and Fisher 1989; Tyler, in press). If people come into the situation already viewing the authorities with whom they will deal as illegitimate, they are more likely to interpret the actions of the authorities as unfair. Hence, a particular police officer or judge will be hindered or aided in dealing with people by the prior views those people bring into the situation.

7. Why do people focus on procedural fairness, rather than on the fairness of their outcomes, when reacting to their experiences? One possibility is that people lack the information needed to compare their outcomes to those of others (Tyler 1988). In the case of people's dealings with the police, for example, people may not know what has happened to others who have dealt with the police. Hence, they may be unable to compare their experience to the experience of others.

In other situations, people may have too much outcome information to make distributive justice judgments. In complex organizations people receive a wide variety of outcomes over time. Those outcomes vary greatly in their favorability. One person may be better paid than others, but have a poorer job assignment and a smaller office. For a person to make a comparison of their outcomes to those of others requires them to engage in a complex calculation combining past, current, and future benefits received relative to those received by others. People often find it easier to focus on the decision-making procedures used to allocate resources, assuming that the distribution of benefits will be fair if the procedures used to make decisions are fair (Lind and Tyler 1988).

8. The questions used to make these assessments are detailed in Tyler, Rasinski, and McGraw 1985. In the case of government benefits, respondents were told that "the government provides citizens with many types of services and benefits, such as social security, medicare and medicaid, housing mortgage subsidies, veterans benefits, student loans, and unemployment and workman's compensation." Self-interest was established by asking respondents "how many" such benefits they received, both in absolute terms and relative to others and to the past. Distributive fairness was assessed by asking respondents to compare what they received to what they "deserved." Finally, procedural justice was assessed by asking respondents to evaluate the fairness of the procedures the government used to decide who will receive benefits.

Evaluations of President Reagan were assessed by having respondents rate the quality of his performance in office. The best predictor of performance evaluations was procedural fairness (beta = .47; $p < .001$), with distributive fairness producing an independent effect (beta = .11; $p < .05$). Performance ratings were also influenced by party, liberalism, and sex. Self-interest had no significant influence on performance ratings. Legitimacy was assessed using standard trust-in-government items. The only factor influencing legitimacy was procedural justice (beta = .61; $p < .001$).

9. The legitimacy that authorities have may initially lie in their social role. Legal authorities, for example, have legitimacy because of the widespread feeling among members of the public that they ought to be obeyed because of the social role that they occupy (Tyler, in press). In addition, particular political or legal authorities can gain support for their actions by behaving in a way that citizens view as fair.

A more general question raised by these findings is what makes a third party an authority to people with a problem or a dispute to be resolved. To what extent is it the social position that the third party occupies, for example, that they are a police officer or a judge? To what extent is it an inference that the third party has personal characteristics, such as sincerity or competence? In other words, to what extent does legitimacy reside in a social role or in the characteristics of the person who occupies that role (Merry and Silbey 1984)?

10. For complete details about question wording and results see Rasinski and Tyler 1988. Self-interest was established by asking respondents how much they had benefited from the policies of the Reagan administration, and how much they thought they would benefit if each candidate were elected. Distributive justice was assessed by asking respondents how fairly each candidate would distribute benefits if elected. Procedural justice was assessed by asking respondents how fairly each candidate would make policies if elected.

The dependent variable was vote choice. Two surveys examined the determinants of vote choice—the first early in the campaign, the second just prior to the election. Both found procedural justice effects. In addition, the second survey found self-interest effects. Neither found distributive justice effects. Party identification and race also influenced vote choice.

11. The participation effects we find in the legal arena are much like those in management studies, which show workers accepting change with less resistance if they have participated in decisions. This participation effect also appears under conditions of "pseudoparticipation" in which workers actually have no power in decisions, but are led to believe that their input will have an impact. For an early, but excellent, summary of this literature see Verba 1961.

We also need to be sensitive to the possibility of "frustration effects" which would occur if people felt that their participation was a sham. While it is clear that such effects might occur, Lind and Tyler 1988 find little evidence of them. It is clear, however, that the extent of such effects has important political implications (Tyler and McGraw 1986).

12. In the area of distributive justice, people recognize that different questions are relevant to attaining distributive justice when decision makers are trying to obtain different goals (see Barrett-Howard and Tyler 1986; Tyler 1986b).

13. Increased attention to issues of fairness is also important within psychol-

ogy. Such attention will also help psychologists develop a conception of the person which is adequate to more fully explain peoples' evaluations and behaviors (Sampson 1977, 1983).

Chapter 11

1. Martha Derthick and Paul J. Quirk, *The Politics of Deregulation* (Washington, D.C.: Brookings Institution, 1985).

2. George J. Stigler, "The Theory of Economic Regulation," *Bell Journal of Economics and Management Science* 2 (1971): 3–21. There is also an earlier and quite different capture theory: see Marver H. Bernstein, *Regulating Business by Independent Commission* (Princeton: Princeton University Press, 1955).

3. Ibid., p. 3.

4. Sam Peltzman, "Toward a More General Theory of Regulation," *Journal of Law and Economics* 19 (1976): 211–40.

5. Roger G. Noll and Bruce M. Owen, *The Political Economy of Deregulation: Interest Groups in the Regulatory Process* (Washington, D.C.: American Enterprise Institute, 1983).

6. See, respectively, Michael Levine, "Revisionism Revisited? Airline Deregulation and the Public Interest," *Journal of Law and Economics* 44 (1981): 179–95; and Gary S. Becker, "A Theory of Competition among Pressure Groups for Political Influence," *Quarterly Journal of Economics* 98 (1983): 371–400.

7. David R. Mayhew, *Congress: The Electoral Connection* (New Haven: Yale University Press, 1974); Morris Fiorina, *Congress: Keystone of the Washington Establishment* (New Haven: Yale University Press, 1977).

8. Fiorina, *Congress,* esp. chaps. 2 and 4.

9. The airline and trucking industries argued that small towns and rural areas would suffer under deregulation, but reform advocates presented a good deal of argument and evidence to the contrary, and managed to avoid any strong perception of regional conflict. See Derthick and Quirk, *Politics of Deregulation,* chap. 4.

10. Voters who were literally out to maximize their individual economic welfare presumably would care only about how issues and candidates' positions affect their specific interests, such as the income earned in their industries or occupations. If they wanted to vote that way, the necessary information would be easily produced and distributed. In fact, interest groups notoriously are unable to control the votes of their members.

Chapter 12

1. Samuel Huntington, "Congress Responds to the Twentieth Century," in David B. Truman, ed., *The Congress and America's Future,* 2d ed. (Englewood Cliffs, N.J.: Prentice-Hall, 1973), 15.

2. I develop my views on this question further in Steven Kelman, *Making Public Policy* (New York: Basic Books, 1987), 213–22. By an idealized process, I mean, among other things, one that weighs each individual's benefits equally. The philosophical literature criticizing utilitarianism as a sufficient ethical standard against which to judge public policies is large. Good places to start are John Rawls, *A Theory of Justice* (Cambridge: Harvard University Press, 1971), particularly pp.

22–33, and Joel Feinberg, *Social Philosophy* (Englewood Cliffs, N.J.: Prentice-Hall, 1973), particularly chaps. 4, 6, 7.

3. I argue for these contentions in Kelman, *Making Public Policy,* chap. 9.

4. See Harold D. Lasswell, *Psychopathology and Politics* (Chicago: University of Chicago Press, 1977), but see James David Barber, *The Lawmakers: Recruitment and Adaptation on Legislative Life* (New Haven: Yale University Press, 1965), and Richard F. Fenno, *Congressmen in Committees* (Boston: Little, Brown, 1973).

5. For a study emphasizing this finding, see Robert H. Salisbury, "The Urban Party Organization Member," *Public Opinion Quarterly* 29 (Winter 1965–66): 550–64. See also Barber, *The Lawmakers.*

6. Robert E. Lane, *Political Man: Why and How People Get Involved in Politics* (New York: Free Press, 1959), 127.

7. See David P. Campbell, *Handbook for the Strong Vocational Interest Blank* (Stanford: Stanford University Press, 1971). To determine what answers incline a student toward given occupations, the test is first administered to a "sample of successful, satisfied men performing [an] occupation in a typical manner. The more a student's answers resemble those of people already in the jobs, the more inclined they are seen as being for the job" (p. 25).

8. Hanna Fenichel Pitkin, *The Concept of Representation* (Berkeley: University of California Press, 1967), 277–78.

9. Arthur Maass, *Congress and the Common Good* (New York: Basic Books, 1984).

10. Bernard Asbell, *The Senate Nobody Knows* (New York: Doubleday, 1978), 210.

11. Elizabeth Drew, *Senator* (New York: Simon and Schuster, 1979), 61.

12. John F. Bibby, ed., *Congress Off the Record* (Washington, D.C.: American Enterprise Institute, 1983), 15.

13. Richard Fenno, *Congressmen in Committees* (Boston: Little, Brown, 1973).

14. R. Douglas Arnold, "The Local Roots of Domestic Policy," in Thomas Mann and Norman Ornstein, *The New Congress* (Washington, D.C.: American Enterprise Institute, 1981), 263.

15. Donald E. Stokes, "Parties and the Nationalization of Electoral Forces," in William N. Chambers and Walter Dean Burnham, eds., *The American Party Systems* (New York: Oxford University Press, 1967), 182–202. The study unfortunately goes only through 1960.

16. See Arnold, "Local Roots," 281–83.

17. Ibid., 287.

18. This point is made by Randall B. Ripley, *Congress: Process and Policy,* 3rd ed. (New York: Norton, 1983), 174.

19. Roger N. Davidson and Walter J. Oleszek, *Congress and Its Members* (Washington, D.C.: Congressional Quarterly Press, 1981), 112.

20. See Quirk, chap. 11, this vol., and Martha Derthick and Paul J. Quirk, *The Politics of Deregulation* (Washington, D.C.: Brookings Institution, 1985).

Chapter 13

1. See Margolis, chap. 14, this vol.; J. Elster, *Ulysses and the Sirens* (1979).

2. See J. Elster, *Sour Grapes* (1983); Akerlof & Dickens, The Economic Con-

sequences of Cognitive Dissonance, 72 *Am. Econ. Rev.* 307 (1981); M. Lerner, *The Belief in a Just World: A Fundamental Delusion* (1980).

3. See, for recent discussion, Holmes, Precommitment and the Paradox of Democracy, in *Constitutionalism and Democracy* 195 (J. Elster & R. Slagstaad eds. 1988).

4. See, e.g., J. Buchanan & G. Tullock, *The Calculus of Consent* (1952); R. Dahl, *A Preface to Democratic Theory* (1956). A quite different position, raising issues beyond the present discussion, is reflected in efforts to see the Constitution itself as a reflection of political self-interest, of which C. Beard, *An Economic Interpretation of the Constitution of the United States* (1913), is the most celebrated example.

5. See, e.g., Dahl, *supra* note 4; A. Bentley, *The Process of Government* (1908); Stigler, The Theory of Economic Regulation, 2 *Bell J. Econ. & Mgmt. Sci.* 3 (1971); Becker, A Theory of Competition among Pressure Groups for Political Influence, 98 *Q. J. Econ.* 371 (1983).

6. See, e.g., R. Epstein, *Takings* (1985).

7. See Becker, *supra* note 5. Claims of this sort raise important issues for constitutional law. If politics consists of self-interested struggle, and if that struggle has normative appeal, judicial efforts to require public-regarding justifications for legislation appear incoherent. See Posner, The DeFunis Case and the Preferential Treatment of Minorities, 1974 *Sup. Ct. Rev.* 1; Linde, Due Process of Lawmaking, 55 *Neb. L. Rev.* 197 (1975).

8. See, e.g., Farber & Frickey, The Jurisprudence of Public Choice, 65 *Tex. L. Rev.* 873 (1986).

9. See Elster, *supra* note 2; J. Mansbridge, *Beyond Adversary Democracy* (1980).

10. The extent of the republican influence is of course sharply disputed. For various views, see T. Pangle, *The Spirit of Modern Republicanism* (1988); J. Pocock, *The Machiavellian Moment* (1975); G. Wood, *The Creation of the American Republic, 1776–1787* (1969); J. Diggins, *The Lost Soul of American Politics* (1984); Sunstein, Interest Groups in American Public Law, 38 *Stan. L. Rev.* 29 (1985).

11. See, e.g., Dahl, *supra* note 4; Macey, Competing Economic Views of the Constitution, 56 *Geo. Wash. L. Rev.* 50 (1987).

12. See *The Federalist* No. 10; D. Epstein, *The Political Theory of the Federalist* (1984); Sunstein, *supra* note 10.

13. See Sunstein, *supra* note 10.

14. See *The Federalist* No. 10.

15. As we will see, the prohibition is not vigorously policed by the judiciary, a phenomenon that probably reflects the Court's sensitivity to its own institutional position. The prohibition is thus part of a category of "underenforced" constitutional norms—norms that have constitutional status but that courts, precisely because they are courts, enforce less aggressively than they might. For discussion, see Sager, Fair Measure: The Legal Status of Underenforced Constitutional Norms, 91 *Harv. L. Rev.* 1212 (1978).

16. It is in part for this reason that the influential treatment in J. Ely, *Democracy and Distrust* (1980), is untrue to the original constitutional structure or to current law.

17. Williamson v. Lee Optical, 348 U.S. 483 (1955).

18. Other examples are not difficult to find. See United States v. Carolene Products, 304 U.S. 144 (1938), discussed in Miller, The True Story of Carolene Products, 1987 *Sup. Ct. Rev.* 397.

19. Most of the examples involve sex discrimination; the Court examines the process to see if the legislature has responded to pressure or tradition, or instead investigated the facts. See, e.g., Califano v. Webster, 430 U.S. 313 (1977); Califano v. Webster, 430 U.S. 199 (1977).

20. The Supreme Court has recently said that the same degree of scrutiny will be applied, see Richmond V. Croson, 109 S. Ct. 706 (1989), but there can be little doubt that affirmative action—whatever its permissible contours—is treated more generously than ordinary discrimination. See, e.g., United States v. Paradise, 107 S. Ct. 1053 (1987); Local 128 v. EEOC, 106 S. Ct. 3019 (1986); Fullilove v. Klutznick, 448 U.S. 448 (1980).

21. See Washington v. Davis, 426 U.S. 229 (1976).

22. Note in this regard the possibility that the rationality idea is part of the category of underenforced constitutional norms—underenforced because of institutional limits of the judiciary. See Sager, *supra* note 15.

23. See Sunstein, Lochner's Legacy, 87 *Colum. L. Rev.* 873 (1987).

24. See Roe v. Wade, 410 U.S. 113 (1973).

25. See Hawaii Hous. Auth. v. Midkiff, 104 S. Ct. 2321 (1984).

26. See Penn Cent. Transp. Co. v. New York City, 438 U.S. 104 (1978).

27. See generally Sunstein, *supra* note 23.

28. See Miller, *supra* note 18.

Chapter 14

1. In considering emphathetic interdependence, I take account only of situations in which actors positively value benefits received by others. Under conditions of severe competition, which is characteristic of power conflicts and particularly of arms races, the reverse may be true: gains for one side are seen as losses for the other. Crowding effects and other negative externalities can lead people to value gains by others negatively, both within domestic society (Hirsch 1976) and in the world political economy. By the argument I make here, negative evaluations of others' welfare gains should make international regimes harder to institute. It should also be noted that in discussing empathetic interdependence I assume that the parties involved have similar values: "benefits" in the eyes of one are also regarded as beneficial by the others. Otherwise, supposed empathy could become a rationale for domination, as in the ideology of "the white man's burden," which justified much nineteenth-century imperialism.

2. Bounded rationality may help to account for myopic rather than farsighted decision-making, since the costliness of calculation is likely to reduce the range of relevant issues and interests considered.

3. Not being able to prove the existence of God in rational terms, Pascal argued that it is nevertheless rational to believe in God, since if there were no such being, we would have lost relatively little by being pious in life, compared to the eternity lost if we disbelieved, only to discover after death that a God of heaven and hell existed. This argument can, of course, be put in game-theoretic terms,

with piety as the minimax solution. But Pascal's further twist on the argument was that if one behaved in a pious way, with all the necessary outward shows of faith, genuine faith might well follow. See Nannerl O. Keohane, 1980, p. 278.

4. Helen Milner made this observation to me, suggesting that the history of the development of credit markets could be informative. The analogy seems to hold. Richard Ehrenberg reports that the development of credit arrangements in the Bourses reduced transaction costs (since money did not need to be transported in the form of specie) and that "during the Middle Ages the best information as to the course of events in the world was regularly to be obtained in the fairs and the Bourses" (1928, p. 317). The Bourses also supplied credit ratings, which provided information but also served as a crude substitute for effective systems of legal liability.

Chapter 15

1. This paper was stimulated by a critique of the possibility that social motivation could account for voting, in Schwartz 1987. For a sample voter named Ellie, Schwartz gives a version of the argument I review in section 2. For a sample voter named Smith, I gave essentially the same argument in Margolis 1982/1984: 84–86. Hence the Ellie Smith of the current chapter.

2. Group selection has become a noticeably more fashionable idea in biology over the past few years. Most biologists remain skeptical of its significance, but with an exception for the only species of interest here. For if group selection could be important anywhere, the most obvious case would be that of a species with the intelligence to allow it to profit from large-scale, open-ended cooperation.

Perhaps a parallel case, where the absence of a well-specified maximand makes it hard for economists to find a model credible, is provided by Richard Herrnstein's work on "meliorating" behavior, where creatures appear to seek allocations of resources that equalize average, instead of marginal, return. Herrnstein provides striking experimental results that start with goats and pigs and in recent years have been extended to (among other creatures) Harvard mathematics professors. As with the dual-utilities model, one can make sense of this as the outcome of a Darwinian process (Vaughan and Herrnstein 1987).

3. It is analytically convenient to go through the argument as if the voter were making an explicit calculation. But rationality does not require an explicit calculation, and all versions of the rational actor approach would be transparently unsound if it did. All we need require (of the dual-utilities model *or* of the standard model) is that its inferences be plausibly consistent with a judgment that Ellie might make if we prompted her to go carefully through such a calculation. Here, as on all such questions, the dual-utilities setup requires no less, but also no more, by way of explicit reasoning than the standard economic model requires in analyzing market behavior. In order to make a rational judgment, Ellie does not need to estimate explicitly the value of her vote any more than she needs to estimate explicitly the consumer surplus and transaction costs to yield a rational judgment on a private purchase. It is enough that Ellie's choice, whether about voting or about some market good, be reasonably consistent with what we can infer about her valuations from her observed behavior in other contexts. A similar proviso applies on other points, for example, with respect to how *rigorous* a standard of consist-

86

ency an empirically useful assumption of rationality requires. Again, I do not argue for relaxing the usual degree of rigor to make room for a nonstandard model. On the contrary, the point is to caution against adopting a different, *more* rigorous test for the nonstandard model than for the standard alternative.

Chapter 16

1. Stigler 1981: 189; also pp. 175–76. Mueller 1986: 14. Mueller began his presidential address by commenting: "The assumption that individuals, be they voters, politicians or bureaucrats, act rationally in their own self-interest is the most important and obvious characteristic of public choice, distinguishing it from its sister disciplines in the social sciences" (1986: 3). See also Mueller 1989: 363–69. Gordon Tullock makes the even stronger claim that "the average human being is about 95 percent selfish in the narrow sense of the term" (1976; also cited in Mansbridge, chap. 1, this vol.).

2. Elster (1983/1987: 10) distinguishes between "economic man," whose preferences "are not only consistent, but also complete, continuous and *selfish*" (emphasis in original), and "rational man," who has only consistent preferences and consistent plans. See also Taylor 1988: 66. Even Downs (1957: 6) specifies the rules of "rationality" without referring to self-interest. Goodin, summing up the rules of rationality (specified in 1976: 10–17) as "choosing means appropriate to the realization of [one's] goals" (p. 9), specifically leaves the goals open. Gary Becker (1974, 1976) explicitly focuses on ways individuals incorporate the goods of others in their own welfare. He omits self-interest when writing that "the combined assumptions of maximizing behavior, market equilibrium, and stable preferences, used relentlessly and unflinchingly, form the heart of the economic approach" (1976: 4). Richard Posner (1986) concludes that "the happiness (or for that matter the misery) of other people may be a part of one's satisfactions" (p. 4). "Economists . . . describe [love] as a form of altruism. Altruism is the condition in which the welfare of one person is a positive function of (i.e., increases with) the welfare of another. If H loves W, then an increase in W's happiness or utility or welfare (synonyms) will be felt by H as an increase in his own happiness or utility or welfare. Altruism facilitates cooperation; it is a cheap and efficacious substitute for (formal) contracting" (p. 129). Sen (1987: 16) concludes: "Universal selfishness as *actuality* may well be false, but universal selfishness as a requirement of *rationality* is patently absurd."

3. "If multiple goals are allowed, means appropriate to one may block attainment of another; hence no unique course can be charted for a rational decision-maker to follow" (Downs 1957: 5). Downs uses the word "goal" here and "motive" later (pp. 28ff.), though in ordinary discourse "motive" has a more subjective implication.

4. Gilman 1915/1979; see also Held, chap. 18, this vol. The cultural problem in the West and perhaps elsewhere may be exacerbated by subcultural characteristics: most information on non-self-interested motives derives from disciplines other than the ones most modelers know well.

5. Frank 1985 (esp. chap. 5) explains the empirical fact of earnings schedules in automobile dealerships, real estate firms, and chemistry departments being flatter than predicted by relative sales or marginal product with the theory that top

earners in these hierarchies are willing to take cuts in salary to preserve their positions as big frogs in small ponds.

6. Margolis (pers. comm. with author) points out that a prisoners' dilemma game designed so that one player chooses first and the second player knows that choice would not change the material payoffs to the second player but would eliminate that player's fear of being exploited.

7. Uhlaner 1988. See also suggestions in Monroe 1988b.

8. Browning and Jacobs 1964, on the basis of a very small sample, suggest that politicians may desire "affiliation" as much as power; Kingdon 1988, reinforcing this perception, discusses in sensitive detail the difficulty of separating one motive from another.

9. McClelland 1975 and Winter 1973 consider the desire to help a desire for power.

10. Kalt and Zupan 1984: 280, commenting on Stigler 1972: 104.

11. See chap. 1, this vol., nn. 63 and 64, on the findings of Radke-Yarrow, Zahn-Waxler, Hoffman, Eisenberg, and others.

12. See Heimer and Stinchcombe 1980.

13. Monroe 1988a suggests that this conception of self motivated many who risked their lives to save Jews in World War II. In discussing Monroe's paper at the 1988 APSA meetings, William Riker called this motive "a perfect natural for modeling."

14. However, reanalyzing the data in Riker and Ordeshook 1968 reveals that what they call "citizen duty," the name devised by Campbell et al. (1960) for an index of agreement with several questions on the importance of voting, explains only about 8 percent of the variance in whether people voted or not. (How much people cared about the election explained about 2 percent of the variance, and how close people thought the election would be had an insignificant effect.)

15. It is a measure of the prevailing direction of empirical interest in these issues that the sole investigation of the reason many people give for voting ("What if everyone didn't vote?") is Quattrone and Tversky's imaginative study (1984) of "magical thinking," which could, on their own account, explain only a very small fraction of the decision to go to the polls.

16. See, e.g., Monroe 1988a.

17. Compare Barry's (1965: 25) use of indifference curves to model a hypothetical trade-off between equity and efficiency. But as we will see, Kingdon points out how hard it is to distinguish in practice between commitment to an ideal and following constituents' wishes.

18. See Quirk, chap. 11, this vol.; Kalt and Zupan 1984: 297–98. Nelson and Silberberg 1987 also argue that "ideological shirking" is more visible and therefore more costly on specific, as opposed to general, bills.

19. I owe this concern to a conversation with Michael Taylor. See also Taylor's critique (1983: 150–52) of Margolis.

20. E.g., Latane and Darley 1970.

21. Eugene Silberberg, pers. comm. with author.

22. Self-interest and altruism are often congruent, however. See Mansbridge, chap. 8, this vol.

23. Mansbridge, chap. 1, n. 61, this vol.

24. Taylor 1987: 111. See also Taylor 1988: 90–91. Taylor argues that self-interest will tend to prevail when an individual's incentives are "substantial" and "a lot (for him) turns on his choice." But he does not present evidence suggesting that self-interest will prevail when the incentives for *both* altruism and self-interest are substantial, and a lot on *both* sides turns on the choice. Taylor also argues that behavior is most likely to be self-interested when options are limited, incentives are well defined and apparent, and prior to the choice there have been many similar occasions of choice. Here again his evidence is weak. What happens when options are limited presumably depends on the options. The argument for the next three conditions seems to rest on the unsubstantiated premise that correctly recognizing the alternatives will lead one to choose self-interest over altruism.

25. See above, n. 18.

26. See Maslow 1954/1970.

27. Oliner and Oliner 1988 did show, however, major differences between the two groups in reports of how close their families had been, whether their parents had added reasoning to physical and verbal punishment, the values of ethical universality and care their parents taught, the number of Jewish contacts they had before the rescue, the size of the town they lived in, and the democratic character of the political party to which they and their families belonged. See Monroe et al. 1988 for the use of rescuers to refute a "luxury" model of altruism.

28. For an enlarged reciprocity model, see "What Goes Around, Comes Around," in Stack 1975.

29. E.g., James Buchanan, Joseph Kalt, Mark Zupan, Lester Thurow. See Mansbridge, chap. 1, this vol.

30. Kingdon 1988: 15. Kingdon adds that supporting coalitions work much the same way, as do bureaucrats, whose dedication to agency mission and desire to maximize agency budget often point them in the same direction. He also adds (p. 21) that legislators sometimes cannot discern constituency preference.

31. Kingdon 1988: 18, 19. This formulation assumes that constituents are also concerned with good public policy and not only with narrow self-interest.

32. For the contemporary analysis of interests, see, e.g., Connolly 1972, Habermas 1968/1971, Mansbridge 1980/1983.

33. The fading of prediction as the sole goal of formal modeling may be judged by comparing the second and third editions of Richard Posner's *Economic Analysis of Law*. In the second edition (1977: 13), Posner wrote, citing Milton Friedman's classic (1953: 4) argument that the task of positive economics is to make correct predictions: "The true test of a theory is its utility in predicting or explaining reality." By the third edition (1986: 16), Posner had cut the word "predicting," dropped the reference to Friedman, and softened the claim, saying only, "An important test of a theory is its ability to explain reality."

Chapter 17

1. George Stigler, "Smith's Travels on the Ship of State," in A. Skinner and T. Wilson, eds., *Essays on Adam Smith* (Oxford: Clarendon Press, 1975), 237, 243, 239, 244, 245, 246.

2. Thus, Jacob Viner, too, is mistaken when he argues that, in the *Wealth of Nations,* "every possible impulse and motive to action is included under self-

interest except a deliberate intention to promote the welfare of others than one-self." Viner, "Adam Smith and Laissez Faire," *The Long View and the Short: Studies in Economic Theory and Policy* (Glencoe, Ill.: Free Press, 1958), 227.

3. Adam Smith, *The Wealth of Nations* (New York: Modern Library, 1937), 582, my emphasis.

4. Ibid., 362, my emphasis.

5. Ibid., 365, 553, 751.

6. Ibid., 279, 389.

7. J. A. W. Gunn, "'Interest Will Not Lie': A Seventeenth-Century Political Maxim," *Journal of the History of Ideas* 29 (1968): 558.

8. Thomas Macaulay, "Mill's Essay on Government: Utilitarian Logic and Politics," in J. Lively and J. Rees, eds., *Utilitarian Logic and Politics* (Oxford: Clarendon Press, 1978), 125.

9. David Hume, *Enquiries concerning the Human Understanding and concerning the Principles of Morals*, ed. L. A. Selby-Bigge (Oxford: Clarendon Press, 1966), 298; cf. Third Earl of Shaftesbury (Anthony Ashley Cooper), *Characteristicks* (London: J. Purser, 1737–38), 1:115; Francis Hutcheson, *An Essay on the Nature and Conduct of the Passions and Affections*, 3rd ed. (1742; rpt., Gainesville, Fla.: Scholars' Facsimiles and Reprints, 1969), ix.

10. Ibid., 296.

11. David Hume "Of the Dignity or Meanness of Human Nature," in *Essays: Moral, Political and Literary* (Indianapolis: Liberty Classics, 1985), 85; cf. Shaftesbury, *Characteristicks*, 1:120.

12. The distinction between calculating and noncalculating behavior, of course, does not correspond neatly to the distinction between interested and disinterested behavior. As economists love to point out, altruists, too, weigh costs and benefits and try to allocate scarce resources in an efficient manner. Similarly, the desire to taste the inferiority of others is not self-interested in a narrow sense, but it can stimulate the most elaborate of Machiavellian calculations. Contrariwise, the "pleasure principle" seems to refer to a form of self-interested motivation that is almost wholly free of rational forethought or the comparison of alternatives. Disinterested motives can be calculating and interested motives can be something close to "second nature." Here, then, is a simple fourfold table, suggested to me by Albert Hirschman, the implications of which need to be developed:

	Interest	Other Motives
Calculating	1	2
Noncalculating	3	4

In what follows, I stress the contrast between cell 1 and cell 4.

13. Hume, *Enquiries*, 301.

14. Ibid., 216, 234n.

15. We may take pleasure in expressing an emotion or conforming to a norm, according to Hume, but this pleasure is secondary and derivative, not primary or causally decisive. We get the pleasure because we do the action; we do not do the action because we get the pleasure ("Of the Dignity or Meanness of Human Nature," 85).

16. Hume, *Enquiries*, 226.

17. Ibid., 218; Hutcheson mentions "disinterested hatred" (*Nature and Conduct of the Passions*, 105).

18. Samuel Johnson similarly claims that "the great law of mutual benevolence is oftener violated by envy than by interest." Johnson, *Rambler*, no. 183 (17 December 1751), in *Rasselas, Poems and Selected Prose*, ed. Bertrand H. Bronson (New York: Holt, Rinehart, and Winston, 1958), 125.

19. Hume, *Enquiries*, 251n., 302.

20. David Hume, "Of the Delicacy of Taste and Passion," in *Essays*, 4.

21. Adam Smith, *The Theory of Moral Sentiments*, ed. D. D. Raphael and A. L. Macfie (Oxford: Clarendon Press, 1976), 34–43.

22. Ibid., 40; Smith's "unsocial passions" are modeled on Shaftesbury's "unnatural affections" that "lead neither to a *publick* nor a *private* Good" (*Characteristicks*, 2:163).

23. Hume, *Enquiries*, 301, my emphasis.

24. Ibid., 281; "Who sees not that vengeance, from the force alone of passion, may be so eagerly pursued, as to make us knowingly neglect every consideration of ease, interest, or safety; and, like some vindictive animals, infuse our very souls into the wounds we give an enemy" (p. 302).

25. Montesquieu, "De l'esprit des lois," in *Oeuvres complètes*, book 12, chap. 4 (Paris: Pléiade, 1951), 2:434.

26. See, for example, Robert Burton, *The Anatomy of Melancholy* (New York: Farrar and Reinholt, 1927), 231–33.

27. David Hume, "Of Parties in General," in *Essays*, 54–63; in what follows, I have also drawn upon idem, "Of the Parties of Great Britain," in *Essays*, 64–72.

28. Hume, "Of Parties in General," 56, 58. Cf. "this propensity of mankind to fall into mutual animosities"; James Madison, *The Federalist Papers*, no. 10 (New York: Mentor, 1961), 79.

29. Hume, *Enquiries*, 275.

30. Hume, "Of Parties in General," 55.

31. "Popular sedition, party zeal, a devoted obedience to factious leaders; these are some of the most visible, though less laudable effects of this social sympathy in human nature" (Hume, *Enquiries*, 224).

32. Hume, "Of Parties in General," 57.

33. Ibid., 301.

34. Hume, "Of Parties in General," 59.

35. Cf. "It is not from the separate interests, real or imaginary, of the majority, that minorities are in danger; but from its antipathies of religion, political party, or race." J. S. Mill, "Tocqueville on Democracy in America," in *Essays on Politics and Society*, ed. J. M. Robson (Toronto: University of Toronto Press, 1977), 176–77.

36. Hume, "Of the Parties of Great Britain," 614; this is a nice reversal of the

contemptuous view, expressed by traditional or prebourgeois elites, that "the great mob of mankind" had only interests, while pride, moral insight, and so forth were reserved for the upper classes.

37. Ibid., 65; note that a reductionist approach to motivation would make this sort of causal analysis impossible; Gary Becker's argument that even the most irrational person will, all things being equal, buy less of a product if the price goes up similarly assumes the independent existence of compulsive and impulsive behavior; Becker "Irrational Behavior and Economic Theory," *Journal of Political Economy* 70, 1 (February 1962): 1–13. Of course, if Becker wanted to claim that negatively sloping demand curves were the only factors realistically-minded students of behavior should take into account, then his position would be quite unlike Hume's.

38. Hume, "Of Parties in General," 58.

39. Ibid., 63.

40. David Hume, "Whether the British Government Inclines Most to Absolute Monarchy or to a Republic," in *Essays,* 51; cf. "One person with a belief, is a social power equal to ninety-nine who have only interests" (J. S. Mill, "Considerations on Representative Government," in *Essays on Politics and Society,* 381).

41. Hume, "Of Parties in General," 59.

42. Ibid., 63.

43. Hume, "Of the Parties of Great Britain," 610.

44. "Born originals, how comes it to pass that we die copies?" in Edward Young, "Conjectures of Original Composition" (1759), in *The Complete Works* (London: W. Tegg and Co., 1854), 2:561.

45. "This is not only conspicuous in children, who implicitly embrace every opinion propos'd to them; but also in men of the greatest judgment and understanding, who find it very difficult to follow their own reason or inclination, in opposition to that of their friends and daily companions." David Hume, *A Treatise of Human Nature* (Oxford, Clarendon Press, 1978), II, 1, xi, p. 316.

46. Hume, "Of the Parties of Great Britain," 610.

47. Ibid., 68.

48. Albert O. Hirschman, *The Passions and the Interests: Political Arguments for Capitalism before Its Triumph* (Princeton: Princeton University Press, 1977); for Hume's contrast between calm and violent passions, see the *Treatise,* II, 1, i, p. 276.

49. In fact, there does not seem to be anything specifically modern or protocapitalist about the attempt to repress violent passions by appealing to material interests. Archaic legal codes—discussed, for example, in Homer (*Iliad* 18, 497–508)—were typically concerned not with the punishment of the guilty but rather with establishing monetary equivalents for broken teeth, gouged eyes, and amputated fingers. Individuals were encouraged not to retaliate for injury but to come to the king's court where the culprit might be made to pay an indemnity. The long history of *wergild* compensation suggests that, long before the seventeenth century, Europeans were hoping to replace the blood feud by the cash nexus. They did not have the language—although it cannot be a coincidence that the word *interest* originally meant compensation for damages—but they did have the idea of overcoming the passions with the interests.

50. Shaftesbury, *Characteristicks*, 1:116.

51. According to Marchamont Needham, "if you can apprehend wherein a man's interest to any particular game on foot doth consist, you may surely know, if the man be prudent, whereabout to have him, that is, how to judge of his design." *Interest Will Not Lie, or a View of England's True Interest* (1659), cited in J. A. W. Gunn, *Politics and the Public Interest in the Seventeenth Century* (London: Routledge and Kegan Paul, 1969), 44.

52. "He that falls by the attacks of interest, is torn by hungry tigers; he may discover and resist his enemies. He that perishes in the ambushes of envy, is destroyed by unknown and invisible assailants, and dies like a man suffocated by a poisonous vapour, without knowledge of his danger, or possibility of contest." Johnson, *Rambler*, no. 183 (17 December 1751), in *Rasselas, Poems and Selected Prose*, 126.

53. R. H. Tawney, *Religion and the Rise of Capitalism* (New York: Harcourt, Brace, and World), 1926.

54. Some of Hirschman's other writings are particularly useful in this regard, notably his analysis of "the tunnel effect" in "The Changing Tolerance for Income Inequality in the Course of Economic Development," in *Essays in Trespassing: Economics to Politics and Beyond* (Cambridge: Cambridge University Press, 1981), 39–58.

55. Compare the shorter and sweeter list given in Joseph Butler, *The Analogy of Religion* (Oxford: Clarendon Press, 1896), 121n.

56. In the *Wealth of Nations,* Smith also explains how three historically powerful moral codes have successfully repressed the taste for conduct conducive to material gain. He discusses (1) the aristocratic belief that economic effort is defiling, (2) military traditions of unquestioning obedience, and (3) religious commitment to otherworldiness and self-abnegation. Moreover, the third book of the *Wealth of Nations* revolves around the distinction between two types of character, between the maximizer and the nonmaximizer, between the calculating and the noncalculating spirit. By temperament, inclination, and training, the nobles of Europe are unsuited to improve the land. Heedlessness of profit is built into their character or "turn of mind." They do not scrutinize their preferences and their resources and rationally choose a noncalculating life. They simply have no taste for calculation (*Wealth of Nations,* 364, 279, 384–85, 379, 389, 578–79).

57. Indeed, the entire argument of the *Wealth of Nations* depends on an underlying contrast between interest and envy. Smith denounced the "invidious and malignant project" whereby Britain excluded other nations from the colony trade (p. 561). By beggaring its neighbors, a country actually impoverished itself. Merchants supported trade barriers because of "private interest," but governments and peoples were drawn to mercantilism by motives which, while no more admirable, were *much less* rational. Politicians tended to be mercantilists not by interest but by "national prejudice and animosity" (p. 441). Smith's polemical intent was not merely to turn attention from short-run to long-run interests. More profoundly, he hoped to draw the political classes of Great Britain away from envy and unreasoning animosity and toward interest—away from the ideal of relative and toward that of absolute wealth.

58. Smith, *Theory of Moral Sentiments,* 52–53; cf. Hume, *Enquiries,* 247.

59. Francis Bacon, "Of Death," in *The Essayes or Counsels, Civill and Morall,* ed. Michael Kiernan (Cambridge: Harvard University Press, 1985), 9–10; Bacon describes vengefulness, in particular, as a bewitching and self-destructive passion: "a Man that studieth *Revenge,* keepes his owne Wounds greene, which otherwise would heale, and doe well" ("Of Revenge," ibid., 17); similarly: "Anger is like Ruine, which breakes it Selfe, upon that it falls" ("Of Anger," ibid., 170); envy, "the vilest Affection, and the most depraved," arises only when we compare ourselves to others ("Of Envy," ibid., 31, 29); we poison our own existence by focusing obsessively—as we do not have to do—on a person whose success has no causal relation to our lack of success; what offends most is not inequality but leap-frogging, seeing others advance while we stand still (p. 28); it is palpably absurd, but nevertheles people do "thinke other Mens harmes, a Redemption of their owne Sufferings" (p. 28). Finally, Bacon also discusses the irrational tendency to believe that an achievement which has cost us a great deal of effort must therefore be extremely valuable. *The New Organon,* ed. Fulton H. Anderson (Indianapolis: Bobbs-Merrill, 1960), 54 (LIV).

60. Aristotle, for example, devoted careful attention to the unreasoning and self-forgetful passions (*Rhetoric,* book II, 1377^b–90^b); particularly noteworthy is his claim that a person exclusively concerned with his private advantage could never successfully insult another, because social slights must be seen to be gratuitous, not instrumental (1378^b–79^a); see, also, the treatise on the passions in Thomas Aquinas, *Summa Theologica* (Westminster, Md.: Christian Classics, 1948), 2:691–790 (pt. I–II, questions 22–48).

61. D. D. Raphael and A. L. Macfie, "Introduction," in Smith, *Theory of Moral Sentiments,* 5.

62. Diogenes Laertius, "Zeno," in *Lives of Eminent Philosophers,* trans. R. D. Hicks (Cambridge: Harvard University Press, 1920), 2:214–23 (vii, 110–17).

63. In the most complete ancient catalog of such disruptive motivations, Cicero included the following: envy, compassion, anxiety, grief, depression, vexation, despondency, sluggishness, shame, fright, consternation, bewilderment, malice, rapture, ostentation, anger, hatred, and greed. *Tusculan Disputations,* trans. J. E. King (Cambridge: Harvard University Press, 1971), 345 (IV.7).

64. Ibid., 349 (IV.9).

65. Seneca, "On Anger," in *Moral Essays,* trans. John Basore (Cambridge: Harvard University Press, 1970), 1:107 (I.1).

66. The irrational craving for approval and the irrational dread of insults, too, will lead individuals to neglect their own well-being (Seneca, "On Firmness," in *Moral Essays,* 103 [xix]). People like to have their interests satisfied, of course, but they prefer to have their vanity caressed. They are much more concerned that you remember their names than that you give them material assistance; Quintus Cicero (attribution doubtful), "Handbook of Electioneering," in Cicero, *Letters to Quintus, Brutus, and Others,* trans. Mary Henderson (Cambridge: Harvard University Press, 1979), 779 (41–42); also: "people are charmed more by looks and words than by the substantial benefit received" (783 [46]).

67. Stoic "apathy" is not complete impassivity or insensibility but merely the absence of uncontrollably irrational impulses. J. M. Rist, *Stoic Philosophy* (Cambridge: Cambridge University Press, 1969), 35.

68. This pair of motivations is discussed by economists today as aversion to, or preference for, risk.

69. Thomas Schelling, *The Strategy of Conflict* (Cambridge: Harvard University Press, 1963), 143.

70. Jon Elster, "Sadder but Wiser? Rationality and the Emotions," *Social Science Information* 24, 2 (1985): 381.

71. Hume notes that the "amours" of Henry IV of France "frequently hurt his interest" (*Enquiries,* 258); in the Western code of love, moreover, there seems to be a powerful taboo against the appearance of economic exchange between lovers; thus, according to Michel de Pure, "l'interest ne sert jamais de rien à l'amour" and "l'interest est impuissant pour l'amour; il est sterile et ne produit rien dans un coeur"; *La prétieuse ou le mystère des ruelles* (1657; Paris: Droz, 1939), 3:78.

72. Some individuals become so upset when they are cheated that they will incur a significant financial loss to eradicate the unpleasant sensation of having been fleeced. But this psychological attachment to the norm of "justice" may well be pathological. It certainly should not be adduced as evidence for the nobility of the human spirit.

73. John Trenchard and Thomas Gordon, *Cato's Letters* (New York: Da Capo Press, 1971), 2:52 (5 August 1721).

74. Leo Strauss, *The Political Philosophy of Hobbes* (Chicago: University of Chicago Press), 1973.

75. *Galatians* 5:26.

76. David Hume, "Of Superstition and Enthusiasm," in *Essays,* 77.

77. *Romans* 8:6–7.

78. 2 *Timothy* 3:2.

79. Augustine, *The City of God,* trans. Philip Levine (Cambridge: Harvard University Press, 1966), 4:404 (XIV, 28).

80. Hume, "Of Superstition and Enthusiasm," 75.

81. Voltaire, "Lettres philosophiques," in *Mélanges,* ed. Jacques van den Heuvel (Paris: Pléiade, 1961), 104–33.

82. Since curiosity was sometimes regarded as a Christian sin, we should note that the word *interesting,* too, became fashionable around 1700. Hume and Smith repeatedly note that we can be "interested" in other people even when our "interests" are not at stake. News in general, for example, is "extremely interesting even to those whose welfare is not immediately engaged" (*Enquiries,* 223).

83. Karl Marx, "On the Jewish Question," *The Marx-Engels Reader,* ed. Robert Tucker (New York: Norton, 1978), 52; it seems that the notion of "long-term interest" was originally introduced by theologians to refer to the "pursuit of happiness" in the afterlife as opposed to concern for short-run interests here below.

84. Thomas à Kempis, *The Imitation of Christ* (Harmondsworth, England: Penguin, 1984), 137; "Whosoever will come after me," said Jesus, "let him deny himself" (*Mark* 8:34).

85. À Kempis, *Imitation of Christ,* 33.

86. Walter Hilton, *The Stairway of Perfection* (New York: Doubleday, 1979), 116–18. Despite the Christian injunction to "love thy neighbor," people were generally asked to love others not for themselves, but only as "carriers"—we should love others not as unique individuals, but only God in them.

87. Hume, *Enquiries,* 270.

88. J. S. Mill, "Considerations on Representative Government," in *Essays on Politics and Society,* 407.

89. Interest in others may be stimulated, for example, by a realistic reminder of the ephemeralness of one's own self: "all selfish interests must be terminated by death." J. S. Mill, "Utilitarianism," in *Essays on Ethics, Religion and Society,* ed. J. M. Robson (Toronto: University of Toronto Press, 1969), 215.

90. Mill, "Considerations on Representative Government," 410.

91. Voltaire, "Lettres philosophiques," 113.

92. "Intérêt," in *Encyclopédie, ou Dictionnaire raisonné des sciences, des arts et des métiers* (Neufchastel: Faulche, 1765), 8:818–19; for polemical reasons, the author accepts a purely negative definition of the word *interest* (as gross selfishness based on a neglect of others and indifference to the rules of justice), reserving positive connotations for *self-love.*

93. Hirschman, *Passions and Interests,* 16; Dale Van Kley, "Pierre Nicole, Jansenism, and the Morality of Enlightened Self-Interest," in Alan Kors and Paul Korshin, eds., *Anticipations of the Enlightenment in England, France, and Germany* (Philadelphia: University of Pennsylvania Press, 1987), 69–85.

94. This idea can be traced back at least to Erasmus.

95. Cf. "the Affection toward Self-Good, may be a good Affection, or an illone" (Shaftesbury, *Characteristicks,* 2:24. See also Rousseau's famous contrast between, on the one hand, a sickly and culturally induced *amour-propre* and, on the other, a wholesome (and biologically original) *amour de soi;* "Discours sue l'origine de l'inégalité," in *Oeuvres complètes,* vol. 3, ed. Bernard Gagnebin and Marcel Raymond (Paris: Pléiade, 1964), 219–20.

96. I am thinking, of course, of the butcher, the brewer, and the baker. But are their hearts really devoid of all motives except self-interest? Perhaps. On examination, however, Smith's language proves ambivalent. He may be making no claim about actual motives, but only about knowable and predictable motives: "We *address ourselves,* not to their humanity but to their self-love" (*Wealth of Nations,* 14, my emphasis). In a commercial society based on an extensive division of labor, we are all involved in long chains of interdependence with people whose characters we will never have an opportunity to judge. Smith's attitude toward self-interest, in other words, may well have been misinterpreted in the same manner as Machiavelli's remarks about the essential wickedness of man. Machiavelli did not advance an empirical generalization but rather a prudential maxim. It was prudent for the Prince to expect the worst. This reading of Smith is also suggested by Hume's claim that the precept "every man must be supposed a knave" is "true in politics" but "false in fact" ("Of the Independency of Parliament," in *Essays,* 43). Our belief that the butcher, the brewer, and the baker are motivated solely by self-interest may be similarly true in the market, while false in fact.

97. Albert O. Hirschman, "The Concept of Interest: From Euphemism to Tautology," in *Rival Views of Market Society* (New York: Viking, 1986), 35–55.

98. Both of the following arguments are stressed by Hirschman.

99. Trenchard and Gordon, *Cato's Letters,* 4:96 (23 February 1722).

100. Mill, "Considerations on Representative Government," 406.

101. R. Hooker, *Of the Laws of Ecclesiastical Polity* (London: Everyman, 1954),

1:192, (I, X, 6); it was also generally believed, as mentioned in note 36, that the upper classes alone could feel and act on exalted and dangerous passions such as pride (cf. Hirschman, *Passions and Interests,* 108–12; idem, "Concept of Interest: From Euphemism to Tautology," 40–41).

102. James Harrington, "The Commonwealth of Oceana," in *The Political Works of James Harrington,* ed. John Pocock (Cambridge: Cambridge University Press, 1977), 173.

103. J. A. W. Gunn, *Politics and the Public Interest in the Seventeenth Century* (London: Routledge and Kegan Paul, 1969).

104. Trenchard and Gordon, *Cato's Letters,* 2:22 (8 July 1721). The earlier Hobbesian claim that monarchy was the best system for making the interests of the ruler coincide with the interests of the ruled (Thomas Hobbes, *Leviathan* [Oxford: Clarendon Press, 1965], 144 [chap. 19]) was an open invitation to such a democratic response.

105. About merchants seeking to sell dear, Smith notes that "their interest is, in this respect, directly opposite to most of the great body of the people" (*Wealth of Nations,* 461); about employers and employees, he said: "their interests are by no means the same" (p. 66); see also ibid., 361–62, 460, 568, 578–79, 582, 603, 605, 625, 765.

106. Or of one kind of democracy—if we accept the distinction drawn in Jane Mansbridge, *Beyond Adversary Democracy* (Chicago: University of Chicago Press, 1983).

107. "The only Secret . . . in forming a Free Government, is to make the Interests of the Governors and of the Governed the same, as far as human Policy can contrive" (Trenchard and Gordon, *Cato's Letters,* 2:232 [6 January 1721]).

108. Ibid., 3:15 (17 March 1721).

109. James Mill, *An Essay on Government* (Indianapolis: Bobbs-Merrill, 1955), 82.

110. J. S. Mill, "Bentham," in *Essays on Ethics, Religion and Society,* 109.

111. J. S. Mill, "De Tocqueville on Democracy in America [I]," in *Essays on Politics and Society,* 71.

112. Mill, "Bentham," 109.

113. Smith, *Wealth of Nations,* 651.

114. J. S. Mill, "Thoughts on Parliamentary Reform," in *Essays on Politics and Society,* 330; cf. idem, "Considerations on Representative Government," 444.

115. John Locke, *Two Treatises of Government,* ed. Peter Laslett (New York: Mentor, 1965), 347–48 (II, vi, 56), my emphasis.

116. Mill even writes of the "inherent tendency of man" to disguise his self-interest as a duty and a virtue. What concerns him is not imposture, but the way individuals deceive themselves—"the artifices by which we persuade ourselves that we are not yielding to our selfish inclinations when we are" ("Bentham," 109–10).

Chapter 18

1. As Carole Pateman writes, "One of the most striking features of the past two decades is the extent to which the assumptions of liberal individualism have permeated the whole of social life." Carole Pateman, *The Problem of Political Obligation: A Critique of Liberal Theory* (Berkeley: University of California Press,

1985), 182–83. All those fields influenced by rational choice theory—and that includes most of the social sciences—thus "hark back to classical liberal contract doctrines," Pateman writes, "and claims that social order is founded on the inter-actions of self-interested, utility-maximizing individuals, protecting and enlarging their property in the capitalist market" (183).

2. E.g., Thomas Hobbes, *Leviathan*, ed. C. B. Macpherson, (Baltimore: Penguin, 1971); John Locke, *Two Treatises of Government*, ed. Peter Laslett (New York: Mentor, 1965); Jean-Jacques Rousseau, *The Social Contract*, ed. Charles Frankel (New York: Hafner, 1947); The U.S. Declaration of Independence; and of course a literature too vast to mention. As Carole Pateman writes of this tradition, "a corollary of the liberal view . . . is that social contract theory is central to liberalism. Paradigmatically, contract is the act through which two free and equal individuals create social bonds, or a collection of such individuals creates the state" (*Problem of Political Obligation*, 180).

3. E.g., Adam Smith, *The Wealth of Nations*, ed. M. Lerner (New York: Random House, 1937) and virtually the whole of classical and neoclassical economics.

4. The phrase has been entrenched in judicial and social discussion since Oliver Wendell Holmes used it in *Abrams v. United States* (250 U.S. 616, 630 [1919]).

5. E.g., John Rawls, *A Theory of Justice* (Cambridge: Harvard University Press, 1971); Robert Nozick, *Anarchy, State, and Utopia* (New York: Basic Books, 1974); and Ronald Dworkin, *Taking Rights Seriously* (Cambridge: Harvard University Press, 1977).

6. E.g., David A. J. Richards, *A Theory of Reasons for Action* (New York: Oxford University Press, 1971); and David Gauthier, *Morals by Agreement* (New York: Oxford University Press, 1986).

7. For a recent sample, see the symposium "Explanation and Justification in Social Theory," in *Ethics* 97, 1.

8. Virginia Held, *Rights and Goods: Justifying Social Action* (New York: Free Press/Macmillan, 1984).

9. Rousseau, *Social Contract*.

10. J.-J. Rousseau, *Emile*, trans. B. Foxley (New York: Dutton, 1911).

11. See especially Nancy Chodorow, *The Reproduction of Mothering: Psycho-analysis and the Sociology of Gender* (Berkeley: University of California Press, 1978); and Joyce Trebilcot, ed., *Mothering: Essays in Feminist Theory* (Totowa, N.J.: Rowman and Allanheld, 1984).

12. See, e.g., Susan Peterson, "Against 'Parenting,'" in Trebilcot, *Mothering*.

13. By then "parenting" might also be acceptable to those who find it presently misleading.

14. Smith, *Wealth of Nations*, bk. 1, chap. 1.

15. See, e.g., Annette Baier, "Hume: The Women's Moral Theorist?" in Eva Kittay and Diana Meyers, eds., *Woman and Moral Theory* (Totowa, N.J.: Rowman and Littlefield, 1986).

16. David Hume, *Essays Moral, Political, and Literary*, vol. 1, ed. T. H. Green and T. H. Grose (London: Longmans, 1898), 176.

17. Charlotte Perkins Gilman, *Herland* (1915; rpt., New York: Pantheon, 1979), 60.

18. Ibid., 66.

19. Jane Flax, "The Family in Contemporary Feminist Thought: A Critical Review," in Jean Bethke Elshtain, ed., *The Family in Political Thought* (Amherst: University of Massachusetts Press, 1982), 252.

20. The collection of readings in Barrie Thorne, ed., *Rethinking the Family* (New York: Longmans, 1982) is a useful source. Joyce Trebilcot's *Mothering* is another helpful collection. And among the best sources of suggestions are feminist utopian novels, e.g., Marge Piercy's *Woman on the Edge of Time* (New York: Fawcett, 1976).

21. See especially Held, *Rights and Goods,* chap. 5.

22. In some societies, social pressures to conform with the norms of reciprocal care—of children by parents and later of parents by children—can be very great. But these societies are usually of a kind which are thought to be at a stage of development antecedent to that of contractual society.

23. The gerontologist Elaine Brody says about old people that "what we hear over and over again—and I'm talking gross numbers of 80 to 90 percent in survey after survey—is 'I don't want to be a burden on my children.'" Interview by Lindsy Van Gelder, *Ms.,* January 1986, 48.

24. For a different view see Howard Cohen, *Equal Rights for Children* (Totowa, N.J.: Littlefield, Adams, 1980).

25. For a more developed discussion of this issue, see Held, *Rights and Goods.*

26. For related discussions, see Nancy Hartsock, *Money, Sex, and Power: Toward a Feminist Historical Materialism* (New York: Longmans, 1983); and Sara Ruddick, "Maternal Thinking," in Trebilcot, *Mothering.*

27. For examples of the view that women are more deficient than men in understanding morality and acting morally, see, e.g., Mary Mahowald, ed., *Philosophy of Woman: Classical to Current Concepts* (Indianapolis: Hackett, 1978). See also Lawrence Kohlberg, *The Philosophy of Moral Development* (San Francisco: Harper and Row, 1981), and L. Kohlberg and R. Kramer, "Continuities and Discontinuities in Child and Adult Moral Development," *Human Development* 12 (1969): 93–120.

28. For further discussion, see Virginia Held, "Feminism and Moral Theory," in Kittay and Meyers, eds., *Women and Moral Theory.*

Reference List

Adkins, A. W. H. 1963. "'Friendship' and 'Self-Sufficiency' in Homer and Aristotle." *Classical Quarterly* 13:30–45.

———. 1972. *Moral Values and Political Behavior in Ancient Greece.* New York: W. W. Norton.

Akerlof, George. 1983. "Loyalty Filters." *American Economic Review* 73:54–63.

Akerlof, George, and W. Dickens. 1981. "The Economic Consequences of Cognitive Dissonance." *American Economic Review* 72:307–19.

Alexander, R. D. 1975."The Search for a General Theory of Behavior." *Behavioral Science* 20:77–100.

Andenaes, J. 1974. *Punishment and Deterrence.* Ann Arbor: University of Michigan Press.

Anderson, Charles W. 1979. "The Place of Principles in Policy Analysis." *American Political Science Review* 73:711–23.

Aoki, K. 1982. "A Condition for Group Selection to Prevail over Counteracting Individual Selection." *Evolution* 36:832–42.

Appleby, Joyce Oldham. 1978. *Economic Thought and Ideology in Seventeenth Century England.* Princeton: Princeton University Press.

Aquinas, Thomas. 1948. *Summa Theologica.* Westminster, Md: Christian Classics.

Archibald, G. C., and D. Donaldson. 1976. "Non-Paternalism and the Basic Theorems of Welfare Economics." *Canadian Journal of Economics* 9:492–507.

Aristotle. 1946. *Politics.* Trans. Ernest Barker. London: Oxford University Press.

———. 1954. *Ethics.* Trans. Sir David Ross. Oxford: Oxford University Press.

Arnold, R. Douglas. 1988. "Congress and Policy Decisions: Strategic Action and the Public Interest." *Newsletter of the Legislative Studies Section, American Political Science Association* 11:123–28.

Arnold, R. Douglas, and F. H. Hahn. 1971. *General Competitive Analysis.* San Francisco: Holden Day.

Arrow, Kenneth. [1951] 1963. *Social Choice and Individual Values.* New Haven: Yale University Press; 2nd ed., New York: Wiley.

———. 1973. "Social Responsibility and Economic Efficiency." *Public Policy* 21:303–17.

———. 1975. "Gifts and Exchanges." In E. S. Phelps, ed., *Altruism, Morality, and Economic Theory.* New York: Russell Sage Foundation.

Asbell, Bernard. 1978. *The Senate Nobody Knows*. New York: Doubleday.

Aubrey, John. [1697/1813] 1982. *Brief Lives*. Ed. Richard Barber. Totowa, N.J.: Barnes and Noble Books.

Augustine. 1966. *The City of God*. Trans. Phillip Levine. Cambridge: Harvard University Press.

Axelrod, Robert. 1981. "The Emergence of Cooperation among Egoists." *American Political Science Review* 75: 306–318.

———. 1984. *The Evolution of Cooperation*. New York: Basic Books.

———. 1986. "An Evolutionary Approach to Norms." *American Political Science Review* 80:1095–1111.

Axelrod, R., and W. D. Hamilton. 1981. "The Evolution of Cooperation." *Science* 211:1390–96.

Bacon, Francis. [1597] 1985. "Of Death." In *The Essayes or Counsels, Civill and Morall*, ed. Michael Kiernan. Cambridge: Harvard University Press.

Bagehot, Walter. [1867] 1966. *The English Constitution*. Ithaca, N.Y.: Cornell University Press.

———. [1873] 1962. *Lombard Street*. Homewood, Ill.: Richard D. Irwin, Inc.

Baier, Annette. 1986. "Hume: The Women's Moral Theorist?" In Eva Kittay and Diana Meyers, eds., *Women and Moral Theory*. Totowa, N.J.: Rowman and Littlefield.

Baier, K. 1958. *The Moral Point of View*. Ithaca, N.Y.: Cornell University Press.

———. 1977. "Rationality and Morality." *Erkenntnis* 11:197–223.

Baldwin, David A. 1979. "Power Analysis and World Politics: New Trends versus Old Tendencies." *World Politics* 31:161–194.

Bandura, A. 1972. *Social Learning Theory*. Hillsdale, N.J.: General Learning Press.

Banfield, Edward C. [1958] 1963. *The Moral Basis of a Backward Society*. Chicago: Free Press.

———. 1985. *Here the People Rule*. New York: Plenum.

Banfield, Edward C., and James Q. Wilson. 1963. *City Politics*. Cambridge: Harvard University Press.

———. 1964. "Public-Regardingness as a Value Premise in Voting Behavior." *American Political Science Review* 58:876–87.

Barber, Benjamin R. 1984. *Strong Democracy: Participatory Politics for a New Age*. Berkeley: University of California Press.

Barker, Ernest. [1942]. 1967. *Reflections on Government*. Reprint. Oxford: Oxford University Press.

Baron, Marcia. 1984. "The Alleged Moral Repugnance of Acting from Duty." *Journal of Philosophy* 91:197–220.

Barrett-Howard, E., and T. R. Tyler. 1986. "Procedural Justice as a Criterion in Allocation Decisions." *Journal of Personality and Social Psychology* 50:296–304.

Barry, Brian. 1965. *Political Argument*. New York: Humanities Press.

———. [1970] 1978. *Sociologists, Economists, and Democracy*. Reprint. Chicago: University of Chicago Press.

———, ed. 1986. "Symposium on Explanation and Justification in Social Theory." *Ethics* 97:1–277.

Barry, Brian, and Russell Hardin. 1982. *Rational Man and Irrational Society*. Beverly Hills, Calif: Sage.

Baumol, W. J. 1959. *Business Behavior, Value and Growth*. New York: Macmillan.

Beard, C. [1913] 1963. *An Economic Interpretation of the Constitution of the United States*. New York: Macmillan.

Beck, Nathaniel. 1975. "The Paradox of Minimax Regret." *American Political Science Review* 69:918.

Beck, Paul Allen. 1974. "A Socialization Theory of Partisan Realignment." In Richard G. Niemi, *The Politics of Future Citizens*, 199–219. San Francisco: Jossey-Boss.

Becker, Gary S. 1962. "Irrational Behavior and Economic Theory." *Journal of Political Economy* 70:1–13.

———. 1974. "A Theory of Social Interactions." *Journal of Political Economy* 82: 1063–93.

———. 1976. *The Economic Approach to Behavior*. Chicago: University of Chicago Press.

———. 1983. "A Theory of Competition among Pressure Groups for Political Influence." *Quarterly Journal of Economics* 98:371–400.

Becker, Howard S. 1960. "Notes on the Concept of Commitment." *American Journal of Sociology* 64:32–40.

Beitz, Charles. 1979a. "Bounded Morality: Justice and the State in World Politics." *International Organization* 33:405–424.

———. 1979b. *Political Theory and International Relations*. Princeton: Princeton University Press.

Bellah, R. N., R. Madsen, W. M. Sullivan, A. Swidler, and S. M. Tipton. 1985. *Habits of the Heart: Individualism and Commitment in American Life*. Berkeley: University of California Press.

Bentham, Jeremy. [1818–19] 1843. "Extracts." In *Collected Works*. Vol. 10. Ed. John Bowring. New York: Russell and Russell.

Bentley, Arthur. [1908] 1949. *The Process of Government*. Reprint. Bloomington, Ind.: Principia Press.

Berelson, B. R., P. F. Lazarsfeld, and W. N. McPhee. 1954. *Voting: A Study of Opinion Formation in a Presidential Campaign*. Chicago: University of Chicago Press.

Berlin, Isaiah. [1958] 1969. "Two Concepts of Liberty." In *Four Essays on Liberty*. Reprint. Oxford: Oxford University Press.

Bernheim, B. Douglas, and Oded Stark. 1988. "Altruism within the Family Reconsidered: So Nice Guys Finish Last?" *American Economic Review* 78:1034–45.

Bernstein, Marver H. 1955. *Regulating Business by Independent Commission*. Princeton: Princeton University Press.

Bessette, Joseph M. 1979. "Deliberation in Congress." Paper delivered at the annual meeting of the American Political Science Association, Washington, D.C.

———. 1982. "Is Congress a Deliberative Body?" In Dennis Hale, ed., *The United States Congress: Proceedings of the Thomas P. O'Neill Symposium*. Chestnut Hill, Mass.: Boston College.

———. Forthcoming. *Democratic Deliberation*.

Bicchieri, M. G., ed. 1972. *Hunters and Gatherers Today*. New York: Holt, Rinehart, and Winston.

Binmore, K. G. 1975. "An Example in Group Preference." *Journal of Economic Theory* 10:377–85.

Blarney, P. H. 1976. "Comment: Genetic Bases of Behavior—Especially of Altruism." *American Psychologist* 31:358.

Block, Fred L. 1977. *The Origins of International Economic Disorder.* Berkeley: University of California Press.

Blum, Lawrence A. 1980. *Friendship, Altruism and Morality.* Boston. Routledge and Kegan Paul.

Bobo, L. 1983. "Whites' Opposition to Busing: Symbolic Racism or Realistic Group Conflict?" *Journal of Personality and Social Psychology* 45:1196–1210.

———. 1988. "Group Conflict, Prejudice, and the Paradox of Contemporary Racial Attitudes." In P. Katz and D. Taylor, eds., *Eliminating Racism: Profiles in Controversy.* New York: Plenum.

Bohm, P. 1972. "Estimating Demand for Public Goods: An Experiment." *European Economic Review* 3:111–30.

Boorman, S., and P. Levitt. 1980. *The Genetics of Altruism.* New York: Academic.

Boyd, R., and P. J. Richerson. 1985. *Culture and the Evolutionary Process.* Chicago: University of Chicago Press.

———. 1988a. "An Evolutionary Model of Social Learning: The Effects of Spatial and Temporal Variation." In T. R. Zentall and B. G. Galef, eds., *Social Learning: Psychological and Biological Perspectives.* Hillsdale N.J.: Lawrence Erlbaum Assoc.

———. 1988b. "The Evolution of Reciprocity in Sizable Groups." *Journal of Theoretical Biology* 132:337–56.

———. In press. "Social Learning as an Adaptation." In A. Hastings, ed., *Some Mathematical Problems in Biology.* New Haven: American Mathematical Society.

Brennan, Geoffrey, and James M. Buchanan. 1981. "The Normative Purpose of Economic 'Science': Rediscovery of an Eighteenth Century Method." *International Review of Law and Economics* 1:155–66.

———. 1988. "Is Public Choice Immoral? The Case for the 'Nobel' Lie." *Virginia Law Review* 74:179–89.

Brewer, Marilyn B., and Roderick M. Kramer. 1986. "Choice Behavior in Social Dilemmas: Effects of Social Identity, Group Size, and Decision Framing." *Journal of Personality and Social Psychology* 50:543–49.

Brigham, J., and D. W. Brown. 1980. *Policy Implementation: Penalties or Incentives?* Beverly Hills, Calif.: Sage.

Brody, R. A., and P. M. Sniderman. 1977. "From Life Space to Polling Place: The Relevance of Personal Concerns for Voting Behavior." *British Journal of Political Science* 7:337–60.

Brown, J. S., M. J. Sanderson, and R. E. Michod. 1982. "Evolution of Social Behavior by Reciprocation." *Journal of Theoretical Biology* 99:319–39.

Browning, Rufus P., and Herbert Jacob. 1964. "Power Motivation and the Political Personality." *Public Opinion Quarterly* 28:75–90.

Brownmiller, Susan. [1975] 1976. *Against Our Will.* New York: Bantam Books.

Buchanan, James M. 1975. "The Samaritan's Dilemma." In Edmund S. Phelps, ed., *Altruism, Morality, and Economic Theory.* New York: Russell Sage Foundation.

———. 1986. "Then and Now, 1961–1986: From Delusion to Dystopia." Paper presented at the Institute for Humane Studies.

Buchanan, James M., and Gordon Tullock. [1952] 1965. *The Calculus of Consent: Logical Foundations of Constitutional Democracy.* Reprint. Ann Arbor: University of Michigan Press.

Burton, Robert. 1927. *The Anatomy of Melancholy.* New York: Farrar and Rineholt.

Buss, L. 1987. *The Evolution of Individuality.* Princeton: Princeton University Press.

Butler, Joseph. [1726] 1949. *Fifteen Sermons Preached at the Rolls Chapel.* Ed. W. R. Matthews. London: Bell. Also excerpted in L. A. Selby-Bigge, *British Moralist* (Oxford: Clarendon Press, 1897).

———. 1896. *The Analogy of Religion.* Oxford: Clarendon Press.

———. 1960. *The New Organon.* Ed. Fulton H. Anderson. Indianapolis: Bobbs-Merrill.

Caditz, J. 1976. *White Liberals in Transition.* New York: Spectrum Press.

Calhoun, John C. [1853] 1953. *A Disquisition on Government.* Ed. C. Gordon Post. New York: Liberal Arts Press.

Campbell, A., P. E. Converse, W. E. Miller, and D. E. Stokes. 1960. *The American Voter.* New York: Wiley.

Campbell, D. T. 1965. "Ethnocentric and Other Altruistic Motives." In D. Levine, ed., *Nebraska Symposium on Motivation, 1965.* Lincoln: University of Nebraska Press, 1965.

———. 1975. "On the Conflicts between Biological and Social Evolution and between Psychology and the Moral Tradition." *American Psychologist* 30:1103–26.

———. 1982. "Legal and Primary-Group Social Controls." *Journal of Social and Biological Structure* 5:431–38.

———. 1983. "The Two Distinct Routes beyond Kin Selection to Ultrasociality." In Diane Bridgeman, ed., *The Nature of Prosocial Development.* New York: Academic Press.

———. 1986. "Rationality and Utility from the Standpoint of Evolutionary Biology." *Journal of Business* 59:355–63.

Caporael, L. R. 1987. "*Homo sapiens, Homo faber, Homo socians:* Technology and the Social Animal." In W. Callebaut and R. Pinxten, eds., *Evolutionary Epistemology: A Multiparadigm Program,* 233–44. Dordrecht City: Reidel.

Caporael, L. R., R. M. Dawes, J. M. Orbell, and A. J. C. van de Kragt. 1989. "Selfishness Examined: Cooperation in the Absence of Egoistic Incentives." *Behavioral and Brain Sciences* 4:683–98.

Casper, J. D., T. R. Tyler, and B. Fisher. 1988. "Procedural Justice in Felony Cases." *Law and Society Review* 22:483–507.

Cataldo, E. F., and J. D. Holm. 1983. "Voting on School Finances: A Test of Competing Theories." *Western Political Quarterly* 36:619–31.

Cavalli-Sforza, L. L., and M. W. Feldman. 1981. *Cultural Transmission and Evolution.* Princeton: Princeton University Press.

Chodorow, Nancy. 1978. *The Reproduction of Mothering: Psychoanalysis and the Sociology of Gender.* Berkeley: University of California Press.

Cicero. 1971. *Tusculan Disputations*. Trans. J. E. Knog. Cambridge: Harvard University Press.

———. 1979. *Letters to Quintas, Brutus, and Others*. Trans. Mary Henderson. Cambridge: Harvard University Press.

Citrin, J., and Green, D. P. 1988. "The Self-Interest Motive in American Public Opinion." Manuscript. University of California, Berkeley.

Clarke, L. 1987. *Broadening the Battlefield: The H-Blocks and the Rise of Sinn Fe'in*. Dublin: Gill and Macmillan.

Cohen, Howard. 1980. *Equal Rights for Children*. Totowa, N.J.: Littlefield, Adams.

Cohen, Ronald. 1972. "Altruism: Human, Cultural, or What?" *Journal of Social Issues* 28:39–57.

Collard, David A. 1975. "Edgeworth's Propositions on Altruism." *Economic Journal* 85:355–60.

———. 1978. *Altruism and Economy: A Study in Non-Selfish Economics*. Oxford: Martin Robinson.

Conlan, Timothy J., David R. Beam, and Margaret T. Wrightson. 1988. "Tax Reform Legislation and the New Politics of Reform." Paper delivered at the annual meeting of the American Political Science Association.

Conley, J. 1988. "Ethnographic Perspectives on Informal Justice: What Litigants Want." Paper presented at the annual meeting of the Law and Society Association, Vail, Colo.

Connolly, William A. 1972. "On 'Interests' in Politics." *Politics and Society* 2:459–77.

Connor, W. Robert. 1971. *The New Politicians of Fifth Century Athens*. Princeton: Princeton University Press.

Conover, Pamela Johnston. 1985. "The Impact of Group Economic Interests on Political Evaluations." *American Politics Quarterly* 13:139–66.

———. 1987. "Approaches to the Political Study of Social Groups: Measures of Group Identification and Group Affect." Paper prepared for the National Election Studies conference on Groups and American Politics.

———. 1988. "Who Cares? Sympathy and Politics: A Feminist Perspective." Paper delivered at the annual meeting of the Midwest Political Science Association, Chicago, Ill. April 14–18.

Conover, Pamela Johnston, S. Feldman, and K. Knight. 1986. "Judging Inflation and Unemployment: The Origins of Retrospective Evaluations." *Journal of Politics* 48:565–88.

———. 1987. "The Personal and Political Underpinnings of Economic Forecasts." *American Journal of Political Science* 31:559–83.

Conover, Pamela Johnston, and Virginia Gray. 1983. *Feminism and the New Right: Conflict over the American Family*. New York: Praeger.

Converse, P. E. 1964. "The Nature of Belief Systems in Mass Publics." In D. E. Apter, ed., *Ideology and Discontent*. New York: Free Press of Glencoe.

Crosby, F. 1976. "A Model of Egoistical Relative Deprivation." *Psychological Review* 83:85–113.

———. 1982. *Relative Deprivation and Working Women*. New York: Oxford University Press.

Dahl, R. 1956. *A Preface to Democratic Theory.* Chicago: University of Chicago Press.

Darhrendorf, R. 1959. *Class and Class Conflict in Industrial Society.* Stanford: Stanford University Press.

Damas, D. 1971. "The Copper Eskimo." In M. G. Bicchieri, ed., *Hunter Gatherers Today.* New York: Holt, Rinehart, and Winston.

Dawes, Robyn M. 1980. "Social Dilemmas." *Annual Review of Psychology* 31:169–93.

Dawes, Robyn M., and Richard H. Thaler. 1988. "Cooperation." *Journal of Economic Perspectives* 2:187–96.

Deci, Edward L. 1971. "Effects of Externally Mediated Rewards on Intrinsic Motivation." *Journal of Personality and Social Psychology* 18:105–15.

———. 1972. "Intrinsic Motivation, Extrinsic Reinforcement, and Inequity." *Journal of Personality and Social Psychology* 22:113–20.

Deci, Edward L., Gregory Betley, James Kahle, Linda Abrams, and Joseph Porac. 1981. "When Trying to Win: Competition and Intrinsic Motivation." *Personality and Social Psychology Bulletin* 7:79–83.

Derthick, Martha, and Paul J. Quirk. 1985. *The Politics of Deregulation.* Washington, D.C.: Brookings.

Deutsch, M. 1960. "The Effects of Motivational Orientation upon Trust and Suspicion." *Human Relations* 13:123–39.

———. 1973. *The Resolution of Conflict: Constructive and Destructive Processes.* New Haven: Yale University Press.

Diggins, John P. 1984. *The Lost Soul of American Politics: Virtue, Self-Interest, and the Foundations of Liberalism.* New York: Basic Books.

Dixit, Avinash. 1980. "The Role of Investment in Entry Deterrence." *Economic Journal* 90:95–106.

Douglas, Mary, and Aaron Wildavsky. 1982. *Risk and Culture.* Berkeley: University of California Press.

Dover, Kenneth. 1974. *Greek Popular Morality in the Time of Plato and Aristotle.* Berkeley: University of California Press.

Downs, A. 1957. *An Economic Theory of Democracy.* New York: Harper and Row.

———. 1989. "Social Values and Democracy." Paper delivered at the annual meeting of the American Political Science Association.

Drew, Elizabeth. 1979. *Senator.* New York: Simon and Schuster.

———. 1983. "Portrait of a Lobbyist." In Allan J. Cigler and Berdett A. Loomis, eds., *Interest Group Politics.* Washington, D.C.: Congressional Quarterly Press.

Dreze, J., and D. de la Vallée Poussin. 1971. "A Tatonnement Process for Public Goods." *Review of Economic Studies* 38:133–50.

Duesenberry, J. S. 1949. *Income, Saving and the Theory of Consumer Behavior.* Cambridge: Harvard University Press.

Durham, W. H. 1978. "Toward a Coevolutionary View of Human Biology and Culture." In A. Caplan, ed., *The Sociobiology Debate.* New York: Harper and Row.

———. 1982. "Interactions of Biological and Cultural Evolution: Models and Examples." *Human Ecology* 10:289–323.

Dutta, B., and P. K. Pattanaik. 1975. "On Nicely Consistent Voting Systems." Typescript. Delhi School of Economics.

Dworkin, Ronald. 1977. *Taking Rights Seriously*. Cambridge: Harvard University Press.

Easton, D. 1965. *A Systems Analysis of Political Life*. Chicago: University of Chicago Press.

Eaton, B. C., and R. G. Lipsey. 1981. "Capital, Commitment, and Entry Equilibrium." *Bell Journal of Economics* 12:593–604.

Edgeworth, F. Y. 1881. *Mathematical Psychics: An Essay on the Application of Mathematics to the Moral Sciences*. London: C. K. Paul and Co.

Ehrenberg, Richard. 1928. *Capital and Finance in the Age of the Renaissance: A Study of the Fuggers and Their Connections*. Trans. H. M. Lucas. New York: Harcourt, Brace.

Eisenberg, Nancy, ed. 1982. *The Development of Prosocial Behavior*. New York: Academic Press.

Eisenberg, Nancy, and Paul Miller. 1987. "Empathy, Sympathy and Altruism: Empirical and Conceptual Links." In Nancy Eisenberg and J. Strayer, eds., *Empathy and Its Development*. New York: Cambridge University Press.

Eisenberg, Nancy, and J. Strayer, eds. 1987. *Empathy and Its Development*. New York: Cambridge University Press.

Ekman, Paul. 1985. *Telling Lies*. New York: W. W. Norton.

Eliot, Jonathan. [N.d.] 1974. *Debates in the Several State Conventions on the Adoption of the Federal Constitution*. Philadelphia: Lippincott Press; reprint, New York: Lenox Hill/Burt Franklin.

Elkin, Stephen L. 1987. *City and Regime in the American Republic*. Chicago: University of Chicago Press.

Elster, Jon. [1979] 1984. *Ulysses and the Sirens: Studies in Rationality and Irrationality*. Reprint. New York: Cambridge University Press.

———. [1983] 1987. *Sour Grapes: Studies in the Subversion of Rationality*. Reprint. Cambridge: Cambridge University Press.

———. 1985. "Sadder but Wiser? Rationality and the Emotions." *Social Science Information* 24:381.

———. 1986. "Introduction." In Jon Elster, ed., *The Multiple Self*. Cambridge: Cambridge University Press.

———. 1989a. *The Cement of Society*. Cambridge: Cambridge University Press.

———. 1989b. *Nuts and Bolts for the Social Sciences*. Cambridge: Cambridge University Press.

Ely, J. H. 1980. *Democracy and Distrust: A Theory of Judicial Review*. Cambridge: Harvard University Press.

Epstein, D. 1984. *The Political Theory of the Federalist*. Chicago: University of Chicago Press.

Epstein, R. 1985. *Takings: Private Property and the Law of Eminent Domain*. Cambridge: Harvard University Press.

Eshel, I. 1972. "On the Neighborhood Effect and the Evolution of Altruistic Traits." *Theoretical Population Biology* 3:258–77.

Etzioni, Amitai. [1961] 1975. *Comparative Analysis of Complex Organizations*. 2d ed. New York: Free Press.

———. 1988. *The Moral Dimension: Toward a New Economics*. New York: Free Press.

Farber, D., and P. Frickey. 1986. "The Jurisprudence of Public Choice." *Texas Law Review* 65:873–927.

Feather, N. T. 1964. "Subjective Probability and Decisions under Uncertainty." In W. J. Gore and J. W. Dyson, eds., *The Making of Decisions*. New York: Macmillan.

Feinberg, Joel. 1970. *Moral Concepts*. New York: Oxford University Press.

Feldman, S. 1982. "Economic Self-Interest and Political Behavior." *American Journal of Political Science* 26:446–66.

———. 1984. "Economic Self-Interest and the Vote: Evidence and Meaning." *Political Behavior* 6:229–52.

Fenno, Richard F. 1973. *Congressmen in Committees*. Boston: Little, Brown.

Ferejohn, John A., and Morris P. Fiorina. 1974. "The Paradox of Not Voting: A Decision-Theoretic Analysis." *American Political Science Review* 68:525–35.

———. 1975. "Closeness Counts Only in Horseshoes and Dancing." *American Political Science Review* 69:920–25.

Fiorina, Morris. 1974. *Representatives, Roll Calls, and Constituencies*. Lexington, Mass.: Lexington Books/D. C. Heath.

———. 1977. *Congress: Keystone of the Washington Establishment*. New Haven: Yale University Press.

———. 1986. "Information and Rationality in Elections." Occasional Paper No. 86-4. Center for American Political Studies, Harvard University.

Fireman, Bruce, and William Gamson. 1979. "Utilitarian Logic in the Resource Mobilization Perspective." In Mayer M. Zald and John D. McCarthy, eds., *The Dynamics of Social Movements*. Cambridge, Mass.: Winthrop.

Fisher, Roger, and William Ury. [1981] 1983. *Getting to Yes*. Reprint. New York: Penguin.

Fishkin, James S. 1982. *The Limits of Obligation*. New Haven: Yale University Press.

Flacks, Richard. 1988. *Making History: The Radical Tradition in American Life*. New York: Columbia University Press.

Flax, Jane. 1982. "The Family in Contemporary Feminist Thought: A Critical Review." In Jean Bethke Elshtain, ed., *The Family in Political Thought*. Amherst: University of Massachusetts Press.

Foley, D. K. 1970. "Lindahl's Solution and the Core of an Economy with Public Goods." *Econometrica* 38:66–72.

Fox, A. 1974. *Beyond Contract: Work, Power and Trust Relations*. London: Faber.

Frank, Robert H. 1985. *Choosing the Right Pond: Human Behavior and the Quest for Status*. New York: Oxford University Press.

———. 1987. "If *Homo Economicus* Could Choose His Own Utility Function, Would He Want One with a Conscience?" *American Economic Review* 77:593–604.

———. 1988. *Passions within Reason: The Strategic Role of the Emotions*. New York: W. W. Norton.

Friedland, Roger, and A. F. Robertson, eds. 1989. *Beyond the Marketplace: Rethinking Economy and Society.* New York: Aldine and de Gruyter.

Friedman, Milton. 1953. "The Methodology of Positive Economics." In *Essays in Positive Economics.* Chicago: University of Chicago Press.

Frisch, Ragnar. [1971] 1976. "Co-operation between Politicians and Econometricians on the Formalization of Political Preferences." In Frank Long, ed., *Economic Planning Studies.* International Studies in Economics and Econometrics, no. 8. Boston: D. Reidel. Originally published as "Samarbied Mellom Politikere og Okonometrikere om Formuleringen av Politiske Preferenenser."

Frohlich, Norman, Joe A. Oppenheimer, and Oran R. Young. 1971. *Political Leadership and Collective Goods.* Princeton: Princeton University Press.

Gaertner, W. 1973. "A Dynamic Model of Interdependent Consumer Behaviour." Mimeo. Bielefeld University, Bielefeld, West Germany.

Gambetta, Diego, ed. 1988. *Trust.* New York: Basil Blackwell.

Gatlin, D. S., M. W. Giles, and E. F. Cataldo. 1978. "Policy Support within a Target Group: The Case of School Desegregation." *American Political Science Review* 72:985–95.

Gauthier, David. 1985. *Morals by Agreement.* Oxford: Oxford University Press.

Gibbard, A. 1973. "Manipulation of Voting Schemes: A General Result." *Econometrica* 41:587–601.

———. 1976. "Social Decision, Strategic Behavior, and Best Outcomes: An Impossibility Result." Discussion Paper No. 224. Northwestern University Center for Mathematical Studies in Economics and Management Science.

Gilman, Charlotte P. [1915] 1979. *Herland.* Reprint. New York: Pantheon.

Goodin, R. E. 1976. *The Politics of Rational Man.* London: John Wiley and Sons.

Goodin, R. E., and K. W. S. Roberts. 1975. "The Ethical Voter." *American Political Science Review* 69:926–28.

Gordon, R. A. 1976. "Rigor and Relevance in a Changing Institutional Setting." *American Economic Review* 66:1–14.

Gorman, W. M. 1975. "Tricks with Utility Functions." In M. Artis and A. R. Nobay, eds., *Essays in Economic Analysis.* Cambridge: Cambridge University Press.

Gough, J. W. [1936] 1957. *The Social Contract: A Critical Study of Its Development.* Reprint. Oxford: Oxford University Press.

Gouldner, Alvin. 1960. "The Norm of Reciprocity." *American Sociological Review* 25:161–178.

Green, D. P. 1988. "Self-Interest, Public Opinion, and Mass Political Behavior." Ph.D. diss., University of California, Berkeley.

Green, J., and J. J. Laffont. 1974. "On the Revelation of Preference for Public Goods." Technical Report No. 140. Institute for Mathematical Studies in the Social Sciences, Stanford University, Stanford, Calif.

Groves, T., and J. Ledyard. 1975. "Optimal Allocation of Public Goods: A Solution to the 'Free Rider Problem.'" Discussion Paper No. 144. Center for Mathematical Studies in Economics and Management Science, Northwestern University, Evanston, Ill.

Gunn, J. A. W. 1968. "'Interest Will Not Lie': A Seventeenth-Century Political Maxim." *Journal of the History of Ideas* 29:558.

———. 1969. *Politics and the Public Interest in the Seventeenth Century*. London: Routledge and Kegan Paul.

Guthrie, Woody. [1943] 1968. *Bound for Glory*. Reprint. New York: E. P. Dutton.

Habermas, Jurgen. [1968] 1971. *Knowledge and Human Interests*. Trans. Jeremy J. Shapiro. Boston: Beacon Press.

Hamilton, W. D. 1964. "The Genetical Theory of Social Behavior." *Journal of Theoretical Biology* 7:1–32.

———. 1975. "Innate Social Aptitudes in Man: An Approach from Evolutionary Genetics." In R. Fox, ed., *Biosocial Anthropology*. London: Malaby Press.

Hampton, Jean. 1986. *Hobbes and the Social Contract Tradition*. New York: Cambridge University Press.

Hanen, Marsha, and Kai Nielsen, eds. 1987. *Science, Morality and Feminist Theory*. Calgary, Alberta: University of Calgary Press.

Hardin, Garrett. 1968. "The Tragedy of the Commons." *Science* 162:1243–48.

Hardin, Russell. 1982. *Collective Action*. Baltimore: Johns Hopkins University Press.

———. 1988. *Morality within the Limits of Reason*. Chicago: University of Chicago Press.

Harrington, James. [1656] 1977. "The Commonwealth of Oceana." In John Pocock, ed., *The Political Works of James Harrington*. Cambridge: Cambridge University Press.

Harris, L., and Associates. 1973. *Confidence and Concern: Citizens View American Government*. U.S. Senate, Committee of Governmental Operations, Subcommittee on Intergovernmental Relations. Washington, D.C.

Harsanyi, John. 1955. "Cardinal Welfare, Individualistic Ethics, and Interpersonal Comparisons of Utility." *Journal of Political Economy* 63:315–21.

———. 1977. *Rational Behavior and Bargaining Equilibrium in Games and Social Situations*. Cambridge: Cambridge University Press.

———. 1980. "Rule Utilitarianism, Rights, Obligations, and the Theory of Rational Behavior." *Theory and Decision* 12:115–33.

Hart, H. L. A. 1961. *The Concept of Law*. Oxford: Oxford University Press.

Hartsock, Nancy. 1983. *Money, Sex, and Power: Toward a Feminist Historical Materialism*. New York: Longmans.

Havelock, Eric A. [1957] 1964. *The Liberal Temper in Greek Politics*. Reprint. New Haven: Yale University Press.

Hawthorne, M. R., and J. E. Jackson. 1987. "The Individual Political Economy of Federal Tax Policy." *American Political Science Review* 81:757–74.

Hechter, Michael. 1987. *Principles of Group Solidarity*. Berkeley: University of California Press.

Heider, F. 1958. *The Psychology of Interpersonal Relations*. New York: Wiley.

Heimer, Carol, and Arthur Stinchcombe. 1980. "Love and Irrationality: It's Got to Be Rational Because It Makes Me So Happy." *Social Science Information* 19:697–754.

Heinberg, John Gilbert. 1926. "History of the Majority Principle." *American Political Science Review* 20:52–68.

Held, Virginia. 1973–74. "Marx, Sex, and the Transformation of Society." *Philosophical Forum* 5:1–2.

———. 1987a. "Feminism and Moral Theory." In Eva Kittay and Diana Meyers, eds., *Women and Moral Theory*. Totowa, N.J.: Rowman and Littlefield.

———. 1987b. "Non-Contractual Society." In Marsha Hanen and Kai Nielsen, eds., *Science, Morality and Feminist Theory*. Calgary, Alberta: University of Calgary Press.

Herman, Barbara. 1983. "Integrity and Impartiality." *Monist* 66:233–50.

Herzberger, H. G. 1973. "Ordinal Preference and Rational Choice." *Econometrica* 41:187–237.

———. 1984. *Rights and Goods: Justifying Social Action*. New York: The Free Press.

Herzog, Don. 1989. *Happy Slaves*. Chicago: University of Chicago Press.

Heyd, David. 1982. *Supererogation*. Cambridge: Cambridge University Press.

Hilton, Walter. 1979. *The Stairway of Perfection*. New York: Doubleday.

Hirsch, Fred. 1976. *Social Limits to Growth*. Cambridge: Harvard University Press.

Hirschman, Albert O. [1945] 1980. *National Power and the Structure of Foreign Trade*. Berkeley: University of California Press.

———. 1973. "An Alternative Explanation of Contemporary Harriedness." In *Essays in Trespassing: Economics to Politics and Beyond*. Cambridge: Cambridge University Press, 1981.

———. 1977. *The Passions and the Interests: Political Arguments for Capitalism before Its Triumph*. Princeton: Princeton University Press.

———. 1981. "Morality and the Social Sciences: A Durable Tension." In *Essays in Trespassing: Economics to Politics and Beyond*. Cambridge: Cambridge University Press.

———. 1985. "Against Parsimony." *Economics and Philosophy* 1:7–21.

———. 1986. "The Concept of Interest: From Euphemism to Tautology." In *Rival Views of Market Society*. New York: Viking.

Hirshleifer, Jack. 1984. "The Emotions as Guarantors of Threats and Promises." UCLA Department of Economics Working Paper.

———. 1985. "The Expanding Domain of Economics." *American Economic Review* 75:53–70.

Hobbes, Thomas. [1651] 1947; 1950. *Leviathan*. London: J. M. Dent and Sons; New York: E. P. Dutton.

Hoess, R. 1959. *Commandant at Auschwitz: Autobiography*. London: Weidenfeld and Nicholson.

Hoffman, Martin L. 1981. "Is Altruism Part of Human Nature?" *Journal of Personality and Social Psychology* 40:121–37.

———. 1982. "Development of Prosocial Motivation: Empathy and Guilt." In Nancy Eisenberg, ed., *The Development of Prosocial Behavior*. New York: Academic Press.

———. 1987. "The Contribution of Empathy to Justice and Moral Judgment." In N. Eisenberg and J. Strayer, eds., *Empathy and Its Development*. New York: Cambridge University Press.

Hofstadter, Richard. 1955. *The Age of Reform*. New York: Vintage Books.

Hollis, M., and E. J. Nell. 1975. *Rational Economic Man*. New York: Cambridge University Press.

Holmes, Oliver Wendell. 1919. Opinion in *Abrams v. United States*, 250 U.S. 616:630.

Holmes, Stephen. 1988a. "Precommitment and the Paradox of Democracy." In J. Elster and R. Slagstaad, eds., *Constitutionalism and Democracy*. New York: Cambridge University Press.

———. 1988b. "Self-Interest in the *Wealth of Nations*." Typescript.

Hooker, Richard. [1907] 1954. *Of the Laws of Ecclesiastical Polity*. London: Everyman; New York: Dutton.

Houthakker, H. S. 1950. "Revealed Preference and the Utility Function." *Economica* 17:159–74.

Huddy, L. 1989. "Generational Agreement on Old Age Policies: Explanations Based on Realistic Interest, Symbolic Political Attitudes, and Age Identity." Ph.D. diss., Department of Psychology, University of California, Los Angeles.

Huddy, L., and D. O. Sears. 1989. "Opposition to Bilingual Education: Symbolic Racism or Realistic Group Conflict?" Typescript. Department of Psychology, University of California, Los Angeles.

Hume, David. [1739–40] 1888. *A Treatise of Human Nature*. Ed. L. A. Selby-Bigge. Oxford: Oxford University Press.

———. [1741] 1898. *Essays Moral, Political, and Literary*. Vol. 1. Ed. T. H. Green and T. H. Grose. London: Longmans.

———. [1748, 1751] 1966; 1975. *Enquiries concerning Human Understanding and concerning the Principles of Morals*. Ed. L. A. Selby-Bigge; 3rd edition ed. P. H. Nidditch. Oxford: Oxford University Press.

Hurwicz, L. 1972. "On Informationally Decentralized Systems." In R. Rader and B. McGuire, eds., *Decisions and Organizations*. Amsterdam: North-Holland Publishing.

Hutcheson, Francis. [1725] 1897. "An Inquiry Concerning Moral Good and Evil." In L. A. Selby-Bigge, M.A., *British Moralists*. Oxford: Clarendon Press.

———. [1728] 1969. *An Essay on the Nature and Conduct of the Passions and Affections*. 3d ed. Gainesville, Fla.: Scholars' Facsimiles and Reprints.

Inglehart, Ronald, and Jacques-Rene Rubier. 1978. "Economic Uncertainty and European Solidarity: Public Opinion Trends." *Annals of the American Academy of Political and Social Science* 440: 66–97.

Isaac, R. Mark, Kenneth F. McCue, and Charles R. Plott. 1985. "Public Goods: Provision in an Experimental Environment." *Journal of Public Economics* 26:51–74.

Jarvis, J. U. M. 1981. "Eusociality in a Mammal: Cooperative Breeding in Naked Mole Rat Colonies." *Science* 212:571–73.

Jefferson, Thomas. [1774–1826] 1953. *Farm Book*. Ed. Edwin Marry Betts. Princeton: Princeton University Press.

Jeffrey, R. C. 1974. "Preferences among Preferences." *Journal of Philosophy* 71:377–91.

Jellison, J. M., and J. Green. 1981. "A Self-Presentation Approach to the Fundamental Attribution Error: The Norm of Internality." *Journal of Personality and Social Psychology* 40:643–49.

Jenckins, J. Craig. 1981. "Sociopolitical Movements." In Samuel Long, ed., *The Handbook of Political Behavior,* vol. 4. New York: Plenum Press.

Jencks, Christopher. 1979. "The Social Basis of Unselfishness." In Herbert J. Gans, Nathan Glazer, Joseph Gusfield, and Christopher Jencks, eds., *On the Making of Americans: Essays in Honor of David Riesman.* Philadelphia: University of Pennsylvania Press.

———. 1987. "Who Gives to What?" In Walter W. Powell, ed., *The Nonprofit Sector: A Research Handbook.* New Haven: Yale University Press.

Jessor, T. 1988. "Personal Interest, Group Conflict, and Symbolic Group Affect: Explanations for Whites' Opposition to Racial Equality." Ph.D. diss., Department of Psychology, University of California, Los Angeles.

Johansen, L. 1966. *Public Economics.* Amsterdam: North-Holland Publishing.

———. 1976. "The Theory of Public Goods: Misplaced Emphasis." Typescript. Institute of Economics, University of Oslo.

Johnson, James. 1988. "Symbolic Action and the Limits of Strategic Rationality: On the Logic of Working Class Collective Action." In Maurice Zeitlin, ed., *Political Power and Social Theory,* vol. 7. Greenwich, Conn.: JAI Press.

Johnson, J., R. Johnson, E. Holubec, and P. Roy. 1984. *Circles of Learning: Cooperation in the Classroom.* Washington, D.C.: Association for Supervision and Curriculum Development.

Johnson, Samuel. [1751] 1958. "Rambler No. 183." In *Rasselas, Poems, and Selected Prose,* ed. Bertrand H. Bronson. New York: Holt, Rinehart, and Winston.

Kagan, Jerome. 1984. *The Nature of the Child.* New York: Basic Books.

Kahneman, Daniel, Jack L. Knetsch, and Richard Thaler. 1986a. "Fairness and the Assumptions of Economics." *Journal of Business* 59:285–300.

———. 1986b. "Fairness as a Constraint on Profit Seeking: Entitlements in the Market." *American Economic Review* 76:728–41.

Kahneman, D., P. Slovic, and A. Tversky, eds. 1982. *Judgment under Uncertainty: Heuristics and Biases.* New York: Cambridge University Press.

Kalt, Joseph, and Mark A. Zupan. 1984. "Capture and Ideology in the Economic Theory of Politics." *American Economic Review* 74:279–300.

———. Forthcoming. "The Apparent Ideological Behavior of Legislators." *Journal of Law and Economics.*

Kanger, S. 1976. "Choice Based on Preference." Typescript. Uppsala, Uppsala University, Sweden.

Kant, Immanuel. [1795] 1949. "Eternal Peace." In Carl J. Friedrich, ed., *The Philosophy of Kant: Immanuel Kant's Moral and Political Writings.* New York: Modern Library.

———. [1797] 1965. *The Metaphysical Elements of Justice.* Ed. John Ladd. Indianapolis: Bobbs-Merrill Educational Publishing.

Kanter, Rosabeth Moss. 1972. *Commitment and Community: Communes and Utopias in Sociological Perspective.* Cambridge: Harvard University Press.

Kaplan, H., and K. Hill. 1985. "Food Sharing among Ache Foragers: Tests of Explanatory Hypotheses." *Current Anthropology* 26:223–45.

Kau, James, and Paul Rubin. 1982. *Congressman, Constituents, and Contributors.* Boston: Martinus Nijhoff.

Kelman, Steven. 1987. *Making Public Policy: A Hopeful View of American Government.* New York: Basic Books.

———. 1988. "Why Public Ideas Matter." In Robert B. Reich, ed., *The Power of Public Ideas.* Cambridge, Mass.: Ballinger.

Kempis, Thomas A. 1984. *The Imitation of Christ.* Harmondsworth, England: Penguin.

Kendall, Wilmoore. 1965. *John Locke and the Doctrine of Majority Rule.* Urbana: University of Illinois Press.

Keohane, Nannerl O. 1980. *Philosophy and the State in France: The Renaissance to the Enlightenment.* Princeton: Princeton University Press.

Keohane, Robert O. 1984. *After Hegemony: Cooperation and Discord in the World Political Economy.* Princeton: Princeton University Press.

Keohane, Robert O., and Joseph S. Nye, eds. 1972. *Transnational Relations and World Politics.* Cambridge: Harvard University Press.

Kiewiet, D. Roderick. 1983. *Macroeconomics and Micropolitics: The Electoral Effects of Economic Issues.* Chicago: Chicago University Press.

Kiewiet, D. Roderick, and D. Rivers. 1984. "A Retrospective on Retrospective Voting." *Political Behavior* 6:369–93.

Kinder, Donald R., and D. Roderick Kiewiet. 1979. "Economic Discontent and Political Behavior: The Role of Personal Grievances and Collective Economic Judgments in Congressional Voting." *American Journal of Political Science* 23:495–527.

———. 1981. "Sociotropic Politics." *British Journal of Political Science* 11:129–61.

Kinder, Donald R., and W. R. Mebane, Jr. 1983. "Politics and Economics in Everyday Life." In K. R. Monroe, ed., *The Political Process and Economic Change.* New York: Agathon Press.

Kinder, Donald R., and D. O. Sears. 1981. "Prejudice and Politics: Symbolic Racism versus Racial Threats to the Good Life." *Journal of Personality and Social Psychology* 40:414–31.

———. 1985. "Public Opinion and Political Action." In G. Lindzey and E. Aronson, eds., *Handbook of Social Psychology,* vol. 2. 3rd ed. New York: Random House.

Kingdon, John W. 1988. "Ideas, Politics, and Public Policies." Paper delivered at the annual meeting of the American Political Science Association.

Kishlansky, Mark A. 1977. "The Emergence of Adversary Politics in the Long Parliament." *Journal of Modern History* 49:617–40.

———. 1986. *Parliamentary Selection.* Cambridge: Cambridge University Press.

Kittay, Eva Feder, and Diana T. Meyers, eds. 1987. *Women and Moral Theory.* Totowa, N.J.: Rowman and Littlefield.

Kluegel, J. R., and E. R. Smith. 1983. "Affirmative Action Attitudes: Effects of Self-interest, Racial Affect, and Stratification Beliefs on Whites' Views." *Social Forces* 61:797–824.

Knoke, David, and Christine Wright-Isak. 1982. "Individual Motives and Organizational Incentive Systems." *Research in the Sociology of Organizations* 1:209–54.

Knorr, Klaus. 1975. *The Power of Nations: The Political Economy of International Relations.* New York: Basic Books.

Kohlberg, Lawrence. 1981. *The Philosophy of Moral Development.* San Francisco: Harper and Row.

Kohlberg, Lawrence, and R. Kramer. 1969. "Continuities and Discontinuities in Child and Adult Moral Development." *Human Development* 12:93–120.

Kolm, Serge-Cristophe. 1983. "Altruism and Efficiency." *Ethics* 94:18–65.

Kornai, J. 1971. *Anti-Equilibrium.* Amsterdam: North-Holland Publishing.

Korner, S. 1971. *Experience and Conduct.* Cambridge: Cambridge University Press.

Kramer, G. H. 1971. "Short-term Fluctuations in U.S. Voting Behavior, 1896–1964." *American Political Science Review* 65:131–43.

———. 1983. "The Ecological Fallacy Revisited: Aggregate- versus Individual-Level Findings on Economics and Elections and Sociotropic Voting." *American Political Science Review* 77:92–111.

Kramer, R. M., and M. B. Brewer. 1986. "Social Group Identity and the Emergence of Cooperation in Resource Conservation Dilemmas." In H. Wilke, D. Messick, and C. Rutte, eds., *Experimental Social Dilemmas,* 205–34. Frankfurt am Main: Verlag Peter Lang.

———. Forthcoming. "Helping the Group or Helping Oneself? Cognitive-Motivational Determinants of Cooperation in Resource Conservation Dilemmas." In David Schoeder, ed., *Social Dilemmas: Social Psychological Perspectives* (tentative title).

Kramnick, Isaac. 1982. "Republican Revisionism Revisited." *American Historical Review* 87:629–64.

Krebs, Dennis L. 1970. "Altruism: An Examination of the Concept." *Psychological Bulletin* 73:258–302.

———. 1971. "Infrahuman Altruism." *Psychological Bulletin* 76:411–14.

———. 1982. "Psychological Approaches to Altruism: An Evaluation." *Ethics* 92:447–58.

Krebs, J. R., and N. B. Davies. 1981. *An Introduction to Behavioral Ecology.* Sunderland, Mass.: Sinauer.

Kreps, David M., Paul Milgrim, John Roberts, and Robert Wilson. 1982. "Rational Cooperation in the Finitely Repeated Prisoners' Dilemma." *Journal of Economic Theory* 27:245–52.

Kuhn, Thomas S. 1970. *The Structure of Scientific Revolutions.* 2d. ed. Chicago: University of Chicago Press.

Laffont, J. J. 1974. "Macroeconomic Constraints, Economic Efficiency and Ethics." Mimeo. Harvard University.

Landis, J. M., and L. Goodstein. 1986. "When Is Justice Fair? An Integrated Approach to the Outcome versus Procedure Debate." *American Bar Foundation Research Journal* 20:675–708.

Lane, Robert E. 1962. *Political Ideology: Why the American Common Man Believes What He Does.* Glencoe, Ill.: Free Press.

———. 1986. "Procedural Justice: How One Is Treated vs. What One Gets." Typescript. Department of Political Science, Yale University.

Langer, E. J. 1975. "The Illusion of Control." *Journal of Personality and Social Psychology* 32:311–28.

Latane, Bibb, and John M. Darley. 1970. *The Unresponsive Bystander: Why Doesn't He Help?* Englewood Cliffs, N.J.: Prentice-Hall.

Lau, R. R., Thad A. Brown, and David O. Sears. 1978. "Self-Interest and Civilians' Attitudes toward the Vietnam War." *Public Opinion Quarterly* 42:464–83.

Lau, R. R., R. F. Coulam, and D. O. Sears. 1983. "Proposition 2½ in Massachusetts: Self-Interest, Anti-Government Attitudes, and Political Schemas." Paper presented at the annual meeting of the Midwest Political Science Association.

Lau, R. R., and D. O. Sears. 1981. "Cognitive Links between Economic Grievances and Political Responses." *Political Behavior* 3: 279–302.

Lau, R. R., D. O. Sears, and T. Jessor. 1989. "Fact or Artifact Revisited: Survey Instrument Effects and Pocketbook Politics." Paper presented at the annual meeting of the Midwest Political Science Association.

Laver, Michael. 1981. *The Politics of Private Desire.* New York: Penguin.

Lea, S. E. G. 1978. "The Psychology and Economics of Demand." *Psychological Bulletin* 85:441–66.

Ledyard, John O. 1984. "The Pure Theory of Large Two Candidate Elections." *Public Choice* 44:7–41.

Ledyard, John O., and D. J. Roberts. 1974. "On the Incentive Problem for Public Goods." Discussion Paper No. 116. Center for Mathematical Studies in Economics and Management Science, Northwestern University.

Lee, R. 1979. *The Dobe !Kung.* New York: Holt, Reinhardt, and Winston.

Leibenstein, Harvey. 1966. "Allocative Efficiency vs. X-Efficiency." *American Economic Review* 56:392–415.

———. 1976. *Beyond Economic Man.* Cambridge: Harvard University Press.

Lerner, Melvin J. 1965. "The Effect of Responsibility and Choice on a Partner's Attractiveness Following Failure." *Journal of Personality and Social Psychology* 33:178–87.

———. 1980. *The Belief in a Just World: A Fundamental Delusion.* New York: Plenum Press.

Levin, B. R., and W. L. Kilmer. 1974. "Interdemic Selection and the Evolution of Altruism: A Computer Simulation Study." *Evolution* 28:527–45.

Levine, Michael. 1981. "Revisionism Revisited? Airline Deregulation and the Public Interest." *Journal of Law and Economics* 44:179–95.

LeVine, R. A., and D. T. Campbell. 1972. *Ethnocentrism: Theories of Conflict, Ethnic Attitudes, and Group Behavior.* New York: Wiley.

Lewis, Ewart. 1954. *Medieval Political Ideas.* Vol. 1. London: Routledge and Kegan Paul.

Lewis-Beck, M. S. 1985. "Pocketbook Voting in U.S. National Election Studies: Fact or Artifact?" *American Journal of Political Science* 29:348–56.

———. 1986. "Comparative Economic Voting: Britain, France, Germany, Italy." *American Journal of Political Science* 30:315–46.

"Lincoln's Theory of Selfishness." 1897. *The Outlook,* vol. 56.

Lind, E. A., R. J. MacCoun, P. A. Ebener, W. L. F. Felstiner, D. R. Hensler, J. Resnik, and T. R. Tyler. 1988. *The Perception of Justice: Tort Litigants' Views of*

Settlement Conferences, Court-Annexed Arbitration, and Trial. Santa Monica, Calif.: Institute for Civil Justice, Rand Corporation.

Lind, E. A., and T. R. Tyler. 1988. *The Social Psychology of Procedural Justice.* New York: Plenum.

Lindahl, E. 1919. *Die Gerechtigkeit der Besteurung.* Lund: Gleerup.

Linde, H. 1975. "Due Process of Lawmaking." *Nebraska Law Review* 55:197–255.

Lipset, S. M. 1981. *Political Man.* Baltimore: Johns Hopkins University Press.

Listhaug, D., and A. H. Miller. 1985. "Public Support for Tax Evasion: Self-Interest or Symbolic Politics?" *European Journal of Political Research* 13:265–82.

Locke, John. [1689] 1955. *A Letter Concerning Toleration.* Ed. Patrick Romanell. New York: Bobbs-Merrill.

———. [1689] 1965. *Two Treatises of Government.* Ed. Peter Laslett. New York: New American Library.

———. [1691] 1823. "Some Considerations of the Consequences of the Lowering of Interest." In *Works,* vol. 5. London: Thomas Tegg.

Lockridge, Kenneth A., and Alan Krieder. 1966. "The Evolution of Massachusetts Town Government, 1640–1740." *William and Mary Quarterly* 33:548–74.

Lovejoy, Arthur O. 1961. *Reflections on Human Nature.* Baltimore: John Hopkins University Press.

Luce, R. D., and H. Raiffa. 1957. *Games and Decisions: Introduction and Critical Survey.* New York: Wiley.

Luce, R. D., and P. Suppes. 1965. "Preference, Utility, and Subjective Probability." In R. D. Luce, R. R. Bush, and E. Galanter, eds., *The Handbook of Mathematical Psychology.* New York: Wiley.

Lumsden, C. J., and E. O. Wilson. 1981. *Genes, Mind, and Culture.* Cambridge: Harvard University Press.

Maass, Arthur. 1983. *Congress and the Common Good.* New York: Basic Books.

Mabbott, J. D. 1971. "Is Plato's *Republic* Utilitarian?" Revised for Gregory Vlatos, ed., *Plato: A Collection of Critical Essays.* Notre Dame, Ind.: University of Notre Dame Press. Originally published in *Mind,* n.s. (1937):386–93.

Macaulay, J., and L. Berkowitz. 1970. *Altruism and Helping Behavior.* New York: Academic Press.

Macaulay, Thomas. 1978. "Mill's Essay on Government: Utilitarian Logic and Politics." In J. Liveley and J. Rees, eds., *Utilitarian Logic and Politics.* Oxford: Clarendon Press.

Mackie, J. L. 1977. *Ethics: Inventing Right and Wrong.* Harmondsworth, England: Penguin Books.

McClelland, David. 1975. *Power: the Inner Experience.* New York: Irvington Publishers.

McClelland, David, and R. I. Watson, Jr. 1973. "Power Motivation and Risk-taking Behavior." *Journal of Personality* 41:121–39.

McClendon, M. J. 1985. "Racism, Rational Choice, and White Opposition to Racial Change: A Case Study of Busing." *Public Opinion Quarterly* 49:214–33.

McClendon, M. J., and F. P. Pestello. 1983. "Self-Interest and Public Policy Attitude Formation: Busing for School Desegregation." *Sociological Focus* 16:1–12.

McClintock, Martha. 1981. "Social Control of the Ovarian Cycle." *American Zoologist* 21:243–56.

———. 1987. "A Functional Approach to the Behavioral Endocrinology of Rodents." In David Crews, ed., *Psychology of Reproductive Behavior: An Evolutionary Perspective*. Englewood Cliffs, N.J.: Prentice-Hall.

McConahay, J. B. 1982. "Self-Interest versus Racial Attitudes as Correlates of Anti-Busing Attitudes in Louisville: Is It the Buses or the Blacks?" *Journal of Politics* 44:692–720.

MacCoun, R. 1988. "Perspectives on Procedure: Arbitration Hearings as Viewed by Plaintiffs, Defendants, and Their Attorneys." Paper presented at the annual meeting of the Law and Society Association, Vail, Colo.

Macey, J. 1987. "Competing Economic Views of the Constitution." *George Washington Law Review* 56:50–80.

McFadden, D. 1975. "Economic Applications of Psychological Choice Models." Paper presented at the Third World Economic Congress.

McGuire, Michael, M. Raleigh, and G. Brammer. 1982. "Sociopharmacology." *Annual Review of Pharmacological Toxicology* 22:643–61.

MacIver, Robert. 1947. *The Web of Government*. New York: Macmillan.

MacLean, Paul D. 1973. *A Triune Concept of the Brain and Behavior*. Toronto: University of Toronto Press.

McPherson, Michael S. 1984. "Limits on Self-Seeking: The Role of Morality in Economic Life." In David C. Colander, eds., *Neo-classical Political Economy*. Cambridge, Mass.: Ballinger.

Madison, James, Alexander Hamilton, and John Jay. [1787–88] 1987. *The Federalist Papers*. Ed. Isaac Kramnick. New York: Penguin.

Madsen, Douglas. 1985. "A Biochemical Property Relating to Power Seeking in Humans." *American Political Science Review* 79:448–57.

———. 1986. "Power Seekers Are Different: Further Biochemical Evidence." *American Political Science Review* 80:261–70.

Mahowald, Mary, ed. 1978. *Philosophy of Women: Classical to Current Concepts*. Indianapolis: Hackett.

Majumadar, T. 1976. "The Concept of Man in Political Economy and Economics." Mimeo. New Delhi: Jawaharlal Nehru University.

Malinvaud, E. 1971. "A Planning Approach to the Public Goods Problem." *Swedish Journal of Economics* 73:96–112.

———. 1972. "Prices for Individual Consumption, Quantity Indicators for Collective Consumption." *Review of Economic Studies* 39:385–406.

Mannheim, Karl. [1936] 1966. *Ideology and Utopia*. Reprint. New York: Harcourt, Brace and World.

Mansbridge, Jane J. [1980] 1983. *Beyond Adversary Democracy*. Reprint with new preface. Chicago: University of Chicago Press.

———. 1985. "Myth and Reality: The ERA and the Gender Gap in the 1980 Election." *Public Opinion Quarterly* 49:164–78.

———. 1986. *Why We Lost the ERA*. Chicago: University of Chicago Press.

———. 1988. "Motivating Deliberation in Congress." In Sarah Baumgartner Thurow, ed., *Constitutionalism in America*, vol. 2. New York: University Press of America.

Marglin, S. A. 1974. "What Do Bosses Do? The Origins and Functions of Hierarchy in Capitalist Production." *Review of Radical Political Economics* 6:60–112.

Margolis, Howard. 1977. "Probability of a Tie Vote." *Public Choice* 31:135–38.

———. [1982] 1984. *Selfishness, Altruism, and Rationality: A Theory of Social Choice.* Reprint. Chicago: University of Chicago Press.

———. 1987. *Patterns, Thinking and Cognition.* Chicago: University of Chicago Press.

Marris, R. 1964. *The Economic Theory of Managerial Capitalism.* London: Macmillan.

Marwell, Gerald, and Ruth Ames. 1979. "Experiments on the Provision of Public Goods. I. Resources, Interest, Group Size, and the Free-Rider Problem." *American Journal of Sociology* 84:1335–60.

———. 1981. "Economists Free Ride; Does Anyone Else?" *Journal of Public Economics* 15:295–310.

Marx, Karl. 1978. "On the Jewish Question." In Robert Tucker, ed., *The Marx-Engels Reader.* New York: Norton.

Marx, Karl, and Friedrich Engel. [1848] 1954. *The Communist Manifesto.* Reprint. Chicago: Regnery.

Maslow, Abraham H. [1954] 1970. *Motivation and Personality.* 2nd ed. New York: Harper and Row.

Mayer, Lawrence S., and I. J. Good. 1975. "Is Minimax Regret Applicable to Voting Decisions?" *American Political Science Review* 69:916–17.

Mayhew, David R. 1974. *Congress: The Electoral Connection.* New Haven: Yale University Press.

Meggit, M. 1977. *Blood Is Their Argument.* Palo Alto, Calif.: Mayfield.

Merry, S. E. 1985. "Concepts of Law and Justice among Working-Class Americans: Ideology as Culture." *Legal Studies Forum* 9:59–69.

———. 1986. "Everyday Understandings of the Law in Working-Class America." *American Ethnologist* 13:253–70.

Merry, S. E., and S. Silbey. 1984. "What Do Plaintiffs Want? Reexamining the Concept of Dispute." *Justice System Journal* 9:151–78.

Mill, James. [1819] 1955. *An Essay on Government.* Indianapolis: Bobbs-Merrill.

Mill, John Stuart. [1835, 1840] 1977. "Tocqueville on Democracy in America [I] and [II]." In J. M. Robson, ed., *Essays on Politics and Society.* Toronto: University of Toronto Press.

———. [1838] 1969. "Bentham." In J. M Robson, ed., *Essays on Ethics, Religion and Society.* Toronto: University of Toronto Press.

———. [1859] 1947. *On Liberty.* New York: Appleton-Century-Crofts.

———. [1859] 1977. "Thoughts on Parliamentary Reform." In J. M. Robson, ed., *Essays on Politics and Society.* Toronto: University of Toronto Press.

———. [1861] 1969. "Utilitarianism." In J. M. Robson, ed., *Essays on Ethics, Religion and Society.* Toronto: University of Toronto Press.

———. [1861] 1977. "Considerations on Representative Government." In J. M. Robson, ed., *Essays on Politics and Society.* Toronto: University of Toronto Press.

———. [1865] 1968. *Auguste Comte and Positivism.* Ann Arbor: University of Michigan Press.

Miller, G. 1987. "The True Story of Carolene Products." *Supreme Court Review*, 397–428.

Mirrlees, J. A. 1973. "The Economics of Charitable Contributions." Paper presented at the Econometric Society European Meeting, Oslo.

Mischel, Walter. 1968. *Personality and Assessment*. New York: Wiley.

Monroe, Kristin Renwick. 1979. "Econometric Analyses of Electoral Behavior: A Critical Review." *Political Behavior* 1:137–73.

———. 1987. "Altruism and Rationality: The Challenge for Political Economy." Paper delivered at the annual meeting of the American Political Science Association.

———. 1988a. "A Far Better Thing: Selfless Behavior, Rationality, and Perception." Paper delivered at the annual meeting of the American Political Science Association.

———. 1988b. "A Fat Lady in a Corset." Paper delivered at the annual meeting of the Midwest Political Science Association.

Monroe, Kristin Renwick, Michael C. Barton and Ute Klingemann. 1988. "Altruism and the Theory of Rational Action: An Analysis of Rescuers of Jews in Nazi-Europe." Paper delivered at the Conference on the Economic Approach to Politics, University of California, Irvine.

Montesquieu, Baron de. [1748] 1951. "De l'esprit des lois." In *Oeuvres complètes*. Paris: Pléiade.

Morgenthau, Hans J. [1948] 1966. *Politics Among Nations*. 4th ed. New York: Knopf.

Mueller, Dennis C. 1979. *Public Choice*. Cambridge: Cambridge University Press.

———. 1986. "Rational Egoism vs. Adaptive Egoism." *Public Choice* 51:3–23.

———. 1989. *Public Choice II*. Cambridge: Cambridge University Press.

Mueller, J. E. 1973. *War, Presidents, and Public Opinion*. New York: John Wiley and Sons.

Muir, William K., Jr. 1982. *Legislature: California's School for Politics*. Chicago: University of Chicago Press.

Muller, E. N., and T. O. Jukam. 1977. "On the Meaning of Political Support." *American Political Science Review* 71:1561–95.

Musgrave, R. 1959. *The Theory of Public Finance*. New York: McGraw-Hill.

Myers, Milton L. 1983. *The Soul of Modern Economic Man: Ideas of Self-Interest, Thomas Hobbes to Adam Smith*. Chicago: University of Chicago Press.

Nagel, Thomas. 1970. *The Possibility of Altruism*. Oxford: Oxford University Press.

Nelson, Douglas, and Eugene Silberberg. 1987. "Ideology and Legislator Shirking." *Economic Inquiry* 25:15–28.

Noll, Roger G., and Bruce M. Owen. 1983. *The Political Economy of Deregulation: Interest Groups in the Regulatory Process*. Washington, D.C.: American Enterprise Institute.

Nozick, Robert. 1974. *Anarchy, State, and Utopia*. New York: Basic Books.

Nunney, L. 1985. "Group Selection, Altruism, and Structured Deme Models." *American Naturalist* 126:212–30.

Nutzinger, H. G. 1976. "The Firm as a Social Institution: The Failure of a Contractarian Viewpoint." Working Paper No. 52. Alfred Weber Institute, University of Heidelberg.

Oberschall, Anthony. 1973. *Social Conflict and Social Movements*. Engelwood Cliffs, N.J.: Prentice-Hall.

Offe, Claus, and Helmut Wiesenthal. 1980. "Two Logics of Collective Action: Theoretical Notes on Social Class and Organizational Form." In Maurice Zeitlin, ed., *Political Power and Social Theory*, vol. 1. Greenwich, Conn.: JAI Press.

Okin, Susan Moller. 1979. *Women in Western Political Thought*. Princeton: Princeton University Press.

Okun, Arthur. 1981. *Equality and Efficiency*. Washington, D.C.: Brookings.

Oliner, Samuel P., and Pearl M. Oliner. 1988. *The Altruistic Personality*. New York: Free Press.

Olson, Mancur. [1965] 1971. *The Logic of Collective Action*. Reprint. Cambridge: Harvard University Press.

———. 1982. *The Rise and Decline of Nations*. New Haven: Yale University Press.

Oppenheimer, Joe A., Norman Frolich, and Cheryl Eavy. 1986. "Laboratory Results on Rawls' Principle of Distributive Justice." *British Journal of Political Science* 17:1–21.

———. 1987. "Choices of Principles of Distributive Justice in Experimental Groups." *American Journal of Political Science* 31:606–36.

Orbell, J. M., A. J. C. van de Kragt, and R. M. Dawes. 1988. "Explaining Discussion-induced Cooperation in Social Dilemmas." *Journal of Personality and Social Psychology* 54:811–19.

Orren, Gary R. 1988. "Beyond Self-Interest." In Robert B. Reich, ed., *The Power of Public Ideas*. Cambridge, Mass.: Ballinger.

Osgood, Robert E. 1953. *Ideals and Self-Interest in American Foreign Relations*. Chicago: University of Chicago Press.

Otterbein, K. F. 1968. "Internal War: A Cross-Cultural Study." *American Anthropologist* 70:277–89.

Pangle, T. 1988. *The Spirit of Modern Republicanism*. Chicago: University of Chicago Press.

Parfit, Derek. 1984. *Reasons and Persons*. Oxford: Clarendon Press.

Pateman, Carole. 1985. *The Problem of Political Obligation: A Critique of Liberal Theory*. Berkeley: University of California Press.

Pattanaik, P. K. 1975. "Strategic Voting without Collusion under Binary and Democratic Group Decision Rules." *Review of Economic Studies* 42:93–104.

Pearson, Lionel. 1962. *Popular Ethics in Ancient Greece*. Stanford, Calif.: Stanford University Press.

Peleg, B. 1976. "Consistent Voting Systems." Institute of Mathematics, Hebrew University, Jerusalem.

Peltzman, Sam. 1976. "Toward a More General Theory of Regulation." *Journal of Law and Economics* 19:211–40.

———. 1984. "Constituent Interest and Congressional Voting." *Journal of Law and Economics* 27:187–210.

Peoples, J. E. 1982. "Individual or Group Advantage? A Reinterpretation of the Mating Ritual Cycle." *Current Anthropology* 23:291–310.

Peterson, Susan. "Against Parenting." In Joyce Treblicot, ed., *Mothering: Essays in Feminist Theory*. Totowa, N.J.: Rowman.

Phelps, E. S., ed. 1975. *Altruism, Morality, and Economic Theory.* New York: Russell Sage.

Piercy, Marge. 1976. *Woman on the Edge of Time.* New York: Fawcett.

Pitkin, Hanna Fenichel. 1964. Hobbes's Concept of Representation, I and II." *American Political Science Review* 58:328–40, 902–18.

———. 1981. "Justice: On Relating Public and Private." *Political Theory* 9:327–52.

———. 1984. *Fortune Is a Woman.* Berkeley: University of California Press.

Pitkin, Hanna Fenichel, and Sara M. Shumer. 1982. "On Participation." *Democracy* 2:43–54.

Plato. 1961. *Collected Dialogues.* Ed. Edith Hamilton and Huntington Cairns. Princeton: Princeton University Press.

Pocock, J. G. A. 1975. *The Machiavellian Moment.* Princeton: Princeton University Press.

Pollak, R. A. 1976. "Interdependent Preferences." *American Economic Review* 66:309–20.

Pollock, Gregory B. 1988. "Population Structure, Spite, and the Iterated Prisoner's Dilemma." *American Journal of Physical Anthropology* 77:459–69.

Ponza, M., G. J. Duncan, M. Corcoran, and F. Groskind. 1988. "The Guns of Autumn? Age Differences in Support for Income Transfers to the Young and Old." *Public Opinion Quarterly* 52:441–66.

Pope, Alexander. [1733] 1966. "An Essay on Man." In Herbert Davis, ed., *Pope Poetical Works.* New York: Oxford University Press.

Posner, Richard A. 1974a. "The DeFunis Case and the Preferential Treatment of Minorities." *Supreme Court Review* 1974:1–32.

———. 1974b. "Theories of Economic Regulation." *Bell Journal of Economics and Management Science* 5:335–58.

———. 1977, 1986. *Economic Analysis of Law.* 2d and 3rd eds. Boston: Little Brown.

Prais, S. J., and H. S. Houthakker. 1955. *The Analysis of Family Budgets.* Cambridge: Cambridge University Press.

Pulliam, H. R., and C. Dunford. 1980. *Programmed to Learn: An Essay on the Evolution of Culture.* New York: Columbia University Press.

Purcell, Edward, Jr. 1973. *The Crisis in Democratic Theory: Scientific Naturalism and the Problem of Value.* Lexington: University of Kentucky Press.

Quattrone, George A., and Amos Tversky. 1984. "Causal versus Diagnostic Contingencies: On Self-Deception and on the Voter's Illusion." *Journal of Personality and Social Psychology* 46:237–48.

———. 1988. "Contrasting Rational and Psychological Analyses of Political Choice." *American Political Science Review* 82:719–36.

Quirk, Paul J. 1988. "In Defense of the Politics of Ideas." *Journal of Politics* 50:31–41.

Radke-Yarrow, Marian, Carolyn Zahn-Waxler, and Michael Chapman. 1983. "Children's Prosocial Dispositions and Behavior." In P. H. Mussened, ed., *Handbook of Child Psychology,* vol. 4. 4th ed. New York: John Wiley and Sons.

Rapoport, Anatol. 1960. *Fights, Games and Debates.* Ann Arbor: University of Michigan Press.

Rapoport, Anatol, and A. M. Chammah. 1965. *Prisoner's Dilemma.* Ann Arbor: University of Michigan Press.

Rasinski, K. A. 1987. "What's Fair Is Fair—or Is It? Value Differences Underlying Public Views about Social Justice." *Journal of Personality and Social Psychology* 53:201–11.

Rasinski, K. A., and T. R. Tyler. 1988. "Fairness and Vote Choice in the 1984 Presidential Election." *American Politics Quarterly* 16:5–24.

Rawls, John. 1971. *A Theory of Justice.* Cambridge: Harvard University Press.

Reich, Robert B., ed. 1988. *The Power of Public Ideas.* Cambridge, Mass.: Ballinger.

Rice, Otis. 1982. *The Hatfields and McCoys.* Lexington: University of Kentucky Press.

Richards, David A. J. 1971. *A Theory of Reasons for Action.* New York: Oxford University Press.

Richerson, P. J., and R. Boyd. 1987. "Simple Models of Complex Phenomena: The Case of Cultural Evolution." In J. Dupré, ed., *The Latest on the Best: Essays on Evolution and Optimality.* Cambridge: MIT Press.

———. 1989. "The Role of Evolved Predispositions in Cultural Evolution: Or Human Sociobiology Meets Pascal's Wager." *Ethology and Sociobiology* 10:195–215.

Richter, M. K. 1971. "Rational Choice." In J. S. Chipman et al., eds., *Preference, Utility and Demand Theory.* New York: Harcourt, Brace, Jovanovich.

Riker, William H., and Peter C. Ordeshook. 1968. "A Theory of the Calculus of Voting." *American Political Science Review* 62:25–42.

———. 1973. *An Introduction to Positive Political Theory.* Englewood Cliffs, N.J.: Prentice-Hall.

Riskin, C. 1973. "Maoism and Motivation: A Discussion of Work Motivation in China." *Bulletin of Concerned Asian Scholars* 5:10–24.

Rist, J. M. 1969. *Stoic Philosophy.* Cambridge: Cambridge University Press.

Robinson, Joan. 1969. *The Cultural Revolution in China.* Harmondsworth, England: Penguin.

Rodgers, Daniel T. 1987. *Contested Truths.* New York: Basic Books.

Rogers, A. 1988. "Does Biology Constrain Culture?" *American Anthropologist* 90:819–31.

———. Forthcoming. "Group Selection by Selective Emigration: The Effects of Migration and Kin Structure." *American Naturalist.*

Rogowski, Ronald. 1981. "Representation in Political Theory and in Law." *Ethics* 91:395–430.

Rousseau, Jean-Jacques. [1755] 1964. "Discours sur l'origine de l'inégalité." In Bernard Gagnebin and Marcel Raymond, eds., *Oeuvres complètes.* Paris: Pleiade.

———. [1762] 1911. *Emile.* Trans. B. Foxley. New York: Dutton.

———. [1762] 1947. *The Social Contract.* New York: Hafner.

Rubin, Paul, and Chris Paul. 1979. "An Evolutionary Model of Taste for Risk." *Economic Enquiry* 17:585–96.

Ruddick, Sara. 1984. "Maternal Thinking." In Joyce Treblicot, ed., *Mothering: Essays in Feminist Theory.* Totowa, N.J.: Rowman.

Ruggie, John Gerard. 1983. *The Antimonies of Interdependence: National Welfare and the International Economy.* New York: Columbia University Press.

Runciman, W. G., and A. K. Sen. 1965. "Games, Justice and the General Will." *Mind* 74:554–62.

Rushton, J. Phillippe. 1982. "Altruism and Society: A Social Learning Perspective." *Ethics* 92:425–46.

Russett, Bruce M., and Elizabeth C. Hanson. 1975. *Interest and Ideology: The Foreign Policy Beliefs of American Businessmen.* San Francisco: W. H. Freeman.

Sager, L. 1978. "Fair Measure: The Legal Status of Underenforced Constitutional Norms." *Harvard Law Review* 91:1212–64.

Sahlins, Marshall. 1972. *Stone Age Economics.* Chicago: Aldine-Atherton.

Sampson, E. E. 1977. "Psychology and the American Ideal." *Journal of Personality and Social Psychology* 35:767–82.

———. 1983. *Justice and the Critique of Pure Psychology.* New York: Plenum.

Samuelson, P. A. 1950. "The Problem of Integrability in Utility Theory." *Economica* 17:355–85.

———. 1954. "The Pure Theory of Public Expenditure." *Review of Economics and Statistics* 36:387–89.

———. 1955. *The Foundation of Economics.* Cambridge: Harvard University Press.

———. 1956. "Social Indifference Curves." *Quarterly Journal of Economics* 70:1–22.

Sandel, Michael J. 1982. *Liberalism and the Limits of Justice.* Cambridge: Cambridge University Press.

Sanders, J., and L. Hamilton. 1987. "Is There a 'Common Law' of Responsibility?" *Law and Human Behavior* 11:277–97.

Sarat, A. 1977. "Surveying American Legal Culture: An Assessment of Survey Evidence." *Law and Society Review* 11:427–88.

Satterthwaite, M. A. 1975. "Strategy-Proofness and Arrow's Conditions: Existence and Correspondence Theorems for Voting Procedures and Social Welfare Functions." *Journal of Economic Theory* 10:187–217.

Savage, L. J. 1954. *The Foundations of Statistics.* New York: Wiley.

Schelling, Thomas C. [1960] 1963. *The Strategy of Conflict.* Reprint. Cambridge: Harvard University Press.

———. 1978a. "Altruism, Meanness, and Other Potentially Strategic Behaviors." *American Economic Review* 68:229–30.

———. 1978b. *Micromotives and Macrobehavior.* New York: W. W. Norton.

Schick, F. 1976. "Rationality and Sociality." Mimeo. Philosophy of Science Association, Rutgers University, New Brunswick, N.J. Later expanded into *Having Reasons: An Essay on Rationality and Sociality.* Princeton: Princeton University Press, 1984.

Schlozman, K. L., and S. Verba. 1979. *Injury to Insult: Unemployment, Class, and Political Response.* Cambridge: Harvard University Press.

Schmalensee, Richard. 1978. "Entry Dererrence in the Ready to Eat Cereal Industry." *Bell Journal of Economics* 9:305–27.

Schmeidler, D., and H. Sonnenschein. 1974. "The Possibility of Nonmanipulable Social Choice Functions." Northwestern University Center for Mathematical Studies in Economics and Management Science, Evanston, Ill.

Schumpeter, Joseph A. [1942] 1962. *Capitalism, Socialism and Democracy.* Reprint. New York: Harper and Row.

Schwartz, Barry. 1986. *The Battle for Human Nature.* New York: W. W. Norton.

Schwartz, Nancy L. 1988. *The Blue Guitar.* Chicago: University of Chicago Press.

Schwartz, R. D. 1978. "Moral Order and Sociology of Law." *Annual Review of Sociology* 4:577–601.

Schwartz, R. D., and S. Orleans. 1967. "On Legal Sanctions." *University of Chicago Law Review* 34:274–300.

Schwartz, T. 1986. "Von Wright's Theory of Human Welfare: A Critique." In L. A. Hahn and P. A. Schilpp, ed., *The Philosophy of Georg Henrik von Wright.* LaSalle, Ill.: Open Court/Library of Living Philosophers.

Schwartz, Thomas. 1987. "Your Vote Counts on Account of the Way It Is Counted: An Institutional Solution to the Paradox of Not Voting." *Public Choice* 54:101–21.

Scitovsky, T. 1976. *The Joyless Economy: An Inquiry into Human Satisfaction and Consumer Dissatisfaction.* London and New York: Oxford University Press.

Sears, D. O. 1975. "Political Socialization." In F. I. Greenstein and N. W. Polsby, eds., *Handbook of Political Science,* 2:93–153. Reading, Mass.: Addison-Wesley.

———. 1983. "The Persistence of Early Political Predispositions: The Roles of Attitude Object and Life Stage." In L. Wheeler and P. Shaver, eds., *Review of Personality and Social Psychology,* 4:79–116. Beverly Hills, Calif.: Sage Publications.

Sears, D. O., and H. M. Allen, Jr. 1984. "The Trajectory of Local Desegregation Controversies and Whites' Opposition to Busing." In N. Miller and M. B. Brewer, eds., *Groups in Contact: The Psychology of Desegregation,* 123–51. New York: Academic Press.

Sears, D. O., C. P. Hensler, and L. K. Speer. 1979. "Whites' Opposition to 'Busing': Self-Interest or Symbolic Politics?" *American Political Science Review* 73:369–84.

Sears, D. O., and L. Huddy. 1987. "Bilingual Education: Symbolic Meaning and Support among Non-Hispanics." Paper presented at the annual meetings of the American Psychological Association and the American Political Science Association.

———. 1990. "On the Origins of the Political Disunity of Women." In P. Gurin and L. Tilly, eds., *Women in Twentieth Century American Politics.* New York: Russell Sage Foundation.

Sears, D. O., and D. R. Kinder. 1971. "Racial Tensions and Voting in Los Angeles." In W. Z. Hirsch, ed., *Los Angeles: Viability and Prospects for Metropolitan Leadership.* New York: Praeger.

———. 1985. "Whites' Opposition to Busing: On Conceptualizing and Operationalizing Group Conflict." *Journal of Personality and Social Psychology* 48:1141–47.

Sears, D. O., and R. R. Lau. 1983. "Inducing Apparently Self-Interested Political Preferences." *American Journal of Political Science* 27:223–52.

Sears, D. O., R. R. Lau, T. R. Tyler, and H. M. Allen, Jr. 1980. "Self-Interest vs. Symbolic Politics in Policy Attitudes and Presidential Voting." *American Political Science Review* 74:670–84.

Sears, D. O., L. Steck, R. R. Lau, and M. T. Gahart. 1983. "Attitudes of the Post-Vietnam Generation toward the Draft and American Military Policy." Paper presented at the annual meeting of the International Society of Political Psychology, Oxford, England.

Sears, D. O., T. R. Tyler, J. Citrin, and D. R. Kinder. 1978. "Political System Support and Public Response to the 1974 Energy Crisis." *American Journal of Political Science* 22:56–82.

Selby-Bigge, L. A. [1893] 1975. "Introduction." In David Hume, *Enquiries concerning Human Understanding and concerning the Principles of Morals.* 3rd edition, ed. P. H. Nedditch. Oxford: Oxford University Press.

———. 1897. *British Moralists.* Oxford: Clarendon Press.

Sen, Amartya. 1966. "Labour Allocation in a Co-operative Enterprise." *Review of Economic Studies* 33:361–71.

———. 1967. "Isolation, Assurance and the Social Rate of Discount." *Quarterly Journal of Economics* 80:112–24.

———. 1970. *Collective Choice and Social Welfare.* San Francisco: Holden-Day.

———. 1971. "Choice Functions and Revealed Preference." *Review of Economic Studies* 38:307–18.

———. 1973a. "Behavior and the Concept of Preference." *Economica* 40:241–59.

———. 1973b. *On Economic Inequality.* Oxford: Clarendon Press.

———. 1974. "Choice, Orderings and Morality." In S. Korner, ed., *Practical Reason.* Oxford: Clarendon Press.

———. 1976. "Liberty, Unanimity and Rights." *Economica* 43:217–45.

———. 1977. "Rationality and Morality: A Reply." *Erkenntnis* 11:225–32.

———. 1985. "Goals, Commitment, and Identity." *Journal of Law, Economics and Organization* 1:341–55.

———. 1987. *On Ethics and Economics.* Oxford: Blackwell.

Seneca. 1970. "On Anger." In *Moral Essays,* vol. 1. Trans. and ed. John Basore. Cambridge: Harvard University Press.

Shaftesbury, Anthony Ashley Cooper, Third Earl of. [1711] 1737–38. *Characteristicks.* 3 vols. London: J. Purser. Also excerpted in L. A. Selby-Bigge, M.A., ed., *British Moralists.* Oxford: Clarendon Press, 1897.

Shapiro, R. Y., and H. Mahajan. 1986. "Gender Differences in Policy Preferences: A Summary of Trends from the 1960s to the 1980s." *Public Opinion Quarterly* 50:42–61.

Shaw, G. B. [1901] 1966. *Three Plays for Puritans.* Harmondsworth, England: Penguin.

Sidgwick, H. [1874.] 1907. *The Method of Ethics.* 7th ed. London: Macmillan.

Silberston, A. 1970. "Price Behaviour of Firms." *Economic Journal* 80:511–75.

Simon, H. 1957. *Models of Man.* New York: Wiley.

———. 1979. "Rational Decision-making in Business Organizations." *American Economic Review* 69:493–513.

———. 1985. "Human Nature in Politics: The Dialogue of Psychology with Political Science." *American Political Science Review* 79:293–304.

Sinclair, Barbara. 1983. *Majority Leadership in the U.S. House*. Baltimore: Johns Hopkins University Press.

Skinner, Quentin. 1966. "The Ideological Content of Hobbes's Political Thought." *Historical Journal* 9:286–317.

Slatkin, M., and M. J. Wade. 1978. "Group Selection on a Quantitative Character." *Proceedings of the National Academy of Sciences* 75:3531–34.

Slavin, R. E. 1983. *Cooperative Learning*. New York: Longman.

Smith, Adam. [1759] 1966; 1976. *The Theory of Moral Sentiments*. New York: Augustus M. Kelley; D. D. Raphaek and A. L. Macfie, eds., Oxford: Clarendon Press.

———. [1776] 1937. *The Wealth of Nations*. New York: Random House.

Smith, Steven S., and Christopher J. Deering. 1984. *Committees in Congress*. Washington, D.C.: Congressional Quarterly Press.

Smith, V. L. 1976. "Incentive Compatible Experimental Processes for the Provision of Public Goods." Mimeo. Economic Society Summer Meeting, Madison, Wisc.

Sniderman, P. M., and R. A. Brody. 1977. "Coping: The Ethic of Self-Reliance." *American Journal of Political Science* 21:501–21.

Sorauf, Frank H. 1957. "The Public Interest Reconsidered." *Journal of Politics* 29:616–39.

Spencer, H. [1879] 1887. *The Data of Ethics*. London: Williams and Norgate.

Spitz, Elaine. 1984. *Majority Rule*. Chatham, N.J.: Chatham House.

Spragens, Thomas A., Jr. 1973. *The Politics of Motion*. Lexington: University Press of Kentucky.

Stack, Carol B. 1975. *All Our Kin: Strategies for Survival in a Black Community*. New York: Harper and Row.

Staub, Ervin, Daniel Bar-Tal, Jerzy Karylowski, and Janusz Reykowsk, eds. 1984. *Development and Maintenance of Prosocial Behavior: International Perspectives on Positive Morality*. New York: Plenum Press.

Stephens, Stephen V. 1975. "The Paradox of Not Voting: Comment." *American Journal of Political Science* 69:914–15.

Steuart, James. [1767] 1966. *An Inquiry into the Principles of Political Economy*. Ed. Andrew S. Skinner. Chicago: University of Chicago Press.

Stigler, G. 1971. "The Theory of Economic Regulation." *Bell Journal of Economics and Management Science* 2:3–21.

———. 1972. "Economic Competition and Political Competition." *Public Choice* 13:91–106.

———. 1975. "Smith's Travels on the Ship of State." In A. Skinner and T. Wilson, eds., *Essays on Adam Smith*. Oxford: Clarendon Press.

———. 1981. "Economics or Ethics?" In Sterling M. McMurrin, ed., *The Tanner Lectures on Human Values,* vol. 2. Cambridge: Cambridge University Press.

Still, Jonathan W. 1981. "Political Equality and Election Systems." *Ethics* 91:375–94.

Strauss, Leo. 1973. *The Political Philosophy of Hobbes*. Chicago: University of Chicago Press.

Strom, Gerald S. 1975. "On the Apparent Paradox of Participation: A New Proposal." *American Journal of Political Science* 69:908–13.

Sunstein, C. 1984. "Naked Preferences and the Constitution." *Columbia Law Review* 84:1689–1732.

———. 1985. "Interest Groups in American Public Law." *Stanford Law Review* 38:29–58.

———. 1987. "Lochner's Legacy." *Columbia Law Review* 87:873–919.

Susskind, Lawrence, and Jeffrey Cruikshank. 1987. *Breaking the Impasse: Consensual Approaches to Resolving Public Disputes.* New York: Basic Books.

Suzumura, K. 1976. "Rational Choice and Revealed Preference." *Review of Economic Studies* 43:149–58.

Tajfel, H. 1974. "Social Identity and Intergroup Behavior." *Social Science Information* 13:65–93.

———. 1982. *Social Identity and Intergroup Relations.* Cambridge: Cambridge University Press.

———, ed. 1978. *Differentiation between Social Groups: Studies in the Social Psychology of Intergroup Relations.* London: Academic Press.

Tajfel, H., and J. Turner. 1979. "An Integrative Theory of Intergroup Conflict." In W. Austin and N. S. Worchel, eds., *The Social Psychology of Intergroup Relations.* Monterey, Calif.: Brooks/Cole.

Tawney, R. H. 1926. *Religion and the Rise of Capitalism.* New York: Harcourt, Brace, and World.

Taylor, Charles. 1989. "Irreducibly Social Goods." In *Proceedings of the Conference on Rationality, Individuality and Public Policy.* Canberra: Australian National University.

Taylor, Michael. 1976. *Anarchy and Cooperation.* London: John Wiley and Sons.

———. 1987. *The Possibility of Cooperation.* New York: Cambridge University Press.

———. 1988. "Rationality and Revolutionary Collective Action." In Michael Taylor, ed., *Rationality and Revolution.* Cambridge: Cambridge University Press.

———. 1989. "Structure, Culture and Action in the Explanation of Social Change." *Politics and Society* 17: 115–62.

Taylor, Paul. 1980. "Interdependence and Autonomy in the European Communities: The Case of the European Monetary System." *Journal of Common Market Studies* 18:370–387.

Thaler, Richard. 1985. "Mental Accounting and Consumer Choice." *Marketing Science* 4:199–214.

Thibaut, J., and L. Walker. 1975. *Procedural Justice.* Hillsdale, N.J.: Erlbaum.

Thorne, Barrie, ed., 1982. *Rethinking the Family.* New York: Longmans.

Thucydides. 1966. *The Peloponnesian War.* Trans. Rex Warner. Baltimore: Penguin.

Thurow, Lester C. 1983. *Dangerous Currents.* New York: Random House.

Titmuss, Richard M. [1970] 1971. *The Gift Relationship.* Reprint. London: Allen and Unwin; New York: Pantheon.

Tittle, C. R. 1980. *Sanction and Social Deviance.* New York: Praeger.

Touraine, Alain. [1984] 1988. *Return of the Actor: Social Theory in Postindustrial Society.* Trans. Myrna Godzich. Minneapolis: University of Minnesota Press.

Trenchard, John, and Thomas Gordon. 1971. *Cato's Letters*. New York: Da Capo Press.

Trivers, R. L. 1971. "The Evolution of Reciprocal Altruism." *Quarterly Review of Biology* 46:35–57.

———. 1985. *Social Evolution*. Menlo Park, Calif.: Benjamin/Cummings.

Tronto, Joan. 1988. "Beyond Gender Difference to a Theory of Care." *Signs* 12:644.

Truman, David. 1959. *The Governmental Process*. New York: Knopf.

Tufte, E. R. 1978. *Political Control of the Economy*. Princeton: Princeton University Press.

Tullock, Gordon. 1975. "The Paradox of Not Voting for Oneself." *American Journal of Political Science* 69:919.

———. 1976. *The Vote Motive*. London: Institute for Economic Affairs.

———. 1979. "Public Choice in Practice." In Clifford S. Russell, ed., *Collective Decision Making: Applications from Public Choice Theory*. Baltimore: Johns Hopkins University Press.

Turnbull, Colin. 1972. *The Mountain People*. New York: Simon and Schuster.

Turner, J. 1975. "Social Comparison and Social Identity: Some Prospects for Intergroup Behavior." *European Journal of Social Psychology* 5:5–34.

Turner, J., and H. Giles. 1981. *Intergroup Behavior*. Chicago: University of Chicago Press.

Tyler, Tom R. 1984. "The Role of Perceived Injustice in Defendants' Evaluations of Their Courtroom Experience." *Law and Society Review* 18:51–74.

———. 1986a. "Justice and Leadership Endorsement." In R. R. Lau and D. O. Sears, eds., *Political Cognition*. Hillsdale, N.J.: L. Erlbaum.

———. 1986b. "When Does Procedural Justice Matter in Organizational Settings?" In R. Lewicki, M. Bazerman, and B. Sheppard, eds., *Research on Negotiation in Organizations*, vol. 1:7–23. Greenwich, Conn.: JAI Press.

———. 1988. "What Is Procedural Justice?: Criteria Used by Citizens to Assess the Fairness of Legal Procedures." *Law and Society Review* 22:301–55.

———. 1989a. "The Quality of Dispute Resolution Processes and Outcomes: Measurement Problems and Possibilities." *Denver University Law Review* 66:419–36.

———. 1989b. "The Psychology of Procedural Justice: A Test of the Group Value Model." *Journal of Personality and Social Psychology* 57:830–38.

———. In press. *Why People Obey the Law*. New Haven: Yale University Press.

Tyler, T. R., J. Casper, and B. Fisher. 1989. "Maintaining Allegiance toward Political Authorities: The Role of Prior Attitudes and the Use of Fair Procedures." *American Journal of Political Science* 33:629–52.

Tyler, T. R., and K. McGraw. 1986. "Ideology and the Interpretation of Personal Experience: Procedural Justice and Political Quiescence." *Journal of Social Issues* 42:115–28.

Tyler, T. R., K. Rasinski, and E. Griffin. 1986. "Alternative Images of the Citizen: Implications for Public Policy." *American Psychologist* 41:970–78.

Tyler, T. R., K. Rasinski, and K. McGraw. 1985. "The Influence of Perceived Injustice on Support for Political Authorities." *Journal of Applied Social Psychology* 15:700–725.

Tyler, T., and R. Folger, 1980. "Distributional and Procedural Aspects of Satisfaction with Citizen-Police Encounters." *Basic and Applied Psychology* 1:281–92.

Uhlaner, Carole J. 1986. "Political Participation, Rational Actors, and Rationality: A New Approach." *Political Psychology* 7:551–73.

———. 1988. "Relational Goods and Participation: Incorporating Sociability into a Theory of Rational Action." Revision of paper presented at the annual meeting of the International Society for Political Psychology, Amsterdam, 1986.

Urmson, J. O. 1958. "Saints and Heroes." In A. I. Melden, ed., *Essays in Moral Philosophy*. Seattle: University of Washington Press.

van de Kragt, A. J. C., J. M. Orbell, and R. M. Dawes. 1983. "The Minimal Contributing Set as a Solution to Public Goods Problems." *American Political Science Review* 77:112–22.

van de Kragt, A. J. C., J. M. Orbell, R. M. Dawes, S. R. Braver, and L. A. Wilson II. 1986. "Doing Well and Doing Good as Ways of Resolving Social Dilemmas." In H. Wilke, D. Messick, and C. Rutte, eds., *Experimental Social Dilemmas*. Frankfurt: P. Lang.

Van Kley, Dale. 1987. "Pierre Nicole, Jansenism, and the Morality of Enlightened Self-Interest." In Alan Kors and Paul Korshin, eds., *Anticipations of the Enlightenment in England, France, and Germany*. Philadelphia: University of Pennsylvania Press.

Van Maanen, J., and E. H. Schein. 1979. "Toward a Theory of Organizational Socialization." In B. Staw, eds., *Research in Organizational Behavior*. Greenwich, Conn.: JAI Press.

Vaughan, William, Jr., and Richard Herrnstein. 1987. "Stability, Melioration and Natural Selection." In L. Green and J. Kagel, eds., *Advances in Behavioral Economics*. Norwood, N.J.: Ablex.

Verba, S. 1961. *Small Groups and Political Behavior*. Princeton: Princeton University Press.

Verba, Sidney, and Norman H. Nie. 1972. *Political Participation in America: Political Democracy and Social Equality*. New York: Harper and Row.

Vidich, Arthur J., and Joseph Bensman. 1968. *Small Town in Mass Society: Class, Power and Religion in a Rural Community*. Princeton: Princeton University Press.

Vlastos, Gregory. [1971] 1978. "Justice and Happiness in the *Republic*." In Gregory Vlastos, eds., *Plato: A Collection of Critical Essays,* vol. 2. Notre Dame, Ind.: University of Notre Dame Press.

Vogler, David J., and Sidney R. Waldman. 1985. *Congress and Democracy*. Washington, D.C.: Congressional Quarterly Press.

Voltaire. [1909] 1961. "Lettres philosophiques." In Jacques van den Heuvel, ed., *Mélanges*. Paris: Pleiade.

Von Neumann, J., and O. Morgenstern. [1944] 1947. *Theory of Games and Economic Behavior*. 2d ed. Princeton: Princeton University Press.

Wade, M. J. 1978. "A Critical Review of Group Selection Models." *Quarterly Review of Biology* 53:101–14.

Wallach, M. A., and L. Wallach. 1983. *Psychology's Sanction for Selfishness: The Error of Egoism in Theory and Therapy*. San Francisco: W. H. Freeman.

Walster, E., G. Walster, and E. Berscheid. 1978. *Equity: Theory and Research*. Boston: Allyn and Bacon.

Walzer, Michael. 1967. *Revolution of the Saints*. Cambridge: Harvard University Press.

Warrender, Howard. 1957. *The Political Philosophy of Hobbes*. Oxford: Oxford University Press.

Watkins, J. 1974. Comment on Amartya Sen, "Choice, Orderings, and Morality." In S. Korner, ed., *Practical Reason*. Oxford: Blackwell, pp. 67–77.

Weatherford, M. Steven. 1983. "Economic Voting and the 'Symbolic Politics' Argument: A Reinterpretation and Synthesis." *American Political Science Review* 77:158–74.

———. 1988. "Self-interest, Commitment and Economic Policy Choice." Paper delivered at the annual meeting of the American Political Science Association.

Webster, Noah. [1785] 1937. *Sketches of American Policy*. Ed. Harry R. Warfel. New York: Scholar's Facsimiles and Reprints.

Weisbrod, B. A. 1977. "Comparing Utility Functions in Efficiency Terms." *American Economic Review* 67:991–95.

Weller, Jack, E. 1965. *Yesterday's People: Life in Contemporary Appalachia*. Lexington: University of Kentucky Press.

Williams, B. 1973. "A Critique of Utilitarianism." In J. J. C. Smart and B. Williams, *Utilitarianism: For and Against*. Cambridge: Cambridge University Press.

Williamson, Oliver E. 1965. *The Economics of Discretionary Behavior*. Englewood Cliffs, N.J.: Prentice-Hall.

———. 1976. "The Evolution of Hierarchy: An Essay on the Organization of Work." Fels Discussion Paper No. 91. University of Pennsylvania, Philadelphia.

———. 1977. "Predatory Pricing: A Strategic and Welfare Analysis." *Yale Law Journal* 87:284–340.

Wilson, D. S. 1983. "The Group Selection Controversy: History and Current Status." *Annual Review of Ecology Systematics* 14:159–87.

Wilson, E. O. 1971. *The Insect Societies*. Cambridge: Harvard University Press.

Wilson, James. [1790–91] 1967. "Lectures on Law." In *The Works of James Wilson*, vol. 1. Ed. Robert Green McCloskey. Cambridge: Harvard University Press.

Wilson, James. Q. 1962. *The Amateur Democrat*. Chicago: University of Chicago Press.

———. 1973. *Political Organizations*. New York: Basic Books.

———. 1983. *Thinking about Crime*. Rev. ed. New York: Basic Books.

Wilson, James, Q., and E. C. Banfield. 1971. "Political Ethos Revisited." *American Political Science Review* 65:1048–62.

Wilson, James Q., and Peter B. Clark. 1961. "Incentive Systems: A Theory of Organization." *Administrative Science Quarterly* 6:129–66.

Winter, David G. 1973. *The Power Motive*. New York: Free Press.

Winter, S. G. 1969. "A Simple Remark on the Second Optimality Theorem of Welfare Economics." *Journal of Economic Theory* 1:99–103.

Wit, A. P., and H. A. M. Wilke. 1988. "The Effect of Social Categorization on Cooperation in Three Types of Social Dilemmas." In A. van Knippenberg et al., eds., *Fundamentele Sociale Psychologie*. Vol. 2. Tilburg, Netherlands: Tilburg University Press.

Wolfers, Arnold. 1962. *Discord and Collaboration: Essays on International Politics*. Baltimore: Johns Hopkins University Press.

Wolfers, Arnold, and Laurence Martin, eds. 1956. *The Anglo-American Tradition in Foreign Affairs*. New Haven: Yale University Press.

Wolin, Sheldon S. 1960. *Politics and Vision*. Boston: Little, Brown.

Wong, S. 1975. "On the Consistency and Completeness of Paul Samuelson's Programme in the Theory of Consumer Behavior." Ph.D. diss., Cambridge University.

Wood, Gordon S. 1969. *The Creation of the American Republic, 1776–1787*. New York: W. W. Norton.

———. 1987. "Interests and Disinterestedness in the Making of the Constitution." In Richard Beeman et al., eds., *Beyond Confederation*. Chapel Hill: University of North Carolina Press.

Woodhouse, A. S. 1957. *Puritanism and Liberty*. Chicago: University of Chicago Press.

Wrightsman, L. S. 1966. "Personality and Attitudinal Correlates of Trusting and Trustworthiness in a Two-Person Game." *Journal of Personality and Social Psychology* 4:328–32.

Young, Edward. 1854. "Conjectures of Original Composition." In *The Complete Works*. London: W. Tegg and Co.

Young, J., E. Borgida, J. Sullivan, and J. Aldrich. 1987. "Personal Agendas and the Relationship between Self-Interest and Voting Behavior." *Social Psychology Quarterly* 50:64–71.

Zahn-Waxler, Carolyn, E. Mark Cummings, and Ronald Iannotti, eds. 1986. *Altruism and Aggression*. New York: Cambridge University Press.

Zuckerman, Michael. 1970. *Peaceable Kingdoms*. New York: Knopf.

Contributors

Robert Boyd, who has a B.A. in physics and a Ph.D. in ecology, is associate professor of anthropology at the University of California at Los Angeles. He is coauthor, with Peter J. Richerson, of *Culture and the Evolutionary Process* (1985).

Robyn M. Dawes is the head of the Department of Social and Decision Sciences and professor of psychology at Carnegie Mellon University. His books include *Mathematical Psychology: An Elementary Introduction* (with Coombs and Tversky, 1970), *Fundamentals on Attitude Measurement* (1972), and *Rational Choice in an Uncertain World* (1988).

Jon Elster is professor of political science at the University of Chicago and research director of the Institute for Social Research, Oslo. His books include *Ulysses and the Sirens: Studies in Rationality and Irrationality* (1979/ 1984), *Sour Grapes: Studies in the Subversion of Rationality* (1983), and *Making Sense of Marx* (1985).

Robert H. Frank is professor of economics at Cornell University. He is the author of *Choosing the Right Pond* (1985) and *Passions within Reason* (1988). He served as chief economist for the Civil Aeronautics Board from 1978 to 1980, and taught for two years in Sanischare, Nepal.

Carolyn L. Funk is a graduate student in social psychology in the Department of Psychology, University of California, Los Angeles.

Virginia Held is professor of philosophy at the City University of New York. She is author, coauthor, editor, or coeditor of eight books, including *The Public Interest and Individual Interests* (1970) and *Rights and Goods: Justifying Social Action* (1984).

Stephen Holmes is professor of political science and law at the University of Chicago. He is the author of *Benjamin Constant and the Making of Modern Liberalism* (1984).

Christopher Jencks is professor of sociology at Northwestern University, and member of the research faculty at the Center for Urban Affairs and Policy Research, Northwestern University. He has authored *The Academic Revolution* (with David Riesman, 1968), *Inequality* (1972; corecipient of the American Sociological Association's Sorokin Award in 1974), and *Who Gets Ahead?* (1979).

Steven Kelman is professor of public policy at the John F. Kennedy School of Government, Harvard University. He is the author of *Regulating America, Regulating Sweden: A Comparative Study of Occupational Safety and Health Policies* (1981), *What Price Incentives: Economists and the Environment* (1981), and *Making Public Policy: A Hopeful View of American Government* (1987).

Robert O. Keohane is Stanfield Professor of International Peace at Harvard University. He is the author of *After Hegemony: Cooperation and Discord in the World Political Economy* (1984) and *International Institutions and State Power: Essays in International Relations Theory* (1989), and co-author, with Joseph S. Nye, Jr., of *Power and Interdependence: World Politics in Transition* (1977; 2d ed. 1988).

Jane J. Mansbridge is professor of political science and sociology, and member of the research faculty at the Center for Urban Affairs and Policy Research, Northwestern University. Her books are *Beyond Adversary Democracy* (1980/1983) and *Why We Lost the ERA* (1986; corecipient of the American Political Science Association's Kammerer Award in 1987 and Schuck Award in 1988).

Howard Margolis is senior lecturer with the Committee on Public Policy Studies at the University of Chicago. He is the author of *Selfishness, Altruism and Rationality* (1984) and *Thinking, Patterns and Cognition* (1987).

John M. Orbell is professor of political science at the University of Oregon. He has published in the *American Political Science Review*, the *British Journal of Political Science*, *Public Choice*, and other scholarly journals.

Paul J. Quirk has a joint appointment as associate professor in the Department of Political Science, University of Illinois at Chicago, and in the

Institute of Government and Public Affairs, University of Illinois. His books are *Industry Influence in Federal Regulatory Agencies* (1981) and *The Politics of Deregulation* (with Martha Derthick, 1985; recipient of the National Academy of Public Administration's Brownlow Award, 1986).

Peter J. Richerson is professor in the Division of Environmental Studies and director of the Institute of Ecology at the University of California at Davis. He works on problems of spatial and temporal variation in plankton communities, and on the theory of cultural evolution. He is coauthor, with Robert Boyd, of *Culture and the Evolutionary Process.*

David O. Sears is professor of psychology and political science and dean of social sciences at UCLA. His books include *Public Opinion* (with R. E. Lane, 1964), *Social Psychology* (with J. L. Freedman, A. Peplau, and S. Taylor, six editions from 1970 to 1987), *The Politics of Violence: The New Urban Blacks and the Watts Riot* (with J. B. McConahay, 1973), *Tax Revolt: Something for Nothing in California* (with J. Citrin, 1982/1985), and *Political Cognition: The 19th Annual Carnegie Symposium on Cognition* (with R. Lau, 1986). Awards include the Edward L. Bernays Foundation Psychology and Social Issues Book Award and the 1978 Gordon Allport Intergroup Relations Prize.

Amartya Sen is Lamont University Professor at Harvard University, and teaches in the Departments of Economics and Philosophy. He was previously Drummond Professor of Political Economy at Oxford University and Fellow of All Souls College. His publications include, inter alia, *Choice of Techniques* (1960), *Collective Choice and Social Welfare* (1970), *On Economic Inequality* (1973), *Poverty and Famines* (1981), *Choice, Welfare and Measurement* (1982), *Resources, Values and Development* (1984), *The Standard of Living* (1987), and *On Ethics and Economics* (1987).

Cass R. Sunstein is the Karl N. Llewellyn Professor of Jurisprudence, Law School and Department of Political Science, University of Chicago. He has also been Samuel Rubin Visiting Professor at Columbia Law School and visiting professor of law at Harvard Law School. Sunstein is the author of *After the Rights Revolution: Reconceiving the Regulatory State* (1990) and coauthor of *Constitutional Law* (1986).

Tom R. Tyler is professor of psychology and political science at Northwestern University, research fellow at the American Bar Foundation, and a member of the research faculty at the Northwestern University Center for Urban Affairs and Policy Research. He is coauthor of *The Social Psychology of Procedural Justice* (1988) and author of *Why People Obey the Law: Procedural Justice, Legitimacy and Compliance* (forthcoming).

Alphons J. C. van de Kragt, from the University of Oregon, published in the *American Political Science Review, Public Choice,* and other scholarly journals. This is the eighth paper he, Orbell, and Dawes published together prior to his death on October 14, 1989.

Index